Luminos is the Open Access monograph publishing program from UC Press. Luminos provides a framework for preserving and reinvigorating monograph publishing for the future and increases the reach and visibility of important scholarly work. Titles published in the UC Press Luminos model are published with the same high standards for selection, peer review, production, and marketing as those in our traditional program. www.luminosoa.org

Inland from Mombasa

Inland from Mombasa

East Africa and the Making of the Indian Ocean World

David P. Bresnahan

UNIVERSITY OF CALIFORNIA PRESS

University of California Press
Oakland, California

© 2025 by David Bresnahan

This work is licensed under a Creative Commons (CC BY-NC-ND) license.
To view a copy of the license, visit http://creativecommons.org/licenses.

Suggested citation: Bresnahan, D. P. *Inland from Mombasa: East Africa and
the Making of the Indian Ocean World*. Oakland: University of California
Press, 2025. DOI: https://doi.org/10.1525/luminos.211

Library of Congress Cataloging-in-Publication Data

Names: Bresnahan, David P., author.
Title: Inland from Mombasa : East Africa and the making of the Indian
    Ocean world / David P. Bresnahan.
Description: Oakland, California : University of California Press, [2025] |
    Includes bibliographical references and index.
Identifiers: LCCN 2024016786 (print) | LCCN 2024016787 (ebook) |
    ISBN 9780520400481 (paperback) | ISBN 9780520400498 (ebook)
Subjects: LCSH: Mijikenda (African people)—History. | Indian Ocean
    Region—Economic aspects. | Mombasa (Kenya)—History.
Classification: LCC DT433.545.M54 B74 2025 (print) | LCC DT433.545.M54
    (ebook) | DDC 967.62/360049639—dc23/eng/20240724

LC record available at https://lccn.loc.gov/2024016786
LC ebook record available at https://lccn.loc.gov/2024016787

33 32 31 30 29 28 27 26 25 24
10 9 8 7 6 5 4 3 2 1

CONTENTS

Acknowledgments	*vii*
Note on Language	*xi*
Introduction	*1*
1. Unmoored from the Ocean	*20*
2. Looking Inland, to the World	*42*
3. The Inland Underpinnings of Indian Ocean Commerce	*68*
4. Inland Villages and Oceanic Empires	*94*
5. From Mijikenda City to Busaidi Backwater	*114*
Conclusion	*132*
Appendix 1: Placing East African Languages in Time and Space	*141*
Appendix 2: Mijikenda Dialects	*146*
Appendix 3: Lexical Reconstructions and Distributions	*149*
Notes	*157*
Bibliography	*193*
Index	*219*

ACKNOWLEDGMENTS

My curiosity about the history of Mombasa's interior began when I was an MA student interested in the Mijikenda *kaya* forests. I didn't intend to become a historian of precolonial East Africa, but that initial introduction left me with too many unresolved questions about inland communities' engagements with Swahili towns like Mombasa during the distant past. Why did the material and religious practices of people living so close to the ocean look so different from those of Swahili ports? Why weren't inland communities like Mijikenda more integrated into the histories of early Swahili towns despite this proximity? If I've come anywhere close to answering these questions, it is only because of the support and generosity of many people.

My debts begin with language teachers, foremost among them Ramadhani Bakari Mbimbi, who patiently guided me through a summerlong Digo tutorial back in 2011 and who has remained a pillar of support in the years since. I also am grateful to my Swahili teachers over the years: Ann Biersteker, Peter Mwangi, Peter Githinji, Judith Namayengo, and the late Frank Ngugi Wang'endo. On the logistical end, I wish to thank Pwani University in Kilifi and RISSEA (now the National Museums of Kenya Heritage Training Institute) in Mombasa for institutional affiliations during my research, as well as the helpful staff at the Fort Jesus Museum Library. During research in Kenya between 2012 and 2014 I relied on the support of many individuals who provided contacts, transport, advice, and hospitality. I want to especially thank Stephen Katana, Fred Kai, Nancy Ngowa, Athman Lali Omar, Khalid Kitito, William Tsaka, the late Kaingu Tinga, Agnes Anzazi, Abdurahim Bakathir, Jumaine Makoti, Suleiman Baraka Duke, George Kai, David Thuvu, and James Chamanje.

viii   ACKNOWLEDGMENTS

Many others shared advice and research materials. Tom Spear shared boxes of research materials and encouraged me to pursue a project that revisited his earliest work, and Daren Ray offered generous encouragement as we worked on parallel projects. The late Samuel Ngala shared his unpublished manuscript on Mijikenda religion and was endlessly generous with his time and knowledge. Mitsuru Hamamoto gave me an electronic database of Duruma vocabulary that he assembled over decades, and Zeb Dingley shared a trove of digitized materials. Yaari Seligman offered advice on conducting linguistic research prior to the start of my own that proved to be invaluable. Odha Swaleh assembled word lists in Pokomo on my behalf after my research plans for northern Kenya didn't work out. I've continued to learn about Pokomo language and history from him in the years since.

Many have shaped my thinking about this project over the years. Nick Creary and Diane Ciekawy pushed me to begin thinking of myself as a real scholar while I was a very green MA student at Ohio University. Even earlier, my undergraduate adviser David Brown encouraged me to give it a go when most would not have. At UW–Madison, Florence Bernault, Jim Sweet, and Emily Callaci provided the perfect balance of encouragement and critique. I am most grateful to my PhD adviser Neil Kodesh, both for his guidance and support and for letting me work through things at my own pace, even if that meant taking long chunks of time away from writing. My ideas were also shaped during my time in Madison through feedback and conversations with Steve Pierce, Patrick Otim, Phil Janzen, Jake Blanc, and John Boonstra. This book also owes a big debt to Leslie Hadfield and Dima Hurlbut for initiating the annual(ish) Rocky Mountain Workshop on African History in Salt Lake, which has offered feedback on parts of three different chapters. Finally, I need to thank my colleagues at the University of Utah's Department of History for their collegiality, support, and critical feedback on a draft of this book's first chapter during our works-in-progress seminar.

Others had a hand in turning draft_a_million.docx into a book. Kathleen Kearns's developmental feedback helped me get the first draft ready for submission, and three anonymous peer reviewers provided critical commentary that made it better. At UC Press, I wish to thank Eric Schmidt, Jyoti Arvey, and Stephanie Summerhays for helping turn the raw product into a book. Sections of chapters 4 and 5 are adapted from my essay "In Mombasa They Are 'Like Prisoners' to the Mijikenda: Martiality, Trade, and Inland Influences on a Swahili Port City," in *Making Martial Races: Gender, Society, and Warfare in Africa*, edited by Myles Osborne (Ohio University Press, 2023). This material is used with the permission of Ohio University Press, www.ohioswallow.com. Comments on a draft of that essay in a workshop Myles Osborne organized at CU Boulder were invaluable for developing my arguments for chapter 4.

I received financial support for research and writing from the University of Utah Department of History, the University of Wisconsin–Madison Department of History and Program in African Studies, the Scott Kloeck-Jenson Fellowship, and the Office of the Vice Chancellor for Research and Graduate Education at the University of Wisconsin–Madison (with funding from the Wisconsin Alumni Research Foundation). I am especially thankful for the generous support from the University of Utah history department's ESSR Environmental History Research Grant, which provided funding to make the book open access. I also wish to thank our department's executive secretary, Brayden Bracken, for helping to manage the payments for research-related expenses over the past few years.

Most of all, I need to thank my parents, Debbie and Dave Bresnahan, and my siblings, Sara, Emily, and Conor, for their love and support over the years. I owe a huge thanks to my in-laws, Sue Richards and Larry Tyler, especially for their considerable help with childcare during the pandemic, which made some of this book's revisions possible.

A line in these acknowledgments could hardly suffice to express my gratitude to Caitlin Tyler-Richards, but I'll try: every part of this book and of life is better because of you. Finally, I wish to thank two great dogs and one great toddler for enriching all aspects of life outside of these pages.

I dedicate this book to my late grandfather, Robert Zallo, both for his love of a story and because I know that me writing a book is one story he would have enjoyed telling.

NOTE ON LANGUAGE

ORTHOGRAPHY

In the chapters and appendices, I've tried to follow standard orthographic conventions of lexicographers for Mijikenda and other East African languages.

The voiced bilabial fricative (β) is written as ph.

The voiced dental fricative (ð) is written as dh.

The voiceless dental fricative (θ) is written as th.

Proto-Sabaki had a seven-vowel system (inherited from proto-Bantu), which was reduced to five vowels in all languages except for Elwana. Due to this book's significant reliance on Derek Nurse and Thomas Hinnebusch's work on Sabaki, I've opted to follow them in representing vowels for reconstructed words as follows: a, e, i, i̧, o, u, u̧.

Capitalized W (e.g., *kuWila, "to owe") indicates uncertainty about the proto-Sabaki phoneme derived from proto-Bantu *b, which was articulated as either a labiodental approximate (ʋ) or a bilabial approximate (w).

STARRED FORMS

All reconstructed vocabulary—meaning the proposed phonetic shape and meaning of a word within a protolanguage—is marked with an asterisk: e.g., *muji, meaning "village" in proto-Sabaki.

Words in italics indicate the attested form of a word (in dictionaries, ethnographic sources, and/or modern speech): e.g., *mudzi* or *mji*, meaning "town" or "village" in Mijikenda and Swahili, respectively.

PROPER NOUNS

Bantu languages use prefixes to indicate the conceptual domain of a noun. For simplicity's sake, I eliminate the prefixes when referring to specific languages or population groups. For example: Swahili rather than *Kiswahili* (the Swahili language) and *Waswahili* (the Swahili people).

Introduction

A few kilometers inland from the port city of Mombasa, the coastal plain begins to rise into a fertile upland ridge. Lithic-using groups settled here, as early as seventy-eight thousand years ago, around limestone cliffs dotting the coastal upland's forested eastern flanks.[1] Early in the first millennium CE, ironworking farmers also made the coastal forests of Mombasa's interior their home. Not all remained inland, however. During the second half of the millennium, settlements flourished along the coast and its offshore islands. Within a few centuries, the descendants of these coastal settlers, by then speaking an early form of Swahili, began converting to Islam, a religion introduced through interactions with visiting merchants from Persia and southern Arabia. Towns like Mombasa and Kilwa emerged as important trading hubs within the network of port cities that are today grouped together under the heuristic of the Indian Ocean world. This is a book about this interconnected oceanic world, told from the vantage point of Mijikenda-speaking groups who remained on the forested upland ridges in Mombasa's interior.

While Mombasa occupies an important place in East Africa's global history, its interior registers inconsistently within historical accounts of the city. Arabic geographic texts reference Mombasa as early as the twelfth century, describing the island's interior as "uninhabited" forest occupied by "every kind of wild beast."[2] When the North African traveler and scholar Ibn Battuta visited Mombasa in 1331, he remarked on its characteristically Islamic appearance, noting the city featured well-built mosques and a pious local population. But perplexingly, he also commented that the island city had "no mainland."[3] Mombasa is bordered by two estuarian creeks that form a horseshoe around the island, separating it from the mainland by only a few hundred meters at the narrowest points. Battuta's dhow likely entered on the northeastern part of the island, following the creek to

2 INTRODUCTION

Mombasa's largest settlement, located around the Friday mosque.[4] Standing on the island side of Mombasa's old harbor today, you can easily see the bustle on the opposing side of the waterway. Since the island city so clearly has a mainland, scholars have suggested that Ibn Battuta did not actually mean that Mombasa lacked one, but instead had meant that Mombasa had no "hinterland," or that it "possesse[d] no territory on the mainland."[5] Battuta only spent one day in Mombasa amid nearly thirty years of global travels, so it is just as likely that he forgot specific details of its geography.[6] The forgetful mind of a weary traveler is perhaps the most likely explanation for Battuta's odd remark. Still, his suggestion that the town had no hinterland or rural dependency was in some ways prescient. Mombasa's mainland was populated by Mijikenda-speaking groups who had been active in oceanic trade for centuries by the time of Battuta's travels.[7] Yet their relationship to the port city can hardly be categorized as that of a hinterland dependency.

Later accounts provide a clearer sense of Mijikenda speakers' varied and important roles in the town, despite their invisibility in earlier records. They supplied Mombasa's merchants with ivory, gum copal, and other valued trade goods, and they formed political and military alliances with the town's elites.[8] Sometimes they also raided the island, crossing the narrow ford separating Mombasa and its mainland, to secure preferred terms in these partnerships. One Portuguese writer reported that during the early seventeenth century, 10 percent of Mombasa's budget was allocated to textiles for neighboring inland villages, given as tribute and compensation for these alliances. The people of Mombasa, according to the author, were "like prisoners" to Mijikenda communities due to their constant raiding, their tight control over interior trade goods, and their demands for textiles.[9] Inland leaders were given audiences with Mombasa's elites when they visited the city, and some even traveled abroad to southern Arabia as delegates.[10] Even farther afield, in Portuguese Goa, officials wrote of the people of Mombasa's interior, recognizing their importance to the flow of trade goods across the ocean basin and the trajectories of its politics.[11]

The disconnect between Mijikenda speakers' active role in East Africa's oceanic connections and their comparative marginality in many accounts of these connections—evidenced in Ibn Battuta's commentary—are central to the questions animating this book. Battuta's odd quip on Mombasa's absent mainland captures a ubiquitous tendency in the conceptual frames that scholars use—to this day— to write about histories of the Indian Ocean. Abdul Sheriff and Edward Alpers have described the Indian Ocean as a "Muslim Lake" and an "Islamic Sea," respectively.[12] To Janet Abu-Lughod, the premodern Indian Ocean was constituted by an "archipelago of 'world cities.'"[13] More recently, Sebastian Prange developed the concept of "monsoon Islam" to emphasize the agency of Muslim merchants in the history of oceanic trade in India's Malabar coast.[14] This scholarship underscores the critical role of Islam and port cities for the development of transregional connections in the Indian Ocean. However, many places adjacent to port cities

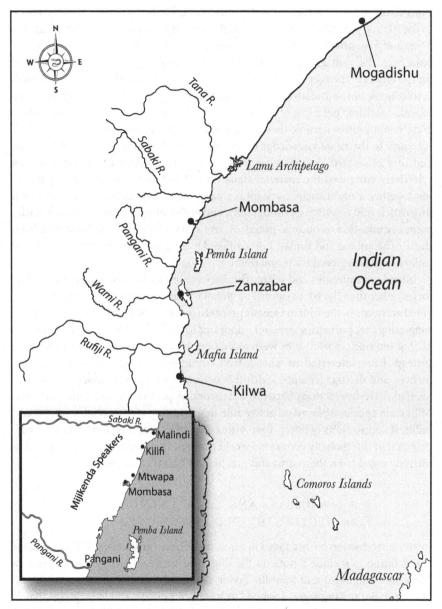

MAP 1. The East African coast. Inset shows Mombasa region and Mijikenda settlement area. Map created by John Wyatt Greenlee, Surprised Eel Mapping.

remain an uneasy fit within the conceptual imaginaries that render the Indian Ocean a "Muslim Lake." As a result, the social actions, cultural ideas, and ambitions of those living in the Indian Ocean's "hinterlands" have become a backdrop to the Islamic port cities that remain focal points of global histories of this region.[15]

Inland from Mombasa is a longue durée history of the Swahili port city of Mombasa from the vantage point of the Mijikenda-speaking communities that lived on the city's rural edges. I argue that Mijikenda speakers influenced East Africa's connections to the Indian Ocean precisely because they turned away from the Islamic-maritime practices of this transregional arena. As the book shows, Mijikenda communities shrunk their settlements as Mombasa urbanized; they were receptive to the ritual knowledge of outsiders, but they never converted to Islam; and they pioneered long-distance trade routes in East Africa's interior, but they selectively embraced the material signatures of Indian Ocean wealth. By bringing together a multidisciplinary source base, including evidence from historical linguistics, oral traditions, ethnography, and archaeology, I show that their settlement organization, economic practices, and ritual ideas, though distinctive from those of Mombasa and similar ports, offered a critical means to participate in and influence transregional trade and politics.

Inland communities and village dwellers are most often the focus of local histories rather than the transregional or global narratives that have traditionally oriented accounts of the Indian Ocean's past.[16] In foregrounding the interior, I am not suggesting that port cities were not important to the Indian Ocean region's history, or that interior communities were more powerful or somehow more important. Instead, I am interested in what inland communities' highly selective engagements—and disengagements—with this oceanic world reveal about the dynamics that drive interactions between a network of port cities. In Mombasa's case, Mijikenda speakers played an active role in generating commercial, cultural, and political connections between East Africa and other world regions. But they participated in this globally connected world through social actions and pursuits that often diverged from the norms and practices of Islamic port cities.

MOMBASA AND THE MIJIKENDA: CONNECTING DIVIDED HISTORIOGRAPHIES

In the introduction to his 1891 Giryama dictionary, missionary William Taylor saw it fitting to include a note on the linguistic similarities between Giryama (a Mijikenda language) and Swahili. Taylor explained that "Giryama and Swahili," like other Bantu languages, seemed "to have been once a single language that at some time or another became split into two ever-increasingly divergent dialects." But despite their similarities, in the missionary's estimation, "there could hardly be a huger contrast" between the people who spoke these languages. The Swahili were "a seafaring, barter-loving" people who had embraced Islam and incorporated

INTRODUCTION 5

"immigrants from Persia, Arabia, and Western India" into their communities. By contrast, he found Giryama communities to be "small, compact; essentially inland" and "uncommercial." They were "confined as to habitat" (compared to Swahili settlements dotting East Africa's littoral) and, as a result, they remained "conservative of manners, custom, and the Bantu religion." Taylor concluded that the discrepancies between Mijikenda and Swahili could only be the result of a "history—so very different in surroundings and fate": the speakers of one language influenced by their external connections to the world, and the speakers of the other language living virtually unchanged since the two languages diverged from one another.[17]

Even without the cultural lens of a nineteenth-century missionary, a visitor to Mombasa today might also conclude that Swahili and Mijikenda communities had experienced radically different historical circumstances. Today, Mombasa's population swells to well over a million people on the island and the surrounding mainland. The Kenya-Uganda Railway, Moi International Airport, and bustling shipping port at Kilindini Harbor all signal the city's connections to international centers. A stroll through Mombasa's Old Town neighborhood provides a vivid reminder of the antiquity of these connections.

One is likely to first enter Old Town on the southeastern part of the island, where the centuries-old Portuguese garrison Fort Jesus dominates the sight line. The cannons and massive weathered walls of the fort, which was constructed in the 1590s, signal Mombasa's important place in Indian Ocean politics during the early modern period. Moving past Fort Jesus, one enters the Kibokoni neighborhood of Old Town. Ignoring the curio shops that mark the entryway to Kibokoni today, a visitor might notice a fenced-in graveyard with burial stones and tombs honoring the Mazrui family, the Omani dynasty that governed Mombasa from the 1730s until the 1830s. Arabic inscriptions on doors and the resonance of the call to prayer attest to Old Town's thoroughly Islamic character, something observed by visitors like Ibn Battuta as far back as 1331. Mombasa's old port—popularly known as dhow harbor—further conjures the city's long-standing connections to the Indian Ocean, even if the iconic dhow sailboats from which the harbor takes its name are now little more than relics of an earlier era of transoceanic trade.

Mombasa makes its first-known appearance in textual accounts of the Indian Ocean in Muhammad al-Idrisi's twelfth-century description of the world's geography. Based on knowledge obtained from merchants and travelers in Sicily, the account accompanies the geographer's famed world map, known as the *Tabula Rogeriana*. According to al-Idrisi, Mombasa was at the time a small town compared to other coastal towns like Malindi and Unguja.[18] Mombasa's comparative humbleness to other ports is supported by Ibn Battuta's accounts of his travels to the island two centuries later. Mombasa was legible within the religious registers of the Indian Ocean by the time of Battuta's visit, evident in its "pious" Muslim population and "admirably constructed" mosques.[19] But the traveler spent just one night in the town, using it as a stopover between lengthier trips to the bustling

6   INTRODUCTION

port centers of Mogadishu and Kilwa, where he hobnobbed with local sultans and itinerant scholars from the Hijaz. Mombasa became far more prominent in the century or so after Ibn Battuta's brief visit. In the fifteenth century, Ahmad ibn Majid, a geographer from Julfar (a port city in the Persian Gulf) wrote that the East African coast featured "many ports for travellers, the best known of which are Moqadīshū, Barāwa, Mombasa, and the land of Sofāla."[20] By the time Portuguese ships reached East Africa in 1498, Mombasa was the most prosperous town along the entire coast.[21]

The fact that Mombasa was one of the main geographic reference points in Arabic writings on East Africa across the early second millennium indicates the town's clear significance to the region's oceanic connections. Archaeological records offer some insights into local developments that overlapped with these scattered references.[22] The earliest human settlers around the island were lithic-using Early, Middle, and Late Stone Age groups, some of whom lived immediately across the creek to the south of Mombasa and likely crossed onto the island intermittently.[23] In the early first millennium, ironworking communities (presumed to speak a language ancestral to Swahili and Mijikenda) planted settlements along the forested ridges immediately inland from the coast, with some moving onto the island itself by the latter part of the millennium.[24] The earliest known settlement on Mombasa dates to the eleventh century, on the northern part of the island. By the thirteenth century, the island's archaeological records begin to show clearer signs of characteristic Swahili ports, specifically coral stone architecture. An increasing number of imported ceramics in archaeological assemblages during this same time demonstrates the town's growing material connections to the Arabian Peninsula, Persia, and China.[25] Between the twelfth and sixteenth centuries, Mombasa's interior developed as a significant region for ivory procurement (in addition to circulations in other inland trade goods such as beeswax and rhinoceros horn), which no doubt supported the town's growing maritime interactions and its emergence as a leading port.[26]

While Mombasa's history fits well within narratives of Indian Ocean port cities, the communities living adjacent to the town are far less integrated into this history. Mijikenda speakers' oral traditions explain that they migrated to the Mombasa region from a mythical northern homeland called Shungwaya, after which they settled in hilltop forested settlements called kayas. "Mijikenda" literally means the "nine towns." In standard renderings of the traditions, there were nine kayas, with one representing each of the nine modern Mijikenda subgroups.[27] Analyses of the migration myths—and their veracity—have long been a focal point of scholarship on Mijikenda communities. This work is best represented by Thomas Spear's 1978 book The Kaya Complex, which argued, based on details in the oral traditions, that Mijikenda communities only reached Mombasa's interior around the sixteenth century.[28] Subsequent scholars, most prominently Justin Willis, have critiqued Spear's interpretation of the origin traditions. However, Willis did not focus on

INTRODUCTION 7

periods prior to the nineteenth century, instead looking at the origin traditions as vehicles for constructing a Mijikenda ethnic identity during the colonial period.[29] Ultimately, the heavy focus on the veracity of oral traditions erased places just kilometers inland from Mombasa from deeper narratives of the littoral's past.[30]

Research by archaeologists Henry Mutoro and Richard Helm and historian Daren Ray has begun to rectify the exclusion of Mijikenda and other inland speech communities from Mombasa's earlier history. Excavations in southeast Kenya have established a complex settlement history that runs far deeper into the past, encompassing far larger scales and interactions than the temporal and geographic frameworks adopted by Spear and other early scholars.[31] Employing a mixed methodology, including evidence from historical linguistics, Ray has illuminated longer-term collaboration strategies between inland and coastal groups, challenging the scholarly tendencies to bifurcate histories of "the Swahili" and "the Mijikenda." In doing so, Ray expands coastal Kenya's littoral history into its near interior and historicizes long-term processes of community formation from the distant past to the present.[32] Together, these scholars' close engagements with deeper histories of coastal-interior entanglements offer an important foundation for my own analysis, which addresses the ways that inland social ideas and actions—including those diverging from oceanic norms—influenced the broader commercial and political milieu of the western Indian Ocean.

My analysis also benefits from—and builds off—a broader shift among archaeologists and historians toward studying the role of local political economies and material ambitions in eastern and southern Africa's oceanic connections. In both coastal and interior regions, people integrated trade goods into their own suite of social ideas and practices. They "domesticated" foreign objects, incorporating them into contexts like feasts and ancestral veneration rituals, while adapting material goods to suit local tastes and fashion preferences. When imported goods didn't suit their individual goals, they rejected them.[33] In many cases, trade goods moved along multidirectional exchange networks, not solely, or even primarily, oriented around provisioning oceanic trade.[34] This literature shows that even people who did not have direct interactions with coastal merchants, and who did not envision themselves as part of any cosmopolitan imaginary, were, nonetheless, key agents of larger interconnections.

Inland from Mombasa adds to this growing literature on eastern Africa's interior connections in three ways. First, by employing evidence from language, I bring greater focus to the social ideas conditioning inland trading interactions with Mombasa. I show that over centuries, Mijikenda speakers continuously adapted and innovated strategies for conducting trade over longer distances; they cultivated rituals for interacting with coastal merchants; and, often in concert with other inland groups, they adapted their healing ideas and settlement designs in response to new forms of wealth entering their villages. Second, I examine the above developments from a relatively situated vantage point, looking primarily

8 INTRODUCTION

at one port city and one adjacent speech community. In doing so, I bring a fine-grained resolution to the specific ways that a port city's growing connections hinged on the agency and ambitions of its neighbors immediately inland. Third, I illuminate how inland agents' influences extended beyond their role as consumers or suppliers of trade goods and into other arenas of interaction such as global politics. As the last two chapters show, Mijikenda speakers built political capital from their advantageous trading position and influenced the trajectories of multiple oceanic empires in the process. Yet the full dynamics of Mijikenda speakers' influence in the western Indian Ocean is impossible to discern from written sources and archaeological evidence alone. To bring inland histories into broader narratives of the Indian Ocean requires anchoring in the methodologies of early African history, specifically comparative historical linguistics.

STUDYING LESS-DOCUMENTED HISTORIES USING WORDS

Scholars often struggle to incorporate smaller-scale societies into global histories because places that existed outside of mercantile, religious, or imperial networks typically lack a strong documentary presence. Thus, until recently, most scholarship on East Africa and other regions of the Indian Ocean portrayed inland communities as rural dependencies, sometimes affected by global networks but without any historical agency of their own.[35] To recover the historical connections between societies in Mombasa's interior and the Indian Ocean, I employ a multidisciplinary source base, drawing insights from historical linguistics, comparative ethnography, oral traditions, archaeology, and written records. An analysis of word histories generated through historical linguistics provides an especially important body of evidence. Word histories render legible the innovations, adaptations, and ancient knowledge that shaped the trading practices, rituals, and politics of Mijikenda speakers and other societies within inland-facing East African networks since the first millennium. Combining word histories with evidence from archaeology, oral traditions, ethnography, and documentary records enables me to bring together the narratives of these small-scale communities with those of the Swahili coast and wider Indian Ocean region.

Like all the world's languages, Mijikenda and Swahili both have rich histories that can offer entry points into the social and cultural worlds of the people who spoke these languages. Throughout the book, I refer to most actors as speakers of specific languages, e.g., "Mijikenda *speakers*" or "Swahili *speakers*." I do so to distinguish the historical speakers of a language (or protolanguage) from any modern claims about identity or ethnicity. Mijikenda, for instance, developed as an ethnic identity during the early to mid-twentieth century.[36] By contrast, the Mijikenda language has been spoken by communities inland from Mombasa since the late first millennium, diverging into mutually intelligible dialects over the course of the

INTRODUCTION 9

second millennium. Thus, when I refer to Mijikenda speakers, I mean individuals who spoke different Mijikenda dialects.[37]

Mijikenda and Swahili both descend from an ancestral language that linguists call proto-Sabaki or, simply, Sabaki. Sabaki is a protolanguage, meaning it is the proposed ancestral form of a language from which later languages emerged. Proto-Sabaki itself is a member of a larger group of languages called Northeast Coast Bantu (all proposed to descend from proto–Northeast Coast, which was spoken about two thousand years ago in eastern Tanzania). On an even larger linguistic scale, Mijikenda and Swahili are part of the Bantu family of languages, which includes hundreds of languages, all related to a common protolanguage—proto-Bantu—which was spoken more than five thousand years ago in modern-day Cameroon.[38]

One of the most familiar examples of a language family is the Romance family, which includes Italian, Romanian, Portuguese, Spanish, and French. All these languages are related because they share a common protolanguage: proto-Romance (or Vulgar Latin), which itself is part of a larger web of language families and relationships stretching back to proto-Indo-European. Using Romance languages as a point of comparison, proto-Bantu is akin to proto-Indo-European while the Sabaki family is like proto-Romance.[39] In this schema, the linguistic relationship between Mijikenda and Swahili is roughly equivalent to that of French and Spanish. Like these two western European languages, Mijikenda and Swahili both feature notable internal diversity due to the differentiation and diffusion of speakers over time, manifesting in modern dialects.

Proto-Sabaki emerged from other Northeast Coast languages during the early first millennium. By the sixth or seventh century, Sabaki began to diverge into daughter languages of its own, first Elwana and Swahili, then Upper Pokomo, followed by Comorian by at least the eighth century, and Lower Pokomo and Mijikenda shortly thereafter. The earliest form of Swahili, or proto-Swahili, was spoken along large expanses of the littoral, forming two closely related dialect clusters (Northern and Southern Swahili) by the ninth century. Early Mijikenda, meanwhile, would have been spoken in southeast Kenya's coastal hinterlands by the end of the first millennium before gradually differentiating into a chain of closely related dialects during the second millennium.[40]

Similar to how scholars of Indo-European languages traced the ancient roots of words in languages spoken across Eurasia, linguists working on Bantu languages have spent more than a century reconstructing the lexicon, grammar, and sounds of ancient languages spoken in Africa.[41] Historians of Africa (and elsewhere) employ these reconstructed linguistic materials to study the histories of past societies for whom there are few documentary records.[42] Their methodology is premised on the idea that words in each of the world's languages refer to things— whether they're material objects, abstract concepts, or practices—that were known to the speakers of that language. To treat a word as historical evidence, historical

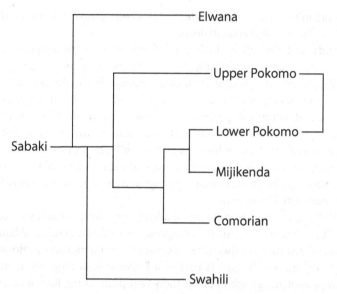

FIGURE 1. Divergence of Sabaki languages.

linguists analyze its phonetic shape and distribution in modern languages, using a classification of the languages where the word is spoken as a guiding framework.[43] Not all words' histories can be reconstructed. But assuming a scholar has adequate linguistic data and assuming the word has been affected by sound changes in the languages under study, it is sometimes possible to determine the past language (or protolanguage) in which a word was first spoken and its status in that language. Furthermore, by studying a word's meaning in extant languages, dictionaries, and ethnographic sources, as well as its derivational features, historical linguists can hypothesize its earliest meaning and determine whether that meaning has changed over time. Some words are inherited from distant linguistic ancestors while others are the product of innovations in an individual language (or language family). In other cases, speakers of a language may begin using a word after borrowing it from another language. Whenever people invented a new technology, idea, or social practice, they also needed to create or adopt a new word (or adapt an existing word) to refer to it. Thus, that same word's derivation can provide clues into concepts and associations that underlie its meaning. Bringing together these details—that is, a word's history in a particular language or group of languages, its derivation, and changes to its meaning over time—can provide scholars with rich materials for historical analysis.[44]

Let's consider as an example a word that is shared in both Mijikenda and Swahili: *muzimu* (or *mzimu*). If we look up these words in some of the earliest Swahili dictionaries from the nineteenth century, we find descriptions like "a place where sacrifices are offered to an evil spirit which is thought to haunt it; e.g., near an *mbuyu* [baobab] tree," and "a native place of worship, i.e. where offerings and prayers are made to the spirits, whether of ancestors or others," located around "a rock, a cave, tree, or ruin."[45] In Mijikenda, *muzimu* similarly represented "nature spirits . . . which live permanently in caves or at the baobab trees."[46] From these materials, we can quickly conclude that a type of spirit called *muzimu* or *mzimu* occupied natural spaces like caves or baobab trees around the East African coast during the nineteenth century and later. We can also see that sometimes people made offerings to appease these spirits. Looking beyond Mijikenda and Swahili, however, we can see that this type of spirit—and the practices surrounding them—have much deeper histories.

Muzimu is derived from the proto-Bantu root *-djm-, which linguists have reconstructed as meaning "be extinguished, extinguish, get lost."[47] The proto-Bantu lexicon also included a noun derived from this root: *mudjmù or "spirit" (the ancient form of the Swahili and Mijikenda terms), which historical linguists propose specifically connoted an "ancestral spirit" or "spirit of a long departed person."[48] Speakers of Bantu languages create nouns by attaching prefixes and suffixes to root words, in this case the noun prefix mu- and the suffix -u. Studying these units of grammar along with the root makes it possible to discern the meanings that speakers embedded in this cluster of sounds that signaled a "spirit" dating back at least five thousand years. The prefix mu- indicates the term's noun class—a classification system that speakers of Bantu languages use to group nouns based on their semantic characteristics. In Bantu languages this noun class mostly consists of trees and plants, body parts, and other natural phenomena. However, scholars have proposed that this noun class also included "entities with vitality," which were "neither human nor prototypically animal," such as supernatural phenomena (ancestral spirits) and human collectives (villages and clans).[49]

On an etymological level, spirits designated by the term *muzimu* were understood to be entities that were "extinguished" or "lost" yet still lived or had vitality. If this seems contradictory at face value (after all, how can something lost or extinguished have vitality?) it makes much more sense when viewed in the context of human relationships with *mizimu* (the word's plural form). This is where comparative ethnographic evidence becomes useful, allowing us to connect words and their meanings to specific practices in the social worlds of speakers of distant languages. In the recent past, communities across the continent understood spirits or ancestral ghosts (called by names derived from the proto-Bantu word *mudjmù) to play a role in their physical worlds. In Ganda-speaking communities (Uganda) these spirits often appeared as snakes and resided around bodies of water, while among Tonga speakers (Zambia) they acted as guardians and shared kinship relations with entire households.[50] In both Swahili and Mijikenda, *mizimu* were linked to specific places on the landscape, often caves, holes in trees, or small shrines that people built themselves.[51] Looking at other Northeast Coast languages, we find that many of the ideas and practices surrounding these ancestral spirits mirror those

12   INTRODUCTION

of Mijikenda- and Swahili-speaking communities. For instance, in communities that spoke Zaramo (a Ruvu language spoken in central coastal Tanzania) healers propitiated *mizimu* that lived in small huts or trees (often baobabs) with offerings, including strips of cloth and medicine gourds. In Seuta languages spoken in northeast Tanzania, *mizimu* dwelled in groves of trees, around prominent rocks, or at ancestral gravesites where they needed to be supplicated with offerings.[52]

From this comparative evidence, we can conclude that practices of constructing shrines in small huts or in natural spaces and presenting offerings to the spirits occupying these spaces date to at least proto–Northeast Coast, approximately two thousand years ago. This is just one example, but it illustrates how studying the words people used in the past can provide a rich background for writing social histories for distant societies. Such evidence is not limited to the ritual realm. As we'll see, historical linguistics can yield similar insights into the social incorporation practices of past societies, changes and continuities in their livelihood activities, and trading interactions across social and linguistic boundaries. From the viewpoint of port cities or from the deck of a dhow, East Africa's interior was an unknown territory. But by layering linguistic evidence alongside other sources, including archaeological evidence, oral traditions, and written documents, it is possible to view the histories of smaller communities in Mombasa's interior within the much larger purview of the global Indian Ocean.

TAKING AN EARLY AFRICAN HISTORY APPROACH TO GLOBAL AND INDIAN OCEAN HISTORY

The sources and methods detailed above offer us a way to approach the Indian Ocean's history from the perspective of smaller-scale, rural societies often peripheral to studies of this global macro-region. My aim, however, is to do more than simply add East Africa's interior into the existing framework of oceanic history. This book is foremost concerned with Mijikenda speakers' participation in commercial and political dynamics of the Indian Ocean. My use of "participation" as a framework is inspired by scholarship on the Eurasian steppe, which addresses practical, and often highly localized, ways that societies engaged in larger-scale worlds and processes.[53] In some cases, Mijikenda speakers' participation strategies aligned with the norms of individuals and communities engaged in trade in ports like Mombasa. But in other instances, they participated in transregional trade and politics by opting out of the dominant transregional norms and instead emphasizing social, ritual, or commercial links within a distinctively inland milieu.

By following Mijikenda speakers' alternative means of participating in the Indian Ocean world, *Inland from Mombasa* contributes to a recent turn in global history and Indian Ocean scholarship toward studying frictions, disconnections, and contingencies in transregional interactions. Much initial global scholarship—especially work on premodern periods—emphasized past movements of people, commodities, or ideas across oceans or continents.[54] In most cases, the key agents of global histories were cosmopolitans, individuals who shared relationships and cultural affinities with people living in far afield locales, either through their own travels or their embracing of widely circulating cultural phenomena.[55] More recently, a growing number of historians have become critical of this overpowering emphasis on transregional mobility and cosmopolitanism in global history scholarship. In asking why people struggled with, or even rejected, new forms of connection, this emerging body of scholarship argues that disconnections were key constituting features of transregional interactions.[56] In the Indian Ocean, for instance, Nile Green has shown that travelers often struggled to comprehend the differences they encountered from one port to another, even when intermingling with fellow Muslims. To Green, the Indian Ocean was a space of "heterotopia," or a "place of difference/otherness." While some of its participants embraced the material or religious signatures of a shared oceanic imaginary, "cosmopolitanism was only one form of response."[57]

Africanist historians and anthropologists also have had a long-standing interest in the uneven ways the continent fits into narratives of the "global." Scholarship on globalization, for example, has shown that different societies and places in Africa engaged with introduced commodities, religious ideas, and institutions in an unpredictable manner, confounding totalizing narratives of global processes.[58] Moreover, as studies of decentralized societies in precolonial West Africa demonstrate, many communities maintained distinctive social philosophies and village organization strategies while also participating in large-scale networks such as the trans-Saharan gold trade and the Atlantic economy.[59] Societies' lacking of features like political centralization, writing, or "global" religious practices did not prevent them from forging connections with other regions of the continent and world. Instead, healing associations, spirit mediums, and ritual cosmologies cast as "local" by the conventional frames of historical scholarship could in fact constitute larger-scale connections.[60] Yet such "internal" developments in Africa have seldom resonated with global historians' interests in transregional mobilities and cultural flows, despite rich evidence of intra-African connections across physiographic regions and language groups dating back millennia.[61]

Building on the above scholarship, I argue that the very features that make Mijikenda speakers' histories appear insignificant or local within the context of broader narratives of the Indian Ocean were not divorced from East Africa's global connections, but they in fact helped constitute those connections. One of the main reasons that spaces like inland villages remain peripheral to global narratives is a dearth of traditional written evidence. Mijikenda were an oral society, at least during the time periods covered in this book. The earliest written documentation, like the Portuguese records noted in the opening section, offer only a glimpse into Mijikenda speakers' world at a very particular moment: when they visited Mombasa for trade or conflict. No detailed descriptions of inland villages and the social

14   INTRODUCTION

ideas and practices animating them exist for periods prior to the nineteenth century. To understand the ideas and motivations that informed their engagements with the world, it is necessary to look to other types of evidence, including archaeology, oral traditions, and especially historical linguistics.

As discussed in the previous section, historians of Africa's distant past employ comparative historical linguistics to reconstruct large-scale histories of places without ample documentary records. Initial scholarship based on these methods focused on the movement of language groups, most famously in debates on the "Bantu expansions."[62] By the 1990s, however, scholars began using reconstructed word histories to explore social histories and political ideologies of societies that lived thousands of years in the past.[63] More recent scholarship has continued expanding the thematic possibilities of historical linguistic methods, addressing topics like fame and bushcraft, gendered authority and motherhood, and concepts of wealth and poverty.[64] While such scholarship focuses predominantly on histories internal to the African continent, other work has shown potential applications of these methods for studying transcontinental topics like Atlantic slavery.[65] For East Africa, Rhonda Gonzales, Yaari Seligman, and Daren Ray have illuminated the vast inland interactive spheres with which Swahili society was connected in their respective histories of religious life, trade, and community formation for different societies in the coastal interior.[66] Yet, the project of using these methods to incorporate "the perspective of those left out of or marginalized in traditional global history archives and metanarratives" remains at its most nascent stages.[67]

DISAGGREGATING THE CONNECTED HISTORIES OF INDIAN OCEAN PORTS

By bringing the histories of small-scale, inland-oriented societies like Mijikenda into the foreground, we can reimagine a diverse array of people and places playing an active role in forging transregional connections across the Indian Ocean. Historians of the Indian Ocean are increasingly interested in linking histories of specific ports, actors, and networks to broader narratives of the region, bringing a new focus to its heterogeneity and diversity. The earliest studies on the Indian Ocean focused on vast scales. Taking their cue from Ferdinand Braudel's model for understanding the Mediterranean, scholars illuminated the cohesiveness of cultural idioms, economic practices, and religious ideas across the "world" constituted by the Indian Ocean.[68] But in endeavoring to study the Indian Ocean as a world or a unified economic system, scholars inadvertently erased the specificity and diversity of local circumstances in the different societies living along the ocean's shores.[69]

Over the last decade and a half, however, scholars have produced pathbreaking book-length studies of many ports and regions of the Indian Ocean.[70] As the field has shifted toward studying specific sites, diasporic communities, and networks, scholars have demonstrated how people in far-flung port cities built and maintained connections to support trade, kinship ties, and religious communities.[71] In turn, this work has offered an increasingly textured view into the social practices, legal and economic institutions, and technologies that supported people's interactions across the vastness of the Indian Ocean.[72]

And yet the inland regions adjacent to port cities remain peripheral to most studies. For instance, we now have a much better understanding of the social and religious dynamics of port cities on the Malabar coast of India, but we still know very little about the hinterlands from where Malabar's most famous export—pepper—was procured.[73] Similarly, it has been established that by the thirteenth and fourteenth centuries, textiles from Gujarat (in northwestern India) circulated widely across the Indian Ocean and beyond, from Cairo to the Swahili coast, Southeast Asia, and China. Yet the cotton-producing and weaving regions based around villages in India's interior do not figure into analyses of the Indian Ocean prior to the seventeenth and eighteenth centuries.[74] The common refrain is that while interior regions were linked to port cities, we do not have the source materials to fully elucidate the economic, political, and social worlds of these places beyond their vague role as suppliers.[75] Recently, some scholars have successfully shown that East Africa's interior was a distinctive Indian Ocean region by tracing movements of coastal individuals, religious practices, and imaginaries into the Great Lakes region during the nineteenth and twentieth centuries.[76]

But probing the rich role of inland "peripheries"—especially for earlier periods—requires taking a different analytical lens, one that moves beyond the littoral frameworks often associated with the Indian Ocean's past.[77] Differences between the littoral and interior are often used to justify the exclusion of inland societies from oceanic histories. Michael Pearson's concept of a "littoral society" has been an influential model for how scholars frame the geographic parameters of the Indian Ocean's history. Pearson defined littoral societies as those whose livelihoods and cultural identities were connected to oceans and seas and argued that this orientation toward the sea made them distinct from land-facing neighbors. To Pearson, the "shore folk" living in Indian Ocean cities like Mombasa, Surat, Aden, and Calicut had "more in common with other shore folk thousands of kilometers away on some other shore of the ocean than they do with those of their immediate hinterland."[78] Being a member of a littoral society was about more than one's location. It also meant possessing cultural connections to the ocean, such as a shared religious identity or kinship ties with people living in far-flung oceanic locales.[79] In such a framing, settlements on Mombasa's mainland, even those located within view of the Indian Ocean, are peripheral to the world of littoral. So, too, are the expert elephant hunters who supplied East Africa's most prized global trade good; and the cotton weavers in South Asian villages who produced textiles that were desired from Mombasa to Cairo to Southeast Asia.[80]

16   INTRODUCTION

I do not dispute that there are similarities—religious, legal, gastronomical, and so on—shared by people in Mombasa, Muscat, and other port cities. However, these mutual cultural characteristics do not fully explain connections between these places. As Thomas McDow argues, previous scholarship on the Indian Ocean generally lacked any sense of contingency. Writing on the nineteenth century, McDow shows that the movement of Omanis to East Africa to pursue commercial opportunities was not simply the predetermined byproduct of increasing transregional connections. Instead, a drought in Oman's interior in the 1840s pushed many rural date farmers to look for new prospects at sea. In East Africa, a mix of people including Arab migrants, manumitted slaves, and others pursued trading opportunities farther into the continent's interior over the course of the nineteenth century. This was partly due to the growth of long-distance caravan routes, but it also was the result of people needing to "buy time" by creating distance between themselves and their creditors in places like Zanzibar.[81] In other words, trading connections between Oman and East Africa did not just happen naturally as the result of peoples' proximity to the sea, some common religious ideas, or even straightforward commercial aspirations. To understand the ocean as a space of interaction means paying attention to peoples' capacity to make these connections happen, sometimes for reasons that are not immediately apparent.

How, then, did people in Mombasa's interior partake in the boom of transregional connections that characterized Indian Ocean port cities during the second millennium? From one perspective, villages in Mombasa's immediate interior represent what James Scott termed "shadow" or "mirror" societies. For Scott, this refers to communities that position their social ideas, economic activities, or religious practices in contradiction to those of neighboring states or urban centers.[82] In such a framing, Mijikenda speakers' rejection of Islam and emphasis on smaller-scale villages represent an intentional political project based around refusing the norms and values of nearby urban polities. In the chapters that follow, I show these were intentional choices; and, moreover, that key features of inland ritual, social, and economic life were the result of ongoing changes, adaptations, and interactions that "mirrored" parallel processes in the Islamicate Indian Ocean. However, peoples' decisions to organize themselves into small-scale societies or to reject a global religion like Islam were often about more than just resisting the values and norms of neighboring states or urban centers. I argue that Mijikenda speakers' choices were not about rejecting Mombasa and its oceanic connections but instead provided them with a means to participate in and influence trade and politics in the port city and beyond.

Port cities—and spaces like states and urban centers more generally—have always depended on economic, social, and political relationships with societies that have radically different social organization strategies, economic practices, and mobilities. As archaeologists Nicole Boivin and Michael Frachetti argue, "It is difficult to envision how early globalising processes might have unfolded if

INTRODUCTION   17

we *do not* deprivilege states" precisely because of their dependency on smaller-scale societies.[83] The centrality of port cities to scholarship on the Indian Ocean is not going away—nor should it. At the same time, it is important to recognize that people living in the "peripheries" of urban centers were not required to enter trading or social relationships with neighboring urbanites and could sometimes strategically benefit from their lack of affiliations.[84] This reality opens questions about why and how people chose to participate in these relationships. What were their goals? What sorts of social ideas motivated their actions and ambitions? And how did these divergent goals and actions—divergent from an oceanic viewpoint, at least—influence larger processes of social and commercial transformation? As the chapters that follow will show, Mijikenda speakers prominently shaped East Africa's oceanic connections through practices, relationships, and social pursuits that were frequently out of harmony with those of Indian Ocean ports.

ORGANIZATION OF THE BOOK

The book is organized into five chapters with a rough chronology, starting in the first millennium in chapter 1 and ending in the mid-nineteenth century in chapter 5. But the chapters are also arranged thematically, each one tackling a major theme in studies of East Africa's Indian Ocean history, but from an inland vantage point: (1) the early roots of coastal society; (2) the formation of social and ritual connections with other societies; (3) long-distance trade; (4) oceanic imperialism; and (5) nineteenth-century transformations and integrations. Chapters 1 and 2 work together to trace the inland roots of Indian Ocean connections, providing a foundation for chapters 3 through 5, which turn to Mijikenda speakers' relationships with Mombasa and the wider world and develop the book's central arguments.

The book begins, quite intentionally, with a moment of discontinuity in the long-distance networks powered by the Indian Ocean monsoon. At the start of the first millennium, the East African coast was integrated within maritime trading networks. However, these linkages dwindled around the middle of the millennium due to overlapping ecological and political ruptures in the Indian Ocean and Mediterranean regions. Chapter 1 traces how the Sabaki-speaking ancestors of Swahili and Mijikenda capitalized on this down period in oceanic trade. They adapted new foods and agricultural technologies, shifting to cultivation strategies based around cereals, which enabled them to establish settlements across a greater range of ecologies. During this same time, coastal East Africans also developed the ideological tools to build larger communities. Ideas about land ownership, debt, and social reciprocity provided enterprising leaders with new strategies for expanding their communities of dependents. By the time Indian Ocean networks reemerged during the latter part of the first millennium, Sabaki speakers had developed the subsistence practices and social tools they needed to occupy regions along the coast, to participate in expanding scales of exchange, and to build larger settlements.

By the end of the first millennium, coastal East Africa was a world rife with different social and economic possibilities, including but not limited to connections with the oceanic sphere. Chapter 2 explores the distinctive ways that Mijikenda communities built connections and adapted new ritual ideas during the Indian Ocean's emerging golden era. At the start of the second millennium, Mijikenda speakers possessed the same capabilities for organizing larger communities as their Swahili neighbors. However, they instead embraced smaller settlements and emphasized interactions with other communities in the interior. Analyzing evidence from archaeology, historical linguistics, ethnography, and oral traditions, I show that Mijikenda speakers cultivated strong social and ritual ties with neighboring inland groups across the second millennium. In the absence of a larger urban polity, specialized medicinal groups and spaces like forest clearings shaped the contours of political life and created linkages between dispersed homesteads. Because healing was a competitive arena, rural homestead heads sought out new medicines and ritual ideas, generating exchanges and associations with neighboring, non-Mijikenda-speaking groups in the process. Much like the transcultural practices that undergirded affiliations between merchants in Indian Ocean port cities, this budding inland interactive sphere created opportunities for inland communities to influence East Africa's connections to the world.

While the book's first two chapters set a foundation for understanding Mombasa's oceanic history from an inland perspective, the remainder of the book shifts to the specific ways that people living in inland villages influenced trading and political connections in the Indian Ocean. Chapter 3 examines how communities in Mombasa's interior shaped its maritime economy between the late first millennium and the early nineteenth century. By the fifteenth century, Mombasa was East Africa's most important port, a position that stemmed from its role in supplying valued trade goods for other parts of the Indian Ocean, especially ivory and gum copal. Extending the analysis from the previous chapter, I trace how the ties that Mijikenda speakers cultivated with their inland neighbors influenced maritime exchange circuits and laid the foundations for long-distance caravan routes. Over centuries, inland societies exchanged knowledge and built networks that supported long-distance trade. They developed social strategies for forming partnerships across sociolinguistic lines and came to share a mutual commercial vocabulary for things like markets, trade party leaders, and long-distance caravans. While Mijikenda speakers and their inland interlocutors supplied Mombasa with key oceanic trade goods, export goods like ivory moved along complex interior mosaics that were not primarily oriented around supplying the demands of the Indian Ocean economy. Tracking the story of Indian Ocean trade through the lens of East Africa's interior offers a novel perspective on the dynamics that drive connections between Mombasa and other Indian Ocean port cities.

The final two chapters explore Mijikenda speakers' influence on global politics during the eras of Portuguese and Omani imperialism. Chapter 4 traces inland communities' influence on these major oceanic empires. Building on chapter 3, I show how Mijikenda speakers' commercial influence in Mombasa extended into the realm of politics, giving them a powerful sway over the city. Between the sixteenth and eighteenth centuries, different maritime empires aspired to control the port city. Mombasa's fate ebbed and flowed around Mijikenda speakers' decisions to collaborate—or not—with these foreign interlocutors. The chapter illuminates how Mijikenda communities wielded their control over access to inland trade goods and critical food provisions to extract tributes from imperial powers and demand a voice in Mombasa's affairs. As fleets from Portuguese India and Oman attempted to control trade in Mombasa, they sent textiles to inland leaders, which formed the foundation of commercial, military, and diplomatic partnerships. Ultimately, I argue that inland communities' political decisions and commercial inventiveness were central to transimperial conflicts in the western Indian Ocean.

Chapter 5 examines how Mijikenda speakers understood their relationship with Mombasa, looking specifically at the rituals and practices that they used to maintain independence from the port city. Trade and political partnerships around Mombasa were constituted by two interlinked concepts: *heshima*—tributes that Mijikenda speakers received from Mombasa—and *kore*—a person exchanged to settle a debt. For centuries, Mijikenda communities maintained their relationships with Mombasa by claiming tributes, or *heshima*, while coastal merchants occasionally seized *kore* to ensure that these partnerships remained fair and balanced. I argue that Mijikenda communities remained fully independent from Mombasa so long as they continued to receive *heshima* from their urban partners, whether they were Swahili speakers, Omanis, or Europeans. However, between the 1830s and 1850s, Mombasa became formally part of the Busaidi Sultanate of Muscat and Zanzibar. This change undermined Mijikenda speakers' control over inland trade routes and, in the process, altered the balance between *heshima* and *kore*. The Busaidi era is typically seen as a period of intensive global integration, during which East Africa's interior became more directly connected to the Indian Ocean economy. In following these shifts in the region's political and economic history, I demonstrate how a familiar story of increasing global connections during the nineteenth century looks radically different from the vantage point of communities on Mombasa's mainland.

The book concludes by zooming out to other locations around the Indian Ocean to explore the influence of smaller-scale, inland societies on other ports and regions. Rather than simply comparing these case studies, I imagine the connections we might discern between these overlooked people and places living across this macro-region by paying attention to these out-of-harmony "peripheries."

1

Unmoored from the Ocean

Fifty million years ago, the tectonic plate that constitutes the Indian subcontinent collided with the Eurasian landmass. Over tens of millennia, the convergence of these two pieces of land pushed up the surrounding earth vertically, forming the Himalayan Mountains and Tibetan Plateau. These ancient subterranean events may seem worlds away from port cities like Mombasa, which only began to flourish millennia later. Yet their histories are intimately linked by the Indian Ocean's monsoon winds—an environmental force brought into being by these distant geological events.[1] The monsoon winds are powered by interactions between the mountain plateau and the ocean. In the northern hemisphere's summer months, the plateau heats up, drawing moist air from the ocean toward the Asian landmass. In the winter months, the high plateau cools the air above it, creating a high-pressure zone that pushes air above the Tibetan Plateau and out toward the ocean.[2] This seasonal push and pull generates alternating wind patterns that have, for millennia, facilitated transregional seaborne travel in the Indian Ocean. Between November and January, the winds allow ships to follow predictable wind patterns and currents to travel from South Asia to Arabia and East Africa. From April to August, the winds reverse, facilitating return trips and connecting communities in coastal East Africa to a vast network of port cities.

For at least two millennia, the seasonal reversal of the Indian Ocean's monsoon trade winds has enabled coastal East African communities to develop commercial ties with merchants from across the wider macro-region. But as a historical force, the monsoon is not timeless or unchanging. While ancient tectonic collisions created the Indian Ocean's famed trade winds, a cooler and drier climate regime during the middle centuries of the first millennium weakened the southwest (or Asian) monsoon and disrupted maritime trading networks that previously connected large expanses of Afro-Eurasia.[3] At the start of the first millennium, the East African coast was part of commercial networks linking the Indian Ocean and Mediterranean.[4] However, when Sabaki-speaking groups (the linguistic ancestors to Swahili and Mijikenda speakers) established settlements on the coast during the mid-first millennium, they did not encounter the Indian Ocean as maritime-oriented traders.

This chapter narrates history of Sabaki society from the vantage point of a farm field, a short distance inland from the coast. My emphasis on coastal East African societies' rural roots has many precedents in the literature. In the 1980s and 1990s, historians, archaeologists, and linguists began to dislodge older colonial scholarship that cast Swahili culture as a Middle Eastern import. Keeping local evolutions at the center of the story, this work detailed how small-scale fishing and farming villages founded in the first millennium grew into flourishing urban centers through centuries of contact with foreign merchants.[5] While this scholarship represented a watershed for emphasizing the African roots of Swahili society, it treated the region's pre-Swahili past mainly as a point of departure for understanding the later emergence of oceanic trading networks. More recent archaeological work has started to dislodge the teleological narratives, showing the complex trajectories of coastal villages from the late first millennium onward.[6] This chapter builds on this newer scholarship by tracing East Africa's varied engagements with oceanic worlds and pushing this narrative back in time to the centuries prior to the emergence of Swahili society. For the region's early Bantu-speaking settlers, this was not a period characterized by blossoming oceanic trade, but instead by climatic and commercial uncertainties.

By focusing on social and economic activities during a down period in oceanic interactions, this chapter illuminates the generative possibilities of disconnecting from global networks. As I will show, during the early to mid-first millennium, coastal East Africans renovated their subsistence economy, assembling knowledge for cultivation strategies based around cereals. These innovations facilitated settlement across a greater variety of ecologies, including the littoral, while also enabling coastal East Africans to experiment with their social form. By the end of the millennium, as maritime trading networks reemerged in full force, coastal East Africans had cultivated the necessary ideological and subsistence roots to live closer to the coast and build larger and denser settlements. These subsistence innovations also made it possible for Sabaki speakers and their descendants to participate in expanding scales of trade, in both the oceanic sphere and in East Africa's interior. Following the considerable social and economic innovations during this moment of discontinuity alerts us to a world of multiple possibilities, where the ultimate

22   UNMOORED FROM THE OCEAN

emergence of Islamic, maritime-oriented urban towns along the East African coast was only one potential outcome.

THE *PERIPLUS* AND THE "PRE-SWAHILI" COAST

No source better represents East Africa's early interactions with maritime trading networks than the first-century Greco-Roman merchant's guide, the *Periplus Maris Erythraei*. The text, and the trading world it depicts, offer useful starting points for this chapter because it describes thriving oceanic connections that were fleeting rather than timeless. Written by an anonymous Greek speaker living in Alexandria around the middle of the first century, the *Periplus* reports on port cities stretching from the Red Sea to the coast of eastern Africa, southern Arabia, the Persian Gulf, and South Asia. As a merchant's guide, it offers details on everything from the products that could be sold and procured at each port to its receptiveness to hosting foreign merchants.[7] The East African coast—called Azania in the *Periplus*—takes up a small yet notable fraction of the guide. According to the text's author, the Azania coast started to the south of the port city of Opônê, located at Ras Hafun, in modern Somalia.[8] After Opônê, mariners encountered a sparsely populated coastline, featuring natural harbors that acted as stopping points for ships, but there were no prominent settlements besides Menuthias, a wooded island occupied by fisherfolk.[9] Shortly after Menuthias, merchants reached Rhapta, "the very last port of trade on the coast of Azania."[10]

As the primary Azanian trading town, Rhapta occupies an important place for understandings of East Africa's earliest connections to the Indian Ocean. According to the *Periplus*, the people of Rhapta participated in seasonal trade with visiting merchants, exchanging locally procured items like ivory and tortoise shell for imported spears, axes, and glassware. The seasonal nature of Indian Ocean trade meant that the merchants who plied their wares along the Azanian coast had to spend months at a time in the town, probably arriving in November or December and departing no earlier than April or May. The text makes clear that foreign merchants were well integrated into the social life of Rhapta. They commonly married into local families and spoke Azanian languages. Furthermore, the seasonal visitors cemented their "good will" among locals with gifts of "wine and grain," which stood apart from common trade goods. Apart from trade, visiting merchants also collected taxes on behalf of the governor of Mapharitis, in southern Yemen, indicating East Africa's political links with Arabia. However, according to the text, the Azanians remained in control of their own political affairs.[11]

With its overseas ties and multicultural households, Rhapta represents the characteristic global port town. But despite all the ways that the town conjures a familiar Indian Ocean milieu, much of the place's history remains elusive. Beyond the *Periplus*, only one other historical text mentions Rhapta: Ptolemy's *Geography*, which was written around 150 CE.[12] Ptolemy described Rhapta as a "metropolis," a label that he used for only five other towns in the entire Indian Ocean region, placing Rhapta in company with Meroe and Aksum (NE Africa); Saphar and Saubatha (Arabia); and Minnagar (South Asia).[13] Even with Rhapta's status as a metropolis, archaeologists have yet to identify its location from material records. Based on geographic details offered in the *Periplus*, most believe that Rhapta was located along the central coast of Tanzania.[14] However, the earliest archaeological evidence for foreign imported goods (ceramics and glassware) in this region all date to around the fifth or sixth century.[15] After *Geography*, the next known textual reference to the East African coast is from the sixth-century text *Christian Topography*, written by the Alexandrian merchant Cosmas Indicopleustes. In contrast to earlier references to the "metropolis" of Rhapta, *Christian Topography* contains only a passing reference to the East African coast, suggesting that Mediterranean interest in the region had waned significantly by the mid-first millennium.[16]

Scholars have a long-standing interest in connecting the traders of Rhapta to the merchants who lived in future Swahili towns. It is tempting to see Rhapta as a precursor to the cosmopolitan port cities that orient our understanding of the East African coast today. However, Rhapta's current state of archaeological invisibility makes it hard to draw direct linkages. Moreover, the sociolinguistic identities of these first-century coastal traders remain unclear. The region's earliest occupants were Late Stone Age groups who fished, hunted small game, and foraged for shellfish along the coast and immediate offshore islands.[17] In the last centuries BCE, Southern Cushitic-speaking agropastoralists also began occupying parts of the coastal region and neighboring hinterlands.[18] By contrast, the earliest evidence of Bantu-speaking settlements within the coastal region dates to the very beginning of the first millennium. Most of these sites are located twenty kilometers or more inland from the coast.[19] While Swahili speakers' Northeast Coast ancestors may have occupied the hinter-coastal region by the time of the *Periplus*, they were relative newcomers. Rhapta appears to have already been a well-established trading hub by the first century, making the pre-Swahili and *Periplus* connections fraught, even apart from the archaeological uncertainties.

To put these sources in a larger context, societies on the coast of East Africa were part of developments that brought together the Mediterranean and Indian Ocean worlds in the early first millennium CE. During this time, the western Indian Ocean experienced relatively stable temperatures and rainfall. Predictable alterations in the monsoon winds aided the growth of the long-distance maritime trade networks described in the *Periplus* while also supporting statecraft in multiple regions connected to the Indian Ocean rim, contributing to the Gupta, Funan, and Sassanian polities.[20] However, there was a major downturn in these Afro-Eurasian exchange networks around the middle of the first millennium, partly due to dramatic changes in the climate. The northern hemisphere experienced a prolonged period of aridity starting around the sixth century, sometimes referred to as the Late Antique Little Ice Age.[21] Paleoenvironmental records from India and southern Arabia similarly point to environmental fluctuations during this time, including a "severe weakening" of the southwest monsoon, which started around the fifth and sixth centuries and lasted until the ninth.[22] These changes in the climate overlapped with bubonic plague outbreaks and the fragmentation of several major states in both the Indian Ocean and Mediterranean.[23]

Coastal East Africans' interface with global exchange networks was unquestionably affected by both the extensive commercial interconnectivity of the early centuries CE and its subsequent decline. As a result, the earliest historical texts on coastal East Africa refer to a thriving market center at Rhapta. But by mid-millennium, the region received only a passing mention by Cosmas. Rhapta itself quite literally disappeared from the map. Today, scholars can only speculate about the location of the once great market town. By the tenth century, when the Baghdadi geographer al-Masudi supplied the next similarly detailed description of coastal East African society, an entirely new set of towns acted as the staging ground for maritime trade in the region.[24]

While the merchants of the bustling metropolis of Rhapta offer us the earliest view of maritime commercial activity in coastal East Africa, they occupied a fleeting world. The *Periplus*, and other high points of maritime connectivity, such as the arrival of Islam and the growth of Swahili ports, offer important vantage points into coastal East Africa's global past.[25] As recent archaeological research has emphasized, however, developments in subsistence, including the translocation of crops and animals in the Indian Ocean, were also a critical component of maritime connectivity.[26] To understand coastal East Africa's urbanization and participation in long-distance trade, it is necessary to first look to steady modifications of subsistence techniques and technologies in prior centuries, processes that historian Jan Vansina famously referred to as the "slow revolution" in agriculture.[27] The next section traces the formative phases of this gradual revolution in subsistence. Over the course of the first millennium, coastal East African societies assembled knowledge of their environment and adapted their food production technologies to suit their local needs. In their experiments with different subsistence techniques, early coastal Bantu groups helped to set the stage for the emergence of port cities along the Swahili coast. But not because they were especially well oriented toward the ocean.

A "SLOW REVOLUTION" IN FIRST-MILLENNIUM COASTAL EAST AFRICA

Northeast Coast speakers' arrival to East Africa's hinter-coastal region around the start of the first millennium CE would have entailed ongoing renovations to their subsistence practices as they adapted to different environments. During the more recent past, seasonal fluctuations in rainfall oriented the agricultural labors of communities living along the northern part of East Africa's littoral.[28] Cultivators spent the drier months of January and February burning brush and breaking up ground in preparation for planting. They planted crops in March, just prior to the arrival of the long rains that last from April to May. After spending the rainy months tending to and protecting their fields, they undertook the major harvest in August, followed by a period for threshing and winnowing to transform the yields into edible foods. Harvesting and processing bled into a short and intense rainy season in October and November.[29] By the end of the short rains, alterations in the seasonal trade winds facilitated travels for merchants from India and the Arabian Peninsula to coastal towns stretching from Mogadishu to Kilwa.

The apparent synergies between agricultural cycles and economic activities were the result of generation upon generation of knowledge accrual and innovations. Coastal East Africa's first Bantu-speaking settlers would not have experienced the Indian Ocean as maritime traders and travelers but as observers of a changing climate and ecology as they settled in closer proximity to the littoral. In the process, they assembled knowledge of local vegetation, soils, and rainfall patterns, establishing their settlements based around a variety of calculations: Where could they effectively grow food? Could they easily procure wild resources nearby? What possibilities existed for exchanges with neighboring communities? When they encountered limitations—perhaps recognizing that certain staple foods grew more effectively than others within these ecological niches—successful communities adapted by adopting or inventing new cultivation techniques and technologies.

To understand the dynamic nature of the agricultural economy in coastal East Africa's early history, it is helpful to take a long-term view of Bantu speakers' food procurement practices. The earliest Bantu-speaking groups based their cultivation strategies around root crops that were well suited for the equatorial forests where Bantu languages were first spoken.[30] After 1000 BCE, speakers of Bantu languages (who spoke a protolanguage called Mashariki) began populating drier savanna regions of eastern Africa where they learned about new crops, including sorghum and millet varieties, from speakers of Sudanic and Sahelian languages.[31] However, shifting their cultivation strategies from tubers to grains was not as simple as replacing one crop with another. Adopting new foods entailed a transformation in food production practices, from the tools and techniques used to manage agricultural grounds, to methods for preparing their harvests for cooking and consumption. Planting root vegetables, as their linguistic ancestors had in the equatorial forests, was not very labor intensive. It involved "minimal clearing of land, cutting larger vegetation . . . but leaving stumps in place" and planting by making "small incisions in the soil" using the blade of a planting axe.[32] Cereal cultivation, by contrast, demanded significantly more exertion: clearing land, burning vegetation to destroy invasive weeds, and breaking up earth to prepare it for planting. Such methods demanded not only new tools, techniques, and field types but also an ability to mobilize labor to clear, plant, and maintain those fields. As a result of the unique challenges of

26 UNMOORED FROM THE OCEAN

grain cultivation, root crops retained primacy in Mashariki speakers' subsistence practices until late in the last millennium BCE.[33]

As Northeast Coast speakers began to occupy regions nearer to the littoral, they adopted ecological and subsistence knowledge from in situ communities.[34] For instance, Northeast Coast speakers' interactions with speakers of a Southern Cushitic language produced a new word for sorghum, *mutama, which replaced an older term, *-pú, which their Mashariki ancestors had adopted from Central Sudanic languages.[35] Their willingness to borrow a new term indicates that as communities moved away from their Mashariki homelands, sorghum became less important as a crop. Perhaps the most interesting addition to Northeast Coast speakers' knowledge base was their adoption of a new word to refer to the short rainy season, *-buli, which was also a Southern Cushitic loanword.[36] This loaning may have been linked to the changing seasonality of rainfall as Northeast Coast speakers settled in northern central Tanzania's coastal hinterlands.[37]

After a short proto-period, probably lasting no more than a few centuries, the proto–Northeast Coast community began to diverge into four daughter languages: Sabaki, Pare, Ruvu, and Seuta. For Sabaki speakers, this divergence likely began as their nascent speech community slowly pushed northward into the coastal hinterlands of southeastern Kenya, possibly in search of more productive lands for cultivation.[38] Paleoecological records indicate that much of East Africa experienced a drier climate during the first half of the first millennium, with "severe and widespread drought" over the first two centuries.[39] The drier climate would have driven communities to favor settlements in ecological niches that granted access to a wide variety of resources.

Southeast Kenya's moist coastal forests were resilient to climate extremes, making them an appealing environment for ironworking settlers and hunting and foraging groups alike. Paleoecological records dating back fourteen thousand years indicate that the forested coastal uplands experienced a relatively stable climate, with "increasing rainfall and forest expansion" starting about two thousand years ago.[40] The region's climate records contrast to increasing aridity in other parts of East Africa during the same time.[41] Archaeological evidence from southeast Kenya shows that the earliest farming communities in this region concentrated their settlements in "the moist, fertile forest margins of the eastern coastal uplands."[42] Nearby freshwater streams and forests would have provided the occupants of these sites with access to wild resources for hunting and foraging and timber for building and making charcoal to fuel iron furnaces.[43] Predictable rainfall and the availability of abundant forest resources would have also offered new opportunities to experiment with subsistence techniques like farming.

While they pushed north out of the Northeast Coast homeland, Sabaki speakers widened their vocabulary for describing the work of clearing land and preparing fields for planting.[44] Their inherited vocabulary for cultivation was already extensive, including many retained techniques for preparing land: "cultivating with a

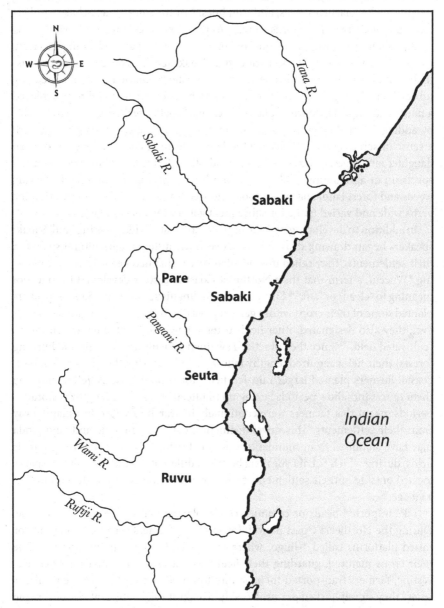

MAP 2. Approximate areas of Northeast Coast subgroups: proto-Sabaki, proto-Pare, proto-Seuta, and proto-Ruvu. Map created by John Wyatt Greenlee, Surprised Eel Mapping.

28   UNMOORED FROM THE OCEAN

hoe" (*-lim-), "flinging up earth" (*-fụkul-), and "uprooting" (*-ng'ol-). They pursued these labors using most of the same tools as their linguistic ancestors, including digging sticks, machetes, axes, and iron hoes.[45] At the same time, Sabaki speakers created at least two new words to refer to the work of clearing and maintaining land: *-omol-, meaning "to dig out" or "break up," and *-palil-, meaning "to clean, weed."[46] This vocabulary demonstrates that Sabaki speakers developed an increasingly complex technological repertoire to describe intensive labors like breaking up earth or digging up the roots of a tree, both actions that would have achieved a newfound importance when planting cereals. Sabaki speakers generated *-palil- by adding a verbal extension to a root meaning "to scrape," which gave the verb a sense of scraping *into* a field or plot, hence cleaning and weeding. In modern daughter languages, reflexes of *-palil- and other derived vocabulary cover a full spectrum of agricultural skills—including hoeing the surface of a field; clearing weeds and forest land; and piling roots and weeds into heaps—demonstrating the verb's wide and varied usage for subsequent generations of cultivators.[47]

In addition to developing new terms to describe labors like clearing land, Sabaki speakers began drawing distinctions between the different agricultural spaces in their settlements. They called uncultivated spaces that had been cleared for planting *Wucelu, a term that their Northeast Coast ancestors developed from a root meaning to "clean" or "sift."[48] Like their distant linguistic ancestors, Sabaki speakers planted some of their crops within garden plots that they called *mugunda.[49] However, they also designated other fields using a new word, *nkonde, which meant "cultivated field."[50] Since they practiced swidden agriculture (clearing and burning forests) their fields required lengthy fallow periods. During the more recent past, coastal farmers planted larger rain-fed fields for several seasons before allowing them to rest for fallow periods lasting up to fifteen years.[51] The lengthy restorative periods meant that farmers were continually in search of virgin forestland away from their settlements. This novel distinction between *nkonde and *mugunda may have stemmed from mundane cycles of clearing, planting, and resting their fields, during which Sabaki speakers began to differentiate the agricultural spaces located outside of their settlements from the smaller plots within the confines of a village.[52]

Like imported beads or ceramic vessels, planted fields were sources of value. During the Northeast Coast period, for instance, farmers began erecting huts or raised platforms called *-lingo, where they waited out the rainy months while their crops matured, guarding their fields against birds or animals.[53] After harvesting, farmers transported their bounty to raised storage huts in their villages where they stored husked grains. Notably, Sabaki speakers innovated a new name for their granaries during this time, *lucaga, which they used synonymously with the inherited term *lutala (or *kitala).[54] This expanding vocabulary for grain huts may indicate a technological diversification of storage methods as cereals like sorghum and millet became more central to subsistence activities. Ultimately, coastal

East Africans' creation of new structures to guard their fields and store their surpluses offers clear evidence of their investments in agriculture during the early first millennium.

Turning stalks of sorghum or millet into food required a repertoire of intensive processing techniques: threshing to remove the stalks, pounding and grinding broken grains, and winnowing away waste products to yield flour suitable for cooking. Sabaki speakers retained technological knowledge and tools from their linguistic ancestors to suit these tasks, such as winnowing baskets and mortars and pestles.[55] Yet they continued to develop new words to augment their inherited processing techniques and technologies. For instance, Sabaki speakers created a new word to describe a winnowing tray, *lucelo, which they derived from the same root as terms for cleared fields (*Wucelu) and cleaned grain (*mucele).[56] Since winnowing was not a new method, the innovation may indicate novel semantic links Sabaki speakers made between agricultural spaces, processing techniques, and their products.

While we cannot know precisely how extensive grain cultivation was during this period or how it compared to previous eras, the linguistic evidence suggests that Sabaki speakers were processing grain products on a scale that was significantly greater than their linguistic ancestors. In addition to tools for grain processing, they innovated several words that referred to waste products generated through winnowing and threshing: *Wishwa and *luWambe, both of which referred to "chaff," and *ncungu, which referred to waste heaps.[57] The derivations of these terms reveal some of the semantic creativity undergirding grain processing labors. Sabaki speakers produced *ncungu from an older root meaning to "winnow," suggestive of how the slow amassing of hardened husks on the ground through tasks like winnowing helped to conjure new vocabulary for waste heaps. They produced the second term, *luWambe, from a root meaning "to stretch." During the more recent past, reflexes of *luWambe referred to the pungent dust produced when threshing and grinding stalks of sorghum and millet.[58] The term's etymology enables us to envision a threshing hut in the first millennium, when Sabaki speakers began to note the ethereal qualities of waste products that "stretched" through the air while they turned their harvests into a cookable flour. Indeed, the intensification of cereal agriculture didn't just introduce new foods. When assembling the skills needed to make grain cultivation work, coastal East Africans interacted with new visual, tactile, and olfactory sensations, some of which left a mark in the words they used to describe products as banal as chaff.

Sabaki speakers' lexical innovations covered activities encompassing nearly every part of the annual rhythms of agriculture, providing an in-progress view of their efforts to expand their subsistence base vis-à-vis cereals. The cycle began when farmers cleared land, felling trees and breaking apart earth to make the most nutrient-rich soils accessible for planting. During the rainy months, they maintained their cultivated fields, weeding and guarding their crops from predators. After harvesting their yields, they transported the harvest to grain stores and began the process of transforming their monthslong labors into edible foods. The Northeast Coast and Sabaki lexicon help to conjure the sights and sounds of a slow revolution underway: iron hoes chopping into the earth and dirt flinging in the air as fields emerged in virgin forest.

Sabaki speakers, like Bantu speakers elsewhere in Africa, combined farming with other subsistence strategies, including hunting and trapping game, herding domestic animals, and gathering wild resources.[59] Archaeobotanical and zooarchaeological records offer material perspectives of the mixed resource economy during the mid-to-late first millennium. The cultivation of the three major African cereals (finger millet, pearl millet, and sorghum) was underway at Early Iron Age sites in multiple regions of East Africa by the middle of the first millennium. Charred seed remains show that these crops were well established in both the coastal hinterlands and on East Africa's offshore islands by the seventh and eighth centuries at the latest.[60] Farmers supplemented cereals with pulse crops such as cow pea (*lukunde), which they intermixed with grains to add fertility to the soil.[61] Faunal records indicate that Sabaki speakers supplemented their diets with locally available wild resources, including small land mammals like duiker, suni, bushbuck, and reedbuck.[62] They also collected freshwater mollusks and exploited some marine resources, especially shellfish.[63] Ultimately, these wild resources provided a regular supply of supplementary food sources, offering flexibility to people moving into new ecologies and amassing knowledge of local soils and rainfall patterns, all while mastering new agricultural techniques.

TRACKING MATERIAL CHANGES
FROM THE SIXTH CENTURY ONWARD

Scaling out from the perspective of a cleared swidden, we can now briefly consider how coastal East Africans' new subsistence knowledge supported larger changes in the region. We know that the Sabaki world was relatively unmoored from the Indian Ocean activities described in the *Periplus*, but why do the developments in arenas like subsistence during this moment of discontinuity in global trading circuits matter to this bigger picture? For one, the resources that coastal East Africans caught and collected provide vital supplementary food sources as they settled new areas and assembled knowledge of soils and rainfall patterns. In such contexts, intensive agriculture and the work of hunting and trapping were mutually supportive. Traps placed along the margins of agricultural fields protected crops while also providing easy access to a regular food source.[64] By supplementing their diets with other wild products, including freshwater and marine fish and shellfish, as well as gathered resources like wild fruits, grasses, and honey, Sabaki speakers would have been able to experiment more extensively with cereal agriculture. Over time, their mastery of more drought-resistant crops, such as sorghum and millet, enabled coastal groups to establish settlements across a wider range of environments, including the sandy, coral rag soils characteristic of many of the coast's offshore islands.

The formative phases of agriculture ultimately helped to support a range of economic and societal transformations that reverberated far beyond the realm of subsistence. Archaeological records show, for instance, that from about the sixth and seventh centuries, there was a significant increase in the number of ironworking and farming settlements founded on the low coastal plain and immediate offshore islands, both environments poorly suited for cultivation based on root crops.[65] In the centuries that followed, post–Sabaki language groups established new settlements far and wide along the littoral, from southern Somalia to southern Mozambique and stretching off the continental mainland as far as the Comoros Islands. Paleoenvironmental records indicate that after a drier climate phase during the first few centuries CE, much of tropical East Africa shifted to a wetter climate for the remainder of the first millennium.[66] Therefore, this movement into new ecological niches overlapped with a general shift to more favorable climate conditions for agriculture, production, and trade.

The region's interactions with reemerging Indian Ocean networks are increasingly legible in material records over the second half of the millennium. Archaeobotanical records indicate Asian crops like rice and coconut reached the Zanzibar Archipelago by the sixth or seventh century.[67] Faunal records also attest to chickens and black rats—both species introduced through maritime translocations—at settlements on the littoral and in the adjacent hinterlands around the same time.[68] During the seventh and eighth centuries, the occupants of settlements across the littoral region also began obtaining increasing quantities of foreign ceramics and glassware, with most of these imported goods originating in the Persian Gulf.[69]

While the trade goods and biological evidence provide early signatures of coastal East Africa's reemerging connections with the Indian Ocean during the late first millennium, ceramic styles known as the Early Tana Tradition (ETT) attest to concurrent interactions in the region's interior. The ETT refers to a style of pottery produced between the seventh and tenth centuries by potters living in settlements that spanned the littoral as far south as Mozambique, outward into the Indian Ocean to the Comoros Islands, and inland to many sites in the coastal hinterlands. ETT ceramics have a distinctive triangular incised pattern—featured most prominently on necked jars—but with substantial stylistic diversity across the range of settlements that produced this pottery.[70] Despite this stylistic diversity, scholars have shown that variations in the ETT's decorative motifs existed along a continuum. As Jeffrey Fleisher and Stephanie Wynne-Jones have argued, this evidence is indicative of a "vast interaction sphere in which communities were most in contact with those nearest to them, while cognizant of a larger sphere that included them all."[71] ETT ceramics were not traded across settlements in this region. Rather, the style demonstrates shared material practices that connected

32   UNMOORED FROM THE OCEAN

"widely dispersed but culturally compatible communities over several centuries."[72] Thus, even as imported material goods became more common among the occupants of some littoral sites, the regional ceramics illustrate enduring material connections between the coast and settlements in the interior.

Material records document an array of changes in the East African coast from the sixth century onward. From this brief survey of these materials, we obtain a clear picture of the ways that the foundational phases of the slow revolution supported subsequent transformations in settlement geographies and scale, and in production and exchange across the wider region. The remainder of this chapter focuses on the social circumstances that undergirded these shifts. As coastal East Africans cultivated cereals with increasing expertise, they also cultivated new methods for assembling larger groups of people. These methods made possible subtle changes in settlement form and complexity in the centuries prior to the emergence of Swahili port cities.

CULTIVATING "WEALTH IN PEOPLE" IN FIRST-MILLENNIUM EAST AFRICA

The changes in scale and production that are evident in material records from the sixth and seventh centuries were an outgrowth of formative developments in subsistence in prior centuries. But for material changes to happen in the first place, coastal leaders needed to be able to bring people together effectively. Historians and anthropologists have long used the concept of "wealth in people" to understand how rights over people formed the basis of accumulation strategies in precolonial Africa. The concept is based on the observation that political leaders and corporate groups regularly sought to translate things into people to meet their needs for labor or social reproduction.[73] Yet past societies' interest in assembling groups of people was not simply a matter of accumulating followers, it was also a matter of composing communities of people possessing "wealth" in skills and knowledge, as subsequent revisions of the concept illustrate.[74] With the right knowledge and skills among their following, leaders could exploit new ecologies, engage in an array of production and subsistence activities, and build relationships with other settlements.

Using the concept of wealth in people, we can imagine the gradual emergence of large, productive communities on the East African coast by the late first millennium as the result of generation-by-generation accruals of knowledge, skills, and followers over the preceding centuries. The archaeological records described above make apparent the success of some coastal communities at constituting wealth in the form of imported pots, beads, and foodstuffs by the second half of the millennium. Yet "boundaries between social and material concepts of poverty and wealth were porous," as Rhiannon Stephens has shown in a longue durée conceptual history of wealth and poverty in eastern Uganda.[75] In Sabaki society, the development of new subsistence strategies, as well as their material engagements with oceanic trade, overlapped with other experiments in social composition and redistribution practices. The remainder of the chapter turns to these social developments to trace the conceptual underpinnings supporting settlement growth and increasing scales of trade by the second half of the first millennium.

To understand how early coastal communities developed the ideological repertoire to support major changes in their societies, it is first necessary to outline the different strategies they used to organize the members of their settlements. At the start of the first millennium, Northeast Coast speakers organized their communities using at least three different types of descent groups: *lukolo ("clan"), *mulyongo ("lineage"), and *nyumba ("house").[76] The *lukolo was the widest grouping, consisting of multiple lineages, or *mulyongo, each of which were made up of people who reckoned their descent through a common ancestor. This linear conceptualization of the members of a *mulyongo is apparent in the word's derivation from a root that referred to a "line (of objects)," giving it the metaphorical sense of a "line of forebears that leads back to the founding ancestor."[77] Lineages formed alliances with one another through marriages between the member of one *mulyongo with another. After two lineages established a marriage alliance, they would view themselves as being members of the same clan, or *lukolo, which included "their affines and the descendants they shared."[78]

As different societies occupied new environments, they frequently discarded or reworked their strategies of social organization to suit their shifting needs. For instance, among speakers of the Kaskazi branch of Mashariki Bantu (which was spoken during the late centuries BCE), clans and lineages grouped members with either their mother's or father's kin, with *-kòlò referring to a mother's "matriclan" and *-lòngò articulating a "patrilineage."[79] While Northeast Coast speakers likely retained these older meanings, their Sabaki-speaking descendants discarded these concrete associations with matrilineal or patrilineal groupings. Sabaki speakers did retain a separate matrilineal grouping with a third type of descent group, the *nyumba, or "house," which consisted of a woman, her children, and her other dependents. Within most villages, the head of the lineage would have had multiple wives, each with their own *nyumba.[80] This matrilineal grouping provided a way to delineate between different kin and different generations within a settlement. To establish her own house, a woman did not need to be associated with recognized lineages or clans. Therefore, *nyumba also offered an important means for incorporating newcomer women into the organizational structure of extant villages.[81] By marrying into a village, a woman could establish her own house and retain a degree of control over her children and any other dependents who became members of her household.[82]

The multiple strategies for reckoning descent provided leaders with a degree of strategic flexibility, enabling them to adapt their settlements' social organization to changing circumstances.[83] Perhaps the most significant area of transformation for

34   UNMOORED FROM THE OCEAN

Northeast Coast speakers was their reconfiguration of ideas about political leadership. In Mashariki society, there were at least four different words that connoted notions of "chiefship."[84] But by the start of the first millennium, Northeast Coast speakers had discarded almost all these titles, choosing to emphasize the authority of a figure known as the *-éné, meaning "lineage head." Christopher Ehret attributes the shifting language of political leadership among different linguistic groups in eastern Africa to the practical reality of people needing to rework ideas about authority as they diverged and began to occupy new environments during the last millennium BCE. Amid periodic changes in scale and ecology, it would have been difficult to transport all inherited leadership institutions into new locations, especially in cases where settlements were relatively small.[85] Tellingly, the leadership titles that North Coast speakers discarded in favor of *-éné described individuals capable of creating conditions of abundance and cultivating honor for their settlement.[86] Instead, Northeast Coast speakers favored more lineage-based authorities who oversaw the small groups of extended kin that constituted their villages, perhaps indicating that influential members of their communities struggled to achieve recognitions characterizing their forebears' settlements.

In different Bantu languages in eastern and southern Africa, the term *-éné referred to an "owner," but within some regions of eastern and southern Africa it had secondary associations to chiefly authority.[87] The title captured, therefore, the extent that local leaders acted as the "owners" or overseers of the various dependents who constituted their lineage group. But during the Northeast Coast period, speakers reimagined the role of lineage heads as individuals who exerted "ownership" over both followers and land, evident in *-éné's connotation of both "lineage head" and "land-owning lineage."[88] Daren Ray has theorized that this innovation stemmed from ecological challenges during the early first millennium. Recall that root crops and vegetables were still the crux of Northeast Coast speakers' cultivation practices. But in the dry hinter-coastal region of central and northern Tanzania—where they established their early village settlements—the land that was best suited for this type of cultivation was relatively scarce. Due to the high value of productive lands, lineage leaders would have wanted to ensure that premium settlement locations remained under the control of their descendants.[89] As a result, they expanded their rights as "owners" to include both the people within their settlement as well as land the members of their lineage occupied and cultivated.

If the role of the *-éné around the start of the first millennium was as an overseer of limited productive lands, then changes in subsistence activities over subsequent centuries would have had the potential to gradually transform the settlements they managed. As we've seen, during the first millennium, coastal East Africans experimented more intensively with cereals, making hardier, more drought-resistant crops such as sorghum and millet a centerpiece of their diets. By the middle of the first millennium, eastern Africa's climate shifted out of an arid phase, which, when combined with successful adaptations in food procurement, would have enabled

UNMOORED FROM THE OCEAN   35

people to occupy a more diverse range of ecologies. Amid these shifts, some communities would have been able to slowly expand in size. After several generations, the leaders of the most successful villages would have become responsible for larger and more diverse lineages as their rights over land and people were passed from one generation to the next.

On a theoretical level, by the mid-first millennium, coastal East Africans had at hand many of the tools necessary to facilitate transformations in the scale of their communities. Using flexible lineal strategies, they could incorporate new members and build strong alliances across their territory. And with new subsistence practices and leadership ideologies, they could support larger and more enduring settlements. The history of the proto-Sabaki term *mutala, meaning "quarter of a village," helps to bring some changes in scale into focus on a conceptual level. *Mutala is derived from an older root word that meant "village" or "settlement area" in Mashariki Bantu languages.[90] By the start of the current era, Northeast Coast Bantu communities used the same world to describe "areas within a village where men who had more than one wife maintained homesteads."[91] This signals to how lineage heads deployed a "mother-derived grouping" (such as *nyumba) to expand their number of dependent kin within a single village settlement.[92] Over generations, as the members of these kin groupings "established adjacent households" and "accepted new residents," they would have been able to gradually increase the scale of their villages.[93]

This shift in scale is apparent in Sabaki speakers' articulation of *mutala as a "quarter of a village," which extended their ancestors' understanding of a large household and applied it to the distinct areas of villages where such households were established. In subsequent centuries, speakers of Swahili dialects built on these inherited concepts, using the root to describe "neighborhoods" or "wards" of a town (*mitaa* in Modern Standard Swahili), a shift that resonates with the growing urban density of littoral settlements during the second millennium. But notably, other Sabaki languages treated this inherited meaning quite differently. Mijikenda speakers reinterpreted *mutala, which they pronounced *muhala*, as a cleared courtyard at the center of a homestead, fitting a larger shift toward homestead-based settlements in Mombasa's interior during the second millennium (a story detailed in the next chapter). Pokomo and Elwana speakers, meanwhile, dropped the word from their vocabulary altogether.[94]

These semantic shifts—from "village," to "village quarter," to "neighborhood," or, in the case of Mijikenda dialects, "courtyard"—demonstrate how coastal East Africans adapted older ideas about space to accommodate changes in their settlements. Over generations, groups of households made up of extended kin eventually came to connote distinct quarters or neighborhoods within a village. Archaeologist Mark Horton conjectured that the Sabaki period may have marked a shift in settlement design whereby larger villages were arranged in clusters of houses— with each cluster occupied by the members of a lineage group—which encircled

36 UNMOORED FROM THE OCEAN

a communal central courtyard or enclosure.[95] The available archaeological evidence does not provide a clear enough picture of mid-first millennium settlement designs to further test this theory. Nevertheless, following the history of *mutala invites us to imagine distant conceptual experiments with scale and form in first-millennium communities, even in the absence of material data clearly documenting these changes.

THE LANGUAGE OF SOCIAL RECIPROCITY, DEBT, AND MARGINALITY

As villages grew, they needed to be delineated into new units: spaces for men with multiple wives and houses; quarters for descent groups; and, eventually, neighborhoods consisting of extended kin. Changes in scale did not happen automatically, however. By envisioning changes in the scale and form of first millennium settlements, we are also alerted to the multiple tensions that would have existed as lineage heads endeavored to expand their influence. To grow their communities, lineage heads had to accumulate land, food resources, and dependents. At the same time, they relied on the knowledge and skills of their constituents to support their aspirations for accumulation. Because of the flexibility of incorporation strategies, people could leave one settlement and join another. But doing so carried risks since newcomers were often ascribed a marginal status when they joined new communities.[96] As a result, successful leaders had to develop the means to attract, incorporate, and retain members.[97]

Sabaki speakers' efforts to assemble people is apparent in the vocabulary that they innovated or adapted to describe different redistributive practices. Two words referring to different types of collection, *-cum- and *-cang-, allow us to envision the tensions between the accumulative aspirations of lineage heads and the potential fluidity of their following. The first term, *-cum-, is derived from a very old root in Bantu languages that meant to "buy food, collect." Into the early first millennium, Northeast Coast speakers retained the root's older meaning, which "carried pragmatic connotations of agricultural collection."[98] Sabaki speakers later expanded its meaning by creating a new secondary gloss, using *-cum- to speak of both "collecting" and "trading" for profit. Reflexes of *-cum- from different Sabaki daughter languages demonstrate associations between collection and commerce that expanded from the mid-first millennium onward. In Mijikenda, for instance, reflexes of the root refer to gathering or collecting as well as trading and doing business; in Pokomo it described keeping money; and in Comorian and Swahili, reflexes refer to collecting and making profits through industrial activities or trade.[99] Some of these glosses reflect modern categories—e.g., making money. But when viewed alongside the verb's etymology, the glosses hint to a much older conceptual apparatus that linked activities like collecting foods with trade and accumulation.

While Sabaki speakers expanded one notion of collecting to encompass trade, another concept, expressed by the root *-cang-, communicated the redistributive possibilities of assembling resources. The Sabaki verb *-cang-, meaning "to collect," is derived from an ancient Bantu root that meant to "meet, find, mix, assemble."[100] Among Northeast Coast speakers, the verb carried the secondary connotation of "contributing," a meaning that demonstrates that the earliest settlers on the coast retained older associations with sociability—meeting, mixing, assembling—within their concept of "collection." From at least the proto-Sabaki period, speakers attested the verb using the applicative verb extension (pronounced *-cangil-), which gave the term an added emphasis of collecting contributions *for, to,* or *on behalf of* another person or group. The derivational and morphological clues reveal the immense social work that Sabaki speakers imagined when they spoke of "collecting" and "contributing." For instance, speakers of different Sabaki daughter languages associate reflexes of *-cangil- with things like charity, pooling together resources, and welcoming visitors. Although this diversity of meanings makes it difficult to pin down a single proto-Sabaki interpretation for the root, together they demonstrate ancient and widespread associations between collecting, reciprocity, and social composition.

For Sabaki speakers, contributing to other members of their community did not simply entail the transfer of collected items from one person to another. Instead, they articulated collection and distributing contributions as actions that bound together—or perhaps more appropriately, mixed and assembled—the individuals partaking in these acts. The ideologies of giving articulated by *-cangil- stand in striking contrast to older practices, such as those expressed in the Sabaki terms *-tuuzy-, meaning "give as gift," and the derived noun *ntuuzo, or "gift."[101] Both of these inherited terms are derived from a root meaning "put down (a load)." They articulated, therefore, a mode of giving that was, etymologically speaking, unidirectional, such as placing down gifts as tributes or offering rewards. Thus, Sabaki speakers understood actions like *-cangil- to have a very different social affect than forms of redistribution associated with the verb *-tuuzy-. By the mid-first millennium, when coastal communities spoke of making contributions, they directly implicated the reciprocal power of giving and the capacity of the contributions themselves to bring people together.

The linguistic evidence illuminates how people sought to articulate the power of redistribution to assemble people, despite an absence of written or archaeological records attesting to these practices.[102] One Sabaki institution, called the *kikola, shows how speakers developed new methods for facilitating reciprocity and mutual assistance.[103] During the first millennium, *kikola probably referred to an arrangement where members of a settlement shared food resources or labor during times of need. In Mijikenda communities, the *chikola,* or *kikola,* took the form of a collective work party, while in the Comoros Islands, a *shikoa* referred to a community savings arrangement to which members made contributions, creating a larger safety net for the group that people could pull from when needed.[104] For Swahili speakers, meanwhile, the *kikoa* referred to meals eaten as a collective, with each participant in the group meal contributing what they could.[105] In each case, people shared food, labor, and other resources with the understanding that this assistance would be later reciprocated in some form by other participants.

Acts of social reciprocity would have provided ideological tools to both foster connections between people and to improvise new social arrangements and economic practices. For instance, the social safety net offered by arrangements like the *kikola could have enabled people to experiment with new cultivation techniques. Redistributive practices would have also helped lineage leaders expand the number of people in their following by attracting newcomers or preventing members of their settlement from leaving and joining a different lineage. Leaders benefited from the array of resources that newcomers brought into their settlements, whether it was their knowledge of medicines, skills in activities like ironworking or agriculture, or their reproductive capacities.

Newcomers themselves were frequently incorporated unequally, however. As David Schoenbrun explains, the "idea that newcomers could expect lower social standing than others in a community is a long-standing commonplace in ideologies of hierarchy" across much of eastern Africa.[106] The marginal status of new members of a community manifested in the proto-Sabaki term *muja, or "newcomer." The term is widely distributed in Bantu languages in eastern, southern, and equatorial Africa with meanings that indicate a *muja was broadly conceived as a "dependent, servant, slave, or refugee."[107] In Sabaki or early Swahili, speakers compounded *muja with the term *-kazi, or "wife," to create the meaning *mujakazi, a person who historical records describe as a "female slave."[108] *Mujakazi's etymological sense of "newcomer wife" indicates how newcomer women were incorporated into extant communities through marriage, thus resonating with the flexible lineage strategies that coastal groups employed during the first millennium. By marrying female newcomers, lineage heads could establish new houses and grow the number of dependents under their stewardship.

Sabaki speakers drew from older metaphorical associations about the marginal status of newcomers to express ideas about less-fully incorporated members of their settlements. They distinguished newcomers from other marginal individuals, called *mukiWa, which designated a "poor" or "abandoned" person.[109] This term is attested in a number of Bantu languages in East Africa in addition to Sabaki, including other languages descended from Northeast Coast as well as many languages in the Chaga-Taita and Thagicu language families. *MukiWa's block distribution and phonetic shape in different languages spoken between the East African coast and highlands of the Eastern Arc Mountains and Central Kenya indicate that it is an areal term that diffused across this larger region by the early first millennium.

The term's derivation and associated meanings offer insights into the conceptual underpinnings of this type of marginality. For instance, *mukiWa appears to be derived from a passive form of the root -kíd-, meaning "pass over, surpass," giving the term a sense of a person who is "passed over" or "surpassed." Related adjectives and nouns derived from the term suggest that being poor in the sense connoted by *mukiWa meant being bereft or kinless.[110] Thus, a *mukiWa, in contrast to marginal newcomers, was perhaps a person who lacked links to an extant community—someone who had fled from their home or who had been abandoned or cast off.

If *mukiWa is indeed an areal term—meaning a word that spread across a contiguous block of languages—dating to the early centuries of the first millennium, then it hints at some fascinating possibilities for understanding cross-societal concepts of marginality during this period. In the first half of the millennium, as I've outlined, communities adapted to new ecologies, mastered new crops, and managed the vagaries of rainfall. As lineage heads made new investments in land, they also needed to build the necessary knowledge base and skills to pursue an array of tasks: assembling tools; clearing and tending fields; harvesting and processing foods; identifying and exploiting wild resources; and fostering relationships across settlements for trade and social reproduction. A settlement's successes or failures had the potential to generate rivalries between lineage heads competing for followers, as well as novel obligations for local leaders and the members of their communities. Amid these changes, those without social attachments would have endeavored to find new positions for themselves among the most successful extant communities, even if that meant accepting subordinate roles. Becoming a subordinate newcomer was no doubt preferable in nearly any circumstance to being one who was abandoned or "passed over." Strategies of social reciprocity would have been invaluable for attracting and incorporating different sorts of people who themselves accrued social debts by accepting their benefactors' patronage.

Sabaki speakers' attestation of words connoting marginality or outsiderness help us to imagine the uncertainties people felt as they endeavored to incorporate new individuals into their settlements. Considering these apparent tensions, one of the more striking innovations dating to this period is the term *-Wil-, which meant "to owe." To create this meaning, Sabaki speakers added an applicative extension to the verb "to be" that gave *-Wil- the literal meaning of "to be to," "to be for," or "to be with" another person.[111] This innovation illustrates how members of mid-first millennium coastal communities thought of "owing" a person not simply as debt, but instead as a sense of attachment or obligation. While other aspects of Sabaki speakers' lexicon for redistribution—evident in terms like *-cang(il)- and *kikola—speak to the role of sharing or contributing resources for attracting or "assembling" people, *-Wil- enables us to think through the social obligations that undergirded these relationships. The term's etymological sense

40   UNMOORED FROM THE OCEAN

of "being to" another person suggests that redistributive practices generated new types of relationships between a provider and the individual who was *bound to* that person vis-à-vis their debt.[112]

While Sabaki-era communities remained small in scale, the linguistic evidence indicates that they had a number of ways to differentiate among the statuses of people within and along the margins of their communities. Concurrently, they developed novel means to attract, retain, and incorporate people into their settlements. Mutual assistance practices could have supported settlements' growth. At the same time, Sabaki speakers' expanding vocabulary for things like debt and contributions would have alerted people to new social distinctions between providers and dependents, insiders, and more marginal members. People would have grappled with the implications of sharing or hoarding resources, or of accepting the contributions offered to them and the potential obligations they carried. These concerns would have only become more pronounced as lineage heads managed larger groups of people, as distinctions between larger and smaller settlements became more noticeable, and as cross-societal trading activities picked up in the centuries that followed.

During the second half of the millennium, Sabaki speakers' linguistic descendants established settlements far and wide across coastal East Africa. By the eighth century, their settlement zone stretched along the littoral from northern Kenya to southern Mozambique, inland into the immediate coastal hinterlands, and far off the continental mainland on the island archipelago of the Comoros. As we'll see in the next chapter, in all of these areas the earliest Sabaki-descended groups formed settlements that were larger than those occupied by their ancestors just a few centuries earlier. While the subsistence roots set by their Northeast Coast and Sabaki ancestors enabled them to develop settlements across a wide range of ecologies, their ancestors' repertoire of social practices and ideas provided critical foundations for changes in complexity and production across the region.

. . .

From the vantage point of a cosmopolitan port, the emergence of Swahili towns may appear to result from the resurgence of Indian Ocean commercial networks during the late first millennium. This chapter has asked: What if we viewed the region's past instead from the perspective of a farm field? Or from the outskirts of a village where a newcomer weighed the pros and cons of accepting a lineage head's patronage, knowing the types of obligations that it may carry? During the early first millennium, coastal East African linguistic groups adapted to an environment influenced by the Indian Ocean monsoon. However, their relationship to the maritime arena was not one of seamless interaction. The earliest ironworking and farming communities on the coast were small in scale and relatively disconnected from the maritime commercial arena. But their experiments with subsistence prompted developments that ultimately transformed their settlements in a variety of ways. As they mastered new farming techniques, Sabaki speakers began planting their villages across a greater range of microclimates, including establishing permanent settlements on the littoral. Lineage heads who previously managed scarce productive lands achieved new pathways to accrue wealth in lands and influence. In the process, coastal communities experimented with their ideas about reciprocity, obligation, and marginality, all of which provided them with a repertoire of strategies for attracting and integrating new members. Despite their dearth of interactions with the Indian Ocean, Sabaki speakers' innovations forged important subsistence and ideological roots that would significantly shape the world to come.

If we recognize that Sabaki speakers' creative actions set the stage for subsequent transformations across the Swahili coast, then we must also consider why some other Sabaki-descended groups pursued such drastically different paths. Mijikenda communities shared with their Swahili neighbors a social and economic repertoire to support larger, more complex settlements. And like their Swahili siblings, they established many of their earliest settlements with easy access to the Indian Ocean. From the late first millennium, Swahili speakers began building connections within reemerging Indian Ocean networks. As the next chapter will show, Mijikenda speakers did too. However, their participation with this transregional arena took on an entirely different form, being characterized not by urbanism or Islam, but by growing social and ritual ties with other inland communities.

2

Looking Inland, to the World

In 1953, a Kenyan poet and publisher named William Frank wrote a short book titled *Habari na desturi za WaRibe*, or "History and Customs of the Ribe" (Ribe being one of the nine Mijikenda subgroups).[1] The book was part of an East African Literature Bureau book series that aimed to describe the histories and cultures of different East African communities for Swahili readers. Perhaps mindful of this audience, Frank began a chapter focused on village leadership with a comparison to a well-known East African polity: the Buganda Kingdom. Much like Buganda had a king—who was called the Kabaka—the Ribe had their own methods of governance, according to Frank. In contrast to Buganda's monarchy, however, Ribe's political decisions were shared among multiple people—councils of respected and knowledgeable men from different villages. The councils were not open to anyone. As Frank explained, elder men achieved their rank due to their knowledge and wealth. To join they needed ample cattle, goats, and palm wine for ritual ceremonies and sacrifices, as well as large productive farm plots to support people during famines. Textiles and medicinal sacks marked their status. As members of the councils, they held authority to litigate domestic disputes and land cases using specialized medicines. Rather than meeting within their own villages, the men congregated in forest groves, which offered an ideal setting for their esoteric activities.[2]

While the previous chapter focused on social and subsistence adaptations in coastal East African society during a down period in oceanic commerce, this chapter traces the multiple social possibilities that existed during the period that followed. The Swahili story is a familiar one. Between the eighth and fifteenth centuries, people living in coastal towns adopted Islam and built relationships with visiting merchants. They also began altering their built landscape, using blocks of living coral cut from underwater reefs to build homes and mosques. Before long, intricately carved archways marked the entrances to the main mosques of larger towns. Merchant houses featured sculpted niches on their interior walls for displaying foreign ceramics and glassware.[3] Builders applied to the exterior of stone buildings a limestone plaster coating that reflected the sun when viewed from the ocean, making towns visible to approaching ships.[4] The built landscape of port cities like Mombasa, in other words, offers a physical testament to East Africa's significant interface with the Indian Ocean world in the centuries following their ancestors' experiments with grain cultivation.

Similarly, the forest groves where elder men congregated for political and healing activities provide an entry into profound transformations and cross-societal exchanges in Mombasa's interior. By comparing Ribe's village-level strategies to Buganda's royal politics, Frank recognized that smaller-scale networks and social pursuits had commonalities with hierarchical states and urban centers.[5] Villages were once seen to represent the historical roots from which coastal towns emerged and then departed once they began building relationships in a rapidly globalizing Indian Ocean. As the authors of one well-known book on Swahili society put it, opportunities for oceanic trade transformed coastal, Swahili-speaking villages into "urban and mercantile" centers, and, in the process, those opportunities "separated culturally" people living in coastal settlements from those in villages in the nearby rural hinterlands.[6] The past two decades of archaeological research on the coast have overturned this older view, showing that coastal urban centers emerged through varied processes, all the while maintaining enduring ties with adjacent rural settlements and interior regions.[7] This work alerts us to the importance of understanding the histories of coastal towns through their engagements with inland communities, and vice versa. But before scaling outward to explore Mijikenda speakers' interactions with the Indian Ocean world—as I will do in chapters 3 through 5—it is necessary to first look inward, to the deep social histories of settlements in Mombasa's interior.

As the chapter will show, Mijikenda speakers possessed the same capabilities for forming larger communities as their Swahili-speaking neighbors after proto-Sabaki began diverging into separate languages. Rather than fully orienting their worlds toward the religious and social norms of urban ports, they established smaller settlements and gradually cultivated strong ties with neighboring inland groups. They borrowed medicines, adopted new means to propitiate ancestral spirits, and incorporated novel spaces into the contours of their villages and the surrounding forests. In the process, they continually generated associations with other villages and with neighboring, non-Mijikenda-speaking communities. Mijikenda speakers' social and ritual pursuits put them in constant contact with other inland societies, supporting and running parallel to expansions in oceanic trading networks. Islamic or Islamicate practices provided the cultural residue for expanding trading connections between Indian Ocean port cities during the

44   LOOKING INLAND, TO THE WORLD

second millennium.[8] In Mombasa's immediate interior, a quite different constellation of social ideas and ritual exchanges supported Mijikenda speakers' ability to participate in this growing world of transregional connections.

PORT CITIES AND OTHER POSSIBILITIES

Before shifting to look at developments among communities in Mombasa's interior, it is necessary to first take a wider view of changes in coastal East Africa between the late first millennium and early second millennium. This was a period rife with many social possibilities for those living in early settlements along East Africa's littoral and immediate interior. As the last chapter documented, ambitious lineage heads could marshal their followers' skills and knowledge to scale up their activities in areas like craft production, subsistence, and trade. Meanwhile, mutual assistance practices offered the members of lineages a means to recruit and incorporate newcomers, helping the most successful villages to grow. In other cases, some individuals may have split off from their community, joining a new settlement or perhaps starting their own village with a smaller number of dependents. To trace these developments and place Mijikenda and Swahili settlements within a common framework, I will briefly consider some linguistic and archaeological evidence that shows (1) how first-millennium coastal East Africans conceptualized their settlements, and (2) processes of growth and fragmentation within these settlements from the late first millennium onward.

The many different possibilities existing for late first-millennium settlements are encapsulated in the term Sabaki speakers used to refer to towns and villages, *muji. Speaking of coastal "towns" today using English, one's imagination might immediately jump to urban port cities. However, past societies on the East African coast spoke of a spectrum of settlements, from the smallest hamlet to the largest towns, using the same word.[9] After proto-Sabaki diverged into daughter languages, their linguistic descendants continued to use reflexes of *muji to describe cities and villages alike. For example, in Swahili, a *mji* (or *mui*) can refer to everything from major urban centers, such as Mombasa or Nairobi, to small coastal hamlets. Mijikenda speakers, similarly, use a cognate form of the inherited word *mudzi* to describe a family homestead, a village, or a large city. The same holds true in other Sabaki languages where reflexes of *muji are applied to all settlements regardless of their size, location, or significance.[10]

Sabaki speakers categorized the spaces they occupied in expansive rather than restrictive terms. Like their distant linguistic ancestors, they articulated *muji by adding the nominal prefix mu- to the stem, indexing the word in a noun class that included various "entities with vitality," including human collectives like villages. Human collectives "are not in themselves human, but [are] endowed with certain human characteristics," namely, the ability to grow and reproduce.[11] In some Sabaki languages, reflexes of *muji also refer to a placenta, a secondary meaning tied to the practice of burying the placenta in a family's settlement area in a town or village.[12] Through this metaphor, they actualized the blurry boundaries between the people and the physical spaces of settlements, directly connecting human reproduction to the village itself. As human collectives, villages didn't follow a single evolutionary trajectory, naturally expanding over time into cities. Villages could fuse and grow, but they could also split or even die.

Sabaki speakers' expansive concepts of towns and villages contrast with much of the earliest archaeological research on coastal villages, which treated them as "stepping stones" to Swahili urbanism.[13] This was due in part to documented changes on the Swahili coast and the Comoros Islands starting from the late first millennium. Around the middle of the first millennium, most Sabaki settlements remained small in scale. But within a few centuries of their dispersal, Sabaki speakers' descendants began building larger settlements than their predecessors. For instance, during the late first millennium, early migrants to the Comoros established at least one large settlement on each of the four volcanic islands that form the archipelago. In the early second millennium, these settlements began to grow, doubling or even tripling in size between the eleventh and thirteenth centuries. Small villages and hamlets clustered around larger towns, forming ever-denser population centers with main towns featuring coral stone mosques as their focal points.[14] Major Swahili towns like Kilwa experienced similar pathways to growth, expanding from small villages to large urban centers between the ninth and thirteenth centuries.[15]

At some coastal Swahili sites, scholars have identified continuities in their spatial organization as they grew from small villages to urban towns. The classic example is Shanga, a town on the Lamu archipelago in northern Kenya where archaeologists have identified the Swahili coast's oldest known mosque, built in the late eighth century. Even though Shanga was never a major trading port along the lines of Kilwa or Mombasa, it provides an important model for understanding local evolutions in Swahili towns. Mark Horton, the archaeologist who led excavations at Shanga, describes its organization as consisting of smaller settlement areas for separate clans grouped around a central enclosure shaped as a rectangle. Eventually, seven subsettlements surrounded the town center, each with its own gateway to access the central space. The central enclosure—originally demarcated by a timber fence, before it was replaced by coral stone during the tenth century—contained a well, a burial area, and a mosque, indicating that it likely served as a focus for different social, ritual, and commercial activities. Shanga's occupants rebuilt the central mosque many times in the town's history to accommodate a growing number of worshippers. Each rebuilt mosque overlayed earlier structures, with coral stone replacing mud and thatch, ultimately manifesting in the construction of a characteristic congregational mosque around 1000 CE.[16]

Research at Shanga played a critical role in helping scholars understand how Swahili towns emerged from local village roots. However, it also placed the story of coastal society in something of a box, where villages represented "nascent versions of later towns built atop them."[17] More recent archaeological work has shifted this viewpoint, showing that coastal villages featured dynamic and complex settlement histories that cannot be reduced to a single story of growth. Adria LaViolette and Jeffrey Fleisher's work on Tumbe, a settlement on Pemba Island in what is now Tanzania, is especially instructive in this regard. During the eighth century, Tumbe developed into a large, dispersed trading village that was integrated into maritime trading networks. Finds at Tumbe reveal voluminous imported goods like glass beads and foreign ceramics. The site's occupants also produced shell beads for export to other areas along the coast. But notably, archaeologists found no evidence of hierarchies across Tumbe's settlement history. Instead, a wide variety of people—from farmers to craft manufacturers—had access to long-distance trade goods. Maritime trade was fully integrated into a robust domestic economy.[18]

Tumbe is the type of settlement that is supposed to develop into a major urban port. The town was set along a six-hundred-meter stretch of coastline and located on an island that had been a site for Indian Ocean trade since the time of the *Periplus*.[19] At an estimated twenty to thirty hectares in size, Tumbe may have been the largest settlement on the East African coast during the late first millennium. Furthermore, its occupants were already engaged in maritime trade by the eighth and ninth centuries.[20] However, during the mid-tenth century, they abandoned the site entirely and dispersed into the neighboring countryside. The area was left entirely unsettled until a new urban center, called Chwaka, was founded on this abandoned stretch of coastline in the mid-eleventh century, about two hundred meters south of Tumbe. Scholars theorize that Chwaka was founded as a religious center rather than a trading port. People lived close together in densely packed earth and thatch houses. They invested in religious architecture, building four coral stone mosques across the site's history, with the earliest dating to the settlement's founding. As Chwaka's religious architecture became more elaborate, people gradually abandoned the dispersed rural villages that their ancestors had established after Tumbe's abandonment and relocated to the growing town.[21] Ultimately, what we see at Tumbe and Chwaka is not continuity, with a small village growing into a large port city, but rather, we see much more complex processes and fluctuations.

This chapter is primarily concerned with Mijikenda-speaking communities, but it is worth engaging with recent scholarship on urbanism in the Swahili coast because it moves us away from any normative understanding of growth and social evolutions during the post-Sabaki period. Evidence from Pemba and other coastal sites has enabled archaeologists to begin rethinking the development of coastal urban centers "as part of an episodic and halting trajectory of development" rather than a single leap from village to mercantile port city.[22] Looking at the concepts and practices that Sabaki speakers developed prior to the sixth century, one might consider Swahili urbanism a natural evolutionary trajectory from these earlier "roots." In such a schema, inland villages look like historical relics from which Swahili speakers departed after they founded settlements along the littoral, converted to Islam, and became engaged in maritime commerce. But, as coastal archaeologists have emphasized, there was not any standard pathway to urban growth.[23] This reality opens questions about the choices people made for social and material changes to happen: Did people decide to abandon a large, connected town like Tumbe because they saw smaller hamlets as a better option—at least for a time? Mijikenda speakers shared many cultural and linguistic similarities with Swahili speakers in towns like Mombasa. Did they maintain distinctions from the town because doing so suited alternative social ambitions?

Two inland sites located a short distance away from Mombasa called Chombo and Mteza offer entry points for answering these questions. The southern part of Mombasa Island is separated from its mainland by Kilindini Harbor, today the site of the city's main shipping hub. At the harbor's narrowest points, the island and mainland sit only five hundred meters apart before the waterway opens into a large estuarian creek called Port Reitz, which flanks a rolling upland dissected by small rivers and creeks. During the late first millennium, ironworking farmers founded Chombo and Mteza along these fertile ridges, just a short distance inland from Port Reitz. Oral traditions about the two sites link them to a deeper settlement history of the Digo Mijikenda-speaking groups that live in the area. According to oral histories, Chombo was first settled by a Digo matriclan that broke away from a larger settlement called Kaya Kwale. The group at Chombo later split again, with some members moving farther north to establish Mteza.[24] Material evidence from each site places their occupations as roughly contemporaneous, with calibrated radiocarbon date ranges between the late eighth and late tenth centuries.[25] Chombo consisted of three closely linked smaller sites, the largest being 2.2 hectares and the smallest 1.2 hectares. Because archaeologists believe the three sites were settled contemporaneously, they may have been occupied by separate lineages of a larger marriage alliance or clan. Mteza demonstrates a similar organizational schema, consisting of "five closely spaced settlement sites which are located together in an area which has been broadly labeled 'Kaya Mwanyundo' by local Digo elders."[26] Like Chombo, Mteza consisted of a cluster of smaller villages, each between 1.8 and 0.9 hectares, all sitting atop a steep incline overlooking a river valley that ended at Port Reitz Creek, just two kilometers away.

With their proximity to the ocean, the people living at both sites participated in the maritime economy. Archaeologists have recovered imported goods from the two sites, including Indo-Pacific glass beads, cowrie shells, and Chinese Yue stoneware. Copal fragments, rock crystal, and a cylinder-shaped carved ivory box demonstrate their access to some of East Africa's most important exports. In addition to oceanic trade, Chombo and Mteza's economic activities were characteristic of their Sabaki roots. They fished and gathered freshwater and marine resources, hunted small wild game, and kept some domestic animals. At Chombo, occupants smelted iron and produced iron tools for hunting and farming. Lithics recovered

48   LOOKING INLAND, TO THE WORLD

from the site also indicate that its occupants either used stone tools or interacted regularly with neighboring lithic-using groups across the site's history.[27]

No detailed written descriptions exist for inland villages until the nineteenth century, a thousand years after Chombo and Mteza's calibrated date ranges. But the archaeological evidence allows us to think through their connections to other communities, and the ways that they distinguished themselves from contemporaneous Swahili-speaking settlements, like the earliest settlers on nearby Mombasa. We might imagine that people so close to the ocean, with established links to the maritime economy, would have desired to take part in emerging Indian Ocean cosmopolitan schema. However, there's no evidence that Mombasa's neighboring countryside was ever depopulated by people flocking to the town to participate in its mercantile culture. Furthermore, the closely linked settlements at Chombo and Mteza did not gradually form into larger towns. Instead, archaeological evidence indicates that the descendants of those living in these two settlements were far more likely to have lived in villages that were smaller and more dispersed than their predecessors.

Archaeological surveys from southeast Kenya provide a clear picture of these larger trends in settlement size. During the early second millennium, a wide variety of settlement types flourished in southeast Kenya's interior. Some of this region's early villages did grow into multicomponent towns. For instance, a site called Mtsengo, located thirty-five kilometers inland from Mombasa and founded in the late first millennium, reached 7.56 hectares by the fourteenth and fifteenth centuries, making it comparable to contemporaneous medium-sized littoral settlements. Several other sites located along Mombasa's inland ridge grew to a size equivalent to smaller coastal towns, roughly four to five hectares, during a similar time frame. However, most settlements were not large towns. Instead, the average site in southeast Kenya's interior—the core of the Mijikenda settlement region—shrank from 1.26 hectares prior to 1000 CE to 0.59 hectares for sites founded between roughly 1000 and 1650 CE.[28] In other words, sites that were founded after 1000 CE were, on average, less than half the size of those that were founded during the first millennium. After the mid-seventeenth century, the settlement hierarchies discernable in earlier periods—which featured many smaller villages but also some large towns like Mtsengo—broke down further. By the latter half of the second millennium, homestead-based villages were the dominant settlement model across southeast Kenya's immediate interior.[29]

The archaeological surveys show that as Mombasa developed as a major port city, most people living immediately inland from the island would have lived in small, rural hamlets. Population densities increased over time across the inland region. However, when populations grew, most people responded by forming more small settlements rather than growing their hamlets into super villages or towns. This emphasis on smaller-scale villages had a major impact on settlement patterns in Mombasa's immediate interior. During the first millennium, settlements in this region clustered on the forested ridges of the coastal upland. But over time, people expanded their settlement areas beyond the fertile ridges inland from Mombasa into the high coastal plain to the west and north, and the low coastal plain to the south.[30] Processes of splitting and expansion put people in contact with new communities and forced them to adapt their foodways and social strategies to new environments. Shrinking and dispersal, in other words, facilitated both internal changes and external connections.

INCORPORATION, COLLABORATION, AND DISPERSAL IN MIJIKENDA ORAL TRADITIONS

Oral traditions attest to the importance of cross-societal alliances for longer-term processes of community formation in coastal East Africa. As Sabaki-speaking groups planted settlements throughout the East African coast during the first millennium, they collaborated with people from other speech communities, often absorbing strangers into their settlements. The previous chapter detailed some linguistic innovations that supported these incorporative practices. Oral accounts about the origins of towns like Mombasa and of neighboring Mijikenda settlements similarly emphasize interactions with outsiders, reflecting what historian Daren Ray calls a "cosmopolitan ethic."[31] The traditions offer a window into coastal East African intellectuals' own perspectives on various settlement processes and interactions, including the inland shift toward smaller-scale villages, as reflected in the archaeological records detailed above.

Oral traditions about the founding of Mombasa and other Swahili-speaking towns are replete with stories of collaborations with newcomers and foreigners. This is especially true of one well-known narrative, called the "Shirazi tradition." In this tradition, migrants from Shiraz (in Persia) are said to have traveled to East Africa, where they met people living along the coast and offshore islands and began trading with them. The migrants introduced East Africans to Islam and married local women. Their children became the Swahili.[32] In Mombasa, a local epic explains that a queen mother named Mwana Mkisi established the island's first permanent settlement at Kongowea, located on the northern part of the island.[33] Later, a migrant named Shehe Mvita (or Sheikh Mvita) traveled to Mombasa from Persia and established the town's first Islamic lineage, becoming remembered as its founding father in local chronicles.[34] Mombasa continued to grow in the centuries that followed through local migrations. People from other northern Swahili towns flocked to the city and established their own *miji* (or "towns") on the island and on its immediate mainland. Eventually, Mombasa's population consisted of twelve *miji*. The leading elders of each town together represented a political council overseeing the island's affairs with their collective *miji* forming the urban polity of Mombasa—sometimes also called Mvita after the town's founding sheikh.[35] Thus, Mombasa grew into a large town, according to oral traditions, by absorbing migrants who collectively contributed to the religious and political life of the port city.

Mijikenda speakers' oral traditions also emphasize collaborations between migrants and in situ groups. In contrast to the oral accounts of Swahili towns, which explained their origins through an Islamic-oceanic interactive sphere, Mijikenda traditions suggest local understandings of the past rooted in processes of interaction and conflict involving other groups from East Africa's interior.[36] Most traditions begin with them fleeing Shungwaya, their mythical northern homeland, following a dispute with Oromo speakers, often having to do with the kidnapping or murder of an Oromo child for an initiation ritual called *mung'aro*.[37] Aspects of the historical traditions vary over time and space or depending on the individual teller. But the most common narrative is that Mijikenda groups fled from Shungwaya and traveled south, stopping to form shorter-term settlements while en route. Eventually, they established their *kayas*—fortified settlements built atop forest glades along Mombasa's inland ridge—sometimes relying on the aid of hunter-foragers who acted as guides. At each *kaya*, the settlers buried a charm called a *fingo*, which protected their settlement.[38]

The period following the migration—which some historians refer to as the "*kaya* phase"—was a thriving era, according to most traditions. During this time, the nine Mijikenda groups lived in their respective *kayas*, each of which was divided into separate areas for clans or family groups. Each clan had their own clearing, called the *lwanda*, where they met to discuss important matters. Another clearing, called the *moro*, was reserved for the leading elders who met to deliberate on judicial matters and esoteric concerns. The *kaya* phase is said to have lasted into the nineteenth century, when the institutions of the *kayas* began to break down and people started moving out of the forests to establish their own homesteads. After the *kayas* ceased to be primary residences, they were recast as burial grounds and meeting places for initiations or other rituals.[39]

The generic narrative structure of the oral traditions divides the past into three phases: pre-*kaya, kaya,* and post-*kaya*. In this schema, the middle era—or *kaya* phase—represents the peak of Mijikenda "traditional" institutions.[40] At first glance, the narrative structure is at odds with the settlement geography discussed in the previous section. This archaeological evidence shows that people living in southeast Kenya constantly founded new settlements and expanded into new ecologies, especially during the mid-second millennium, precisely when the *kaya* phase is supposed to have begun. Yet traditions regarding the sequencing of these sites demonstrate the reliability of oral historians' knowledge of past settlement processes. According to an analysis by archaeologist Richard Helm, the sites associated with pre-*kaya* and *kaya* traditions are among the oldest in southeast Kenya's coastal hinterlands, with most being founded in the first millennium. Meanwhile, the historical sites that oral histories link to splintering *kayas* were, in general, smaller, located over more diffuse ecologies, and were founded during the last four or five centuries.[41] In other words, oral traditions about splintering *kayas* seem to correlate with the documented proliferation of smaller, homestead-based settlements over the course of the second millennium. These processes accelerated during the seventeenth century, representing the post-*kaya* phase in oral traditions.[42]

While *kaya* traditions and archaeological records indicate longer-term processes of shrinking and dispersal, oral narratives also highlight the role of forest groves as spaces for assembly and cross-societal connections. Oral historians' accounts speak to this most directly in narratives that center foreigners and their knowledge in the making of Mijikenda clans. Consider, for example, the following narrative that Thomas Spear recorded in a conversation with an elder named Kathungi Ndenge about the founding of the *kayas*:

> Some of the smaller clans were formed by foreigners, people from Digo, Taita, and even Laa. We have all kinds of people in Giriama. . . . The Giriama often brought foreign *waganga* [healers] to Giriama; a Taita for his special knowledge, a Digo for rain-making, and a Pemba for his *uganga* [medicine]. These people settled in Giriama; they married and had families; and each of these became their own sub-clan.[43]

In Ndenge's rendering, settlements succeeded by constantly adopting newcomers and their skills and medicinal knowledge, including hunter-foragers (Laa), other Mijikenda (Digo), Swahili (Pemba), and more distantly related Bantu-speaking communities (Taita). As a result of the skills that people brought with them, some were able to eventually bypass the marginal status ascribed to outsiders and start their own clans.

Ndenge's perspective on the importance of collaborations with different groups is hardly an isolated example.[44] In other traditions, autochthonous hunter-foragers—usually called the Langulo or Laa—led the different Mijikenda groups to the protected forest groves where they established their *kayas*. In the process of these interactions, some were incorporated into extant clans or even cast as founders of specific clans and subclans, both called *mbari*.[45] Other clans are said to be founded by members of different Mijikenda groups, and others still purport that their founders were from different parts of Kenya's interior, like the Taita Hills or Mount Kilimanjaro regions.[46] Many clans had their own specialized medicines. Some of these medicines helped them along the migration route from Shungwaya, protecting them and leading them to their *kayas*. Once they settled down in their forested homesteads, different groups possessed specialties like rainmaking, preventing disease, or casting out harmful spirits.[47]

Notions of clanship offered coastal East Africans an ideological framework for cross-societal collaborations. The social organization practices commonly glossed in English as "clans" were flexible and inclusive, as historians of early Africa have observed. Rather than representing people sharing biological descent, clans constituted "networks of knowledge" that members could use to procure material goods, mobilize people, or to gain access to healing associations or medicines.[48]

In Sabaki society, according to Ray, clans were tasked with addressing pressing social and ecological issues such as rainmaking during droughts, resolving disputes, and assembling protective medicines. A village couldn't wait out a drought or a disease outbreak. They needed access to medicines and other forms of specialized knowledge quickly. Access to a network bounded by social ideologies of clanship provided settlements with a framework for obtaining and mobilizing knowledge to mitigate these challenges. While the clans' inclusive nature encouraged collaborations, it also created potential conflicts if specialists in one clan or settlement tried to guard or monopolize their knowledge.[49]

Oral traditions on the "*kaya* phase" attest to processes of assembly and incorporation that are resonant with the social ideas discussed in chapter 1. But as the archaeological evidence demonstrates, over the second millennium, communities in Mombasa's interior built more smaller settlements rather than continuing to recruit outsiders to simply help their villages to grow.[50] Mijikenda historical traditions provide insights into processes reflected in the archaeological surveys. These accounts are replete with stories of clans splitting to form new settlements following disputes, population pressures, or natural disasters like famine. Sometimes family quarrels prompted people to move elsewhere and found new villages.[51] Accusations that a person used harmful magic (*utsai*) or engaged in other antisocial behaviors could also result in them being expelled from one settlement and starting their own, or joining a different settlement.[52] More mundane developments like population pressures and overcrowding could also result in a settlement splitting apart.[53]

In delving into these traditional histories, I am not claiming that they represent the past exactly as it was. Instead, the oral traditions describe "events and processes of dispute and conflict" as people gradually established villages in new environments over the course of the second millennium, accelerating especially around the sixteenth and seventeenth centuries.[54] As Ray explains, Mijikenda oral historians "assembled stories that their audiences could accept as true."[55] Clearly, assembly and fissure were resonant and enduring features in local visions of the past. Both processes necessitated collaboration.

Mombasa's interior features highly varied microclimates, meaning settlements within a small radius could be affected very differently by a drought or famine. During the more recent past, people often moved from one region of the interior to another to seek relief from droughts and food shortages.[56] Mobility during adverse circumstances overlapped with more regular subsistence practices like swidden agriculture, which required that people move their farm plots every few years. Over time, this would have caused a gradual expansion in Mijikenda speakers' settlement geography as people moved into new areas in search of available forestland for cultivation. As communities pressed westward off the fertile coastal ridges and into the drier upland plains, cultivatable land became sparser and planted fields were often less capable of supporting large populations. Knowledge of the local soils, weather patterns, and forest products would have been especially valuable for migrants as they settled in regions with less predictable rainfall. At the same time, ecological pressures would have made it harder to recruit, incorporate, and retain newcomers. This meant that the members of extant settlements needed to constantly innovate or adopt new social and ritual strategies to thrive.

Mijikenda speakers' gradual emphasis on smaller settlements created opportunities to build connections with closely related speech communities and other inland groups. Settlements collaborated with one another regularly, adopting and innovating new knowledge, and incorporating new people and groups into their networks. The oral traditions of people founding *kayas*, incorporating strangers, and exchanging medicines and skills attest to an enlarging interactive sphere in Mombasa's immediate interior during past centuries. Furthermore, the traditions underscore the contingent qualities of collectives like a village, a *kaya*, or a clan. Settlements worked because people had options. To ensure that their village endured, a homestead head (or *mwenye*) needed to be able to maintain the social well-being and prosperity of their dependents.[57] The remainder of the chapter traces how they did so. As Mijikenda speakers started to emphasize homestead-based settlements, they developed healing associations and innovated and adopted various types of forest clearings around their settlements. These ritual spaces and healing groups operated as a crossroads for interactions among their villages and with other inland communities.

ASSEMBLING KNOWLEDGE, ANIMATING THE INLAND LANDSCAPE

Forest shrines and meeting places proliferated as Mijikenda speakers settled down along the ridges inland from Mombasa. They conducted healing rituals and administered judicial oaths in forested clearings on the outskirts of their villages. They left offerings in shrines built in tree stumps and caves to appease natural spirits. Medicines and charms buried around the borders of homes and farm fields ensured healthy yields and social reproduction. Within their homesteads, they erected commemorative wooden posts that represented recently departed ancestors.[58] Mijikenda speakers' array of shrines and meeting spaces reflect enduring concerns with appeasing natural and ancestral spirits, maintaining balance between medicines that could heal and harm, and finding spaces to congregate and build relationships that cut across individual homesteads. To demarcate ritual spaces for different healing activities, they drew from inherited practices while also readily adopting new ideas from other societies in Mombasa's interior, as the linguistic evidence analyzed below will show. Over centuries, Mijikenda speakers developed spaces for healing and ritual critical to their settlements' well-being through knowledge exchanges with other inland societies. Like the oral traditions, this evidence reveals inland villages as adaptive and connected spaces.

54 LOOKING INLAND, TO THE WORLD

Before shifting to linguistic evidence, I need to add a quick note on methodology. As in the last chapter, I use historical linguistic methodologies in the following discussion. However, since I focus on Mijikenda—which is a dialect chain—my approach differs slightly. Words that Mijikenda speakers inherited from their Sabaki ancestors provide a picture of the ritual and intellectual contours of early Mijikenda society. However, linguistic and ethnographic records also contain many words that were not inherited from proto-Sabaki. These words speak to innovations and adaptations that Mijikenda-speaking groups made to meet their own goals. Because Mijikenda dialects exhibit limited lexical and phonological differences, I cannot place most post-Sabaki changes precisely in time. Nevertheless, studying the derivation and distributions of words for different forested spaces, meeting grounds, and ritual markers illuminates a longer-term picture of socio-ritual transformations in this region between the early second millennium and the nineteenth century.

Spatial-ritual practices that Mijikenda speakers inherited from their linguistic ancestors offer a good starting point for considering these transformations over the longue durée. One example is the common practice, mentioned earlier, of burying protective charms called *fingo*. In oral traditions, the founding narrative for each of the main *kayas* includes stories about the original occupants burying *fingo* in the central and most sacred place of their palisaded villages. The term *fingo*, meaning "fetish" or "charm," dates back thousands of years to the earliest Bantu-speaking communities in equatorial Africa.[59] Comparative ethnographic evidence indicates that Northeast Coast speakers buried these protective charms—often in medicinal pots—since at least the start of the first millennium. Since modern Mijikenda dialects retained this word and associated practices, we can conclude that the earliest Mijikenda-speaking communities employed similar protective measures, burying *fingo* pots under the main pathways leading into their villages, the doorways of homes, and along the boundaries of agricultural fields.[60] Thus, oral traditions speak to an assemblage of medicinal practices that existed for many centuries prior to the proto-Mijikenda period.

Other agents animated spaces beyond the settled contours of their villages. For instance, coastal Bantu-speaking groups have constructed shrines in small huts and caves where they presented offerings to spirits (*mizimu) to promote the health and well-being of their settlements since at least the start of the first millennium. These practices endured among early Mijikenda speakers who understood *mizimu* to refer to both the spirits and the shrines. During the more recent past, natural spaces around their villages, such as caves and rock outcroppings, hollowed tree trunks, and forest groves, were all common abodes for *mizimu*. Medicinal experts pacified the spirits by offering foods, textiles, and charms, the latter of which they prepared from forest products and human objects like hair and nail clippings.[61]

Although *mizimu* spirits retained a significant role in some Mijikenda-speaking settlements, they continued adapting their understanding of the invisible forces that resided in wild spaces outside of their settlements. For instance, in Digo and Duruma—the two southernmost Mijikenda dialects—people replaced *muzimu* with a similar space called *muzuka*. This was an inherited term that meant "apparition" in proto-Sabaki (*muzyuka) and often carried associations with malevolent spirits. However, in southern Mijikenda dialects, *muzuka* referred to an abode for the spirits, which they located in natural spaces around their settlements, making it effectively synonymous in meaning and practice to a *muzimu*.[62] While I cannot say precisely when or why they replaced one spirit-shrine with another, this innovation highlights an important trend among communities in Mombasa's immediate interior: a regular willingness to adapt their ritual landscape to meet their needs.

In addition to the shrines, Mijikenda speakers used memorial posts for recently departed ancestors, called *koma*, to ensure their villages' well-being as they regularly moved and rebuilt their settlements.[63] During the recent past, the markers for the *koma* were located within the settlement area itself, which had the effect of repatriating the spirit of the deceased to the homestead.[64] People constructed the posts (also called *koma*) from tree branches, tying colorful cloth strips around the branch to dress the ancestral spirit and mark their gender identity.[65] Not every ancestor received a memorial shrine. They only erected a *koma* if a living person became afflicted by the spirit of a recently deceased ancestor. Building a memorial post provided a physical context for appeasing the ancestor with offerings of food or palm wine. If they moved settlements, they would leave their *koma* in place, meaning the ancestor's spirit would fold into the newly unsettled landscape as forest regrowth overtook the abandoned village.[66] Practices associated with these small wooden posts therefore fit well alongside the available archaeological evidence and oral histories, which suggests regular processes of mobility and fissures between settlements in the region.

Furthermore, these wooden memorial posts show how village rituals connected Mijikenda settlements to more expansive cross-societal interactions and borrowings. The word *koma* is attested across a much larger linguistic geography, including in other Sabaki languages (Pokomo and Swahili); some adjacent Northeast Coast languages; and some neighboring but more distantly related Bantu languages. Because the term is attested across a contiguous linguistic area, it is likely the product of what linguists refer to as an areal spread, referring to a word that spreads among speakers of geographically adjacent languages. Its phonetic shape in these languages indicates that the term, probably with the form *nkoma, diffused very early across this region, possibly as early as the proto-Sabaki period.[67] While reflexes of *nkoma generally connoted the spirit of a deceased ancestor across a contiguous corridor of languages, different linguistic groups adapted the term to their own needs. In Upper Pokomo–speaking communities in northern Kenya, for instance, *nkoma* took the form of impersonal nature spirits that people pacified with offerings before planting and for rainmaking rituals. Dawida

56   LOOKING INLAND, TO THE WORLD

speakers—who lived immediately west of the core Mijikenda settlement region—constructed shrines called *ngoma* (which is cognate with *koma*) containing the exhumed skulls of the ancestors of their lineage.[68]

To maintain relationships with their *koma*, Mijikenda speakers made offerings at the memorial markers, a practice they called *kuhasa* or *kuhatsa*. Much like *koma*, the verb *-hasa* has a history that draws attention to Mijikenda speakers' interactions with neighboring inland societies. The term's original source is the Chaga-Taita root word *-tac-, which meant "to offer, sacrifice."[69] Mijikenda speakers likely adopted this word from Dawida speakers living directly to their west in the Taita Hills, which has long been an important exchange corridor, especially since the early second millennium.[70] In Mijikenda dialects, the loanword *-hasa* replaced their inherited proto-Sabaki term for making a sacrifice (*-tambik-), perhaps indicating that the borrowing marked a novel way of thinking about rituals associated with ancestor veneration. In the Taita Hills, performances of *kutasa* rituals involved spitting libations and specialized utterances to call on the ancestors for blessings.[71] Mijikenda communities adopted similar practices, spitting and casting fluids like palm wine, to honor *koma* and to initiate healing ceremonies in other ritual settings.[72]

Mijikenda speakers made significant investments in ritual spaces in and around their settlements, drawing from many practices that were recognized and shared among language groups and societies across a wider region. In the settled contours of their villages, memorial posts brought balance to the homesteads while buried charms protected homes and crops from harmful magic. Outside of villages, nature spirits hovered around forest groves and caves. In addition to these spaces, ethnographic and oral sources—which I will discuss below—describe various forested meeting spaces and clearings in the bush as key foci of social and ritual activities. For many Bantu-speaking societies, the bush carries powerful associations as the appropriate spatial context for mediations with nonhuman agents, rituals for healing and reproduction, and productive activities like ironworking. These activities distinguished forests and bushland from the settled spaces of the villages, manifesting in what scholars describe as an ancient "village/bush dichotomy."[73] In early Mijikenda society, people continually assembled knowledge to reproduce and reinterpret ancient associations between the bush, healing, and social reproduction of homesteads.

By comparing Mijikenda speakers' inherited vocabulary for the bush with words that they innovated and borrowed, it quickly becomes clear that they greatly expanded the lexicon they used to name meeting spaces and forested clearings from the late first millennium onward. The earliest Mijikenda speakers inherited words that referred to forested spaces, such as the ancient Bantu terms *nyika* and *tsaka*, which they interpreted as "wilderness" and "forest," respectively.[74] However, it is unclear whether their Sabaki ancestors possessed any words referring to cleared activity areas within the bush. One potential candidate is found in the Digo and Duruma term *chiphalo*, which referred to a place for practicing medicines and

TABLE 1 Meeting Places in Mijikenda Dialects

Term in Mijikenda	Meanings	Distribution	Status
moro	Assembly of elders, meeting place in *kaya*	All Mijikenda; also, Pokomo, Mwiini	Loanword from Eastern Cushitic "cattle fold"
rungu, kurungu	Meeting place for elders; shrine for keeping healing pots and drums, located in bush	All Mijikenda; in Digo and Duruma, a shrine for healing pots associated with matrilineal ancestors	Likely derived from Mashariki term associated with "wilderness"
chiphalo	Dancing area, healing grounds located in clearing in bush	Digo, Duruma; also, Gogo, Thagicu languages	Inheritance (or relic areal diffusion?)
p'ala	Healer's workplace, meeting place for secret societies, located in clearing in bush	Giryama	Related to *chiphalo* either as a morphological innovation or relic form
ndala	Healer's workplace, place for recovery after initiations, located in clearing in bush	All Mijikenda except Giryama; also, Bondei to south	Areal innovation with Bondei? (Seuta language adjacent to Digo)
kinyaka, chinyaka	Dancing area located in clearing in bush close to village	All Mijikenda except Digo and Duruma	Loanword from Kamba
rome, dhome	Shaded sitting area for elder men, place for storytelling	All Mijikenda	Loanword from Thagicu (Kamba or Segeju)

performing dances. This term has a scattered distribution in the Kaskazi branch of Mashariki Bantu languages, indicating it may date back over two thousand years.[75] Mijikenda speakers also inherited the Sabaki term *luWanda. In proto-Sabaki this term described an open area, but the Mijikenda form, *lwanda*, connoted a clearing or meeting house for clans of a *kaya* in oral traditions.[76] After Mijikenda emerged as a distinct language, its speakers expanded the number and variety of places for meeting, socializing, and practicing rituals in the forests around their villages, as Table 1 illustrates.

A brief overview of the development of Mijikenda dialects is necessary to contextualize this table.[77] During the late first millennium, communities speaking an early form of Mijikenda lived on the fertile ridges inland from Mombasa. Within a few centuries—likely during the early second millennium—differences began forming between the speech of people living at the northern and southern ends of this speech community.[78] Eventually, distinctions in the speech of people living in different areas became pronounced enough to be considered distinctive dialects,

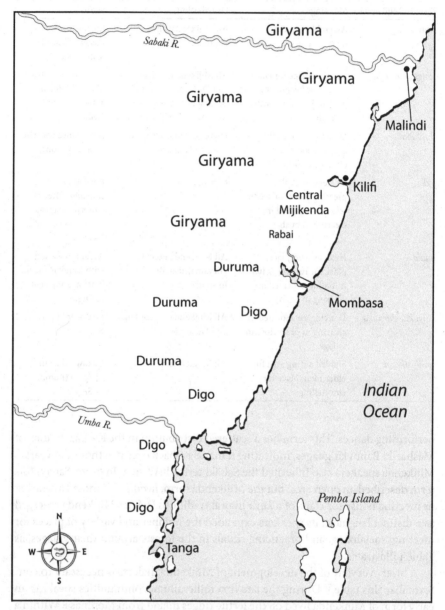

MAP 3. Mijikenda dialects: Digo, Duruma, Rabai, Central Mijikenda, and Giryama (Central Mijikenda includes Chonyi, Jibana, Kambe, Kauma, and Ribe). Map created by John Wyatt Greenlee, Surprised Eel Mapping.

today, consisting of Digo, Duruma, Rabai, Central Mijikenda, and Giryama.[79] Of these, Digo—the southernmost dialect—is the most distinct, both in terms of its lexicon and its grammar.[80] The other dialects, meanwhile, feature fewer lexical differences in terms of their core vocabulary. This indicates that they probably only began to differentiate from one another over the last few centuries.[81] Even after differences in their speech started to develop, people living in all parts of the Mijikenda speech community continued to interact with one another, exchanging words and ideas in the process.[82]

The diversity of words for forested and ritual meeting places in different dialects since proto-Mijikenda reflects the innovative nature of this social-spatial arena. By comparing these words—and the practices associated with them—we can conjecture about larger processes of adaptation, replacement, and borrowing over generations. For instance, in northern Mijikenda dialects, people replaced the term *chiphalo* with a similar space called *chinyaka*, a word they borrowed from Kamba.[83] Giryama speakers, meanwhile, interpreted *chiphalo* with a different noun prefix and suffix, articulating the word *p'ala*, which described a cleared area in the bush for administering medicines, holding feasts, and carving memorial posts.[84] A similar space called *ndala*—which was a healer's workplace, a meeting place, and a recovery ground following initiations—spread among other Mijikenda dialects.[85] All these spaces were distinct from another type of forest shrine called the *rungu*. At the southern edges of the dialect chain, Digo and Duruma speakers built their *rungu* just outside of their villages, using the forest shrines to store medicinal pots (*vifudu*) associated with matrilineal ancestors.[86] In other dialects, the *rungu* was a meeting place in the bush where the members of male healing societies stored special drums—called *mwanza*—that were played when administering judicial medicines.[87]

The derivations of *rungu* and *chiphalo/p'ala* offer a window into the concepts underpinning early Mijikenda speakers' understanding of forested ritual spaces. *Chiphalo* and *p'ala*, for instance, are derived from the root *-pád-, meaning "scrape, scratch." Proto-Sabaki speakers created an array of verbs that described clearing land for agriculture from this stem. Its semantic links to land clearing indicate that although the spaces were in the bush, people considered it a maintained wilderness.[88] *Rungu*, meanwhile, is likely derived from a root that is thousands of years old that means "plain; open space; desert; loneliness."[89] Across eastern Africa, words derived from this root carried associations with potent wilderness spirits. When attested with a different noun prefix in Great Lakes Bantu languages, it referred to "a dispersed territorial spiritual force which assists hunters."[90] A reflex of the same term described a "'potentially malevolent spirit' that moved within unsettled, neglected wilderness areas" among proto-Ruvu speakers in central-eastern Tanzania. Rhonda Gonzales has argued that both the Great Lakes and Ruvu meanings have their origins in the proto-Kaskazi word *mulungu, which described a type of spirit that inhabited unsettled areas and required supplication in the bush.[91]

60 LOOKING INLAND, TO THE WORLD

In *rungu*, Mijikenda speakers brought together ancient ideas about spiritual potency and wilderness into a single spatial context.

Members of inland settlements maintained specialized activity areas for healing activities while restricting access to certain knowledgeable individuals. The female *chifudu* members who kept medicine pots in the *rungu* and the members of male secret societies who carved memorial posts and prepared medicinal oaths in the *p'ala* both pursued wellness for their communities. However, the secretive and restricted nature of their activities also made it possible for practitioners to use healing knowledge to achieve their own individual ambitions, as the next section will detail.

Ultimately, the proliferation of overlapping—and sometimes synonymous— meanings for forested healing grounds, shrines, and other meeting places highlights Mijikenda speakers' unique investments in the ancient village/bush dichotomy. They reworked their understanding of the spaces around their villages by altering the meanings of older words, creating entirely new words, and by adopting words and knowledge from other linguistic communities. Amid these transformations, Mijikenda speakers began conceptualizing forested meeting spaces as the main contexts for political and ritual life, ideas that endured well into the twentieth century in stories about the *kayas*.[92] As their oral traditions suggest, people pursued medicinal knowledge by seeking out experts from other communities. By looking outward for knowledge to solve their most pressing problems, village leaders created links between dispersed homesteads and continually generated associations with other inland groups.

INNOVATING MEDICINES, MAKING CONNECTIONS

The remainder of the chapter situates the meeting spaces that proliferated in Mijikenda society and overlapping physical/spatial changes in inland villages within a broader history of healing and political authority. Forested clearings and ritual meeting grounds were the main spatial contexts for political work in inland villages. The first published Mijikenda language dictionary, for example, defined a *mudzi* (or village) as meaning a "place of abode" and the "people of a place" but also as the elders representing the people, such as when men from different villages assembled under large baobabs.[93] The village itself, as the entry alludes, could be metaphorically understood as existing under the shade of a large tree where elder men congregated to deliberate on important matters. In the absence of a state or larger polity, forest clearings and medicines linked villages in Mombasa's interior.

In arguing that healing and ritual knowledge undergirded growing connections in Mombasa's interior, I build on a wealth of scholarship on public healing in precolonial Africa. Public healing refers to "socially composed" ritual practices that healed collective ailments.[94] Public healers addressed droughts, famines, and disease outbreaks. They also sought to resolve moral afflictions such as those caused

LOOKING INLAND, TO THE WORLD   61

by neglected ancestral spirits; conflicts within a settlement, kin-group, or even an entire state or region; or a leader failing to engage in proper patronage.[95] Public healing activities could forge connections between disparate groups, helping to form new political identities or expand the reach of economic networks. In the Lower Congo, for instance, anthropologist John Janzen has shown that judges and merchants were healers in Lemba, a cult of affliction that acted as an integrative mechanism across a large, politically decentralized region. Lemba was especially critical to the region's participation in international trade between the seventeen and nineteenth centuries as the Lower Congo became a part of the Atlantic world nexus. Lemba practitioners used its medicines to regulate markets, build marriage alliances between clans, and heal afflictions that occurred when merchants accumulated wealth.[96] Ultimately, Janzen's work shows how public healing activities acted as a governing framework across dispersed and disparate communities while also fostering participation in trade. Thus, the Lemba example is instructive for understanding how healing ideas and practices created a connective tissue between villages in Mombasa's interior.

A brief background on Mijikenda speakers' medicinal ideas is necessary to examine the interplay between healing and governance in small-scale villages in southeast Kenya. Mijikenda speakers called medicine *uganga*, an ancient term that dates back thousands of years to the earliest Bantu speakers.[97] In coastal East Africa, *uganga* encompassed a huge range of ritual activities. As Ray explains, *uganga* included "techniques of iron working, rain making, clearing paths, negotiating peace, leading a war party, carving grave markers, moving sacred drums, composing songs, and communicating with ancestors."[98] Since not all individuals or groups possessed equal knowledge for these tasks, medicinal experts needed to collaborate frequently, as oral traditions demonstrate. Experts closely guarded their knowledge to ensure that they could benefit from collaborations with other clans and settlements.[99]

Mijikenda speakers inherited many of the words and practices associated with different types of *uganga* from their Sabaki ancestors. During the proto-Sabaki period, healers called *Waganga were the main proprietors of medicines that they used to address problems of individual health as well as larger social ailments.[100] They also helped to remedy the actions of people who used harmful magic, called *WucaWi, for destructive or antisocial purposes.[101] When practitioners wielded *utsai* (the Mijikenda form of the word *WucaWi) they could damage an individual's health or their possessions, such as crops or cattle. Especially powerful *utsai* could also affect an entire family or a cluster of neighboring settlements.[102] Calamities like drought, disease, and famine all potentially signaled that someone had used harmful medicines for antisocial purposes. Healers curated a variety of protective medicines to combat *utsai*. But the lines between healing and harming were fragile. Public perception of a healer's motivations and intent influenced whether the medicine was designated as *uganga*, a medicine that healed, or *utsai*,

62   LOOKING INLAND, TO THE WORLD

a medicine that caused harm. If healers failed to properly address misfortunes or violated established community norms, they risked being accused of practicing *utsai* themselves.[103]

Due to the porous boundaries between medicines that healed and medicines that caused harm, village leaders needed to be able to root out the cause of any misfortune to maintain social balance. One of the main methods for doing so was by having healers administer "oaths" that were used to determine the cause of moral transgressions or calamities. Sabaki speakers inherited two different terms that referred to oathing practices from their linguistic ancestors, *mwavį and *kilapo. Mijikenda speakers retained only *kilapo, however, which they articulated as *kiraho, chiraho,* or *chirapho* in different dialects. These terms derived from the proto-Bantu root word -dàp-, meaning "to swear."[104] Fitting the word's derivation, the practice itself typically took the form of what anthropological literature refers to as a "poison ordeal." In an ordeal, the accused individual would stand trial against their accusers by offering testimony and "swearing" an oath in support of its truthfulness. After their testimony, the *aganga* (Mijikenda form of *Waganga) administered an oath that typically took the form of poison or an object like a hot axe or needle.[105] In the mid-nineteenth century, for instance, missionary Charles New reported that Central Mijikenda groups used at least four different types of judicial oaths, including the *kiraho cha tsoka*, or "ordeal of the axe," which was administered by "applying a red-hot axe four times to the palm of the hand of the suspected person."[106] Oaths were only effective if the person was guilty of the transgression of which they were accused. The hot axe of a *kiraho cha tsoka* could not burn an innocent person's hands.

While Mijikenda speakers inherited these practices from their Sabaki ancestors, they continued to adapt *virapho* (pl.) practices, ultimately using groups associated with different medicines to foster connections across dispersed homesteads. In addition to curating judicial oaths, Sabaki speakers possessed *virapho* that could protect from misfortune—rather than simply rooting out its cause after the fact.[107] This practice continued among Mijikenda speakers who developed a huge range of *virapho* for guarding their fields, homes, and individual bodies. For instance, people used preventative *virapho* to protect their homes and fields against thieves by casting a spell on someone who entered a field without permission. One common *chirapho* was the *habasi*, a medicine made from a painted baobab shell that caused bleeding or dysentery when a person violated the area it protected. If someone believed a family member or rival was afflicting them with *utsai*, they could also obtain *virapho* to bury around their home or to wear as amulets to proactively prevent or reverse the impact of harmful medicines.[108]

The number and variety of *virapho* proliferated in Mijikenda society over many centuries. When medicines were deemed ineffective, they were discarded, and new ones gained prominence. Over time, those possessing knowledge of the most powerful oaths organized into specialist groups associated with specific medicines.

This ensured the durability of certain *virapho* and promoted these knowledgeable specialists as the proper mediators of healing within their communities.[109] In some cases, the groups were open to anyone capable of paying the membership fees, while others required that an individual already be a recognized member of local elders' councils. These councils featured different ornamentation and specialized ritual objects, including drums, medicine pots, and objects associated with their medicines and oaths. For example, protective medicines such as the *chirapho cha kobe* and the *chirapho cha dzaya* utilized a tortoise shell (*kobe*) and potsherd (*dzaya*), respectively.[110] Ultimately, five different *virapho* specialist groups became widely attested across Mijikenda dialect communities: *chinyenze, gophu, phaya, habasi,* and *chifudu.*[111]

Each of these groups met in forest clearings where they performed rituals that ensured the well-being of their communities and provided members opportunities to cultivate social distinctions. For instance, the *phaya* society curated a powerful oath called the *fisi,* or "hyena oath." This was a "proscriptive oath" that was sworn by members before events like warfare to attest to their collective commitment to the cause at hand. Violations of the oath caused a person to howl like a dying hyena. Drums and shouts during the swearing ceremony were said to mimic the sounds of that animal.[112] The accounts of nineteenth-century missionaries indicate that the sounds of secret meetings penetrated nearby homesteads. Most notorious were the sounds of the *mwanza,* a friction drum played when administering *virapho.* According to New, the sound of the *mwanza* resembled "the rumbling of distant thunder . . . the roaring of a lion, and now what may be imagined of the moaning of some demon in agony." When played in the dead of the night, the "bellowings of this drum, rolling through the forests, up the valleys, echoing and re-echoing among the hills, accompanied by the howls and shrieks" alerted people to the practitioners' esoteric activities.[113] For the nonmembers of these groups, the noises reverberating from the forested clearings and into the settled contours of villages would have signaled activities that were socially valuable yet unknowable. Respected, but also feared.

The medicinal groups assumed a key role in social reproduction and protecting individual homesteads. The *chifudu* group, which was the only group whose membership was restricted to women, provides a useful illustration. The *chifudu* is the most widely practiced medicinal group and the only one attested among speakers of Digo—the southernmost Mijikenda dialect—in historical and ethnographic records.[114] *Chifudu* practitioners specialized in fertility medicines and met at forested shrines (*rungu*) immediately outside of their villages. The name *chifudu* is derived from an ancient Bantu term meaning "tortoise," which also referred to the empty shell of a coconut in Mijikenda and some Swahili dialects.[115] In Mijikenda, the term also referred to the *vifudu* containers, typically gourds or small clay pots, each of which was named after a female ancestor. These pots lived in small huts in the bush where members met to mix medicines and practice *chifudu*

64   LOOKING INLAND, TO THE WORLD

dances, during which they made "hooing" sounds into their pot openings while performing. *Vifudu* members also performed at life cycle events such as weddings and funerals—both occasions that carried heightened risks for moral transgression that could lead to social or ecological calamities.[116] *Vifudu* members' pots and forest shrines thus enabled them to play an active role in ensuring the health and well-being of their villages.

Membership in the healing groups gave initiated experts the means to influence their communities and assemble wealth in an acceptable manner by controlling medicines considered essential to the social health of their settlement. One example of this is the *gophu* (or *gohu*), a group known for their lavish feasts and for curing a disease that resulted from sexual transgressions, known as *vitio*.[117] *Vitio* encompassed disease symptoms like vomiting, diarrhea, and even death that struck when someone had sexual intercourse with the wrong person or at the wrong time prior to performing the proper cleansing rituals.[118] Transition points like the founding of new villages and initiations (as well as marriages and funerals, as mentioned) carried an especially heightened risk for *vitio*.[119] According to oral traditions, *vitio* outbreaks caused some *kaya* settlements to split, making clans and individuals possessing medicines to cure the disease highly valued members of a community.[120] Female *vifudu* members represented one half of this equation, using their pots and dances to protect the clans with which they were associated, especially for matters related to reproduction. *Gophu* members' ability to cure *vitio* created a complementary male realm of reproductive rituals and ensured that initiates in this group retained a significant influence over the health and well-being of their villages.[121]

Gophu and *vifudu* members' skills at protecting and preserving homesteads would have been especially valued amid processes of splitting and settlement diffusion, reflected in archaeology and oral traditions. Notably, Mijikenda speakers adopted some initiation practices associated with the *gophu* around the same time they began emphasizing smaller settlements. It is unclear when the *gophu* society originated, although the name of the group—pronounced *gophu* in southern Mijikenda and *gohu* in northern dialects—follows regular sound correspondences, indicating that the group's name has some antiquity in Mijikenda society. Compellingly, several of the words associated with *gophu* practices—including terms for their initiation feast and a verb referring to receiving initiation honors—are loanwords from speakers of another inland language called Segeju (or Daiso), with whom Mijikenda shared considerable interrelations in the sixteenth and seventeenth centuries. During these interactions, Mijikenda speakers borrowed many loanwords related to trade, animal husbandry, and medicines—some of which I will discuss in chapters 3 and 4.[122] The loanwords thus indicate that Mijikenda speakers adopted at least some of the practices for initiations into this specialized healing group precisely when archaeological records begin to reflect a clear shift toward smaller, more dispersed homestead-based settlements.

Due to the *gophu's* critical role in homestead reproduction, initiated members were memorialized in their villages with carved posts called *vigango*. In comparison to the *koma* posts that represented recently departed ancestors, *vigango* were taller—typically between three and eight feet tall—and featured more intricate designs such as incised triangular patterns on the "body" and rounded or square "heads" with faces.[123] People erected them, as they did *koma*, in their homesteads, dressing the posts with textile strips and venerating them with foods and palm wine. When people established new villages, they were allowed to transport their *vigango* one time. But more often, the posts were left behind like *koma*.[124] Based on these similarities, *vigango* practices appear to have developed out of those associated with the *koma*. However, the new word also signals the distinctive ways that people envisioned the role of the *vigango* posts within their settlements. The word *vigango* is derived from the same root as *uganga*, with an etymological meaning of an object or instrument that is the result of healing. The etymology speaks directly to the role of *gophu* members in protecting homesteads from diseases like *vitio*. The purpose of erecting *vigango* was not to simply memorialize influential elders. Instead, they ensured that homesteads remained protected from harmful diseases during the transition period following their death.

The historical and ethnographic literature gives a sense of what these healing dynamics looked like during the past few centuries. In the more recent past, joining a specialist group like the *gophu* offered ways for people to cultivate distinctions and exert influence over their homesteads, even after their death. But these honors were restricted to those with the ability to pay initiation fees. The hefty fees for the two most influential groups, the *gophu* and the *phaya*, restricted membership to the wealthiest men. In the early twentieth century, for instance, fees for joining the *phaya* were "fourteen lengths of cotton or fourteen rupees; ten calabashes of beer; one large and bearded goat; seven cooking pots of mealie meal; four measures of castor oil seeds; one new axe."[125] Joining one—or even multiple—*virapho* groups made it possible for one to amass wealth while avoiding accusations associated with excess accumulation.[126] The twinning of wealth and gendered forms of healing expertise offered meaningful pathways to accrue power and influence.[127] Moreover, by joining these groups, members could nurture relationships across dispersed settlement geographies. As people spread out into homestead-based settlements, forested clearings in the bush in between settlements acted as nodes of connection and contact between the leading members of different villages, including elder men, as well as female healers and their medicinal pots.

The earliest available documentary records and oral accounts show that some people who participated in *virapho* groups had overlapping roles. For instance, oral traditions indicate that the *phaya* operated as a special body within a local council of elders.[128] The councils, which were made up of elder men from adjacent settlements, were responsible for adjudicating disputes. However, if a person was unhappy with the councils' rulings, they could turn to the expertise of *virapho* specialists. According to the colonial administrator Arthur Champion, after standing before the councils, an individual could inform "the elders that their judgement does not meet with his approval and that he would like to take an oath before them." By invoking this right to a *chirapho* ordeal, the individual could force elders to "summon a medicine man of the class competent to administer the oath in their presence."[129] Ultimately, the elder men that made up the council maintained the legitimacy of their judicial decisions through collaborations with medicinal experts who were also frequently members of the councils themselves.

Mijikenda speakers' emphasis on these healing groups influenced both their political arrangements and accumulative activities. Secret societies like *virapho* groups, as archaeologist Susan Keech McIntosh has observed, acted as a socially sanctioned "arena . . . for the elaboration of individualistic displays of prestige and wealth." In many parts of Africa, participation in such groups enabled members "to channel wealth and ambition in such a way as to impede political consolidation," offering pathways to accrue prestige and influence without requiring they achieve a formal office or position within an established political hierarchy.[130] In Mombasa's immediate interior, specialist healing associations, forest clearings, and protective medicines and oaths similarly stood at the center of social and political life.[131] Participation in these healing associations offered people—primarily men—pathways for translating their wealth into activities where they could accrue knowledge and influence. Their accumulative aspirations also supported the broader social prosperity of their villages. They used specialized knowledge for essential tasks like ensuring social reproduction, appeasing spirits, protecting farm fields and homes, and identifying the cause of misfortunes caused by *utsai*. Critically, they pursued these activities as they also began participating extensively in transregional trade, operating as the gateway between Mombasa and places farther in the interior, as the next chapter will explore in depth.

Through a longue durée lens, we can discern some larger trends among the details covered in the second half of this chapter, even if the available evidence makes it hard to develop a precise chronology for many of these changes. To recap, during the second millennium, communities inland from Mombasa increasingly emphasized homestead-based settlements. They protected their villages by burying medicines around their homes and farm fields and pacifying spirits in natural shrines. Over centuries, they diversified the ritual contours of their homesteads by building multiple types of memorial posts for deceased ancestors and designating forested areas in the bush for practicing *uganga*. When challenges arose, they resolved natural calamities, disputes, and any potential harm caused by *utsai* by consulting medicinal experts within and outside of their communities. In the process, they emphasized one important type of medicine called *viraho*, or *virapho*, which, like their ancestors, they used to adjudicate disputes and assemble protective medicines. Eventually, specialist groups made up of people who could afford the fees necessary to join their ranks became the main guardians of the most powerful oaths and protective medicines. They congregated in special meeting places outside of the settled areas of their villages, varieties of which proliferated in Mombasa's interior.

. . .

While Mombasa emerged as a major Islamic port city, its inland neighbors showed little apparent interest in the ideas and practices that constituted the connective tissue of Indian Ocean societies. Instead, they innovated and adapted new ritual ideas, spaces, and practices, building on inherited frameworks of *uganga* and *virapho* to create social worlds that suited their own needs. The changes detailed in this chapter occurred as Mijikenda speakers pressed into new ecologies, entered new spheres of contact, and began emphasizing homestead-based villages rather than larger multicomponent towns. Forest clearings, specialized medicines, and healing groups undergirded connections between dispersed villages, influential elders, and, in some cases, entirely disparate communities. In the process of borrowing ritual ideas and practices from other inland groups, Mijikenda speakers generated relationships with communities with whom they also traded to obtain some of East Africa's most lucrative export goods. As the next chapter will show, by pursuing ambitions that put them out of harmony with the Indian Ocean's core cultural norms, people living in a small region in Mombasa's interior began to influence much larger spheres of interaction.

3

The Inland Underpinnings of Indian Ocean Commerce

During the second millennium, Mijikenda-speaking groups pressed into new regions of the coastal uplands, establishing settlements over a variety of environments and absorbing new people and new ritual ideas into their social worlds. Their emphasis on a smaller-scale village organization and knowledge exchanges with other inland societies overlapped with their growing role as traders in some of East Africa's most valued exports, as the previous chapter noted. Villages in Mombasa's immediate interior increasingly began to represent a gateway between the worlds of the coast and interior, mediating the flow of ivory and gum copal into the port city. As a gateway society, Mijikenda speakers' aspirations and initiatives prominently shaped Mombasa's connections to the world.[1]

This chapter takes an inland perspective to understanding Mombasa's emergence as a major Indian Ocean trading port. It reconstructs the inland interactive sphere supporting the town's maritime trading connections from the early second millennium to the start of the nineteenth century. No detailed descriptions of inland trading routes exist for periods prior to the mid-nineteenth century. But societies in Africa's interior contributed substantially to maritime trade, something archaeologists working in eastern and southern Africa have increasingly emphasized over the past two decades. As this work shows, intra-African circulations in products like salt, clay pots, metals, domestic animals, and wild animal products pulled oceanic trade goods into interior regions. The material interests and ritual economies of people living in smaller-scale societies and participating in multidirectional trading networks were critical to the emergence of transregional trade between Africa and other parts of the Indian Ocean.[2] Evidence from comparative historical linguistics, meanwhile, can illuminate the social ideas and motivations of those contributing to the interior exchange networks documented

THE INLAND UNDERPINNINGS OF COMMERCE   69

by archaeologists. Members of distant speech communities frequently innovated novel techniques to support long-distance trading activities. But their involvement in long-distance trade was not always motivated by straightforward commercial aspirations, as Yaari Felber-Seligman and Kathryn de Luna have shown for eastern and southern Africa, respectively.[3]

I add to this existing work by homing in on one port city's relationship with one adjacent inland community, taking a scaled-down view of the ideas, practices, and networks motivating trade circulations in Mombasa. As the above scholarship demonstrates, it was never a foregone outcome that interior trade goods would reach coastal ports. Treating inland participation in Indian Ocean commerce as something that was contingent opens questions about why Mijikenda speakers chose to engage with emerging maritime trading networks at all. In the narrative that follows, I highlight the iterative nature of trade in Mombasa's interior, showing how Mijikenda speakers responded to changes in their own villages and across the broader coastal and interior regions. Over centuries, they adapted and innovated novel methods for conducting long-distance trade, building on the relationships and ritual networks detailed in the last chapter.

To reconstruct the inland underpinnings of Mombasa's oceanic connections requires a multidisciplinary source base. The chapter is roughly divided into thirds, with each part anchored in a particular evidentiary base critical for understanding inland contributions to Indian Ocean trade. I begin with the published archaeological materials before moving to written records concerning Mombasa's role as a distribution center for ivory, gum copal, and imported cotton textiles. In the final third of the chapter, I bring these materials together through an analysis of linguistic evidence to show how inland communities generated knowledge to support the trading circulations attested in the archaeological and written records.

Ultimately, the chapter shows that Mijikenda speakers influenced Mombasa's enduring role as a major port city because they pursued a variety of means for participating in trade, both coastal and inland. Inland villages were not drawn into transregional trade as a hinterland dependency of the neighboring port.[4] Instead, Mijikenda speakers' considerable influence on oceanic trade hinged on innovations, networks, and material ambitions that diverged from the Islamicate practices commonly understood as the driving force of connections between different regions of the Indian Ocean.

ECOLOGIES OF INTERIOR TRADE: FROM WILD BACKWATER TO INLAND MOSAICS

Over the course of the second millennium, Mijikenda speakers built expansive connections with each other and with other inland communities, as the previous chapter detailed. They swapped ritual ideas, borrowed new medicines, and established contacts with other inland societies. The ecological diversity of Mombasa's interior encouraged these sorts of collaborations. To begin tracing the growth of inland trading networks and cross-societal collaborations, it is helpful to take an ecological viewpoint, beginning in the forested ridges immediately inland from the coast. If one were to visit the Mombasa region during the early first millennium, they would find that interactions between different sociolinguistic groups occupying the region were quite limited. When ironworking and farming communities first settled in southeast Kenya, the region was already occupied by lithic-using Late Stone Age (LSA) communities who primarily subsisted by hunting and collecting wild resources.[5] Ironworking and farming communities occupied similar environments to LSA hunting and gathering specialists. In some cases, they lived in settlements within walking distance of one another. However, during the early to mid-first millennium, these groups interacted with each other infrequently.[6]

The scope and scale of cross-societal interactions began to change after the midpoint of the millennium. Excavations at LSA sites have recovered ceramics that, based on their style, were either produced by—or were produced to mimic the ceramics of—neighboring farming communities. Chemical analysis of these ceramics indicates that LSA communities consumed cultivated crops, including sorghum, pearl millet, and finger millet, which they likely obtained through exchanges with their farming neighbors.[7] Most of these early exchanges would have been small in scale, taking place primarily between neighboring settlements. Having steadily developed their expertise cultivating sorghum and millet in the preceding centuries, post-Sabaki communities would have been well positioned to use their agricultural surpluses to obtain resources like wild honey and beeswax, skins, and other animal products from their neighbors.[8]

Participants in these inland exchange networks also began developing connections with reemerging oceanic trade during the same late first-millennium time frame. Archaeological records show that both LSA settlements and their ironworking neighbors could access maritime trade goods like cowries, shell beads, and imported glass. Some farming settlements also procured Sassanian and Chinese ceramics, although this imported pottery was quite rare.[9] By the end of the first millennium, early Swahili speakers began living on Mombasa Island. Within a few centuries, their descendants erected houses and mosques using coral stone architectural styles, marking the town as a characteristic Swahili port city.[10] These expanding scales of coastal trade gradually generated new opportunities for interactions farther into East Africa's interior as well. By the end of the first millennium, the inland roots of oceanic commerce slowly took shape, first with small exchanges in foodstuffs, beads, and pottery along Mombasa's forested uplands, and soon extending outward into other environments.

For people in Mombasa, all regions beyond the immediate coast were an unknown and hostile territory. Swahili speakers referred to inland regions away from coastal towns as the *nyika*, a word meaning "wilderness." This *nyika* wilderness encompassed everything from nearby settlements in the coastal uplands

THE INLAND UNDERPINNINGS OF COMMERCE 71

to imagined locales in East Africa's far interior. Swahili speakers even referred to Mijikenda communities—and sometimes other inland groups—by the pejorative name Wanyika, or "wilderness dwellers."[11] Yet the ecologically diverse regions in Mombasa's interior were anything but wild backwaters.

Moving inland from the ocean's edge, the landscape gently rises from the low coastal plain to an upland region which reaches as close as eight kilometers to the littoral.[12] While East Africa's offshore islands and low coastal plain are dominated by dry forest, coral rag, and mangrove thicket, the coastal uplands feature a far greater diversity of vegetation. The eastern part of the inland ridge—where Sabaki speakers planted some of their earliest settlements—includes dry forest, lowland moist savanna, Miombo woodland, and lowland rainforest. Rainfall varies greatly by microclimates, with some locations experiencing high average rainfall, peaking during the two rainy seasons from October to November and April to May. Rivers and streams dissect the landscape, some of which feed into the two large coastal creek estuaries that encircle Mombasa. Other inland creeks connect the low-lying ridges to nearby coastal towns like Mtwapa and Kilifi, granting easy access to these urban centers from the coastal upland. The environment becomes progressively more arid only slightly farther inland. The western flanks of the coastal range give way to a much drier high coastal plain that fringes a large arid zone known as the Tsavo region, or simply the *nyika*.[13]

This arid region formed a key part of Mombasa's inland trading connections. Lying approximately one hundred to two hundred kilometers inland, the Tsavo region has historically been home to some of East Africa's largest elephant populations and today includes Kenya's largest national park.[14] For centuries prior, the Tsavo region constituted a major zone for exchanges in goods like ivory, rock crystal, and iron.[15] Hunters in this region began supplying ivory to coastal markets on a large scale around the twelfth century CE.[16] Ivory procurement overlapped with expanding productive activities and local trade in agricultural goods, domestic animals, wild resources, and iron.

The Tsavo region's economy operated as a mosaic as Chapurukha Kusimba, Sibel Kusimba, and David Wright have argued. Mosaics refer to "a group of societies that inhabit a region together and that practice different economies and religions, speaking diverse languages, but related through clientship, alliances, knowledge sharing, and rituals."[17] Like an artwork mosaic that combines smaller fragments of material to create a unified whole, trading mosaics formed through collaborations among distinct pieces, illuminating interactions between societies with different economic specializations, occupying diverse environments, and of different scales.[18] The mosaic framing alerts us to the fact that trading interactions between coast and interior did not follow a supply-and-demand model driven by the interests and agency of oceanic merchants. Instead, an array of societies, material interests, and trading strategies undergirded the town's transregional connections. In other words, trade thrived in Mombasa's interior precisely because

MAP 4. Mombasa's interior. Map created by John Wyatt Greenlee, Surprised Eel Mapping.

connections to coastal networks were not the only drivers for the production and circulation of interior goods.

The arid interior region developed through its relationship with bordering environments. In addition to the coastal uplands to the east, Tsavo's southern frontiers were marked by three large mountain massifs that make up the Taita Hills. Towering several thousand feet above the dry plain, Taita and neighboring montane forests are often described as archipelagos of highland "islands" for their role as nodal points for cross-societal exchanges in an otherwise arid landscape.[19] The easternmost massif, Kasigau, was located about three days from Mombasa,

THE INLAND UNDERPINNINGS OF COMMERCE   73

making it one of the first stopovers for overland travelers.[20] Within a relatively condensed region, a person could move from the coastal uplands' diverse microclimates into Mombasa, or travel west and quickly reach the Tsavo plains. Moving across this arid zone, that same person would find many rock outcroppings and pastoral camps before reaching the highland mountain massifs of the Taita Hills. In the highlands, they would enter a very different ecology featuring perennial streams, rich iron ore deposits, and high agricultural productivity. The diverse resources of these closely proximate ecologies promoted trade based around circular exchanges and intergroup collaborations rather than being dominated by any one product or place.

PRODUCTION AND EXCHANGE IN MOMBASA'S INTERIOR: THE ARCHAEOLOGICAL EVIDENCE

Archaeological evidence from the Tsavo plains and adjacent highland regions demonstrates the collaborative and integrated nature of trade in Mombasa's interior. Between the late first and mid-second millennium, societies living in this region scaled up their productive potential in multiple areas, including ironmaking, craft production, agriculture, animal husbandry, and ivory procurement. For example, around Mount Kasigau, the easternmost massif of the Taita Hills, archaeologists have located two significant ironworking centers, Rukanga and Kirongwe. Smelting furnaces, slag heaps, tuyere fragments, and abundant finished and unfinished iron products attest to substantial iron smelting and smithing activities at the two sites from about the ninth century.[21] Kasigau's residents also invested in other areas of output, such as agriculture. They built hillside terraces that captured water from the streams that dissected the massif's forested slopes. The irrigation techniques allowed farm fields and fruit orchards to thrive at lower elevations despite minimal rainfall. By growing foods at lower elevations, farmers could trade their agricultural wares more easily with neighboring pastoralists and other occupants of the adjacent plains.[22]

During the same period that Kasigau developed as an iron production center, a variety of site types flourished on the neighboring plains, creating many opportunities for exchanges between different groups. These sites included rock shelters, which served as seasonal residences for hunting specialists; open-air settlements; and pastoralist camps featuring livestock pens constructed from dry stonework. Many rock outcroppings dotting the Tsavo region show evidence of grinding hollows—cup-sized depressions weathered into rocks—indicating the occupants processed foods on-site, including crops procured from settlements in the adjacent highlands. Archaeologists theorize that some of the more prominent open-air sites were regional markets where communities from the hills and plains met to exchange fresh fruits and grains for milk products, honey, animal skins, ostrich shells, and rock crystal.[23]

74   THE INLAND UNDERPINNINGS OF COMMERCE

Signatures of oceanic trade are not absent from these inland settlements. At every single site excavated in Tsavo, the Taita Hills, and adjacent regions like Mombasa's uplands, archaeologists have recovered glass beads, most originating from South Asia.[24] Glass beads were an ideal long-distance trade good. They were easy to transport, hard to break, and easy to adapt into local or even individual styles.[25] As a result, beads flourished as trade goods in East Africa's interior from the first millennium until well into the nineteenth century, circulating alongside local crafts, animal products, and foodstuffs.

Other inland iron production centers flourished around the same time as Kasigau, supplying finished iron products for local use, as well as iron bloom for maritime trade. These included Mtsengo, an early to mid-second-millennium settlement located about thirty-five kilometers northwest of Mombasa, and Gonja, a site in northeastern Tanzania's South Pare Mountains.[26] Like Kasigau, Gonja was located at an ecological borderland, situated 150 kilometers inland from the coast on the eastern edge of a forested mountain massif flanking an arid steppe hundreds of meters below.[27] Large quantities of iron slag, tuyere fragments, and smelting furnace remains show that significant on-site ironworking took place in specialized activity areas. But despite extensive evidence of large-scale iron smelting, archaeologists recovered very few finished iron products from Gonja, indicating that its occupants mainly produced iron for trade.[28]

According to Arabic geographical accounts, both Mombasa and Malindi exported iron for trade during the same period that sites like Kasigau, Gonja, and Mtsengo flourished as iron production centers. In the twelfth century, Muhammad al-Idrisi reported that iron made up Malindi's "largest profits." More than a century later, a geographer from Damascus named Abu al-Fida—whose work built on earlier geographies like al-Idrisi's—wrote that the mountains inland from the coast of modern Kenya featured ample iron mines.[29] East Africa's main oceanic trading partners produced their own iron. However, merchants in Arabia and South Asia may have preferred East Africa's comparatively cheap and high-quality iron bloom and steel.[30] There is evidence of ironworking technology on the Kenya coast during this time, but very little evidence of iron smelting. This dearth of smelting evidence suggests that iron production in coastal towns was probably only sufficient to support local needs at the household level. Most iron exported from East Africa, therefore, must have originated in contemporaneous inland production centers. Before reaching coastal entrepôt, it would have moved across multidirectional trading mosaics alongside goods that included crops, animals, and skins.[31]

While the Arabic geographic accounts provide tantalizing indications of the role of inland production centers in provisioning iron for maritime trade, metal products also circulated for local uses. Metalworkers produced finished iron hoes and weaponry, including arrowheads and spear points for elephant hunters. Based on the quality and sophistication of iron arrowheads recovered from

THE INLAND UNDERPINNINGS OF COMMERCE   75

Rukanga and Kirongwe, scholars theorize that Tsavo's elephant-hunting specialists were a critical market for the metalworkers at these sites.[32] Arrows and iron offer an entry into thinking about exchanges between different societies in the region. For instance, during the more recent past, hunters from this region used potent poisons that they attached to the tips of their arrows when hunting larger animals like elephants. According to oral traditions, they obtained this poison by trade from Mijikenda-speaking partners.[33] Arrow poison was already a well-established tool for warfare by the start of the sixteenth century, when Portuguese records attest to archers from the mainland wielding poison-tipped arrows to defend Mombasa against seaborne attacks. According to one account, Mijikenda communities produced this poison by boiling the fruit of oil palm trees, yielding a substance potent enough that it could "cause immediate death."[34] These sources point to Mijikenda speakers' long-standing expertise at producing arrow poison, dating back centuries, which also helped support Tsavo's place as a major ivory procurement region.

In some cases, the exchanges attested in archaeological records took place through hand-to-hand transactions between individuals with established relationships. But people in Mombasa's interior also congregated in common locations like markets, where people who spoke different languages and practiced unique specializations met to exchange their wares. The dry lowlands feature many isolated rock outcroppings, some of which were used as meeting grounds by at least the start of the second millennium.[35] East Africa's first markets occurred in "buffer zones" between different language groups and resource specialists, something that is apparent in the diffusion of market terms among neighboring linguistic groups.[36] Linguists have documented the proliferation of words referring to "markets" in different East African languages between the late first and early second millennium. For instance, daughter languages in the Seuta and Ruvu subgroups of Northeast Coast Bantu shared a late first-millennium areal term for markets that they derived from an inherited root word that meant "to buy."[37] Similarly, speakers of Thagicu and Chaga languages in East Africa's highlands employed several words borrowed from nearby Nilotic languages to describe markets.[38]

Communities living between Mombasa, the Taita Hills, and Pare Mountains were also a part of this regional trend, using a shared term—pronounced *chete* in Mijikenda dialects—to refer to markets and market days.[39] Variations of the term *chete* are shared in geographically adjacent languages leading inland from Mombasa and neighboring Mijikenda-speaking settlements, into Tsavo's drylands and the montane highlands of the Taita Hills and Pare Mountains. The distribution of the word thus precisely maps onto the production and exchange networks detailed in this section. Compellingly, *chete* may be a loanword from a Southern Cushitic language where the word originally meant "cattle transaction" or "market."[40] The word likely entered Mijikenda dialects via interactions with communities in the neighboring Taita Hills and Tsavo region, which were home to several different

76   THE INLAND UNDERPINNINGS OF COMMERCE

Southern Cushitic-speaking groups during the early to mid-second millennium.[41] With this evidence in mind, we can envision common ideas about markets spreading among different groups living in Mombasa's interior as they traded foodstuffs, iron, beads, and other goods identified in the region's archaeological records. In some cases, these trading connections would have intersected with more esoteric exchanges in medicines and ritual ideas, as the previous chapter detailed.

From the late fifteenth century, Mombasa's connections to oceanic trade are increasingly legible in documentary records. These written sources highlight the town's preeminent position in the Indian Ocean ivory trade and its role as a clearinghouse for Gujarati textiles. It is important to remember that trade in these ocean-crossing goods was never divorced from contemporaneous circulations of foodstuffs, animal products, iron, arrow poisons, and medicines.[42] Cross-societal meeting grounds at isolated rock outcroppings and healing groves in the bush were spatial settings for collaborations that directly and indirectly influenced the circulation of goods and ideas. Mombasa's interior was not a supply land or rural dependency. Instead, trade goods moved to Mombasa Island and reached other faraway port cities due to material practices of communities in the town's interior, which intersected with the interests of, but were not determined solely by, oceanic merchants.

MORE THAN A LIST OF TRADE GOODS: FINDING INLAND CONNECTIONS IN TEXTUAL RECORDS

On April 7, 1498, a Portuguese fleet traveling northbound along East Africa's coastline became the first European vessels to reach Mombasa. Rather than immediately entering the harbor, Vasco da Gama's ships anchored at a distance from the town, where they waited until they were met by smaller boats from the island. The next day, the Portuguese sent two men to the island to meet Mombasa's leader, who offered them a sampling of spices and other goods as gifts. Da Gama remained suspicious of Mombasa's intentions, however, and just a few days later, he pulled up anchor and sailed north to Malindi, a rival town.[43] Portuguese ships returned to Mombasa in 1505 and sacked the city, both in support of their budding alliance with Malindi and as retaliation for the town's perceived antagonism to da Gama's party seven years earlier. Mombasa would go on to have a conflict-ridden relationship with the Portuguese over the next two centuries (a story detailed in the next chapter). In many ways, da Gama's experiences in Mombasa portended these tensions. Nevertheless, it would be a mistake to view Mombasa's first encounter with European mariners only through the lens of conflict. The town's initial interactions with Vasco da Gama's ships also highlight its central place at an intersection of maritime and interior trading networks during the late fifteenth century.

When da Gama's ships dropped anchor outside of Mombasa in 1498, the representatives from the island who came out in small boats to greet him were part of

THE INLAND UNDERPINNINGS OF COMMERCE   77

a long history of protection and patronage that undergirded merchant activity in the Indian Ocean.[44] After Ibn Battuta arrived in Mogadishu in 1331, for instance, his dhow was similarly met by small boats, including one representing the sultan. It was customary, according to Battuta, for the sultan's representative to determine all the details of the ship, including where it came from, its owner, captain, and cargo. Local merchants also sent young men bearing small gifts to visitors, hoping to establish guest-host relationships that could yield profitable trading opportunities.[45] The representatives from Mombasa in 1498 would have met da Gama's ships with similar motivations. Indeed, a day after their arrival, Mombasa's leader sent gifts of fruit and sheep, "together with a ring, as a pledge of safety, letting [da Gama] know that in case of his entering the port he would be supplied with all he stood in need of."[46] The supplies from the city included not just provisions, but also, in a show of the town's commercial strength, "all the spices and merchandise of India" as well as locally procured goods like ivory and ambergris. This sampling of trade goods came with a promise that greater quantities of each ware could be furnished for the foreign fleet.[47] Clearly, Mombasa was a town with connections.

The late fifteenth-century encounter between da Gama's ships and Mombasa provides a jumping-off point for considering the role of Mombasa's interior in shaping these transregional connections. Although communities on the mainland did not figure into the initial Portuguese impressions of the town, references to common trade goods—both exports and imports—in early Portuguese sources make East Africa's interior legible in ways that were seldom the case in earlier records. The ivory sent to da Gama's ships offers the most obvious example, but other sources from the first decades the Portuguese came to coastal cities like Mombasa and Malindi also signal the region's role in providing inland goods like beeswax, resins, and foodstuffs. Most importantly, Portuguese records describe voluminous traffic in cotton cloth, the most important imported good in East Africa's interior. By following this documentary trail of trade goods, it is possible to discern how inland procurement strategies and material practices shaped trading patterns in the Indian Ocean. This section tracks written descriptions of two export goods—ivory and gum copal—to demonstrate the centrality of people in Mombasa's interior to the town's prominence.

Written records on Mombasa and other Swahili towns are sparse before the late fifteenth century, but the existing evidence makes it clear that coastal East African towns were major distribution points for the global ivory trade. The first-century Greco-Roman text the *Periplus* indicates that East Africans had supplied ivory to Indian Ocean markets since the beginning of the current era.[48] By the late tenth century, East African ivory appeared in European markets with increasing frequency.[49] Around this same time, East Africa became the major supply region for Asian markets. In the tenth century, al-Masudi reported that the East African coast was the primary supply region for ivory exported to China and India via Oman.[50] This was primarily due to the superior quality of East African elephants' ivory compared to those from Asia. As explained in a thirteenth-century Chinese merchant's guide, East African tusks were "straight and of a clear white color" with "delicate streaks," while Asian elephants had "small tusks of a reddish tint."[51] So, while ivory bangles had long been popular adornments among South Asian women, the locally available ivory was inferior for artisanal purposes.[52] As a result, the Swahili coast became the world's most important ivory-exporting region by the second millennium.

The best data on East African ivory exports prior to the nineteenth century concerns the southern Swahili coast, especially Portuguese-controlled ports in Mozambique. But sources from the sixteenth and seventeenth centuries indicate that northern towns like Mombasa, Malindi, and Pate were all significant centers for the ivory trade.[53] In 1516, Duarte Barbosa reported that Mombasa's occupants traded extensively with communities on the mainland and that they provided the city with an abundance of ivory and valued products like wax and honey.[54] A century later, an English trader similarly noted that the "coast of Mellinda"—a descriptor that Europeans used to refer to the coastal region encompassing both Mombasa and Malindi—brokered large quantities of ivory that they obtained from adjacent inland communities.[55] Other European visitors similarly note the great quantities of ivory available at northern Swahili towns like Mombasa and Pate that were then traded across the Indian Ocean. As one commentor noted, much of this ivory, after being procured from East Africa's interior, was "shipped from Mombasa to India and to Ormuz"—or Hormuz, in the Persian Gulf.[56]

Mombasa remained a preeminent port for the ivory trade well into the eighteenth century, placing the town at the center of power struggles between different oceanic empires. In 1720, the Scottish sea captain Alexander Hamilton reported that when Oman ousted the Portuguese from Mombasa twenty-two years prior, they found stowed away in the town's fort "a Booty of about two hundred Tons of Teeth, which was worth in India, one hundred twenty-five thousand Pound Sterling."[57] A Portuguese report from around the same time noted that a single ship could return from Mombasa "with more than 300 barrels of ivory."[58] The large elephants in Mombasa's interior were said to produce tusks that were "more precious than gold and diamonds" in Asia, making it a lucrative port of trade for all merchants in the Indian Ocean.[59]

While European records highlight Mombasa's role as a major export region for the global ivory trade during the sixteenth century and later, its preeminence registers more ambiguously in earlier documentary records, such as the thirteenth-century Chinese trade guide, *Zhu Fan Zhi* (or *Records of Various Foreign Peoples*). The two-volume book was written by Zhao Rukua, the superintendent of maritime trade at Quanzhou, China's most prosperous port city. Typical of early guidebooks, the two volumes give an overview of all the peoples and places known to Chinese merchants (in volume one) as well as details on goods that the Chinese imported from overseas, including information on the production, quality, and place of origin for each commodity (in volume two).[60] Specific details on the East African coast are sparse across the two books, limited to short descriptions of Zanzibar, Madagascar, and the coast of Somalia, plus entries on common East African trade goods, such as ivory and ambergris. Zhao never traveled outside of China and, as a result, he incorrectly attributed the origins of many of these goods, including East African ivory. He presumed ivory reaching Quanzhou originated from Arabia since it was sourced from merchants from Mirbat, a town located on the southwestern coast of Oman.[61]

Elephants had long been extinct on the Arabian Peninsula by the thirteenth century. Nevertheless, Zhao Rukua's trading guide included a detailed account of "Arabian" elephant hunting techniques. Compellingly, this description matches—with precision—the elephant hunting techniques of the Waata hunting specialists who occupied the Tsavo region. As described earlier, these hunters pursued elephants using bows with iron tipped arrows, to which they applied a poison made from boiling the bark of the *Acokanthera schimperi* tree. They aimed for the elephant's underbelly so that the arrow would transport the poison into the animal's intestines, and then they followed their target until it collapsed. If hit properly, even a large fleeing elephant would die from the arrow poison within a few hundred yards of being shot. The hunters would then congregate around the carcass while eating and drying the meat, typically removing the tusks and burying them in nearby bush for safekeeping. Eventually, they would exchange their cache of ivory with neighboring Mijikenda communities who supplied them with arrow poison and livestock. Their Mijikenda partners then traded the elephant tusks with merchants in Mombasa.[62]

The historical reconstruction of elephant hunting in Mombasa's interior bears remarkable similarity to the details in *Zhu Fan Zhi*:

> Elephant hunters make use of bows of extraordinary strength and poisoned arrows. When hit by an arrow the elephant runs away, but before he has gone a li or two, or a little more, the arrow poison acts and the animal falls down dead. The hunters follow him, remove the tusks from the carcass and bury them in the ground. When ten tusks or more have been collected, they are brought to the [Arabs] who ship them to [Southeast Asia] for barter.[63]

Although it is impossible to say with certainty that Zhao's description of elephant hunting was based on communities living in Mombasa's interior, it is certainly the most logical explanation. Elephant hunting was a common activity in other parts of eastern and southern Africa, but spears and pit traps were more common techniques in such places.[64] In Zhao's account, even the distance that an elephant could go before succumbing to the poison—one or two *li*, about a quarter to a half a mile—is identical to descriptions in historical records on the efficacy of arrow poisons used in Mombasa's interior. Furthermore, the timing of the account would have overlapped with the scaling-up of iron production in Mombasa's interior,

80   THE INLAND UNDERPINNINGS OF COMMERCE

including the production of sophisticated iron arrowheads around the Kasigau massif, which archaeologists believe were used for elephant hunting.[65] Without realizing it, the author of this eight-hundred-year-old Chinese guidebook told a story about one of the Indian Ocean's most valued trade goods that centered procurement practices in Mombasa's interior.

As gateway societies between Mombasa and the interior, Mijikenda speakers were ideally positioned to broker trade that linked the port city and elephant hunters in the Tsavo plains. Oral traditions are littered with accounts of Mijikenda communities obtaining ivory from hunting specialists to whom they supplied domestic animals, foodstuffs, and arrow poison.[66] Written records from the seventeenth century similarly indicate that ivory procured from elephant-rich environments inland ultimately reached coastal markets through the hands of Mijikenda traders. By purchasing ivory before it reached Mombasa, Mijikenda merchants reportedly "gained fourfold" when trading for cloth in the city.[67] Inland ivory traders strictly controlled the flow of ivory from the interior, sometimes meeting coastal merchants at the estuarian creeks adjacent to Mombasa, where their wares were loaded onto small boats for transport to the town's harbor.[68]

Mijikenda speakers' central role as trade brokers between Mombasa and the interior continued into the early nineteenth century. British records from the 1820s note that inland groups regularly supplied Mombasa with "ivory, gum copal, honey, bees-wax, and cattle: in exchange for which they get cloths, beads, and wire—the two latter articles they carry to the tribes inland."[69] They either brought the ivory to Mombasa themselves or sold it to coastal merchants at an annual market held every August at Kwa Jomvu, a town located about eight kilometers inland from the island.[70] Acting as Mombasa's gateway to interior products, they tightly controlled all aspects of commerce with the town, even refusing to allow traders from other inland regions to pass through their territories to trade directly with Mombasa's merchants well into the nineteenth century.[71]

In addition to ivory, Mijikenda speakers monopolized Mombasa's access to the region's second-most important export good: gum copal. Copal is a resin produced by the *Hymenaea verrucosa* tree, which was burned as incense and used for caulking ships. By the nineteenth century, East African copal was used as a varnish for wooden furniture manufactured in workshops as far away as New England.[72] Copal can be tapped from trees, but the highest quality resin was produced from fossilized deposits buried in the area around living copal trees.[73] The *Hymenaea verrucosa* tree grows only in East Africa's coastal forests, meaning that "copal trees were rare directly on the coastal plain and disappeared west of the coastal hinterland."[74] As a result, even as global demand for the resin reached its peak during the nineteenth century manufacturing boom, copal extraction remained a cottage industry controlled by societies in the coast's immediate mainland.

While ivory is a far more famous global trade good, East African copal has been used locally and traded across oceanic networks for at least a millennium.

THE INLAND UNDERPINNINGS OF COMMERCE   81

Archaeologists have recovered copal fragments from several late first-millennium sites on the East African coast where the resin was burned as incense.[75] Within a few centuries, East African copal was exported to southern Arabia, where it was bought and sold among local aromatic resins like frankincense and myrrh.[76] By the early modern period, copal was one of the coast's most important trade goods. Early Portuguese records mention Mombasa and Malindi trading an abundance of this tar-like product.[77] In 1591, the English ship the *Edward Bonaventure* visited Zanzibar and left with a thousand pounds of copal, which merchants aboard the ship described as a "gray and white gumme like unto frankincense, as clammie as turnpentine, which in melting growth as black as pitch."[78] Over the next few centuries, European ships continued to procure the product to use as a sealant and wood varnish.[79] By the mid-nineteenth century, Zanzibar alone exported more than a million pounds of hardened resin each year, most of which originated in either Mijikenda- or Zaramo-speaking communities and reached the island via local networks.[80]

The copal trade ultimately connected East Africa's coastal forests to manufacturing networks that stretched from East African port cities to northern Atlantic furniture-making centers like Salem, Massachusetts. Societies in East Africa's "copal belt"—Mijikenda in southeast Kenya and Zaramo in northeastern Tanzania—held a near monopoly over the good's circulation. In Swahili, copal is called *msandarusi*. They borrowed this term from Arabic speakers who called it *sindarus* or *sandarus*, a word that referred to a variety of fossilized resins.[81] Notably, both Mijikenda and Zaramo speakers retained their own unique terms to refer to the resin despite its ubiquity as a global trade good. Among Zaramo speakers, copal is called *mnangu*.[82] Mijikenda speakers, meanwhile, called copal *m'mongolo*, a word that they also used for glass, attesting to the visual and tactile similarities between glass and the hardened resin.[83] It is not clear whether there was a word for *Hymenaea verrucosa*—the tree or its products—among the proto–Northeast Coast communities who were the first Bantu speakers to occupy East Africa's coastal forests.[84] Nevertheless, the limited distribution of the Mijikenda and Zaramo words for copal underscores the highly local nature of the resin's procurement prior to being exported to Swahili towns, then to other Indian Ocean locales, and, ultimately, to factories as far away as North America.

Tracing the histories of ivory and gum copal from procurement to export highlights the critical position of Mijikenda-speaking communities in mediating Mombasa's relationship with the interior. It is not especially novel to suggest that East Africa's interior contributed to maritime trade. However, reading textual records with archaeological evidence detailed in the previous section in mind makes it possible to move beyond a generalized picture of inland trade and highlight the specific networks and communities that ensured the continued buzz of maritime trade into and out of Mombasa. For generations, Arabian dhows and Portuguese carracks leaving the port city abounded with ivory, destined to circulate

82 THE INLAND UNDERPINNINGS OF COMMERCE

as far away as eastern China. Inland procurement networks were the motor behind these global flows. While it is important to highlight these contributions, inland communities were more than suppliers for external markets. They also pursued their own material desires.[85] The next section explores Mijikenda speakers' interests in oceanic trade, focusing on Mombasa's most important inland trade good: cotton textiles.

INLAND MATERIAL DESIRES: CONNECTING INDIAN FACTORIES TO RITUALS ON MOMBASA'S MAINLAND

Excavations in Mombasa's immediate interior have recovered maritime trade goods, including Indo-Pacific glass beads and imported glazed ceramics in contexts stretching back to the late first millennium.[86] But cotton textiles were unquestionably the most desired and most critical imported trade good for the Mijikenda speakers interacting with merchants in the port city. Cotton cloth has a long history as a trade good in coastal East Africa, and it is helpful to take a broader view before shifting to its place in Mijikenda settlements. During the early second millennium, there was a thriving textile production industry in coastal towns like Shanga, Kilwa, and Mogadishu. However, local weaving industries declined as imported South Asian textiles became more readily available.[87] By the thirteenth century, Gujarati merchants supplied cloth directly to communities on Zanzibar, visiting annually with a variety of dyed cotton textiles.[88] Trade between Gujarat—in northwest India—and coastal East Africa continued in the centuries that followed. When Portuguese mariners reached the East African coast, they found ships from Cambay—a port city in Gujarat and the preindustrial world's leading center for cloth textile production—anchored at Mombasa and Malindi.[89] Consumer demand for cloth in East Africa, and for ivory in South Asia, fueled these connections.

Cloth had many important uses in coastal East African society. Ports in Indian Ocean Africa were, according to Pedro Machado, "cloth currency zones," where Gujarati textiles became "a primary measure of value for which ivory, slaves, and other commodities were exchanged."[90] Cloth acted as a status marker, and access to imported textiles could transform coastal settlements from humble villages into flourishing urban towns.[91] This is best demonstrated in historical chronicles of Kilwa that recount how the town's founder purchased the island and established its renown as an Islamic port city by providing an infidel king with a bounty of colorful cloth in quantities so great that they "encircled the island." Kilwa's founder ruled for the next forty years, earning the nickname *nguo nyingi*, or "many clothes," for his ability to supply the town's residents with cotton cloth.[92]

Due to the high social and commercial value of imported textiles, port cities levied large fees on visiting merchants that were paid in cloth. In 1506, a Portuguese clerk reported that if a merchant arrived at Mombasa with one thousand

THE INLAND UNDERPINNINGS OF COMMERCE   83

pieces of cloth, Mombasa's *mfalme*, or "king," would take half of the total. After paying this tax, the merchant was then free to sell the remaining cloth in the city.[93] The earliest Portuguese accounts suggest that Gujarati merchants favored port cities with the most direct access to interior trade goods. As a result of its ability to procure ivory and other inland goods, Mombasa emerged as a major regional depot for cloth, brokering trade between South Asian and East African port cities. The town's merchants tightly monopolized the textile trade. During the sixteenth century, traders from other towns like Zanzibar had to travel to Mombasa to purchase cotton textiles.[94]

While Mombasa leveraged control of Gujarati cloth to assert trading dominance along the northern Swahili coast, they were able to do so due to their strong ties with the adjacent mainland. A hefty portion of the town's textiles were set aside for trade and tribute for neighboring inland communities. A spending report from Fort Jesus, the Portuguese fort at Mombasa, shows that in the 1630s, a tenth of their yearly expenditures went to supplying cloth to communities on the mainland.[95] As Portuguese observers saw it, Mijikenda communities cared for little else but textiles, and because of their tremendous influence on the city, they were "given cloths whenever they demand[ed] them."[96] These payments served two main purposes. First, coastal merchants used cotton textiles to obtain trade goods like ivory, resins, and food provisions from the mainland. Second, different constituencies in Mombasa used imported cloth as tributes that they sent to their inland neighbors to maintain peaceful relations (both topics covered in greater detail in chapters 4 and 5).

Textiles are useful for thinking through the ways that Mijikenda speakers engaged with but also diverged from the material practices of the Indian Ocean. Indian textiles were traded widely across the premodern Indian Ocean. Fragments of textiles produced in Gujarat between the thirteenth and fifteenth centuries have been found in Fustat—or Old Cairo—likely having reached Egypt after passing through markets in Aden. Similar finds exist in parts of eastern Indonesia for the same period.[97] In East Africa, the oldest surviving textile fragment—a piece of indigo-dyed cloth from India found at Mtambwe Mkuu on Pemba—is even older, dating to the eleventh century.[98] By the early sixteenth century, Portuguese mariners reported that Mombasa traded "quantities of cotton cloth from Cambay" and that the entirety of the "coast dress[ed] in these cloths and has no other."[99] These textiles were valued on the East African coast and far beyond because of their quality and beauty. Indian textile producers colored their cottons with dyes that could yield a rich palette of reds, yellows, and blues, using block prints to create intricate design patterns. When these textiles began reaching Europe, they famously overrode the inferior and comparatively bland wools and linens that characterized local fashion.[100] The many references to Mijikenda speakers obtaining these cloths connect them to this larger world of material exchanges, which included merchants from northwest

84 THE INLAND UNDERPINNINGS OF COMMERCE

India, consumers in places like Cairo, Timor, and the Maluku Islands, as well as cotton growers and weavers living in villages in India.

From one perspective, the connections between Mijikenda communities, Mombasa, and other Indian Ocean locales may look inevitable.[101] Indian textiles were desired commodities across the eastern hemisphere so, of course, Mijikenda speakers, like many others, sought out opportunities to obtain them. But this macroview of the circulation of cloth is best understood when anchored in local circumstances.[102] Despite the commonality of cloth—as well as things like glass beads and metal bangles—as trade goods and adornments, foreign merchants and local elites did not control the meanings people attached to these items.[103] By studying local valuations of imported textiles in Mombasa's rural mainland, we see that the city's connections to Indian Ocean networks formed in part because Mijikenda communities turned an imported commodity into a locally meaningful object.

To trace the values that the members of Mijikenda communities attached to imported cloth, it is necessary to turn from written texts to evidence from language. Coastal East Africans had a complex vocabulary to describe different types of cloth.[104] They inherited at least one word for cloth from their Sabaki ancestors: *nguWo, which meant "clothing" in proto-Sabaki.[105] Another term with significant antiquity in the region is the Swahili word *kitambi*, which is cognate with a Mijikenda word, *chitsambi* (or *kitsambi*) and Lower Pokomo *kitsambi*. All are derived from a Northeast Coast term for "loincloth" (*-cambo), which was itself derived from the ancient Bantu root *-camb-, meaning to wash one's private areas. In Sabaki languages, speakers added a new noun suffix, marking it as an agent noun and thus distinguishing the cloth from earlier loincloths. The available evidence suggests that this word and its association with textiles likely originated as an early areal term on the Kenya coast, where it was first pronounced *kicambi.[106]

From these humble beginnings, the term's meaning evolved over time, with *kitambi* eventually describing cloth textiles traded along the coast. When the Portuguese briefly regained control of Mombasa from Oman in 1728, they found a huge inventory of "quitambes" in the port's main fort, although most were old and of poor quality.[107] The Portuguese perception of the "quitambes" reflects the term's general meaning as a cloth commodity in Swahili towns. In Mombasa Swahili dialects, for instance, *kitambi* described a long piece of colorful cloth, about five or six arms' length, a meaning that stressed *kitambi* as a unit of measure and a commodity. Over time, the word spread to other parts of the Swahili coast—likely due to Mombasa's role as a cloth distribution center—ultimately becoming a catchall for a wide range of imported textiles.

Mijikenda speakers also reworked the term's meaning from its earliest associations with grass loincloths. However, their own form of the word, *chitsambi*, represented much more than a basic commodity. In the simplest terms, *chitsambi* referred to dyed cotton textiles. Historical records show that Mijikenda speakers considered *vitsambi* (pl.) to have a variety of protective qualities. People wore these textiles during pregnancy, initiation rituals, or if they were afflicted by malevolent spirits.[108] Influential elders marked their status by wearing cloths of specific colors. Access to cloth facilitated membership in the specialized healing groups considered in the previous chapter. In Giryama communities, for instance, people used cotton cloth to join *viraho* groups like the *habasi*, *phaya*, and *kinyenze*, with the initiation fees peaking at seventeen lengths of cloth for the *habasi*.[109]

Imported textiles also played an important role in rituals surrounding ancestors. At death, the bodies of elders were dressed in black cloth and "tied at the waist with red and white sashes."[110] People hung strips of cloth at natural shrines (*mizimu*) and wrapped them around wooden memorial posts (*koma* and *vigango*) that represented departed ancestors. When they tied the colorful cloths around the neck and waist of the wooden posts, they symbolically "dressed" their ancestors and attested to their enduring importance to the lives of their descendants.[111] Through these ritual practices, they "domesticated" the imported goods to suit their own needs and aspirations.[112] Considering the different use values of *vitsambi* alongside larger transformations in ritual life detailed in chapter 2, it shows that Mijikenda speakers' participation in the Indian Ocean was connected to processes and interactions that had little to do with the common signatures of this global interactive sphere. Their reasons for securing access to imported textiles included gendered notions of wealth, household reproduction and rituals associated with healing groups, and ideas about proper ancestor veneration, some of which they adopted through interactions with other inland societies.

How should practices like tying cloth to a grave post, or the protective adornments worn during pregnancy, fit into narratives of transregional oceanic trade? They often don't.[113] But we only need to look to the many historical sources that describe Mijikenda speakers procuring cloth from merchants in Mombasa to discern the critical interplay between inland rituals and the rhythms of oceanic trade. Through their material practices, people living inland from Mombasa transformed a commoditized cloth into an object with immense local value. For Mijikenda speakers, imported goods were not meant to evoke cultural ties with people living in other cosmopolitan centers and far-flung ports.[114] Instead, they used the textiles within local contexts like healing rituals in forest glades, household reproduction, and ancestor veneration practices. In doing so, they imbued the textiles with their own meanings, ultimately envisioning the imported goods as objects that could protect and support the well-being of their communities.

THE LANGUAGE OF LONG-DISTANCE TRADE

As the archaeological and textual evidence shows, coastal-interior trading connections in Mombasa did not happen simply because the Indian Ocean monsoon facilitated easy travel between the East African coast and port cities in western India and southern Arabia. Nor was it just a story of supply and demand. Exchange networks in Mombasa's interior provided the town with a ready supply of goods like ivory, beeswax, and gums, which inland traders were happy to exchange for textiles, beads,

86 THE INLAND UNDERPINNINGS OF COMMERCE

and wire.[115] This trade happened as people in the town's interior ascribed new meanings to imported textiles, exchanged ritual ideas and medicines, and animated the forests surrounding their villages with shrines and meeting grounds. In short, Mombasa's emergence as a hub of commercial activity, and the continued flow of goods into and out of the port city, were connected processes and interactions falling far outside the most familiar participation rubrics of Indian Ocean trade.

The remainder of this chapter uses linguistic evidence, oral traditions, and ethnographic sources to explore the social knowledge that undergirded inland trading practices. I focus in particular on adaptations that Mijikenda speakers and their interlocutors made to partake in trade over expanding scales centuries prior to the advent of Arab-Swahili caravans. Trading practices in Mombasa's interior were iterative by nature. To ensure access to textiles and other important inland goods, Mijikenda speakers and their partners had to adapt and refine their trading practices to suit shifting circumstances. During the first half of the second millennium, inland goods moved along established exchange mosaics in Mombasa's interior. But starting during the seventeenth and eighteenth centuries, inland communities initiated a new type of commerce: long-distance trading parties.

Blood Pacts and the Roots of Cross-Cultural Commerce

The best evidence for changing approaches to inland commerce across the second millennium comes from the words that Mijikenda speakers used to describe their commercial activities. Early Mijikenda speakers mostly employed an economic vocabulary that was retained from proto-Sabaki. This vocabulary indicates that around the start of the second millennium, they conceptualized most of their trading activities along similar lines to their linguistic ancestors. For instance, early Mijikenda speakers' vocabulary included inherited words for "buying" (-gula) and "selling" (-guza), both of which were derived from the same ancient Bantu root meaning "to buy"—with the term -guza, or selling, literally meaning "causing to buy." They also retained terms that referred to borrowing and lending practices, including -azima, which could mean either to "borrow" or "lend," and the verb -aphasa (or -ahasa), which they used to describe obtaining goods on credit.[116] In addition to these trading terms, they retained the Sabaki verb *-cum- (which they pronounced -tsuma) and continued to use it to describe trading for the purpose of making profits.[117]

Much of this inherited commercial vocabulary underscores the importance of interpersonal relationships to trade, captured in the ancient semantic links people made between buying and selling, and lending and borrowing. Notably, however, early Mijikenda speakers lacked words for describing many key aspects of trade during later periods in coastal history such as titles for professional traders and words related to long-distance caravans.

One early strategy for building partnerships across sociolinguistic lines in the absence of long-distance caravans was forming relationships through blood pacts.

THE INLAND UNDERPINNINGS OF COMMERCE   87

In historical accounts, blood pacts helped to establish social relationships between two men, often in the context of trade. The men making a pact would slaughter a chicken or goat. They would then cut themselves and smear their own blood on two pieces of meat taken from the slaughtered animal, in many accounts the heart or the liver. Finally, they would exchange the two pieces of meat and consume that which was covered in the blood of their partner.[118] The pact served two ends. First, it established a trader's social identity as a known individual within the community where they made the pact. Second, by forming a pact a person initiated a contract that ensured their safety and well-being as they traveled in that territory.[119]

The practice of forming blood pacts is called *kurya tsoga* in Mijikenda languages, a phrase that literally meant "to eat the scar" or "eat the pact." The term *tsoga* is derived from the word *-coga—meaning "blood pact" in a connected chain of Northeast Coast daughter languages—which itself is from a Northeast Coast root word meaning to "cut" or "incise."[120] While the verbal form of the word dates to at least the early first millennium, the derived noun may be of more recent vintage. Cognate forms of *-coga are found with the meaning "blood pact" in three subbranches of Northeast Coast Bantu: Sabaki (Mijikenda); Seuta (all); and Ruvu (Kagulu). These meanings appear in a contiguous distribution beginning immediately inland from Mombasa and the Mrima coast and extending into the montane forest regions of northern and central Tanzania. Therefore, *-coga may be the result of an areal spread that, because it diffused early enough, was interpreted with a regular phonetic shape across these closely related languages.[121]

The wide distribution of the reflexes of *-coga illuminates how a bloc of adjacent Northeast Coast daughter languages drew from shared ancestral ideas about cutting and incision to conceptualize a special type of partnership. Blood pacts among these distantly related speech communities likely date back more than a millennium, possibly having originated among the proto-Seuta speech community that began to diverge into separate daughter languages around 1000 CE.[122] In this case, the term and practice in Mijikenda would be the result of long-standing interactions with Seuta-speaking communities to their south.[123] However, they used *kurya tsoga* to establish relationships with a much wider array of societies than just Northeast Coast daughter languages.

Mijikenda oral traditions recount men forming blood pacts across an expansive geographic network. Sometimes they formed pacts within their own clans and with neighboring communities. But more often, they used the practice to cement ties across social and linguistic lines. Oral histories speak of blood pact relationships with Waata hunters and Oromo-speaking pastoralists living in the drylands adjacent to the coastal uplands, as well as Dawida speakers in the Taita Hills and Kamba speakers in central Kenya.[124] From the eighteenth century, Mijikenda trade parties traveled to Kamba-speaking areas (or Ukambani) to exchange cloth, beads, and wire for cattle and ivory. According to Giryama oral histories, men from certain clans had *kurya tsoga* relationships with specific Kamba villages. When trade

88   THE INLAND UNDERPINNINGS OF COMMERCE

parties reached Kamba-speaking areas, the men would split up and stay in the village of their established *kurya tsoga* partners. At the end of the stay, the trade party's members recongregated with their wares and made the journey home together.[125] By the end of the eighteenth century, small groups of Kamba speakers began relocating to the Kenya coast to escape famines in the interior. They built on these preestablished links with Mijikenda traders and founded new settlements in the vicinity of their "blood brothers."[126]

While *kurya tsoga* relationships show the social nature of inland trade, they also highlight the ways that Indian Ocean connections were supported by gendered ideas about homestead reproduction and cross-societal male bonding. As Louise White argues, East Africans' expressions of blood brotherhood were foremost about male bonding. They offered ways for men to develop relationships with established rights and obligation outside of the context of lineage or clan.[127] Although White downplays the importance of trade to these bonds, sources on Mijikenda blood pacts emphasize the intersection of bonding, imagined kinship, and commerce. Accounts in Thomas Spear's collection of oral traditions describe *kurya tsoga* relationships between Mijikenda- and Kamba-speaking traders as being as real as biological kin.[128] According to historian Thomas Herlehy, blood pact partners sometimes solidified these relationships by marrying one another's daughters. In addition to formalizing kinship ties, blood pacts encompassed social practices that enabled men to mitigate various uncertainties. An existing pact could secure a trader the "first preference . . . in any business transaction," making them especially important during times of "economic scarcity or intense competition." During the nineteenth century, some men even turned to their blood brothers for access to food provisions during famines.[129]

The oral traditions describing practices associated with the two-millennia-old root word *-cog- offer an East African example of a key concern in studies of premodern trade: how people established trading links with individuals beyond family members who they could trust based on kinship.[130] In the Indian Ocean, an Islamic institution called the *suhba* provided an important framework for expanding the business of trade beyond recognized kin. The *suhba*, which is sometimes described as a "formal friendship," was a reciprocal trading arrangement where a merchant in one port would sell goods on another merchant's behalf. These economic friendships were underwritten by Islamic law but not limited to Muslim traders. They ultimately enabled people living an ocean apart to sell their own goods and obtain items from other ports by extending their commercial sphere beyond that of their immediate kin network.[131] For Mijikenda speakers, *kurya tsoga* relationships supported similar goals, fostering longer-term relationships with trading partners from other inland regions based on mutual trust and gendered social bonds, which they articulated using the language of fictive kinship.

For a person to engage in a cross-societal arena like long-distance trade, they had to have a sense of how to engage with social and commercial worlds that existed

THE INLAND UNDERPINNINGS OF COMMERCE   89

beyond their home village. A person couldn't just walk out the door one morning and decide they'd like to get their hands on some ivory so they could obtain textiles. Much like elsewhere in the Indian Ocean, trade in East Africa's interior was built out of social relationships and shared knowledge and institutions. A practice like *kurya tsoga* helps to imagine how Mijikenda speakers' longer-term orientation toward southeast Kenya's interior supported a variety of exchanges. Scholars of the Indian Ocean have long assumed that trade goods moved from the interior to the coast through "down the line" exchanges, moving from one village network to another, until they reached the port.[132] However, these movements did not follow random patterns. Instead, trade goods circulated along well-established networks where people exchanged goods and medicines; in spatial contexts like markets; and through technologies like blood pacts, which supported bonds between men from far-apart villages and even entirely different regions.

Making Proto-Caravans: The Knowledge of Long-Distance Trade

Practices like blood pacts supported early inland connections, but over time, the structure of inland trade and the knowledge and practices that supported such trade changed. The remainder of the chapter looks at the growth of long-distance trading practices among inland communities during the second half of the second millennium. These inland initiatives laid the groundwork for later caravan routes. During the sixteenth and seventeenth centuries, Mijikenda speakers began borrowing vocabulary from Thagicu-speaking groups that enabled them to conceptualize positions like merchants and trade party leaders. Notably, these novel forms of trade overlapped with changes in the Tsavo region, which had long formed the backbone of the inland economy. Starting in the seventeenth century, many sites around the Taita Hills were abandoned as people moved their farming villages to the higher slopes of Taita's three massifs. Concurrently, seasonal camps in the adjacent Tsavo plains fell out of use as pastoralist communities retreated to fortified rock shelter sites, possibly to avoid cattle rustling.[133] These changes overlapped with the establishment of Portuguese control over Mombasa at the end of the sixteenth century.

In the context of these larger changes in Tsavo and Mombasa, we can imagine ambitious inland traders being confronted with new challenges: How would they obtain ivory? Where would they find markets for imported beads and wire? And most critically, how would they ensure the continued flow of imported textiles necessary for rituals and healing? These questions underscore both the contingencies of Mombasa's interactions with oceanic merchants and the iterative nature of inland trading practices. Connections between port cities did not simply happen because seasonal winds pushed and pulled dhows from one region of the ocean to another. Inland communities adapted and refined the knowledge and practices that supported exchanges in East Africa's interior. Their initiatives helped to establish and maintain Mombasa's maritime connections over the longue durée.

90 THE INLAND UNDERPINNINGS OF COMMERCE

One good example of the ingenuity of people engaged in the inland commercial sphere is found in the regional circulation of the Thagicu term *-cogora, which meant to "buy, bargain." This term spread as a loanword in multiple parts of Mombasa's interior, including among communities in the Pare Mountains and Taita Hills. While communities living in these highland regions adopted and retained the root in its original verbal form, Mijikenda speakers only retained a noun meaning "bargain" or "price" from the borrowed verb, which they attested as *dhora*, or *rora* in different dialects.[134] Nineteenth-century dictionaries show that Mijikenda speakers compounded this borrowed word with other nouns and verbs to create a rich commercial vocabulary. In W. E. Taylor's *Giryama Vocabulary and Collections*, for instance, the entries for the word *dhora* include the following meanings:

mwenye madhora	"merchant, trader"
munena dhora	"go-between in borrowing"
kuhenda dhora	"to trade"
kutosa dhora	"to finish a bargain"
kutana dhora	"to fail to effect a bargain"
hat'u ha madhorani	"shop"[135]

The available evidence makes it impossible to place these innovations precisely in time. But clearly people creatively adapted this borrowed vocabulary to describe intensive commercial activities and occupations between the sixteenth and seventeenth centuries (when Mijikenda and other inland communities first borrowed the word) and the nineteenth century (when these attestations were recorded in dictionaries).

Mijikenda speakers did not adopt loanwords like *dhora* in isolation. Recall from the previous chapter that interactions with speakers of Segeju (a Thagicu language) also influenced initiation practices among the *gophu* healing groups that prepared medicines that protected homesteads from afflictions. As we'll see in the next chapter, through these interactions, Mijikenda speakers also adopted many loanwords related to specialized cattle keeping: a story that is intimately connected to intensifying cross-societal trade. Other Segeju loanwords in Mijikenda directly relate to long-distance travel. For instance, Mijikenda speakers borrowed the verb -*rumarya*, which meant to "accompany a departing visitor" such as one would do when seeing off a trade party.[136] They also adopted the verb -*dhyana/-ryana*—which, like *dhora*, is also attested in Pare and Dawida—with the meaning to "spy" or "scout."[137] Thagicu speakers used a noun form of the root to describe a "scout" or "tracker." Later, both Kamba and Mijikenda speakers used reflexes of this term to describe the leaders of long-distance trading parties. Thus, an array of interactions and knowledge exchanges, including knowledge related to rituals and animal husbandry, overlapped with, and even directly supported, long-distance trading practices.

THE INLAND UNDERPINNINGS OF COMMERCE 91

By studying historical and ethnographic records on figures like trade party leaders, we can see how inland communities used cross-linguistic knowledge exchanges to support novel types of trade during this moment of regional transformation. The earliest caravan leaders curated a wide range of skills and knowledge, fitting with the term's original denotation of people with expertise in tracking. Among Kamba speakers, for example, the title *mũthiani* was given to the leaders of trade parties, but it was also applied to war leaders and expert hunters.[138] Similarly, for Mijikenda speakers, trade party leaders (called *mudhyani* or *muryani*) led small caravans across the Tsavo plains to obtain ivory and cattle from speakers of Kamba and Chaga, to whom they supplied cloth, beads, wire, and arrow poison.[139] Skills for long-distance travel were considered a form of specialized knowledge, or *uganga*. The leaders of trade and hunting parties protected themselves from wild animals and robbers with powerful medicines. They traveled with protective charms called *virumbi*, which were broadly used for tasks like guarding cattle herds, making war, and detecting changes in the weather. The *adhyani* affixed the charms to special staffs (also called *virumbi*), which signaled their status as the party's leader and helped them to guard their wares en route.[140]

The use of this titled position for a trade party leader—and the practices surrounding it—in Mijikenda and Kamba offers evidence of the professionalization of trading activities in Mombasa's interior prior to the emergence of Arab-Swahili caravans. Relying on their geographic skills, knowledge of protective medicines, and relationships with distant communities, these individuals led the region's earliest long-distance trade parties, facilitating direct interactions between the coast and as far inland as Mount Kilimanjaro. During the nineteenth century, caravans crossing from Swahili ports into the far interior were called *safari*, an Arabic loanword in Swahili.[141] But the earliest trading parties in the region were referred to by a different name: *charo*, an internal innovation in Mijikenda dialects that was later borrowed by many language groups in Mombasa's interior.

Charo's derivation allows us to consider how inland communities perceived trading parties that moved across ever-larger geographic networks. The term was produced from an inherited verb meaning "to burst" or "split."[142] To create the noun, Mijikenda speakers added a class 7 noun prefix plus the nominal suffix -o to the verb root. The noun class in which they indexed *charo* generally includes instrumental artifacts and diminutives, but it can also indicate that a noun possesses the "qualities and attributes" of the root.[143] The prefix reveals that they understood their early trade parties to be entities that possessed the qualities of "bursting" or "splitting." The suffix, meanwhile, suggests that speakers understood *charo* to refer to the "action itself, the result of the action, the place or the instrument" of the same root.[144] Piecing together the derivation details, we are left with two possible interpretations of the word. If "burst" is the main productive root, it would indicate that when people used the word *charo* to refer to trade parties,

92   THE INLAND UNDERPINNINGS OF COMMERCE

they recognized them as entities that both resulted from and had the qualities of speedy movement, i.e., "bursting" across expansive territories. In this interpretation, the expanding scales of trade parties in Mombasa's interior elicited novel sensory understandings of what it meant to move across well-established geographic networks for the purpose of obtaining trade goods. Alternatively, long-distance traders may have understood their trade parties as entities that "split." This interpretation of the root could refer to traders dividing the bounties of their excursion, or perhaps to different party members splitting up to trade with their *kurya tsoga* partners after arriving in inland regions like Ukambani, a practice documented in oral traditions.[145]

Written records and oral traditions suggest that Mijikenda trade parties traveled overland routes between the coast and Chaga- and Kamba-speaking areas by the eighteenth century.[146] From *charo*'s derivation and the places where it was spoken, we can speculate that inland communities developed and adopted this term to describe new types of travel and trading activities that were different in scope and scale from earlier modes of interaction. This region—ranging from Mombasa's immediate interior, across the dry Tsavo plains, and extending into the highland regions of the Taita Hills and Pare Mountains—had long been an important corridor for exchanges between different resource specialists, both in trade and subsistence goods as well as ritual ideas and knowledge. But as the Tsavo region faced new challenges, long-distance trade parties led by skilled scouts became the region's commercial leaders. They helped to maintain the interior's connections to Indian Ocean trading networks. And critically, trading innovations enabled Mijikenda communities to continue procuring goods like textiles and wire from Mombasa while the town remained under foreign rule. Shared terminology for this novel type of long-distance trade extended into all places that Mijikenda traders reached. Derivations of *charo* ultimately referred to long-distance journeys, caravans, and trade parties in languages spoken around Mombasa, in the Taita Hills, in Ukambani in central Kenya, and in Chaga languages spoken around Mount Kilimanjaro.

Charo's wide distribution indicates the geographic networks along which inland goods and knowledge circulated. By the mid-nineteenth century, coastal caravans moved along these exact routes. Early European travelers in East Africa frequently wrote of the outlying regions beyond the coast as wild lands, "hermetically sealed" from cosmopolitan port cities.[147] Yet, when overland *safaris* expanded across East Africa's interior during the mid-nineteenth century, they followed the contours set by inland communities over preceding generations. After Johannes Rebmann became the first European to see Mount Kilimanjaro in 1848, for instance, he characterized Mombasa's interior as a "great wilderness" despite traveling along a well-worn trade route replete with places to encamp and provision.[148] Rebmann even went so far as to claim that the mountain's name was derived from its visible position for these long-distance trading parties. According to his journal, "The

Suahili of the coast call the snow-mountain Kilimanjaro 'mountain of greatness.'" He added that it also meant "mountain of caravans" since it was "a landmark for the caravans seen everywhere from afar." Rebmann derived this second theory from the mountain's name, which he claimed was produced by compounding the words "Kilima, mountain" with "Jaro, caravans."[149] His journal does not indicate whether he arrived at this etymology on his own or through conversations during his travels. Regardless, the offhand comment speaks to a deeper history of inland networking initiatives that prominently shaped the contours of oceanic commercial worlds.

Trading parties departing from Mombasa's near interior employed knowledge that had been assembled over generations. The earliest *charo* trade parties moved at a new pace. But their *mudhyani's* expertise rested on a deeper knowledge of the region's interior, including routes, places to provision, and the location of seasonal markets. To navigate between the diverse societies living in Mombasa's interior, traders had to establish social bonds with other communities en route, using practices like blood pacts. Leaders also needed to possess knowledge of effective medicines for protection from wild animals, robbers, and the elements. Knowledge exchanges related to social rituals, trade goods, and medicines provided critical support for ongoing commercial connections in the port city's interior. Mombasa's connections to maritime trading networks rested on these inland participation strategies, which were centuries in the making.

. . .

Across the second millennium, Mijikenda speakers developed new means to participate in worlds beyond their villages. They established strategies for building social relationships, for exchanging goods and knowledge, and for conducting commerce over long distances, often in collaboration with other—non-Mijikenda-speaking—inland groups. Over centuries, they adapted and refined their trading practices to meet changing circumstances. These initiatives made it possible for their dispersed villages to maintain their influential position as a gateway that mediated the flow of trade goods into Mombasa as it emerged as one of East Africa's most prominent ports. As such, ideas and actions grounded in Mijikenda speakers' social goals and material ambitions became central to Mombasa's enduring connections to faraway port cities in southern Arabia, Persia, and western India. Much like mosques and merchants' houses, inland markets and forest groves were important sites for the development of oceanic commerce, forging connections between disparate inland communities in East Africa's interior. As we will see in the next two chapters, inland influences on Mombasa reverberated far beyond the realm of trade.

4

Inland Villages and Oceanic Empires

In 1720, Portuguese India's outgoing viceroy wrote a lengthy advice letter to his successor. Much of the letter focused on Mombasa, a city that the Portuguese empire had lost to Oman in 1698. The viceroy conspired to retake the city in 1718, but an order of textiles from Cambay meant to accompany his fleet was delayed, causing them to miss the seasonal monsoon. The following year he addressed the textile shortage, assembling a large bounty of cotton cloth to build alliances with Mombasa's locals, but he was again thwarted by a variety of mishaps. Soldiers reserved for the mission had dwindled in number during the intervening year due to disease and degeneracy, and one of the vessels intended for the expedition was shipwrecked in Persia. Despite these trials, the viceroy assured his successor that Mombasa's abundance of ivory, wax, ambergris, and tortoise shell made it all well worth the effort. He added that a properly outfitted fleet could easily retake control of the port city because the "Musunglo on the Mombasa mainland" were "favourably inclined" to the Portuguese.[1]

In just a few paragraphs, the viceroy's advice letter touched on several key themes in the Indian Ocean's historiography. Rivalries between the Portuguese and Omani empires, the role of the monsoon in shaping oceanic travel, and the circulation of ivory and textiles—these themes all emerge from this brief description, unfolding across littoral regions stretching from East Africa to Arabia, Persia, and South Asia. Notably, the "Musungulo" of the town's mainland—an ethnonym that Portuguese writers applied to Mijikenda-speaking communities—also figure prominently into this global narrative. Mombasa's interior influenced trading circulations in the Indian Ocean, as the previous chapter detailed. But this

INLAND VILLAGES AND OCEANIC EMPIRES   95

handing-off letter, written in eighteenth-century Goa, highlights something else: communities on Mombasa's mainland also affected the political trajectories of oceanic empires.

Between the sixteenth and eighteenth centuries, Mombasa became a nexus in conflicts between foreign powers, most significantly Portugal and Oman. Shifting control over Mombasa ebbed and flowed around different inland communities' decisions to collaborate—or not—with those aspiring to control the port city. Because the foreigners' jurisdiction over Mombasa's trade hinged on the support of the mainland, fleets from Portugal and Oman were forced to send textiles to inland leaders. These tributes formed the foundation of commercial, military, and diplomatic partnerships around the city. In faraway locales like Goa and Muscat, officials understood the importance of communities on Mombasa's mainland to their imperial ambitions in East Africa. Mijikenda speakers played their part, using the threat of raids, combined with their monopoly over inland trade goods and food provisions, to extract textiles from oceanic powers and demand a voice in Mombasa's affairs.

As scholarship on other world regions demonstrates, smaller-scale societies living on the periphery of large states or urban centers were frequently able to influence and extract concessions from neighboring polities utilizing geographic, commercial, and political advantages. In upland Southeast Asia, James Scott has shown that valley states were economically dependent on neighboring "hill people" while also being vulnerable to raids from the same nonstate societies. Uplanders traded with neighboring states while using the mobility afforded by swidden agriculture and the defensibility of their terrain to evade state control.[2] Maroon communities in the Americas similarly contributed to European colonial economies while also establishing autonomy from colonial authorities through warfare, banditry, and geographic advantages.[3]

This chapter centers the political decisions and commercial inventiveness of inland communities within the western Indian Ocean's shifting imperial landscapes between the sixteenth and eighteenth centuries. Building on the above scholarship, I show that the very distinctive ways that Mijikenda speakers' social organization and economy departed from oceanic norms enabled them to exert political influence on Mombasa and various imperial powers.[4] They lived in settlements that were difficult to control, being historically mobile and located along forested upland ridges. Moreover, they possessed established strategies for mobilizing people across dispersed village networks for military alliances and raids, using ritual apparatuses detailed in chapter 2. Finally, Mijikenda speakers' access to inland trade goods and provisions offered critical bargaining chips in conflicts and collaborations with the port city and its foreign interlocutors and adversaries. Mijikenda participation in contests over Mombasa illuminates an array of developments in the port

96   INLAND VILLAGES AND OCEANIC EMPIRES

city's interior that influenced the trajectories of global empires in the western Indian Ocean.

MOMBASA AND THE PORTUGUESE EMPIRE

In the 1630s, Portuguese cartographer Pedro Barreto de Resende wrote what became a well-known description of Mombasa. His commentary focused on two broad themes: the city's military capacity—specifically the garrison Fort Jesus—and the relationship between the island town and its neighboring mainland. Constructed in the 1590s, Fort Jesus was an imposing physical symbol of Portuguese military power in East Africa, protecting Mombasa's harbor from seaborne attacks. In addition to the seaward-facing Fort Jesus, the Portuguese also constructed three smaller forts along Makupa Creek on the inland-facing side of the island. While Portugal's nascent Indian Ocean empire faced many challenges, in Mombasa, threats coming from the opposite side of the shallow creek separating the island from its mainland were the most concerning. The people of Mombasa, Resende explained, lived in "continual fear" of neighboring "Muzungullos" (i.e., Musungulos) "crossing to the island."[5] He continued,

> These Muzungullos Caffres were regarded as the vassals of the King of Mombassa, Dom Jeronimo, but their submission was mainly obtained by giving them cloths. They were in reality quite different from vassals . . . they would come to murder in the land of the said Dom Jeronimo, who called himself their king . . . Many Arabian Moors live both to the north and to the south along the coast belonging to the fortress of Mombassa. They are like prisoners of the Muzungullos Caffres, because they have to pay them a large tribute in cloth in order to be allowed to live in security.[6]

Resende's comments offer several important details for understanding Mombasa's relationship with its neighbors, making them a useful starting point for this chapter. First, the Mijikenda-speaking Musungulos enjoyed a substantial influence on the island and the surrounding coastal region, in part through their capacity to inflict violence. Second, although they were nominally attached to Dom Jeronimo— the Portuguese-aligned ruler of Mombasa at that time—as "vassals," from Resende's perspective, the town's leader was greatly limited in his ability to enact authority over the adjacent mainland. Third, and perhaps most compelling considering the trading engagements detailed in the previous chapter, Mombasa maintained peaceful relations with its neighbors by sending them regular tributes, paid in cloth textiles.

By the 1630s, Portugal had already spent over a century maneuvering to control Mombasa's valuable port. As mentioned in the previous chapter, Vasco da Gama first visited Mombasa and several other towns along the East African coast in 1498. The Portuguese returned to East Africa in 1502 and established an alliance with Mombasa's rival town, Malindi, located one hundred kilometers north.[7] Like elsewhere in the Indian Ocean, Portuguese fleets disrupted older trading networks and subjugated port cities by imposing restrictive trading policies, often enforced through warfare.[8] When da Gama's fleet first sailed up the East African coast in early April of 1498, they arrived in Mombasa under the belief that the famed port city was home to a sizable number of Christians. Reaching the town just a few days before Palm Sunday, the Portuguese anticipated spending the upcoming Sunday attending mass in the town's Christian quarter. Instead, their fleet left the town within a few days after suspecting that Mombasa's leader was conspiring to attack them.[9] Seven years later, Portuguese ships returned to Mombasa as aggressors. For one and a half days, they laid siege to the city, burning mud and thatch houses, looting stone buildings, and sinking three Gujarati ships anchored in the harbor. By the time the Portuguese invaders returned to their ships, they had reportedly left fifteen hundred locals dead and the town itself burned to ashes.[10]

Despite their early presence in the region, the Portuguese did not gain a major foothold in Mombasa until the end of the sixteenth century. After sacking the town in 1505, they returned in 1528 and briefly occupied the island before locals regained control the following year.[11] The Portuguese resumed attacks on Mombasa from 1542 to 1543, and again in 1587, but they failed to gain full control over the port city.[12] Even in the aftermath of the attacks, Mombasa maintained a strong position as a trading center. Ultimately, the town's close relationships with its mainland—which provided both trade goods and military support—and its reputation as a major port enabled it to maintain its autonomy while the Portuguese concentrated on controlling traffic in towns like Kilwa and Malindi.

Near the end of the 1500s, the Ottoman empire became increasingly interested in East Africa commerce. Ottoman Turks had been active as traders along the Swahili coast since the 1540s. In 1586, an Ottoman naval commander named Mir Ali Beg began establishing formal alliances with towns stretching from Mogadishu to Mombasa. Hoping to secure their continued autonomy from the Portuguese, Mombasa's leaders welcomed Mir Ali Beg's presence in the town and promised their support. When Mir Ali Beg returned to the Swahili coast for a second time in late 1588, the people of Mombasa helped him erect a stone tower to guard the harbor. The Ottoman commander also supplied five war galleys to protect the city from seaborne attacks. This alliance was brief, however. In March 1589, the Portuguese attacked Mombasa again, driving the Ottoman Turks out of the town.[13] In 1593, they began constructing Fort Jesus. Standing at the entryway of the town's northern harbor, the large military garrison marks an imposing welcome to the port city. For centuries, Mombasa's connections to other parts of the world were primarily based around trading relationships. But by the end of the sixteenth century, the town's place in transimperial conflicts had clearly begun.

TRIBUTES, VIOLENCE, AND THE INFLUENCE OF INLAND COMMUNITIES

Inland communities were key players in imperial shifts in East Africa in the centuries following Fort Jesus's construction. Portuguese accounts from this period capture two primary themes, both of which are apparent in Resende's description of Mombasa. First, Portuguese writers regularly portray Mijikenda speakers and other inland groups as ruthless opportunists. Communities on the mainland were

98   INLAND VILLAGES AND OCEANIC EMPIRES

potential allies in military conflicts, but they also posed a serious threat to cities like Mombasa and Malindi if they turned against the controlling authorities. In contrast to their portrayals of the mainland's cruelty, the foreigners' commentaries also illuminate the exchanges in valued trade goods that occurred alongside martial relationships. The accounts, therefore, help illustrate the different means through which inland communities influenced global empires in East Africa.

After Mombasa became part of the Portuguese Estado da Índia, officials in Goa appointed a Swahili-speaking "king" to oversee local affairs in concert with military officials in Fort Jesus. As with other Indian Ocean port cities, political elites were also leading merchants, and vice versa.[14] As a result, local elites desired to maintain control of some aspects of regional trade. One constantly contentious point in Mombasa's relationship with Portuguese officials was the status of Pemba, an island in the Zanzibar Archipelago that was an important source of food provisions for the town. Mombasa's appointed leader retained control over trade with Pemba, but he was forced to pay Fort Jesus a fee of two hundred bags of rice annually for these privileges. In 1610, a new captain at Fort Jesus increased the annual payments to five hundred bags of rice. However, Mombasa's leader, al-Hasan ibn Ahmed, rejected the price hike, claiming that he needed the provisions to keep soldiers from the mainland as his retainers. Shortly after this, a group of Musungulos—allegedly recruited by Hasan—attacked the Portuguese fort that guarded the creek separating Mombasa's western edges from the mainland, killing nine Portuguese soldiers.[15]

Textiles were central to Hasan's ability to maintain the support of neighboring Mijikenda-speaking communities. Urban-to-rural textile exchanges during this period demonstrate the closely connected nature of military support, trade, and tribute between Mombasa and its mainland. By the start of the seventeenth century, a "time-honored practice" was already in place that dictated "when the Muzungulos came [to Mombasa] the sultan was expected to feed them and give to each one of them a piece of cloth."[16] Yet these transactional alliances were often fragile. In 1614, for instance, as tensions between Hasan and the Portuguese reached an apex, the sultan fled Mombasa and sought refuge at the inland settlement of Rabai. The leaders of Rabai initially welcomed the deposed sultan. However, after captains in Fort Jesus offered them two thousand pieces of cloth to murder Hasan, they betrayed their former ally, allegedly returning his severed head to the Portuguese forts at Makupa Creek.[17] This obligation to compensate communities on the mainland shaped the actions of subsequent Portuguese-appointed rulers, including Hasan's son Dom Jeronimo Chingulia, who governed Mombasa from 1627–1632. Dom Jeronimo set aside a large percentage of the annual duties collected by Mombasa's customs house for the "countries of the interior."[18] In return for a portion of the town's profits—paid in rolls of cloth—the Musungulos abstained from attacking Mombasa and acted as soldiers in campaigns against rival towns.

I want to briefly focus on Dom Jeronimo's tenure as Mombasa's leader because it reveals a chain of connections that linked villages in Mombasa's interior to faraway locales in the Portuguese empire. In comparison to his father, Dom Jeronimo represented a new model of Portuguese-affiliated leader: a Christian king with strong connections to Estado da Índia's oceanic empire. Born Yusuf bin Hasan Chingulia, Dom Jeronimo was sent at a young age to Goa, where he was educated at a school for Portuguese elites. By the time he returned to Mombasa in 1626, he had been baptized a Christian and married to a Portuguese woman. Moreover, he possessed significant military experience, having served in Portuguese armies in the Persian Gulf and Red Sea during the first half of the 1620s.[19] Like his father, Dom Jeronimo found that he could sidestep Portuguese authority by sending regular tributes of textiles to communities on Mombasa's mainland. This was critical as his relationships with Portuguese captains at Fort Jesus became increasingly strained over time, in no small part because of the Musungulos's prominent military role in Mombasa and on Pemba.[20]

Dom Jeronimo's affiliation with Estado da Índia reached a dramatic culmination in August 1631, when he confronted the Portuguese at Fort Jesus, accompanied by sixty inland soldiers. Armed with poison arrows, his Musungulo retainers swiftly drove the Portuguese forces out of Mombasa.[21] Dom Jeronimo then renounced Christianity and proclaimed himself once again to be Yusuf bin Hasan, the Muslim heir to Mombasa and Malindi. Mombasa was critical to Portuguese political and commercial prospects in East Africa, so in the months that followed Yusuf bin Hasan Chingulia's revolt, officials in Goa conspired to retake the town. In January 1632, a large Portuguese fleet returned to the port city. Once again, the support of inland communities was critical to the impending confrontation. The Swahili leader—now referred to only as Chingulia in Portuguese records—reportedly had between five hundred and six hundred Musungulo soldiers posted at different parts of the island. When the Portuguese attempted to attack the city, they were driven off by inland archers' poison arrows.[22]

The Portuguese eventually resorted to forming a blockade by sea, thus cutting off Mombasa's access to imported trade goods, including cloth textiles. Taking a two-pronged approach, they slowly chipped away at the king's mainland support by "sending [the Musungulos] presents of cotton goods" and setting bounties for Chingulia's allies.[23] Ultimately, this approach proved successful. In May 1632, Chingulia fled Mombasa as the Portuguese retook control of Fort Jesus. Mombasa's former leader spent the next five years of his life traveling the Indian Ocean and Red Sea, angling for support to attack Portuguese holdings across East Africa and becoming a fugitive in the eyes of Portuguese officials.[24] However, his Musungulo supporters did not take up this cause. Instead, they abandoned Fort Jesus without any resistance and returned to the mainland, knowing that the end of the Portuguese blockade would reinvigorate their commercial role in the town.

100   INLAND VILLAGES AND OCEANIC EMPIRES

This dynamic—in which the occupants of coastal cities sent cloth payments to inland neighbors for protection and military support—was not limited to Mijikenda speakers and Mombasa. Southeast Kenya's immediate interior also included hunter-forager groups and, from at least the sixteenth century, a Thagicu-speaking group called Segeju or Daiso. Portuguese accounts portray the Segeju, much like the Musungulos, as a constant menace for coastal towns. In 1569, for instance, a Jesuit priest in Malindi wrote of the Segeju (whom he called "Moceguejos"):

> They are very warlike. . . . The Moors here are much molested by these Kaffirs, and to prevent them from spoiling their crops and making war upon them, they buy them off with cloth and other things.[25]

During the 1630s, the Portuguese reportedly had to supply Malindi's governor with "scores of linen cloth" to give to Segeju speakers as gifts.[26] In return, the "warlike" Segeju refrained from attacking the town and provided it with military support when needed.

The Ottomans' defeat by Portuguese armadas in 1589 offers another good example of the roles that different inland communities played in transimperial shifts in the region. In March of that year, Mombasa-aligned Ottomans were preparing to protect the city from an imminent Portuguese seaborne attack when thousands of warriors—whom historical records refer to as the "Zimba"—attacked them from the city's mainland. The Zimba roundly defeated Mir Ali Beg's forces, prompting a total Ottoman retreat from the East African coast and paving the way for the Portuguese to take control of the city. After driving out the Ottoman Turks, the Zimbas turned northward toward Portuguese-aligned Malindi, only to be thwarted by three thousand Segeju fighting on the town's behalf.[27]

It is not clear from the available evidence whether the Zimba were Mijikenda speakers. Contemporaneous historical documents refer to other inland raiders from southern Africa by the same name.[28] So, it is possible this was a group from southeastern Africa that invaded the Mombasa region following an overland migration before quickly retreating from the region. Alternatively, Zimba may have been a catchall term for inland communities that Portuguese writers used to reference the broad similarities they identified between Mombasa's inland neighbors and similarly hostile inland groups on the southern Swahili coast. If this is the case, then, by the 1600s, after the Portuguese became more established in the region, they began referring to mainland communities as the Musungulos.[29] Regardless, the episode centers the role of inland communities in major political shifts in the sixteenth-century Indian Ocean.

Historian Giancarlo Casale has suggested that had the Ottomans successfully established themselves in Mombasa, they may have been able to expand into Malindi and other parts of the Swahili coast. Ottoman control of Mombasa, he argued, could have fundamentally altered the balance of power in the western Indian Ocean, potentially leading to "the premature demise of Portuguese Asia."

INLAND VILLAGES AND OCEANIC EMPIRES   101

Ultimately, according to Casale, "the outcome of a confrontation between two technologically advanced, centralized, and expansive colonial powers" hinged on "a mainland force from the interior of Africa."[30] Irrespective of whether Mombasa falling under Ottoman control would have had these larger ripple effects, communities in the town's mainland continued to play an influential role in transregional connections and politics, as is evident in their centrality to Sultan Hasan's and Yusuf Chingulia's tenures in the decades that followed. In all these instances, communities from the interior acted as a linchpin within a much larger set of relationships that stretched from Mombasa across multiple nodes of the Indian Ocean's commercial and political landscape.

INVISIBLE DEVELOPMENTS IN MOMBASA'S INTERIOR

A surface reading of the written evidence might suggest that those living adjacent to coastal towns like Mombasa and Malindi were little more than opportunistic extortionists, shifting their allegiances for cloth. Portuguese sources certainly give this impression. For instance, when Rabai betrayed Sultan Hasan, an observer wrote that this occurrence was almost expected since the Musungulos "do not keep faith with anyone, nor were they loyal to anything other than their own interest which is clothing."[31] Into the 1700s, Portuguese accounts continued to describe the Mijikenda-speaking Musungulos as warriors who were "famously skilled in the art of archery" but who were also considered untrustworthy since they supported whichever party supplied them with the most cloth.[32] Similarly, the Segeju, according to historical accounts, were a barbarous group of warriors to whom Malindi's officials had to send cloth tributes to prevent them from attacking the town.[33]

In documentary accounts, Mijikenda and Segeju speakers mostly encounter the Portuguese during moments of conflict. Estado da Índia was a militarized trading empire, and descriptions of their conflicts and interactions with inland communities in the Mombasa region need to be understood in this context. But by paying attention to the important role that Mijikenda speakers played in building Mombasa's commercial connections, we might also see these accounts in a different light. By the time Vasco da Gama's fleet reached Mombasa, Mijikenda speakers participated in overlapping local, regional, and global trading networks. Their ready access to valued inland trade goods, such as ivory, beeswax, and copal, facilitated strong trading relationships with coastal markets that continued to thrive even after the Portuguese began controlling the town's harbor.

Established trading relationships did not preclude conflicts and tensions between Mombasa and its interior prior to the Portuguese era. Duarte Barbosa's early sixteenth-century overview of the Indian Ocean described the people of Mombasa as "oft-times at war and but seldom at peace with those of the mainland." Yet, according to Barbosa, people in Mombasa continued to "carry on trade

102 INLAND VILLAGES AND OCEANIC EMPIRES

with [people on the mainland]" for ivory and wax.[34] Trading relationships grew out of long-standing networks and connections in Mombasa's interior. As the previous two chapters detailed, the region inland from Mombasa was an important exchange corridor for centuries prior to the arrival of the Portuguese. The arrival of Segeju-speaking migrants from Central Kenya during the mid-second millennium accelerated certain aspects of these inland exchanges. From Segeju speakers, Mijikenda communities adopted new ritual ideas and trading vocabulary. These exchanges and transformations are largely invisible in written records, but they hint at some of the ways that inland communities' military influence and trading prowess were mutually constitutive. One of the reasons Mombasa's connections to the Indian Ocean grew and endured was because communities in its interior desired cloth. However, these connections also relied on other material desires and transformations, including exchanges in foodstuffs, cattle, and knowledge.

Before continuing to trace the story of imperial shifts in Mombasa, I want to briefly return to the town's interior to explore some of the invisible developments behind these encounters with overseas empires. Here, I build on work by scholars like Jeremy Prestholdt, Pedro Machado, and Yaari Felber-Seligman that has demonstrated that Portuguese imperialism reconfigured—rather than destroyed—older patterns of trade and interaction, sometimes offering new opportunities for both coastal and interior traders alike.[35] For inland communities around Mombasa, this era of oceanic imperialism created opportunities to affiliate with new constituencies and to access valued goods. In pursuing these relationships, Mijikenda speakers and other inland groups not only shaped trade into and out of Mombasa, but they also affected the political fates of multiple oceanic empires. To tell this story, however, requires a larger anchoring in the exchanges unfolding in the interior in the critical yet less obviously "global" realm of animal husbandry.

Keeping Cattle: The Segeju Influence

The previous chapter discussed the trading mosaics that thrived in Mombasa's interior, especially around the arid Tsavo plains during the first half of the second millennium. However, as I alluded, archaeological research shows that, starting in the seventeenth century, many sites on the Taita Hills' lower slopes were abandoned as people moved their farming villages to the upper elevations of the Taita Hills' three massifs. Seasonal camps in the adjacent plains also fell out of use around this same time, and some of Tsavo's pastoralists relocated to fortified rock shelter sites.[36] Archaeologist Chapurukha Kusimba has suggested that these changing settlement patterns might have resulted from an increase in slave raiding and cattle rustling in the interior.[37] Yet documentary records demonstrate that Mijikenda speakers continued to supply Mombasa with trade goods and provisions despite these changes, helping to maintain the town's position as a leading port. They did so by continuing to build relationships with other inland societies from whom they adopted new ritual ideas, trading practices, and technical skills in areas like animal husbandry.

To understand Mombasa's political landscape as the town became a nodal point in global conflicts, let's turn to a somewhat anomalous location: the cattle enclosure of a village in Mombasa's interior. Notably, domestic livestock were a very small part of coastal East Africa's economy during the first millennium. For instance, Sabaki speakers' linguistic ancestors possessed a complex terminology to differentiate animals by age, sex, and breeding status.[38] But proto-Sabaki speakers retained little of this vocabulary, suggesting that domesticates played a minor role in their economy and diet, especially compared to their linguistic ancestors. Faunal records support the linguistic picture, showing that settlements in southeast Kenya kept only a small number of domestic animals during the first millennium.[39] From this evidence we can imagine people gradually shedding knowledge of specialized animal husbandry from their lexicon over generations, mainly because domestic animals were not that important for their diet or for their subsistence economy.

The significance of domesticates in Mombasa's immediate interior changed dramatically over time. Like their Sabaki ancestors, early Mijikenda speakers met their animal protein needs by hunting and trapping small fauna, fishing in nearby creeks and streams, and collecting gastropods. However, starting from the fourteenth and fifteenth centuries, the bones of domestic stock like cattle, sheep, and goats dominated faunal assemblages in the same region.[40] As people pressed into drier environments beyond the fertile inland ridge, they filled enclosures in their villages with new sources of food and wealth: cattle and goats.

While archaeological records show a steady uptick in domestic animals in faunal assemblages from Mombasa's immediate interior, these records tell only part of the story. Because Mijikenda speakers inherited very little specialized knowledge of animal husbandry from their linguistic ancestors, to keep domestic stock in larger numbers they would have either needed to develop knowledge of advanced animal husbandry themselves or adopt this knowledge from someone else. For Mijikenda communities, Segeju-speaking migrants were the key source of animal husbandry knowledge. Portuguese records describe Segeju communities as possessing large cattle herds.[41] Mijikenda historical traditions similarly depict the Segeju as expert cattle herders who accompanied them on the mythical migration from Shungwaya.[42] Linguistic records confirm the Segeju's herding expertise. Table 2 shows some of the loanwords that Mijikenda speakers—as well as other inland speech communities like Pare, Dawida, and Gweno—adopted directly from Segeju.[43]

These loanwords reflect changes in the scale and value of domestic animals in Mombasa's interior. As herds grew, people needed to find ways to constrain competition between male animals and develop more intentional breeding practices. By adopting strategies for differentiating animals by age, sex, and breeding status, people obtained a means to keep greater numbers of animals.[44] Written records

TABLE 2 Domestic Animal Loanwords in Mijikenda and Pare from Segeju

Mijikenda form	English gloss
ndzao; kadzao	Bull; bullock
k'uro ~ kuro	Dog
mwati	Immature female sheep (ewe)
mvarika ~ -pharika	Immature female goat
ndenge; kadenge	Male goat
ndewa	Ox, steer, castrated animal
t'urume ~ turume	Ram; immature male sheep

document Segeju speakers' presence on the East African coast—first around Malindi and shortly after in Mombasa—as early as the 1560s.[45] To the Portuguese, communities like Mijikenda and Segeju were "warrior" groups that had to be placated with cloth. The spread of these loanwords among Mijikenda speakers and other inland communities overlapped with the start of Portuguese imperialism in East Africa. Thus, they alert us to inland knowledge exchanges that, though absent from written coastal accounts, formed a backdrop to alliances and conflicts between oceanic empires and societies in East Africa's interior.

Provisioning Global Trade

By scaling up their ability to keep cattle, inland communities opened up new avenues for trade and exchange. During the nineteenth century, for instance, the expansion of global trade in East Africa's highlands supported the growth of cattle-keeping in communities that were not specialized pastoralists. Caravans flocked to the interior in search of ivory while farming communities sold their agricultural surpluses to these passing traders for cloth and beads. They then used coastal trade goods to obtain cattle from neighboring pastoralists. In the process, cattle herds quickly became key markers of political status. Ultimately, the growth of global trade in East Africa's highlands contributed to the rising value of cattle among nonpastoralist communities.[46] Scholarship on transformations in cattle keeping in East Africa's highlands addresses the nineteenth century, a period for which we have ample written records. But the available linguistic and faunal evidence suggests that similar changes took place among communities in Mombasa's near interior several centuries prior.

The earlier shift in the valuation of cattle in Mombasa's interior was likely due to a combination of factors. First, Mijikenda speakers had direct and early interface with coastal trading networks. Second, around the mid-second millennium, two new communities pushed into southeast Kenya's coastal interior: the Segeju as well as Oromo-speaking pastoralists who were documented living around Malindi by 1624. In the centuries that followed, Oromo communities became important brokers for ivory and cattle with Mijikenda and Waata communities.[47] Finally, the climate may have aided these dynamics. Lake records from East Africa indicate that the coast's near interior experienced a generally wetter climate during the period corresponding to the northern hemisphere's "Little Ice Age," with pluvial conditions between the mid-seventeenth and late eighteenth century.[48] Regular and predictable rainfall would have aided the production of foodstuffs for trade while also creating ample grazing grounds to support larger herds. As Mijikenda speakers established settlements across a wider range of ecologies after the mid-second millennium, they would have gained more and more opportunities to obtain cattle and knowledge from migrant pastoralist groups.

As was the case in Tsavo during prior centuries, oceanic trade goods were enmeshed within these networks. People traded livestock and foodstuffs alongside iron, ivory, and arrow poison, which gave them access to imported goods like glass beads and textiles.[49] Mijikenda communities were not only Mombasa's source of export goods; they were also among the town's main provisioning agents. Nearly all food provisions in Mombasa were brought from either the town's mainland or from Pemba, an island in the Zanzibar Archipelago that is sometimes called Mombasa's breadbasket. Since food from Pemba had to be shipped by sea, land-based provisioning routes were especially important whenever the sea routes were disrupted, giving inland communities a tremendous influence over Mombasa's most basic needs during periods of maritime conflict.

We know less about Mombasa's role in trading foods than we do ivory, but the available evidence indicates that it was a major distribution center for grains and other foodstuffs. In the early seventeenth century, each inland village supplied the city with "twenty bags of meal" annually, and, in turn, the villages were compensated with a fixed rate of cloth.[50] The mainland also provisioned Mombasa with livestock, especially cattle, sheep, and chickens.[51] Mombasa sent some surplus food goods to forts in Portuguese Mozambique. According to Resende, the town's main revenue came from "ivory, amber, and civet," which were shipped to India, but its "large supplies of corn, rice, and cows" made the port "of vital importance to the rulers of the coast." Without Mombasa, he claimed, "it would be impossible to supply the fortress of Mozambique."[52] More detailed records from the early nineteenth century show that provisioning agents from the mainland traveled to Mombasa almost daily, supplying the town with grains, cassava, fruits, vegetables, and cattle.[53] Mijikenda communities were considered "the whole support of the island," so maintaining good relations was essential to the town's survival.[54]

Under Portuguese rule, Mombasa's leaders continued to send large volumes of cotton cloth to communities on the mainland. Despite the disruptions caused by Portuguese incursions, Mombasa remained a major entrepôt for the global ivory trade throughout this period. So, the cloth payments, which the Portuguese characterized as a form of extortion, reflected military partnerships. At the same time, these payments underwrote trading relationships with inland merchants who

106 INLAND VILLAGES AND OCEANIC EMPIRES

supplied them with goods such as ivory and beeswax, as well as essentials like agricultural wares, cattle, and sheep.

Foreign observers found inland communities' influence on port cities like Mombasa and Malindi bewildering. In their eyes, Mijikenda speakers and other groups like Segeju could only be violent "barbarians" at odds with their more "civilized" urban neighbors.[55] The evidence of concurrent transformations in arenas like trade and subsistence within Mombasa's interior alert us to alternative ways of thinking about Mombasa's interactions with its interior. Mijikenda speakers used both their access to trade goods and provisions, as well as their ability to raid Mombasa, to maintain influence in the city. Some of the ritual interconnections detailed in chapter 2 could have also aided in organizing men for activities like warfare. For instance, Mijikenda speakers used a system of age sets, called *rika*, to organize men across different villages and clans into gerontocratic groups.[56] Martial ideas were embedded in the rituals men performed to advance from their youth to elderhood. For instance, during an initiation ritual called the *mung'aro*, junior men kidnapped a male stranger. The initiates killed the victim and removed his genitals for a sacrifice. After the sacrifice, they covered themselves in mud and put on grass skirts, commonly worn by women. At the ritual's conclusion, the initiates donned new adornments: colorful cotton textiles that symbolized their ascension into a new rank.[57] The victim's genitals, according to some accounts, were then kept and used to prepare a war charm.[58] In short, the material signature of oceanic trade and martial rituals were both central to strategies for organizing young men.

The age-set system and associated rituals illuminate how inland communities could have mobilized people across different inland settlements, including for activities like raids. Musungulo leaders assembled hundreds of warriors at a time for raids, as the Portuguese accounts detailed in this chapter indicate. In the 1780s, Oman's imam described the "terrible" Mijikenda who held sway over Mombasa as "a people whom God alone can number" in a seeming reference to their raids on the island.[59] Notably, Mijikenda speakers conducted these raids during a period when archaeological records indicate a clear shift toward smaller settlement patterns.[60] Living in smaller villages, which frequently split and moved around—as oral traditions discussed in chapter 2 indicate—would have offered a means for evading counteroffensives or capture by foreign invaders or partners in Mombasa.[61] Forest groves and associated ritual practices provided the spatial and intellectual framework for connecting and mobilizing people across dispersed communities.[62] Added to all of this, Mijikenda speakers' position as a gateway between Mombasa and its interior meant that they controlled access to valued trade goods and food provisions necessary for the town to function. Village ritual practices, inland knowledge exchanges, long-distance trade, subsistence adaptations, and warfare were all part and parcel of Mijikenda speakers' influence on Mombasa's and the Indian Ocean's trade and politics. The global resonance of these interconnected developments in Mombasa's interior is especially apparent in one well-documented episode: Oman's thirty-three-month siege of Mombasa from 1696 to 1698.

FOOD SUPPLIES AND THE FALL OF FORT JESUS DURING OMAN'S SIEGE OF MOMBASA

Following Oman's rise as a naval power during the second half of the seventeenth century, Mombasa became an even more important theater for western Indian Ocean conflicts. Portugal invaded the coast of southern Arabia in 1507, capturing Muscat and imposing a monopoly over maritime trade in the region. Portuguese suzerainty lasted until 1650, when Sultan bin Saif, who governed Oman's interior, drove the Portuguese from Muscat. This initiated Oman's emergence as a maritime power. Over the next few decades, their fleets waged war by sea against Portuguese-controlled port cities on the Persian side of the Gulf, in India, and East Africa.[63] In 1661, Omani ships attacked Mombasa, allegedly at the request of Mombasa's locals, who hoped to oust the Portuguese from their city.[64] The Omani navy assembled a large contingent of supporters, including Musungulo warriors from the mainland, but the Portuguese maintained control of the town. In 1696, Omani fleets returned to Mombasa and began a prolonged campaign against the Portuguese, which ended when they took control of Fort Jesus in 1698.

A Portuguese text called *História de Mombaça* provides a detailed accounting of the events of 1696 to 1698. The text, written anonymously by a Portuguese academic living in Goa, is based on the testimonies of officers who fled Mombasa during a Portuguese recovery mission shortly before Fort Jesus fell.[65] Although the text primarily focuses on Oman's attempts to capture Fort Jesus, it also illuminates how established commercial and social relationships influenced this period of turmoil in Mombasa. Not surprisingly, Mijikenda speakers' allegiances and support play a key part in the author's narrative of Omani forces capturing Mombasa from the Portuguese empire. When read with the larger context of Mombasa's interior in mind, the account makes it possible to connect the different threads of military support, trade, and provisioning covered thus far in the chapter. To draw out these connections, the remainder of this section offers a blow-by-blow account of the Omani siege while highlighting the central role of one Mijikenda settlement, Chonyi, in the series of events.

The conflict started when the Portuguese assigned Mombasa's commercial administration to a Junta do Comércio (board of trade) in 1695.[66] The Junta granted commercial oversight of Mombasa to a trading company based out of Goa that maintained a monopoly over most of the town's trade goods, including ivory. The trading company became responsible for setting prices on exports, dictating that all trade needed to be conducted through company officials at Fort Jesus.[67] These changing commercial regulations created tensions with some inland merchants, especially ivory traders, because of the company's decision to cut the purchasing price of ivory in half. The company further tightened their grip over commerce by prohibiting local traders from selling ivory to anyone but company officials. Furthermore, they prohibited local merchants from transporting ivory out of Mombasa themselves.[68] Shortly after these new trading arrangements were established, some people in Mombasa turned to Muscat for assistance.

An Omani fleet entered Mombasa's harbor on March 13, 1696. They quickly captured smaller forts on the island, forcing the Portuguese and their local allies into Fort Jesus.[69] According to Portuguese reports, as many as 2,500 people sheltered in the fort. Without the ability to leave Fort Jesus, save for access to a small stretch of protected beach adjacent to the garrison, they quickly ran low on provisions. They requested supplies and support from other Portuguese outposts in East Africa, but Omani ships guarding Mombasa's harbor prevented most supply missions from reaching the fort.[70] Supplies from the mainland were critical as a result.

The Portuguese had already established partnerships with inland traders for both ivory and foodstuffs during their prior century in Mombasa. However, Oman's arrival fractured some of these ties. For instance, according to *História de Mombaça*, the Portuguese lost access to one of the mainland's most important ivory traders when he began trading exclusively with the Omani newcomers.[71] As a result, alliances with another inland trader—called the "King of Chonyi" in the text—were essential to Fort Jesus's survival.[72] The Chonyi leader was less affected by the changing price of ivory than some other inland brokers since he primarily traded livestock, ambergris, tortoiseshell, and beeswax.[73] This put him in an advantageous position in negotiating with Fort Jesus. He agreed to send the garrison provisions, but, capitalizing on their vulnerability, this assistance came at a hefty price. The demands of the "ambitious" Musungulos at Chonyi increased throughout the occupation, growing, according to the Portuguese account, "in the same measure as our need for assistance" in Fort Jesus.[74]

While access to provisions influenced Chonyi's ability to procure cloth from the Portuguese at Fort Jesus, other details from *História de Mombaça* highlight how these demands were given weight by the capacity of the Musungulos in warfare. Soon after Chonyi's leader affirmed his support for Fort Jesus, the Omanis attempted to work with an intermediary from Mombasa, named Mwinyi Chambe, to form their own alliance with Chonyi.[75] However, Chambe had already brokered Chonyi's provisioning agreement with Fort Jesus, and he remained loyal to his Portuguese partners by ensuring the Omani message never left Mombasa.[76]

After failing to establish direct contact with Chonyi through diplomatic channels, the Omanis resolved to instead settle the matter by force. According to the account, they sent an armed party of five hundred of their best soldiers to Chonyi with orders to "destroy them by sword and bloodshed." However, Chonyi received advanced word of the attack from allies in Mombasa and prepared a deadly ambush, using the "dense and almost impenetrable forest" surrounding their settlements as a defensive advantage. Fighting in unfamiliar territory, the Omanis stood little chance. Reportedly only forty to eighty of the original five hundred soldiers survived the ordeal.[77]

When we read these two episodes about the Chonyi together, we can see how an array of exchanges—payments in cloth, trade in food provisions and export goods, and military support—underwrote inland relationships with both foreign and local constituencies in Mombasa. The *História de Mombaça* directly connects the slow demise of the Portuguese in Mombasa to inland trade and provisions. After Chonyi's resounding victory against the Omani soldiers, the Portuguese captain continued sending larger and larger amounts of textiles to the mainland with hope that his inland allies would mount additional offensives and drive the Omani forces from the island entirely. However, the Musungulos "were not willing to strive for another victory," according to the text's author, "because they already had the bounty of our textiles."[78] Inland leaders clearly valued their autonomy within these affiliations with the foreigners and knew their monopoly over provisions and inland trade goods gave them a substantial leverage over both parties. As the siege wore on, Portuguese supply ships continued failing to reach Mombasa, meaning all that sustained the Portuguese were provisions from the mainland.[79] This became a huge problem for the Portuguese by the end of 1697, when people from Chonyi and other inland communities began withholding provisions. In Fort Jesus, they feared that the entire mainland would soon throw its support to Oman.[80]

A series of letters from Chambe and Bwana Dau bin Bwana Shaka—another close Portuguese ally from the northern Swahili town of Faza—illuminates the centrality of Mijikenda-speaking communities at this moment when the Portuguese hold on Mombasa seemed to be slipping. Holed up in Fort Jesus and short on supplies, the two advised Portuguese captains waiting at sea that it would not be long before the Chonyi began "taking up arms in favour of the Arabs." They warned that if this happened, all the other communities on the mainland—most of whom remained neutral in the conflict—would see the Omanis as the obvious victors and would quickly follow Chonyi's lead.[81] Regardless of whether this was entirely true, the two writers employed this rhetoric in multiple letters to Zanzibar and Goa to muster support. Clearly, they believed the looming threat of the Musungulos' shifting alliances would be convincing. While this support never reached the fort, the stories of the Musungulos circulated widely, eventually being reproduced in Estado da Índia's official account of Fort Jesus's fall.

The *História de Mombaça*, written shortly after the events in question, was based on testimonials from informants who escaped prior to the fall of Fort Jesus, which happened sometime before the end of 1698.[82] I am less concerned with the accuracy of the account—which was written an ocean away by a person who had never so much as traveled to Mombasa—than I am with what the source reveals about imperial understandings of the town itself and its inland neighbors. During the seventeenth century, the leaders of Portugal's Indian Ocean empire were concerned with competition from commercial rivals, not only from Oman but also from English and Dutch trading companies.[83] *História de Mombaça* and other written accounts from this era enable us to squarely situate the occupants of settlements in Mombasa's mainland within these transimperial rivalries. It wasn't only trade goods like ivory, gum copal, and textiles that connected East Africa's mainland to other parts of the Indian Ocean. Stories of communities in Mombasa's interior also traveled across expanses of ocean, from Fort Jesus to Muscat and Goa. While foreigners' accounts often portrayed Mijikenda speakers as ruthless barbarians, a careful reading of these documents and their context reveals the remarkable influence of inland communities to the shifting fate of global empires in Mombasa. Portuguese writers clearly understood that the future of Estado da Índia in Mombasa hinged on the status of communities in the town's mainland.

THE MIJIKENDA DELEGATION TO MUSCAT
AND THE TRAJECTORY OF OCEANIC EMPIRES

The perception that Mijikenda-speaking communities were central to Portugal's imperial ambitions in East Africa endured after Mombasa's fall to Oman. For the first few decades of the eighteenth century, officials in Goa continued plotting to retake the town. Rumors of waning local support for the Omanis circulated along the coast as early as 1705. In 1710, a spy from Mombasa working for Portuguese officials in Mozambique reported that the Omanis compensated Mijikenda-speaking villages with "generous amounts of cotton cloth." Nevertheless, the Omanis still needed to keep troops at the forts at Makupa Creek to repel the looming threat of raids from the mainland.[84] Civil wars and succession disputes in Oman between 1718–1728 further exacerbated tensions in East Africa, disrupting trade with Muscat and splitting Omani constituencies in Mombasa into two rival factions.[85]

As Oman's hold on Mombasa waned, Portuguese officials schemed to rebuild their alliances with the Musungulos and thus regain control of the town's trade.[86] Like the former viceroy whose letter opened this chapter, officials in Goa understood well that Mijikenda speakers could be compelled to support them for adequate compensation in Indian textiles. Capitalizing on the internal turmoil in Oman, the Portuguese recaptured Mombasa in March 1728.[87] This time, however, local discontent began almost immediately. Some of the most prominent inland leaders were reluctant to recognize Estado da Índia's authority in the town after representatives from Fort Jesus failed to provide cloth tributes "as was a longstanding custom."[88] Although the Portuguese generals quickly remedied the situation, tensions persisted. By early 1729, communities in the mainland had begun withholding provisions from the fort, which had again reneged on its annual duties in cloth.[89] As had been the case many times prior, Mombasa's political fate was contingent on the flow of textiles from the town to its mainland. Within a few months, most inland communities had shifted their allegiances back in favor of

Oman. In late April, Musungulos led attacks to take over Portuguese forts at Makupa Creek.[90] Shortly after this, a large delegation from Mombasa traveled to Oman to obtain support for expelling the Portuguese from the city once again.[91]

The Mombasa delegation's trip to Muscat offers a remarkable illustration of Mijikenda speakers' influence on the western Indian Ocean's political landscape. According to the *Mombasa Chronicle*, the group consisted of representatives from Mombasa's Twelve Tribes confederations as well as leaders from "the cities of Vanikat," which included "Ribah, Shuni, Kambah, Gauma, Jibanah, Rabayi, Jiryamah, Darvmah-Mutavi, Shibah, Lughuh, Diju."[92] The names of these "cities" include all of the groups known since the middle of the twentieth century as the Mijikenda. The chronicle refers to them collectively as "Vanikat," an Arabic rendering of the Swahili term, Wanyika, or "bush people."[93] As noted in the previous chapter, the name Wanyika (or Nyika) is a pejorative ethnonym that Swahili speakers, Arabs, and Europeans commonly used to describe Mijikenda-speaking communities during the nineteenth and early twentieth centuries. By referring to these communities as "bush people," they emphasized the supposed cultural differences between Mombasa's urban, Muslim residents and their rural, non-Muslim neighbors immediately inland. The paradox this episode presents is that the leaders from the "bush" are shown playing a prominent role in global politics.

This meeting between representatives from the Mombasa region and Muscat took place at a pivotal moment in Oman's history. Only a year prior, the Imamate (or Omani state) had resolved a decade-long civil war that had erupted due to succession disputes. In 1718, Imam Sultan bin Saif II died, and his twelve-year-old son Saif bin Sultan II was appointed Oman's new leader. Due to his age, Saif bin Sultan II was quickly replaced by a series of regents and challengers. None of these individuals lasted long, meaning Saif bin Sultan II was appointed four separate times during his lifetime after different claimants were killed or deposed. The period from 1724 to 1728 was especially volatile, and Oman lost control of most of its overseas territories, including Mombasa. When the leaders of both factions of the civil war died in 1728, Saif bin Sultan II was appointed imam for the fourth and final time. However, he was quickly isolated from Oman's powerful religious leaders in the capital, Nizwa, one hundred kilometers from the coast. As a result, the young leader's authority was limited to coastal regions around Muscat.[94]

We can imagine the delegation from Mombasa arriving in Oman amid this period of internal turmoil. Following the southwest monsoon, they would have reached Muscat as early as May or June, a little over a year after Saif bin Sultan II resumed his position as imam for the fourth time.[95] For the Mombasa delegation, Oman was the natural partner to help rid their city of the Portuguese for good. For Saif bin Sultan II, the Mombasa delegation's arrival would have presented an opportunity for reestablishing Oman's influence in East Africa, which had declined amid recent dynastic struggles. Confined to the coast and controlling Oman's navy, he must have considered the oceanic sphere his best bet for consolidating authority.

112   INLAND VILLAGES AND OCEANIC EMPIRES

Due to Oman's history in Mombasa, the imam's confidants would have undoubtedly been aware of Mijikenda speakers' importance to the city's political fate. The fact that the delegation included "one man from each city," encompassing major settlements inland from Mombasa, was no coincidence.[96] The "Wanyika" delegates' presence demonstrated the mainland's broad support, which was critical to maintaining control of the city. Not surprisingly, the imam responded to their request.

On November 26, 1729, local militias took full control of Fort Jesus. A few weeks later, a large Omani fleet carrying two thousand armed soldiers arrived from Muscat.[97] Compellingly, the *Mombasa Chronicle* explains these shifts through stories of food provisions and alliances with the mainland. According to the text, as local frustrations mounted with Portuguese authorities in Fort Jesus, residents of Mombasa offered to de-husk the rice stored in the fort. Portuguese officials accepted their assistance and sent out "all of the paddy which was in the fort and divided it among the people" in town who promised to return it de-husked. In the chronicle's dramatic accounting, instead of returning the rice, the locals launched a surprise attack, beheading the Portuguese generals and seizing control of the fort.[98]

The chronicle vividly illustrates shifting nodes of political power in Mombasa. When read in context, we can think about the rice in the chronicle as representing not only food but access to resources, trading networks, and military affiliations that undergirded political legitimacy in the town. While there is no other documentation of the people of Mombasa destroying the rice at Fort Jesus, Portuguese accounts directly connect the fort's downfall to a shortage of provisions once they lost the support of the mainland.[99] By taking their food, seizing control of Fort Jesus, and demonstrating the broad support of the mainland with their trip to Muscat, Mombasa's contingent symbolically erased the Portuguese from the town's political landscape. At the hands of an alliance that spanned from southern Arabia to villages in the town's rural interior, Mombasa's Portuguese period was over for good.

...

Portuguese writers considered Mijikenda-speaking communities opportunistic mercenaries who would quickly flip their support for textiles. Consequently, these groups represented an ever-present threat to Mombasa's well-being. As Resende expressed, rather than assuming the proper place as rural vassals to the powerful port city, inland communities held the town's leaders as "prisoners" on the island if they were not properly compensated with payments in cloth. Centuries of inland networking and commercial inventiveness were the invisible backdrop to this tremendous influence. Because Mijikenda speakers held a near monopoly over provisions and interior trade goods, they had a powerful means to influence Mombasa's politics under foreign rule. The imperial contests that linked Mombasa at various points in time to the Ottomans, Portuguese India, and Muscat did not just unfold in the Indian Ocean's seascapes. Oceanic imperialism also implicated trade in foodstuffs, circulating cattle terminology, and inland affiliation strategies.

Mombasa's political fate and imperial arrangements in the western Indian Ocean often hinged on the actions of communities in the town's interior. For centuries, imperial powers established and maintained influence in Mombasa by building alliances with communities on the town's mainland who were their trading partners, military supporters, and rivals—sometimes all at once. Payments in cloth textiles held these relationships together or pulled them apart. The next chapter zooms in on these urban-to-rural tribute practices to trace how Mijikenda speakers themselves understood their relationship with Mombasa and the various global actors that converged at the port city.

5

From Mijikenda City
to Busaidi Backwater

The Mijikenda delegation to Muscat in 1729 was not the first inland cohort to visit the Omani port city, according to a Swahili chronicle written in the nineteenth century. This chronicle tells of a trip by representatives from Chonyi, Jibana, and Ribe more than three decades prior. They traveled to southern Arabia as part of an alliance with Mtwapa and Kilifi—smaller towns immediately north of Mombasa—to visit the imam shortly prior to Oman's siege of Mombasa, which began in 1696. According to the chronicle, when the representatives arrived in Muscat, they each received a gift—a pipe for the Chonyi, a ring for the Jibana, and a chair for the Ribe. The gifts established a *khatti*, or contract agreement, between the imam and his visitors.[1] Shortly thereafter, Oman sent ships to Mombasa to confront the Portuguese. The episode may or may not have happened (and the fact that Chonyi allied against Oman in the subsequent siege raises some questions about its veracity). Nevertheless, the chronicle provides a productive entry point for this chapter because of the specific language it used to describe the imam's gifts for his Mijikenda visitors. According to the Swahili text, by offering the gifts "*Imamu akawaheshimu sana*," or "the imam honored them exceedingly."[2] The chronicle designated these honors using the Swahili term *-heshimu*, meaning "to honor," a word that signified cloth tribute payments that flowed from Mombasa to its interior.

This chapter focuses on the changing political relationships between Mombasa and its interior during the eighteenth and nineteenth centuries. When Portuguese observers described Mombasa, they referred to it as a city situated in the "land of" the Musungulos or a "region called Musungula." Intentionally or not, by positioning Mombasa in the context of its mainland, Portuguese imperialists recognized the ways that Mombasa relied on—and, in many cases, was forced to show deference to—its mainland. This chapter expands on Mijikenda speakers' role in

Mombasa's politics, following two key threads. First, I show how Mijikenda speakers understood their relationship with Mombasa by studying the rituals of honor (*heshima*) that undergirded their partnerships with different maritime actors. Second, I explore the ways that this port-interior relationship changed during the nineteenth century, after Mombasa became part of the growing Indian Ocean empire of Oman's Busaidi dynasty.

I trace this history through records of *heshima* tributes and an interlinked practice called *kore*, an ancient Bantu word that referred to a person exchanged as compensation to settle a debt. For centuries, Mijikenda speakers established favorable terms with coastal traders by claiming *heshima*, often made manifest through tributes in cotton textiles. Merchants in Mombasa occasionally seized *kore* from Mijikenda communities to ensure that exchanges with their inland partners remained balanced and fair. Together, *heshima* and *kore* helped mutually constitute trading practices, partnerships, and political affiliations in the region. Mijikenda communities remained fully independent from Mombasa so long as they continued to receive *heshima* from their urban partners, whether those were Swahili speakers, Omani Arabs, or Europeans. In 1837, however, Mombasa became formally part of the Busaidi Sultanate, a change that altered long-standing practices of *heshima* and *kore*.

As scholars have well documented, the Busaidi era was a period of intensive global integration during which East Africa's interior became more directly connected to the Indian Ocean economy. Long-distance caravans flocked from far and wide into East Africa's interior, reaching the Congo Basin by the second half of the 1800s. Consumer demands for piano keys and billiard balls in industrializing countries in Europe and North America fueled East Africa's ivory trade. East African gum copal proved to be the ideal resin for varnishing wooden furniture in factories as far afield as Salem, Massachusetts, as chapter 3 noted. On the Zanzibar Archipelago and East Africa's mainland, the Busaidi established plantations where enslaved laborers grew cloves and other globally exported cash crops. These new trading connections granted communities in East Africa's interior even greater access to imported goods such as beads, wire, textiles, and guns, ushering manifold social and cultural transformations among different inland societies.[3]

For many living in Mijikenda-speaking villages, this moment of growing global connections was characterized foremost by the Busaidi's movement away from established norms of *heshima* and *kore*. As the previous chapter delineated, Mijikenda speakers had long played a leading role in shaping Mombasa's maritime politics. Inland representatives traveled to Muscat for diplomatic missions while the Portuguese described Mombasa as a port city in the land of the Mijikenda. Inland communities' participation in East Africa's oceanic connections began to change under the Busaidi, however. Slavery became more central to the region's economy, and transformations in trading practices—from its financing, to the merchants participating in trade, to the trade routes themselves—undermined Mijikenda

116   FROM MIJIKENDA CITY TO BUSAIDI BACKWATER

speakers' position as a gateway society mediating the flow of goods between coast and interior. In chronicling these changes, this chapter offers an inland view of a transformative period in East Africa's history, seen through the lens of Mijikenda speakers' most important strategies for participating in oceanic trade and politics.

MOMBASA, THE MAZRUI, AND THE POLITICS OF URBAN-TO-RURAL TRIBUTE

As we saw in the previous chapter, urban-to-rural textile tributes were a key feature of politics in Mombasa. From the viewpoint of foreigners like the Portuguese, tributes were simply transactional matters that enabled them to purchase the loyalties of leaders of inland constituencies. For instance, when the Portuguese regained control of Fort Jesus in 1728, the general overseeing the imperial venture violated "long-standing custom" by failing to send any textiles to the mainland. Communities on the mainland were "reluctant to come and swear obedience" to Fort Jesus as a result. The general quickly reversed course, realizing that peace on the island and access to trade goods were contingent on these gifts. Shortly after sending textiles to the mainland as tribute, three Musungulo leaders arrived in Mombasa promising their "obedience."[4] But as much as the Portuguese needed to obtain their inland partners' cooperation, these alliances would go on only so long as they continued to supply the mainland with cloth.

The directional flow of such tributes, from the urban port to its interior, contrasts with a characteristic rural dependency. In Mombasa's case, global empires and maritime merchants were deferential to smaller, inland-oriented communities. Furthermore, the tributes themselves demonstrated Mijikenda speakers' relative autonomy from their partners in the port city. Although they built allegiances with Mombasa's controlling authorities, different Mijikenda-speaking groups also readily shifted their affiliations at their own will. In this way, they showed that they were never fully beholden to the Portuguese, Omanis, or any other maritime powers with whom they affiliated. To further explore the nature of these relationships, let's turn to the mainland's role in Mombasa's politics.

Although they maintained a degree of independence from Mombasa, Mijikenda speakers still played an important role in the town's politics, beyond their functions as military allies and trading partners. As mentioned in the previous chapter, Portuguese records from as early as 1610 reported that each time prominent "Musungulos" visited Mombasa, the town's leader was obligated to provide them with food and cloth.[5] These obligations applied in other coastal towns within Mombasa's larger orbit. Vumba Kuu, a small Swahili-speaking town located around the modern border of Kenya and Tanzania, offers a useful illustration. Vumba's oral traditions recount that whenever a new sultan was enthroned, the town would invite representatives from Mombasa, along with neighboring Digo and Segeju communities, for feasts and entertainment. The attending Digo and

Segeju elders were given huge quantities of cloth, amounting to "two thousand ells"—approximately three thousand feet—in return for their participation.[6] Even as control over the coast shifted from Portuguese to Omani authorities, these expectations continued. Whenever inland leaders came to Mombasa for "public business," the town's Omani governors were beholden to host and entertain them with feasts, dances, and gifts.[7] In some Mijikenda settlements, a special liaison called *mwana njira* ("child of the path") acted as an agent or go-between with Mombasa's government.[8]

A brief overview of Mombasa under the Mazrui dynasty of Oman (ca. 1730s–1837) helps to situate the enduring significance of town-interior affiliation strategies. After Oman retook control of Mombasa at the end of 1729, the imam appointed a governor (*liwali* in Swahili) to oversee the city. Rivalries between local constituencies undermined the authority of the first few governors, ultimately leading to the appointment of Muhammad bin Uthman al-Mazrui, who became *liwali* sometime after 1735.[9] For the next century, he and his descendants oversaw the city. The Mazrui initially sent annual tributes back to Muscat, but as Saif bin Sultan II's power waned, they became more and more independent. By the 1740s, the Busaidi dynasty assumed control of the Imamate from the traditional ruling dynasty, the Yarubi. However, the Mazrui refused to recognize Busaidi authority. This meant Mombasa quickly found itself a port city under the governorship of an Omani dynasty but without any formal political ties to Oman.[10] The decoupling of the Mazrui from Oman's political leadership made them heavily reliant on different constituencies in Mombasa. Rather than representing foreign overlords, they had to enculturate themselves into Mombasa's social fabric. The Mazrui learned to speak Swahili, married into local families, and adopted the locally practiced branch of Sunni Islam.[11] They also invested heavily in relationships with Mombasa's political elites, especially the members of the two loosely organized political confederations known collectively as the Twelve Tribes (*Thenashara Taifa* in Swahili).

The Twelve Tribes consisted of two rival political factions, the *Thelatha Taifa* (Three Tribes) and *Tisa Taifa* (Nine Tribes), each of which represented different locations around Mombasa. F. J. Berg has proposed that these confederations formed amid disruptions on the East African coast during the sixteenth century, as newcomers incorporated themselves into Mombasa's social fabric following migrations from northern Swahili towns. After 1593, Estado da Índia delegated the administration of Mombasa to the town's rivals from Malindi. In this context, the confederations provided Mombasa's elites with a degree of local political autonomy under foreign rule.[12]

One of the Twelve Tribes' key advantages was that they had established partnerships with neighboring inland communities. According to historical traditions, each group within the *Thelatha Taifa* and *Tisa Taifa* had formalized tributary relationships with specific Mijikenda subgroups that were made meaningful through practices like gift exchanges.[13] These partnerships sustained Mombasa's population

118   FROM MIJIKENDA CITY TO BUSAIDI BACKWATER

amid the political shifts, conflicts, and warfare that affected the town into the nineteenth century.[14] Alliances between Mijikenda groups and various constituencies in Mombasa meant not only military support but also access to foods, trade commodities, and, in some cases, safe refuge.[15] For instance, recall from the previous chapter that during Oman's siege of Mombasa, Portuguese officers who sheltered in Fort Jesus relied on Mwinyi Chambe (a member of the *Thelatha Taifa*) to broker their arrangement to receive provisions from Chonyi. As was the case in this episode, inland communities expected to receive tributes from their partners in Mombasa in return for continued support, including from Mazrui governors by the eighteenth century. These relationships were unquestionably transactional, and members of Mijikenda communities had a considerable say in the terms of the contract.

People living in Mijikenda villages were not just Mombasa's trading partners and military allies. Through political affiliations and tributes, they helped establish the legitimacy of governing authorities in Mombasa and other coastal towns. They maintained these relationships at their own will. The next section considers how Mijikenda speakers understood their relationship with Mombasa's elites and various foreign interlocutors, focusing on the rituals of honor called *heshima* that went along with the cloth tributes.

DEMANDING HONOR: INLAND UNDERSTANDINGS OF TRIBUTES AS AUTONOMY

While the earliest records of Mijikenda speakers' interactions with Mombasa give only a vague sense of the meanings that they assigned to these urban-to-rural tributes, documentary records from the mid-nineteenth century offer a more fine-grained view of these exchanges. When read with the longer role of textiles in Mombasa's politics in mind, the records illuminate how tributes constituted Mijikenda speakers' autonomy from the port city. The most detailed accounts of these practices appear in the writings of Johann Ludwig Krapf, a German missionary who spent close to a decade living in the Mombasa region while proselytizing for the Church Missionary Society of England. When Krapf arrived in Mombasa in 1844, he learned of a practice that he would need to adhere to while traveling on the mainland, called *heshima* in Swahili and *eshima* or *ishima* in Mijikenda languages. From conversations in Mombasa, Krapf learned that this practice referred to displays of honor "connected with the exchange of presents," which acted as "marks of good recognition" when traveling on the mainland.[16] Krapf soon witnessed the practice of *heshima* firsthand when he visited Mombasa's mainland.

After traveling up Tudor Creek by boat, Krapf and his party reached Rabai, one of the nearest Mijikenda-speaking settlements to Mombasa. From there, they traversed forested footpaths, eventually reaching the outermost gate of the settlement of Ribe, where they were instructed to wait for a welcome party. Before long,

FROM MIJIKENDA CITY TO BUSAIDI BACKWATER   119

a band of men emerged from the forest and "displayed their *heshima*," a performance consisting of "shouting, dancing, brandishing their swords and bows." They then led the missionary into the village to the backdrop of shrieks and war yelps until the entire village congregated around him. After this performance, Krapf was taken into the house of a village leader. Assuming the missionary was a merchant, he was expected to offer his own *heshima* in the form of gifts.[17] For coastal merchants, the number of gifts expected as *heshima* varied according to the value of the goods they carried as trade articles. Once the merchants had offered appropriate tribute, they were allowed safe passage through the area, accompanied by a local guide or escort.[18] These rituals were a necessary component of trade practices inland from the coast, which "all the great merchants" adhered to regardless of their status in Mombasa.[19] According to Krapf, if merchants did not participate in the ritual or refused to offer the proper amount of tribute to their inland partners, they were "liable to be robbed."[20]

A brief detour into the meaning of the word *heshima* in Swahili and Mijikenda offers some insights into the different ways that people in coastal East Africa understood these rituals. *Heshima* is an Arabic loanword in Swahili that originally meant "diffidence, timidity, or shame" in Arabic.[21] Coastal East Africans altered the original meaning of the root, reinterpreting the word as both a noun and verb that meant "honor" and "to honor." *Heshima*, according to Krapf's Swahili dictionary, was "rendered by giving a present of respect." This was expressed very directly in the word's verbal form, -*heshimu*, which meant "to respect" or to honor a person "by giving him a present."[22] Most scholarship on *heshima* on the Swahili coast has emphasized how this form of honor operated alongside concepts of social rank and etiquette.[23] In Swahili towns during the nineteenth century, the term *heshima* articulated the "power and fear associated with holding honor," made meaningful through the power that coastal patricians held over slaves and other dependents.[24] A person demonstrated that they possessed honor by acting with behaviors and virtues appropriate to their station in life. In the case of an enslaved person, *heshima* meant showing proper deference and respect to coastal elites. Wealthy coastal patricians, meanwhile, established their honor through proper patronage.[25]

The conceptual links between honor, diffidence, and timidity make sense when viewing *heshima* as a facet of public reputation that was actualized in the relationship between Swahili elites and their dependents. However, taking the term out of a strictly Swahili context puts the relationship between honor and diffidence in an entirely different light. By offering *heshima* in the form of gifts and tributes, traders and travelers in Mombasa's interior honored inland leaders and made known their deference to local authorities. The *heshima* that coastal traders received in return—which consisted of dance performances and shouting—was, by contrast, embedded with gestures to the martial capacities of their hosts.[26] Visiting merchants assumed positions of diffidence or timidity in these rituals, even as the performances of *heshima* occurred under the auspices of mutual respect. Echoing

Portuguese portrayals of Mombasa as a port city in the land of the Mijikenda, the *heshima* rituals affirmed inland authority in the region, with textiles being their key signature.

Heshima is probably an old loanword in both Swahili and Mijikenda. While most Arabic loaning in Swahili occurred during the eighteenth and nineteenth centuries, the phonological shape of *heshima* in Mijikenda dialects indicates that it may date to an earlier period of loaning.[27] The sound "h" was not part of the phonemic inventory in proto-Mijikenda, but it occurs in modern dialects as a reflex of the proto-Sabaki phonemes *t and *p. Their pronunciation of the loanword (*eshima* or *ishima*) suggests that speakers borrowed the word before these sound changes to create the modern sound "h" occurred in Mijikenda languages.[28] Rather than adapting a foreign sound (in Arabic ḥ or ح), early speakers of Mijikenda dropped it entirely from the loanword. The same linguistic code affects one additional Swahili-Arabic loanword in Mijikenda: *ḥasa:ba* (Swahili *-hesabu*), meaning "to count," which speakers of Mijikenda dialects attest as *-esabu* or *-isabu*. The possibility that these two terms date to the same period of loaning seems to indicate that the custom of offering inland communities "honor" developed alongside trading practices.[29]

While the evidence does not allow us to determine whether the cloth payments from the Portuguese era were also called *heshima*, earlier records do clearly demonstrate that similar transfers of gifts and tributes from Mombasa to the mainland predate Krapf's writings by at least several centuries. These shows of hospitality were reciprocal but also contractual. To establish a partnership in the mid-nineteenth century, representatives from the Twelve Tribes paid a set fee of six hundred dollars, which was divided among local homestead heads. For this fee, traders from Mombasa were given food and some commercial benefits when traveling inland from the city with the expectation that they would provide gifts in cloth on each visit. In turn, Swahili merchants gave their inland partners food, lodging, and protection when visiting Mombasa.[30] These town-mainland alliances are sometimes portrayed as patron-client relationships in which the Mombasa groups are the senior partners.[31] But if we consider these relationships in light of *heshima* rituals it becomes possible to imagine how Mijikenda speakers understood these arrangements not simply as a way to command honor and conduct trade, but as a strategy for asserting their autonomy from the town.

Krapf's commentaries make clear that Mijikenda-speaking communities dictated the terms of these arrangements. Everyone in Mombasa, "even the governor," according to Krapf, had to "submit to this custom" of giving *heshima* to communities on the mainland. To Krapf this indicated that Mijikenda communities "consider[ed] themselves entirely independent" from coastal authorities who were obligated to "pay them tribute if not in name."[32] *Heshima* ensured that Mijikenda speakers would be treated with respect when visiting Mombasa. Furthermore, the rituals enabled inland communities to tightly control the flow of goods and people between Mombasa and the interior (and vice versa).[33] Even as Mijikenda communities partnered with some of the most formidable political entities in the Indian Ocean, they never considered themselves to be dependent on or beholden to the authority of any person, city, or larger polity. By demanding that Mombasa's merchants and leaders showed them deference and provided them with regular tributes, they continually affirmed their autonomy from the town's governing authorities. Rural dependencies they were not.

THE RISE OF THE BUSAIDI AND THE SHIFTING TIDES OF WESTERN INDIAN OCEAN POLITICS

Whenever foreign powers arrived in Mombasa, they adopted existing practices of urban-to-rural tribute to cement their relationships with the mainland. In 1824, for instance, the British briefly established a protectorate at Mombasa at the Mazrui's urging. Just a year later, Mombasa installed a new *liwali* (governor), and the Mazrui used this opportunity to ensure that the British would be responsible for paying tributes to the mainland. They invited representatives from more than twenty inland settlements to Mombasa, informing them that "the island and country of Mombasa belongs to the king of England and it was now governed by the English governor."[34] The Mazrui governor instructed James Emery—the British lieutenant overseeing Mombasa—to pay each of the inland representatives in textiles, signifying to all in attendance that the British were now responsible for maintaining these tribute relationships.[35] Like the Portuguese and Omanis before him, Emery was enculturated into established tribute practices, providing the Mijikenda representatives with cloth tributes to demonstrate the British navy's desire to affiliate with communities on the mainland.

The British navy reached Mombasa against the backdrop of major political changes in East Africa and the western Indian Ocean. When the Busaidi took over Oman in the 1740s, their navy was decimated. As a result, the Mazrui maintained control over Mombasa without any challenges from Muscat. But over the course of the 1760s and 1770s, Muscat became one of the most important commercial ports in the western Indian Ocean, operating at the center of a nexus connecting Persia, India, and the Red Sea.[36] The Busaidi also maintained spheres of influence on Kilwa and Zanzibar, the latter town increasingly becoming a focal point of their nascent empire. However, Mombasa remained out of their reach.

The Omanis considered Mombasa key to controlling commerce in East Africa, but Mijikenda communities stood in the way of these aims. According to the Busaidi dynasty's own chronicles, Hamad bin Said (the leader of Oman from 1784–1792) aspired to gain control of two port cities in his lifetime: Mombasa and Bombay. Mindful of Oman's long history with Mombasa, he reportedly told an

122 FROM MIJIKENDA CITY TO BUSAIDI BACKWATER

aide that gaining control of the town would be a major challenge because its "fort is strong, and it is held by the terrible Wanika."[37] In Hamad bin Said's estimation, although the Mazrui governors occupied Fort Jesus, communities on the mainland held the town's fate in their hands. He had never traveled to the city, but small communities living in the mainland certainly shaped the political world that he imagined and aspired to control.

The Omani sultan had good reason to fear Mombasa's "terrible Wanika." As in prior eras, Mijikenda speakers functioned as the Mazrui's soldiers and supporters in Mombasa and beyond, with cloth and *heshima* forming the backbone of their partnerships. During the eighteenth century, Mombasa's sphere of influence included most of the coast of modern Kenya, stretching from Ras Ngomeni (to the north of Malindi) to Pangani (in present-day northeastern Tanzania) and at times including parts of the Lamu Archipelago in northern Kenya.[38] The Mazrui also controlled the key provisioning point of Pemba Island, which provided relief against intermittent droughts. In Muscat, Busaidi leaders were clearly aware of the critical role that Mijikenda speakers had played on the East African coast for centuries. Hamad bin Said never achieved his goal of controlling Mombasa. However, Muscat's growing political and commercial strength by the start of the nineteenth century put his successors in a position to finally make a play for the town.

During the early nineteenth century, the Omani dynasty slowly began exerting influence on towns along the northern Swahili coast. In 1813, representatives from Lamu invited Oman to help protect the town after they defeated a joint alliance of Mombasa and Pate, driving the Mazrui-appointed governors from the Lamu Archipelago.[39] From that point, the Busaidi began encroaching on Mombasa's larger sphere of influence in a series of small wars and conflicts that lasted more than two decades. In 1823, the Busaidi took control of Pemba after defeating the famed military leader Mbaruk Mazrui and a contingent of Mijikenda soldiers serving him on the island.[40] Losing Pemba was a turning point. Soon after, the Mazrui looked to the British navy for assistance, hoping that a protectorate at Mombasa would prevent Busaidi aggression against the town.

The informal protectorate was short lived, however. At the end of July 1826, the British navy left Mombasa following a pressure campaign by allies of Said bin Sultan al-Busaidi (the sultan of Oman, honorifically Seyyid Said), which persuaded British governors in India to not extend formal protection over the town. Within eighteen months, the Busaidi initiated the first of three major campaigns in Mombasa. And in 1837, they finally pushed the Mazrui out of the city after imposing an economic blockade on the port, straining the local alliances that formed the basis of Mazrui governance.[41]

The rivalry between the Busaidi and Mazrui dynasties illuminates the shifting tides of commerce and politics in the western Indian Ocean during the nineteenth century. The Mazrui invested heavily in local relationships. Their goal, as historian Fahad Bishara has argued, was to maintain their place "as rulers of independent port cities" like Mombasa. The Busaidi, by contrast, endeavored to monopolize commerce in East Africa and southern Arabia by controlling the most significant ports in both regions.[42] Thus, the confrontations between the Mazrui and Busaidi in Mombasa represented a turning point in the coast's history whereby a network of loosely linked towns, which thrived by maintaining strong ties with their interiors, were subsumed into an oceanic empire. All of Mombasa's constituencies, including their Mijikenda-speaking allies, were folded into a commercial empire with new goals, technologies, and foci. The Busaidi Sultanate's rise altered the direction of commerce in East Africa, introducing new financial arrangements based on credit and foreign capital.[43] On a local level, these changes altered the nature of Mombasa's relationship with its mainland. Mijikenda speakers slowly lost their ability to influence the town's trading relationships and politics using established strategies like *heshima*.

While norms of honor and reciprocity had structured town-interior relationships in the past, Mijikenda-speaking communities became marginalized in Mombasa's politics under Busaidi rule. For the remainder of this chapter, I will examine how Mijikenda communities understood these changes. In some ways, the Busaidi's ascension represented a profound departure from the earlier forms of interaction between town and interior that stretched back centuries. Under Busaidi rule, Zanzibar became East Africa's main commercial capital while the adjacent Mrima coast emerged as its primary supply land.[44] Furthermore, the capitalization of commerce transformed trading networks in East Africa's interior. Large-scale caravans financed with lines of foreign credit replaced older trade parties like *charo*. For many Mijikenda speakers, integration into world markets manifested as a slow erosion of established norms of honor and reciprocity. They articulated these changes as a betrayal of *heshima*.

SLAVERY AND THE SHIFTING BALANCE BETWEEN HONOR AND DEBT IN BUSAIDI MOMBASA

When the Busaidi dynasty took control of Mombasa in 1837, the larger region was experiencing a famine that was especially harsh for communities on the mainland. Famines, or *ndzala* in Mijikenda, were not atypical in the region. Although Mijikenda speakers produced and traded in food goods, they also faced intermittent food insecurity.[45] Food shortages could force people to relocate to new areas, where they adopted junior roles as dependent outsiders in exchange for food and refuge. During the worst *ndzala*, inland homestead heads pawned junior dependents in Mombasa in exchange for food.[46] These pawning arrangements followed preestablished norms. After each *ndzala*, homestead heads would travel to Mombasa to reclaim their pawns. Inland homestead heads had long practiced such exchanges with the Mazrui governors. However, at the end of the famine of 1836–1837, Mombasa had a new government. When inland homestead heads traveled to Mombasa

124 FROM MIJIKENDA CITY TO BUSAIDI BACKWATER

at the end of this *ndzala*, they found that the town's new authorities had sent some of the pawns to Arabia as slaves.[47]

This section takes the famine and the subsequent rise of the Busaidi in Mombasa as entry points to explore changes in ideas about honor (*heshima*) and debt (*kore*) from the 1830s to 1850s. Stories about Arab traders kidnapping Mijikenda children during famines are common tropes in oral traditions. In the 1970s, Mijikenda elders told Spear many stories about late nineteenth-century famines, during which people were lured onto dhows by the promise of food but were instead abducted and taken away into slavery.[48] When Krapf reached Mombasa in the 1840s, he heard similar stories, including ones about the "great famine" of 1836–1837. Prior to this famine, Mijikenda trading parties made near-daily visits to Mombasa.[49] However, after 1837, some inland communities viewed Mombasa with "aversion and dread," according to Krapf. Instead, Mijikenda traders began redirecting their commercial activities to trade centers at Mtsanganyiko and Takaungu, where the Mazrui relocated after the Busaidi drove them out of Mombasa.[50]

To be clear, I do not know whether the famine of 1836–1837 was the cataclysmic moment Krapf claimed, or whether some pawns being permanently enslaved was entirely unprecedented. Instead, I am interested in the ways these stories about pawns and social debts, honor, and betrayal resonated with documented changes from this same historical moment. The famine overlapped with the exponential growth of coastal East Africa's plantation economy, meaning enslaved people, runaways, and other vulnerable people were increasingly numerous in and around Mombasa. The Busaidi government continued practices of *heshima*, but they also cut into Mijikenda speakers' control over inland trade goods. Entangled stories of *heshima* and *kore*, thus, direct us to local understandings of the Mombasa region's incorporation into the Busaidi's oceanic empire, and Mijikenda speakers' changing influence in the region.

The ideas about honor and debt articulated in the famine of 1836–1837 were closely linked to the practice of pawning junior dependents. Pawning—or the "transfer of 'rights in persons'"—was a widespread and ancient practice in the Mombasa region. Homestead heads held rights over the junior members of their extended family. They could exchange their dependents' rights to settle debts, to obtain provisions during famines, and to pay compensation for crimes.[51] Speakers of Mijikenda languages called these exchanges *kore*, a term derived from the proto-Bantu word *-kódè*, which meant "captive." Ancient speech communities in equatorial Africa created this word from the verb *-kód-*, meaning "touch, seize." Marcos de Almeida has shown that "by adding the final *-e, speakers shifted the perspective from the process to the result of the action of touching or seizing." Based on this derivation and analysis of comparative lexical materials, de Almeida argues that *-kódè* represented a "captive seized for settling debts and offenses between local groups."[52] The meaning "captive" has remained relatively stable on

FROM MIJIKENDA CITY TO BUSAIDI BACKWATER   125

the East African coast over time based on the word's distribution in other Sabaki and Northeast Coast languages.[53]

Like their distant linguistic ancestors, Mijikenda speakers situated *kore* within the interpersonal realm. They used the word for things like transferring a junior family member to another lineage as "compensation" or "blood money," often as part of the apparatus of judicial oaths (*virapho*) described in chapter 2.[54] People also sometimes exchanged *kore* across sociolinguistic communities. Such was the case in pawning during famines or as compensation for a crime or unpaid debts.[55] But ultimately, *kore* operated less as a category of person violently seized or captured than as a person transferred according to established social codes and judicial procedures.

A brief turn to linguistic evidence allows us to contrast *kore* to other relationships of dependency in Mijikenda languages, illustrating how people viewed practices like pawning during food shortages. Notably, many of the common terms that describe forms of slavery in Mijikenda are loanwords from Swahili. For instance, Mijikenda speakers borrowed words meaning "runaway slave" (*mtoro*), "captives" (*mateka*), and "slave" (*mtumwa*).[56] These borrowed words offer evidence of expanding forms of inequality in the Mombasa region and allow us to parse the differences between *kore* and the other meanings introduced into Mijikenda languages during more recent historical periods. For instance, both *mateka* and *kore* described temporary states of bondage, such as being a "captive," but with marked differences. *Mateka*, which was derived from a verb meaning "to plunder," was applied to war captives or hostages, encompassing a form of marginality that was both violent and lacking in personal connections.[57] *Kore*, by contrast, existed between people with established relationships. Furthermore, it was contractual in nature, as is evident in its usage for settling debts or providing compensation.[58] Even though those transferring their junior dependents as *kore* ultimately had no control over those people's fates, in most instances there remained the possibility of reobtaining their rights later.

The linguistic picture reflects the minimal nature of slave raiding in Mombasa's interior prior to the nineteenth century. While early Swahili towns supplied enslaved captives for other parts of the Indian Ocean, most enslaved people were used locally as unequally incorporated dependents. In the sixteenth and seventeenth centuries, Hadhrami merchants living in the Lamu Archipelago started shipping captives from Madagascar to the Comoros Islands and ports in the Red Sea and the Persian Gulf. In towns like Mombasa and Zanzibar, the Portuguese forced enslaved people to work in their forts and as soldiers. But imperial merchants in Portuguese ports generally did not trade slaves to other parts of the Indian Ocean.[59] Historical records indicate that Mijikenda speakers did sometimes sell captives from the interior in Mombasa and capture runaways on behalf of their partners in the town.[60] More often, however, European accounts speak to Mombasa as a place with great potential for the slave trade but minimal actual trade in enslaved captives. In 1773, a French official lamented that Mombasa could "furnish up to six thousand slaves" annually but that the town's merchants preferred to limit their trade with Europeans to ivory, copal, and ambergris.[61] Instead, the Mazrui exploited enslaved people's labor for local public works projects and their militaries while also keeping some enslaved women as concubines.[62]

The role of slavery in East African society changed dramatically by the middle of the nineteenth century. In the 1820s, coastal patricians started investing in large-scale plantations where they grew crops like cloves, coconuts, and sugar.[63] The growing global demands for these cash crops created new markets for enslaved laborers, most of whom were captured in the interior of eastern and southern Africa and violently transported to coastal plantations.[64] While Mijikenda speakers were generally not forced into labor on coastal plantations, the "servile labour force" in nineteenth-century coastal East Africa was far more varied than just plantation slavery. Clients, debtors, and younger members of homesteads were increasingly vulnerable to being enslaved.[65] As a result, kore shifted from an occasional practice rooted in ideas about obligation and proper procedure to a more permanent form of "debt imprisonment."

Up until the mid-1800s, merchants from Mombasa had occasionally used debt imprisonment as a safeguard for their trade relationships with rural partners. According to Krapf, people seized kore "on account of the debt of another countryman or of a relation who owes the taker some money, but has not yet paid him." Once the debt was repaid, the kore was then returned to their family member.[66] Although debt imprisonment was, by Krapf's reckoning, "the only power and means which the government of Mombas[a] possesse[d] to help their subjects to the recovery of their money," it rarely utilized it in practice. By occasionally seizing kore, Mombasa's merchants could provide a "check" against unfair terms from their inland partners. However, in the long run, these practices would not "satisfactorily secure the position of the merchants."[67] As Methodist missionary Charles New similarly expressed, "Even the short-sighted slave-owner of the coast sees that the freedom of the Wanika [Mijikenda], is far more advantageous to him than it would be to capture and enslave them." As New saw it, Mijikenda communities were more valuable as allies than as captives for coastal merchants since they provided trade goods and assistance in warfare.[68]

The missionaries' observations reflect the ways that heshima and kore were mutually constitutive practices. The ideology of heshima provided a way for Mijikenda communities to hold the government in Mombasa accountable for its actions. Kore, meanwhile, enabled Mombasa's merchant class to assure fair terms in trade with inland communities by occasionally claiming debt captives as bargaining chips. This interplay continued after the Busaidi took control of Mombasa, as is evidenced in the writings of Krapf and New, both of whom arrived in the region only after the Mazrui's overthrow. At the same time, their writings suggest that the practice of debt imprisonment was becoming increasingly common. By the 1840s, if a person owed a debt, creditors in Mombasa would seize the first person they met from the interior and imprison them "until the relatives of the prisoner's tribe pay off the debt, or until they can induce the original debtor, to settle his affairs at Mombas[a]."[69] While earlier practices of *kore* were based around preexisting relationships between debtors and creditors, the later forms of debt imprisonment and pawning lacked these intimacies.[70] This shift from pawning to debt imprisonment was a departure from the established notions of accountability and honor that had long undergirded town-inland relationships.

It is important to remember that commentaries like Krapf's are filtered through the eyes of missionaries, who, in many cases, flattened the diverse range of dependent relationships described above into "slavery." Justin Willis points out that "what Krapf saw as a transformation wrought by the Busaidi was a possibility always present in this type of relationship, the terms of which may well have varied from one individual to the next."[71] Moreover, inland homestead heads had a vested interest in portraying Mombasa as a dangerous place. Such portrayals helped them thwart the free movement of people from rural communities into the city. By limiting contact with Mombasa, wealthy men could maintain their hold on economic partnerships with their counterparts in town. Younger women and men sometimes subverted these controls by fleeing from their homesteads to join new patronage networks in Mombasa. In doing so, they could avoid potential vulnerabilities that arose during famines or due to their family member's or patron's debts. Mobility gave dependent members of inland homesteads—especially younger women—a strategy for controlling their own labor. Thus, the relational crises that observers like Krapf described as "slavery" were also connected to larger gendered and generational disputes.[72]

Ultimately, anecdotes about debt imprisonment and changes in *kore* draw attention to continuing insecurities and internal challenges for Mijikenda communities that were amplified by political and economic changes in Mombasa during the 1830s and after. Tracing Mombasa's history through the concepts of *kore* and *heshima* contextualizes memories of the "great famine" of 1836–1837. It helps us to see the famine not as a single cataclysmic event but as a moment that marked the start of the erosion of older practices bound by interlinked ideas about mutual debt and honor. The Busaidi governors continued to offer their inland neighbors *heshima*, at least intermittently, after the famine. I am less concerned with whether these practices were becoming less prominent than with the ways that ideas about honor and mutual respect were embedded in local understandings of East Africa's shifting political and commercial terrain, as is evident in oral traditions, missionaries' accounts, and the Mazrui's own chronicles.[73] By the mid-nineteenth century, Mombasa was becoming less of a port city set in the land of the Mijikenda.

128   FROM MIJIKENDA CITY TO BUSAIDI BACKWATER

Yet Mijikenda speakers' understandings of their autonomy from the town persisted, even amid these transformations.

THE LIMITS OF OMANI AUTHORITY IN MOMBASA'S INTERIOR

In March 1853, Seyyid Said, the sultan of Oman and Zanzibar, traveled to Mombasa to meet with the leaders of several Mijikenda constituencies. This meeting followed a surge of French interest in East Africa, including rumors that the French backed a regime change on Zanzibar.[74] For Seyyid Said, it provided an opportunity to assess and affirm his support in Mombasa and the surrounding region. Krapf also attended this meeting and provided a report on the gathering for Henry Venn, the secretary of the Church Missionary Society. According to Krapf's report, Seyyid Said

> assembled all the chiefs of all the Wanika [Mijikenda] tribes, & asked them in earnest whether they were his subjects or whether they were independent of him. They all declared boisterously that he was their father, their king, that their country and everything belonged to him.[75]

Krapf was perplexed by this declaration. By proclaiming their allegiance to Seyyid Said, the Mijikenda representatives submitted their land and liberty to Oman and Zanzibar. They were, he claimed, "unaware of the consequences" as "the whole Kinika [Mijikenda] land belongs from that day to the Imam of Muscat."[76] While Krapf found this show of allegiance perplexing he also questioned whether this pledge had any actual implications, noting that "the Imam has demanded no tribute from them, so that everything remained in the former state." Instead, Seyyid Said was "content with the nominal allegiance."[77] Johannes Rebmann, Krapf's missionary partner at Rabai, also attended the meeting, and his account reflected similar sentiments. The inland leaders gave their allegiance to Seyyid Said, he explained, "without any show of resistance well knowing that their independence would remain just the same which it was before, as long as no tribute was demanded from them."[78]

The two missionaries' descriptions of this meeting offer a good illustration of how communities adjacent to Mombasa viewed their relationship to the town. In the meeting, the Omani sultan asked those assembled to acknowledge that they were his dependent subjects. The attendees were aware, however, that without any stipulations or exchanges—of either material goods like cloth or of *heshima*—the agreement was an empty gesture. Simply put, they did not see themselves as dependents of Seyyid Said or of any party in Mombasa since they were not required to offer any tributes. The inverse was also true: for centuries, Mombasa's political and merchant classes, both foreign and local, had sent regular tributes to Mijikenda-speaking communities. By offering this *heshima*, Swahili, Arabs, and Europeans assumed an intentionally deferential positioning from the perspectives of their inland partners.

The major transformations unfolding across East Africa's coast and interior during the nineteenth century are well documented in the literature. The development of the plantation economy on Zanzibar, Pemba, and mainland East Africa created a demand for captives from the interior of eastern and central Africa to work as forced laborers on the coast.[79] Some inland societies, like the Yao and Nyamwezi, capitalized on the changing commercial landscape by supplying ivory and enslaved captives for global markets. Through this "nexus of international trade" the interior of eastern and central Africa became integrated into the capitalist world system.[80] African consumers were not passive recipients in the face of these changes. Societies in East Africa's interior influenced global production and exchange by demanding and domesticating imported commodities to fit their own goals and needs.[81] In coastal towns like Pangani and Bagamoyo, the influx of people from the interior during the second half of the nineteenth century begat a remaking of urban citizenship.[82] Coastal traders did employ some Mijikenda speakers as caravan porters, and they continued to obtain goods like copal, copra, and foodstuffs from communities on the mainland.[83] But the Busaidi increasingly directed the focus of the long-distance caravan trade to towns along the Mrima coast, where economic "relationships were less concentrated on the local hinterland."[84]

Mijikenda-speaking communities felt the changes that followed the establishment of Busaidi authority differently than such well-known narratives of social and economic transformation depict. While ideas about generosity and obligation bound patrons and clients *within* coastal centers like Pangani, in Mombasa the politics of obligation extended far beyond the town itself. For centuries, reciprocity had formed the basis of relationships between Mombasa and its neighbors. Tributes undergirded trade partnerships and political and military alliances. The regular transfer of cloth textiles from the town to inland villages not only constituted a symbol of respect but also marked the continued autonomy of the gifts' recipients.

Even in the early years of Busaidi rule, Mijikenda communities held "rights of retaliation" against the Omani government, enabling them to retain control over their territory. As Krapf explained in 1844, although Seyyid Said claimed the region inland from Mombasa as his jurisdiction, they were "not dependent on the Imam." They, he continued, "are on good terms with him and the people of Mombas[a], as he gives them presents from time to time." However, Mijikenda communities maintained their independence from the government on Zanzibar by refusing to participate in transactions with coastal traders, in case "any wrong is committed" against them. In some instances, inland communities would go so far as entirely "closing their chief market places to the Mombassians."[85] By wielding these "rights of retaliation," Mijikenda groups retained a "collective strategy"

130 FROM MIJIKENDA CITY TO BUSAIDI BACKWATER

for ensuring that the Busaidi government respected them and did not violate the expectations of *heshima* and *kore*.[86]

Although *heshima* exchanges continued under Mombasa's new government, inland communities were much more ambivalent toward these partnerships. Contrasting attitudes toward the Mazrui and Busaidi, a French merchant who visited Mombasa in the 1840s wrote that Mijikenda leaders "only took account of orders given to them" by the Busaidi governor "if that was convenient for them." Following centuries of practice, "they never answered his call without having first received the customary piece of fabric."[87] Mijikenda-speaking communities had long counted on tributes to assert their autonomy from Mombasa. But the shift from Mazrui to Busaidi governance gradually eroded well-established reciprocal relationships and redirected control over inland trade networks into new hands. In part, this was the result of the economic focus of the sultanate. On Zanzibar, the Busaidi operated as a loosely organized trading empire with economic activities centered on long-distance caravans and coastal clove plantations worked by enslaved laborers. As a result, by the mid-nineteenth century, Mijikenda traders were increasingly marginalized within the very trade networks that they had helped to develop in the centuries prior.

The Busaidi's growing influence in East Africa did not overhaul connections between Mombasa and its adjacent mainland all at once. Seyyid Said's meeting with inland leaders in 1853 illuminates the unresolved nature of Oman's authority. Although the inland representatives declared that they were the dependent subjects of Seyyid Said and his government, he did not require that they offer any tributes or *heshima*. In many ways, the discordant perceptions of this agreement operate as a metaphor for Busaidi authority in the wider Mombasa region. The rise of Oman's East African empire helped spur the region's integration into emergent global markets. Inland from Mombasa, however, this integration existed alongside the slow erosion of older ideals and past practices.

. . .

In the mid-nineteenth century, East Africa's interior rapidly incorporated into the global economy. Paradoxically, the practices that had long undergirded Mijikenda speakers' participation within the Indian Ocean world were losing their strength. In concluding with this transformative moment in coastal East Africa's past, I do not wish to suggest that the rise of Zanzibar and the Omani empire destroyed Mijikenda speakers' connections to the Indian Ocean altogether. Rather, I want to highlight the ways that this period marked a major shift in their relationships with Mombasa, whereby shared practices with other oceanic societies became increasingly important. By the mid-nineteenth century, participation in coastal commerce increasingly required that people claim membership in urban Islamic society, as Jonathon Glassman has shown.[88] Like others living around nineteenth-century coastal towns, many members of Mijikenda communities pursued opportunities to participate in coastal commerce. Doing so meant discarding some practices that had long been central to their participation in oceanic trade and politics by embracing new religious identities, settlement patterns, and social relationships.

One example of Mijikenda speakers' changing relationship with coastal society was the growing number of Mijikenda Muslims during the second half of the nineteenth century. There is no concrete evidence of Islam being practiced within Mijikenda-speaking communities prior to the nineteenth century, despite their proximity to Mombasa and frequent interactions with Muslims. Some Mijikenda speakers had become Muslims at different points in the past, for sure. In these cases, however, they left their home communities and began new lives in Mombasa and other towns along the coast.[89] This began to change by the 1840s and 1850s, when some Digo-speaking elders living around Mtongwe—a settlement immediately across Kilindini Harbor, to Mombasa's southwest—converted to Islam. Over the next few decades, Digo speakers adopted Islam widely through interactions with Muslim traders from the coast. By the end of the nineteenth century, nearly all the communities to the south of Mombasa had some Muslim converts living in them. Islam was less popular among communities to Mombasa's north and west. Over a similar time frame, however, some Mijikenda converts formed new communities, in most cases moving away from their natal homes and founding settlements near coastal towns or around trading centers that clustered around overland caravan routes.[90] For the first time in Mombasa's history, Islam began to support relationships between members of inland communities and merchants from the coast.

Prior to the 1830s and 1840s, Mijikenda communities closely guarded interior trade routes, and coastal merchants seldom ventured far beyond Mombasa. To access trade goods and provisions from the interior, they relied on established support networks, undergirded by *heshima*. This changed later in the nineteenth century as inland trading centers became the main focal points for interior trade. While wealthy homestead heads had long overseen trading relationships with the coast, the growth of trading centers like Mtsangnyiko and Takaungu gave younger men opportunities to carve out their own spheres of influence by provisioning the Arab, Swahili, and European caravans that had begun traversing the interior.[91] Mijikenda speakers' ongoing participation in maritime trading networks now necessitated adopting a new religious identity, relocating to locales frequented by coastal traders, or supporting coastal caravans as porters. While Mombasa was once seen as a port city set in the land of the Mijikenda, by the mid-nineteenth century, the town's interior was increasingly incorporated into a different interactive sphere: the Busaidi's oceanic empire.

Conclusion

The oral traditions of many Mijikenda communities include a story about a group of elephant hunters settling Mombasa. The basic outline goes as follows: some hunters shot an elephant and tracked it to Mombasa, which was then not settled. They followed the elephant through the forest until it collapsed and died at a cave on the northeastern part of the island. They stayed there and feasted on the elephant's meat. But in time, the hunters realized that they could not grow crops on the island. So, without any other source of food, they abandoned Mombasa and returned to the mainland. This story is usually told to accompany traditions on the settlement of the coastal region during the mythical migration from Shungwaya. In some iterations, the hunters tracked other animals such as buffalo. In others, the Mijikenda hunters are accompanied by hunter-foragers who they called the Laa. Regardless of these minor differences, in every version one thing is consistent: the roving hunters abandon the coast and make their homes along the forested ridges inland from Mombasa.[1]

A Swahili manuscript on Mombasa's origins tells a similar story. In the Swahili narrative, Mombasa's original inhabitants were a mix of people, including migrants from Persia and the Hijaz who lived alongside hunter-foragers north of Mombasa Island. One day, the hunters saw an elephant and followed it until it collapsed on the island. Like the hunters in the Mijikenda story, they stayed on the island feasting on the elephant's meat. However, when finished, instead of abandoning Mombasa, they began exploring and discovered that Europeans were already living on the island. From there, the narrative explains Mombasa's partnerships with the Portuguese who had arrived as traders living at Fort Jesus. After starting as a story of elephant trackers discovering Mombasa, it quickly moves to narratives of oceanic trade and conflicts with Europeans and Omanis, finally culminating with the town's incorporation into the Busaidi Sultanate in the nineteenth century.[2]

CONCLUSION   133

I close this book by juxtaposing these two origin stories because of the vastly different ways that they orient our gaze, despite both featuring a tale of elephant trackers on Mombasa at their core. In the Swahili narrative, we're quickly swept into a rich tapestry of Indian Ocean connections featuring migrants from Persia and Mecca, and trade and conflicts with the oceanic empires of Portugal and Oman. The Mijikenda elephant hunting story does something different. Whether intentionally or not, the oral traditions explain a metaphorical turn inland *away* from Mombasa and its oceanic connections and *toward* more favorable environments immediately inland. If the Swahili narrative places Mombasa's origins within the familiar bounds of an outward-facing Indian Ocean history, the Mijikenda story invites the listener to imagine the littoral from an alternative, inland vantage point. Most importantly, it explains Mijikenda speakers' inland orientation as an intentional choice. It is easy to see connections and collaborations within the oceanic sphere as the result of choices and historical agency. This book has highlighted the ways that people might reject or participate selectively within these very same networks according to their own ambitions.

Over the previous five chapters, I have argued that Mombasa's maritime connections were contingent on its inland neighbor's particular modes of engagement with the norms and practices of the Indian Ocean. Moving away from a focus on diasporic traders and Islamic port cities, I've shown that Mombasa's global connections hinged on an array of developments in the interior. This included the circulation of medicinal ideas among inland societies, as well as material practices with textiles in forest clearings. Mombasa's global history was also shaped by Mijikenda speakers' use of rituals of honor and displays of martiality—which they articulated using an Arabic loanword—to demand tributes and articulate their autonomy from the port city. Stories about inland communities supplying trade goods like ivory and consuming imported goods like textiles make sense within conventional narratives of the Indian Ocean. But if we ask why inland agents acted as they did, then we must acknowledge that global trading patterns and politics were contingent on many things invisible from the perspective of a port: people in rural villages choosing to dress memorial posts for their ancestral spirits with strips of cloth, a healer's aspirations to obtain powerful medicines, or circulating knowledge between different social groups related to meeting places, rituals, or animal husbandry.

Inland developments loom large in Mombasa's history. Mijikenda-speaking groups acted at different moments as the town's suppliers, as its political and military allies, and as aggressors conducting raids on the island. As a result, urban merchants and elites had to regularly accommodate and appeal to their inland neighbors to obtain trade goods, provisions, and military support. Coastal urbanites and the town's foreign interlocutors often disparaged Mijikenda communities, calling them barbarians or bush folk. But they also understood that communities in the interior were critical to the port city's position as a leading commercial hub.

134   CONCLUSION

This book has focused on Mombasa, one node of an interconnected Indian Ocean. It is a specific case study, but I believe that it is not exceptional. People in many parts of the world and at different times in the past have participated in larger interactive spheres while also pursuing goals and interests dissonant to the dominant norms of those arenas. By reimaging what it meant to participate in the Indian Ocean world from the vantage point of Mombasa's immediate interior, I have highlighted the generative potential of developments that might seem out of harmony within a global history literature dominated by stories of cosmopolitan traders, port cities, and states and empires. People living in small, seemingly disconnected places could and did participate in global developments.[3] Not as an exploited periphery, but as active agents, capable of shaping larger-scale processes, even as they pursued goals rooted in their particular social or cultural milieu.

. . .

To conclude, let's take a brief detour away from East Africa and delve into secondary scholarship on three widely circulated Indian Ocean products—pepper, cotton textiles, and birds of paradise feathers—and the people that initiated their entry into large-scale networks. My aim is to draw focus to the people, places, and practices contributing to the movement of each product across and between different scales, from inland villages to port cities in different parts of the Indian Ocean. Together, these examples hint at the possibility of writing histories of large-scale connections while keeping the agency and ambitions of interior regions, villages, and small-scale societies at the center of the narrative.

VILLAGE ECONOMIES AND COTTON TEXTILES

Cotton textiles are synonymous with India's connections with global trade and thus offer a useful starting point. While much of the literature on Indian cottons adopts a large-scale focus—their circulation in Europe, Africa, and other parts of Asia, and their critical role in the Industrial Revolution—textile production started within much smaller, village-based economies. In preindustrial India, cotton spinners bought raw cotton directly from growers and sold it to people in weaving villages where textile production skills had been developed and passed down over generations. Women in peasant households did most of the processing work, cleaning raw cotton and spinning it into yarn before selling it to weavers who used cotton looms to turn the yarn into cloth textiles. Next, agents with established relationships with weaving households and villages purchased the textiles for finishing. Dyes made from indigo, turmeric, safflower, and madder, along with block prints and sketching, gave the finished textiles their colorful design patterns.[4] By the seventeenth and eighteenth centuries, finishing took place in specialized workshops near urban centers, which allowed merchants to cater designs to the consumer demands of external markets.[5] Eventually, the cotton textiles reached the ships of merchants who transported the cloth to locales across the world.

As the above sketch shows, village textile production was highly complex, implicating multiple actors and forms of expertise even within a single weaving village. Notably, those engaged in textile production did not play a direct role in trading the garments they produced.[6] However, they did use their skills to earn social and economic benefits, something evident in "tax reductions . . . grants of agricultural lands, privileges in temple rituals, or positions in temple administration" available to weaving villages by the fourteenth century.[7] While textile production was driven by weavers' goals within this particular milieu, once cotton textiles were taken out of the villages, they had a wide range of use values in the different locales to which they traveled. In addition to their most common use as adornments in India, cotton was also used for recordkeeping, mapmaking, and as decorations in the interiors of homes and royal courts.[8] In Southeast Asia, textiles—both locally produced and imported—were used for "curing diseases, death and other religious rights, the sanctification of icons, ceremonial and diplomatic exchanges, as well as the payment of services and taxes and the decoration of royal compounds."[9] As we've seen, Mijikenda speakers used textiles in initiations and various ritual contexts and as a form of tribute that undergirded their commercial and military partnerships with Mombasa.

Viewing the Indian Ocean's history from the life of an object, we can imagine a textile passing through various hands, from a weaver's loom to a healing ceremony in Indonesia or a forested glade in Mombasa's interior. A dhow's cargo hold or a port's storehouse would have been nodes within our textile's life cycle. But these spaces where it was touched by the hands of actors deemed sufficiently "global" were transitory. To fix our gaze solely on the maritime sphere erases other means by which people participated in and shaped transregional connections. Women processing cotton fibers in villages in India's interior were a critical part of circulations that spanned continents, even if they never interacted with characteristic spaces like a port city. By taking a different orientation within our sources, paying attention to participation strategies that are dissonant to the practices traditionally centered in narratives of the Indian Ocean, scholars might find that the macroregion's history can be as productively analyzed from the vantage point of a weaving village as it can from tracing the movements of diasporic merchants.

FROM THE FOREST SWIDDEN
TO THE "LAND OF PEPPER"

India's Malabar coast offers another compelling case study for thinking about smaller interior networks and Indian Ocean connections. Malabar is popularly known as the "land of pepper" due to the spice that fueled the region's connections to global trading circuits.

Historian Sebastian Prange's book *Monsoon Islam* is the most comprehensive study of the Malabar coast—and perhaps the best study of any single Indian Ocean region—masterfully tracing the role of ports, mosques, palaces, and the sea in the formation of the commercial, religious, and political milieu of port cities in southwest India.[10] Although the book spends only two sentences discussing Malabar's hinterland—the Western Ghats where pepper was procured—in a separate article, titled "Measuring by the Bushel," Prange delves into pepper production based on the sparse available evidence. The insights of that article—while remaining more suggestive than definitive—indicate the critical role of this "hinterland" in the making of Malabar's oceanic connections.

Premodern pepper cultivation unfolded across several spheres: among small-holding farmers who intermixed pepper in garden plots with bananas and coconuts, on larger monocultural plantations controlled by wealthy landowners, and in upland swiddens where forest dwellers cultivated spices and collected forest goods that ultimately reached coastal markets.[11] Malayali traders brokered exchanges between port cities and these different nodes of inland production. Spices did not move directly from the interior to the port but were instead, according to Prange, "assembled at trading locations further inland along roads, rivers or backwaters and only later transported to those markets." He concludes that this "intermediary sphere was sustained by the physical and social barriers that separated the land and society of Malabar's interior from the centres of international demand on its coast."[12] There's no doubt that Malabar's rise to a major region of the Indian Ocean was intimately connected to the development of shared religious, commercial, and political practices among Muslim merchants in coastal ports. But it also hinged on inland networks that had few direct interactions with the worlds of port cities connected by the Indian Ocean monsoon.

The people that first developed knowledge of pepper cultivation remain obscured from the Indian Ocean's history, despite pepper's centrality to Malabar's connections to this global macro-region. Pepper first grew as a wild, gathered product. Communities living in the forested Western Ghats were experts at "locating, gathering, drying, processing, and transporting" pepper to other parts of South Asia.[13] By the early centuries CE, some began cultivating pepper intentionally, incorporating it into their swidden plots along with plants like ginger and cardamom. These spices circulated alongside other forest products, including aromatic woods and resins that were similarly valued far beyond the forested Ghats.[14] Anthropologist Kathleen Morrison argues that early European visitors to South Asia misrecognized pepper and other forest products as "wild" commodities, erasing the people and knowledge behind their production and circulation in the process.[15] Historians have continued along this path, devoting little attention to the circulation of forest products between the uplands and coastal markets prior to their inauguration as "global" trade goods once they reach the port. The

CONCLUSION   137

labors, knowledge, and aspirations of people living in the interior pepper-producing regions remain obscure to global histories as a result.

TO SOUTHEAST ASIA: FOREST PRODUCTS
AND BIRD FEATHERS

There's perhaps no region where forest producers and products played a larger role in global maritime networks than Southeast Asia. For centuries, forest products like sandalwood oils, camphor, beeswax, and resins fueled Southeast Asia's connections to larger exchange networks.[16] Sandalwood oil, for instance, was used in India and China for artisanal purposes and as a medicinal aromatic. Much of the sandalwood reaching these places originated in Timor and then circulated through global transshipment hubs, first in the Srivijaya empire and later at port cities like Melaka. Like the resins, gums, and oils mentioned above, sandalwood was a product of the forests rather than of the sea. From one perspective, sandalwood and other forest products appear as little more than commodities on a list of trade goods, moving from a distant "periphery" to core trading cities. Once the forest goods enter the shipping holds of ocean-bound merchants, their story transforms from local to global. Yet forest products reached port cities through the actions of many other individuals, including forest experts who possessed the specialized knowledge necessary to identify and assemble the forest's bounties, and various agents who moved goods through complex local exchange networks. In most cases, these people had social ideas and community organization strategies quite different from those centered in studies of oceanic trade.[17]

Birds of paradise feathers, which originated in eastern Indonesia and Papua New Guinea, provide another rich illustration of the diverse social ideas and skills undergirding transregional trade. The birds' colorful plumage was valued widely in Indian Ocean ports, in Himalayan kingdoms, and in parts of medieval Europe. These circulations began not with merchants in transshipment hubs, but with skilled Papuan hunters. Hunting birds of paradise was no ad hoc matter. It took place annually when the birds visited the same forest clearings to mate. Knowledge of the preferred clearings and timing of mating rituals was passed down between generations of hunters who staked claims at specific mating trees. Hunters positioned themselves in the trees, waiting until the mating ritual commenced and then shot the birds using blunt arrows. After killing as many birds as possible, they had to prep them immediately on the spot so their skins dried with the colorful plumage intact. They did not develop these immense skills simply because birds of paradise feathers were export goods. Papuans themselves understood the feathers to have protective qualities. Warriors wore the birds' colorful plumage as headdresses when going into battle, and people also adorned themselves with feathers for wedding ceremonies and fertility rituals. As historian Leonard Andaya has

138   CONCLUSION

argued, birds of paradise feathers were not raw economic goods. Instead, the story of this globally circulating good must be understood within local Papuan contexts.[18] As was the case elsewhere, larger processes of global trade and cultural interactions grew out of the cultural ideas and skills of people largely invisible within much of the literature on transregional oceanic connections.

I offer these brief considerations—of bird feathers, sandalwood, pepper, and textiles—as entry points for rethinking histories of connections that spanned world regions. As an example of these histories, let's consider Zhao Rukua's thirteenth-century commercial guide *Zhu Fan Zhi*, which is rife with references to goods that originate in smaller-scale communities living inland from the sea. The goods reported to circulate through the Chinese port city of Quanzhou included East African elephant ivory, Indian spices and textiles, various woods and resins, and avian products, like kingfisher feathers.[19] Descriptions of the origin points of these goods are brief and sometimes incomplete—as we saw with the details on elephant hunting discussed in chapter 3. But in other cases, Zhao was keenly aware of the interior locales from which some goods originated. To cite a few examples, according to *Zhu Fan Zhi*, pepper grew "in the uncultivated wilds, and the villages" of India's interior, where people organized their harvests and processing around monsoonal rains. Camphor originated in the "depths of hills and remotest valleys" of Borneo. There, according to Zhao, large groups traveled into forests to cut bark from trees. They then burned the bark down to a condensed substance that they sealed in jars for trade as an aromatic medicine. Similarly, kingfisher feathers reached Chinese ports after skilled hunters living around lakes and ponds in the interiors of southern Thailand and the Malay Peninsula employed decoys to lure and trap the birds.[20]

Thirteenth-century Quanzhou epitomizes the massive scales of premodern oceanic trade. The port city's success was tied to its robust commercial infrastructure and established diasporic communities of Muslim merchants from southern Arabia, Persia, and Central Asia.[21] Products originating from the Indian Ocean, the Pacific, the South China Sea, and overland Silk Road routes flowed through the city's commercial offices. If we accept that goods moving between far-flung ports played a key role in forging Quanzhou's transregional connections, then we might also consider how people living in the places where these goods originated participated in these connections. As the examples above show, people living in inland regions and small-scale villages were not simply suppliers of trade goods. They were active agents in making these connections, even as their specific strategies for doing so diverged from the dominant norms of large-scale networks under study.

• • •

Sources have always been a major limiting factor to centering the above narratives of the Indian Ocean or other global macro-regions. With few exceptions,

CONCLUSION 139

urban centers, states, and individuals integrated into transregional mercantile networks have better written documentation—and frequently also better archaeological visibility—than smaller-scale or rural communities. These problems are only amplified as we move further back in time. As I've argued, however, the very same social, political, and commercial features that make communities like Mijikenda hard to study were in fact critical to their active role and influence within expansive global arenas like the Indian Ocean. In other words, the challenges of incorporating smaller-scale communities into global histories might also offer us an opportunity to ask new questions about such communities' participation and influence in larger-scale processes. In doing so, scholars of the premodern world can add important insights to existing "turns" in Indian Ocean and global history that have thus far been dominated by modern historians.

Recent scholarship on the Indian Ocean, for instance, has begun to break apart earlier notions of a unified and connected ocean by studying sources written in its numerous languages. Departing from the European source base that dominated earlier studies, recent work brings documentary records in the many African, Middle Eastern, and Asian languages spoken across the Indian Ocean to the fore, illuminating a heterogeneity masked by earlier focus on the unity of littoral societies.[22] Like scholars working in the Indian Ocean's numerous vernaculars, historians of precolonial Africa have a long-standing interest in language. However, reconstructed word histories, rather than written texts, constitute the vernacular source base for studying Africa's distant pasts. Historical linguistics methods are well established among scholars of Africa, and it is possible to imagine their utilization in studies of other Indian Ocean regions as well. With such approaches and methods in hand, scholars may find entirely novel ways to narrate the macro-region's history from the vantage of people and places thus far rendered peripheral—or simply unknowable—in studies written from the purview of urban ports.

By asking what it means to participate in the Indian Ocean, this book reveals how peoples' selective engagements—and disengagements—with global networks and processes could help constitute larger connections. Transregional mobilities and global flows represent key themes of global histories, including the subfield of Indian Ocean studies. Yet recently, some scholars have questioned whether this focus on connectivity comes at the neglect of histories of contestation, exclusion, and rupture that were also part of global processes. Attention to the limits of larger interactive spheres, these scholars argue, will draw attention to varied responses, contingencies, and local attachments so crucial to understanding the global past.[23] As I have shown throughout this book, selective engagements with the dominant global norms could also offer people a critical means for participating in—and shaping—worlds beyond their locale. In the Indian Ocean, mobile commodities, diasporic merchants, and port cities all played a central role in creating enduring transregional interactions. But large-scale connections also hinged on an array of less obviously "global" ideas and practices that circulated in the very places where the reach of oceanic actors—and their cultural norms, religious ideas, and technologies—seems to end. Hunters mastering the behaviors of bird species to procure feathers, forest dwellers experimenting with pepper cultivation in their swiddens, and indeed, people learning a new word—and its associated idea—as they moved between villages in a port's interior were all participating, in one way or another, in the making of expansive worlds.

APPENDIX 1

Placing East African Languages in Time and Space

This appendix offers a brief outline of the settlement geography and chronology of Sabaki languages. Throughout the book, I follow Nurse and Hinnebusch's 1993 classification of Sabaki, *Swahili and Sabaki*. In the book, the linguists propose that Northeast Coast Bantu was spoken by the start of the first millennium and quickly diverged into four separate daughter languages, including proto-Sabaki. By the sixth century, Sabaki had begun to diverge into separate daughter languages. While I agree with their general conclusions, this appendix builds on their work by incorporating new archaeological research since their book's publication and noting some correspondences between linguistic innovations and the material evidence. The following is what I see as the most plausible scenario for proto-Sabaki's time depth and geography based on current evidence.

Sabaki is one of four subgroups of a protolanguage called Northeast Coast Bantu, which also includes the Seuta, Ruvu, and Pare subgroups (see map in chapter 1). After emerging as a distinct language from Northeast Coast, Sabaki languages slowly differentiated themselves from their linguistic cousins through morphological, phonological, and lexical changes.[1] Within a few centuries, Sabaki began to diverge into separate daughter languages including Elwana, Swahili, Comorian, Pokomo, and Mijikenda.[2] Based on a diachronic analysis of Sabaki phonology and morphology, Nurse and Hinnebusch determined that Elwana and Swahili were the first to depart from proto-Sabaki. Comorian, Mijikenda, and Pokomo shared a brief period of innovation, after which Comorian diverged and its speakers made their way from East Africa's mainland to the Comoros Archipelago. In the final stage of Sabaki, Mijikenda and Lower Pokomo diverged from one another.[3]

Where were proto–Northeast Coast and proto-Sabaki spoken?
The above describes Sabaki's position within Northeast Coast as well as the relative chronology of its members' divergence from proto-Sabaki. However, the classification alone does not tell us when or where these languages were spoken. Historical linguists use a

142 APPENDIX 1

theory called the "principle of least moves" (or principle of least effort) to locate proto-languages in space and hypothesize historical movements of languages and/or language speakers.[4] It involves working backward in time from the location of contemporary speech communities to determine their past settlement geographies while following the scientific principle known as Occam's razor, which stipulates that the most probable and least complex explanatory model is usually correct. According to the theory, the most likely location of a protolanguage will be the area with the greatest diversity of languages descended from that protolanguage since this linguistic geography would have required the least amount of movement.[5] Outside of the Sabaki group, nearly all other Northeast Coast languages are spoken today in eastern and central Tanzania, with most clustering between the Rufiji River to the south and the Pangani River to the north. Furthermore, since eastern Tanzania features the greatest diversity of Northeast Coast languages, it is likely that the people who spoke proto-Northeast Coast lived within this broad region. The principle of least moves is slightly more difficult to apply to Sabaki languages due to dispersal of Comorian and Swahili to eastern Africa's offshore islands. But the three Sabaki languages found on East Africa's mainland—Mijikenda, Pokomo, and Elwana—are spoken today between northern Tanzania (north of Tanga) and the Tana River on the northern-central Kenya coast. Following Occam's razor, the simplest explanation is that proto-Sabaki was spoken in eastern Kenya, to the south of the Tana River, after diverging from the other Northeast Coast languages spoken to their south.

Language change happens through a variety of processes. Sometimes people moved, taking their languages with them as they settled in new regions. In other cases, in situ groups adopted new languages or became multilingual as they entered new spheres of interaction. Often it was a mixture of both scenarios. I say this to emphasize that when I describe movements of languages, I'm not talking about bounded speech communities making long-distance migrations from one location to another. More often, language change happened slowly as villages split, as people opened new ecologies for settlement through technological innovations and/or subsistence adaptations, and as these gradual expansions brought different speech communities in contact with one another. In such contexts, they exchanged social ideas, intermarried, and sometimes learned one another's languages.[6]

When did these processes of language change happen?
Some historical linguists use a method called glottochronology to date the divergence of past protolanguages. Glottochronology takes the cognition rates of shared "core" vocabulary between two or more languages to calculate approximate dates for when the languages or a language family diverged from one another. The method assumes that languages tend to replace core vocabulary at a standard rate of about fourteen words every five hundred years. Thus, two languages that share eighty-six cognates on a list of one hundred core vocabulary items are assumed to have diverged around five hundred years ago.[7] The method is controversial among many linguists and difficult to apply to languages of coastal East Africa, which feature many loanwords, making them appear to share more core vocabulary (and thus to have diverged more recently) than was actually the case.[8] Linguists can account for the skews caused by postdivergence contact by eliminating loanwords and looking only at cognate scores of nonadjacent languages that are less likely to have influenced one another through direct contact. Christopher Ehret has done this for Northeast Coast and Sabaki languages. After eliminating skews and calculating the median rates of divergence, Ehret

determined that Northeast Coast Bantu languages diverged from one another around the third century while Sabaki languages began their divergence around the sixth or seventh century.[9] These broad estimates offer a starting point for thinking about the time depth of early Bantu-speaking communities on the East African coast. Notably, the dates produced from median cognate scores are roughly consistent with the available archaeological evidence from the hypothesized Northeast Coast settlement region.

THE ARCHAEOLOGICAL PICTURE

Pots aren't people, as the saying goes. Evidence from material culture cannot, on its own, tell us anything about the languages spoken by the people who produced and used the objects. Thus, as archaeologists of East Africa and other regions have argued, ceramics should not be considered proxies for their users' linguistic or ethnic identities.[10] Nonetheless, in coastal East African historiography, scholars have sometimes associated certain ceramic styles with specific language groups. This has led to flawed or otherwise inconsistent models for understanding the earliest Bantu-speaking groups in the region. Making matters even more complicated, historians, linguists, and archaeologists have frequently drawn on each other's sources in support of their conclusions without adequately accounting for the different types of information the sources convey.[11] Mindful of these limitations, the following narrative is my attempt to summarize some archaeological materials for first-millennium settlements along with a brief analysis of what these materials can and cannot tell us about the speech communities described above.

In the early first millennium, the occupants of ironworking sites (usually called Early Iron Age or EIA) in coastal East Africa produced and used a pottery style that scholars call Kwale Ware. The earliest known Kwale Ware ceramics were used by people living in the coastal hinterlands of central Tanzania. Radiocarbon dates indicate that people first occupied the earliest known EIA sites in this region between the first century BCE and the start of the current era. By the third century, EIA sites with Kwale ceramics started to appear in adjacent regions: in southeast Kenya's coastal hinterlands; in the montane forests of the Pare Mountains and Taita Hills; southward along the coast to Kilwa and then farther south to Mozambique; and on some offshore islands, like the Mafia Archipelago.[12] Scholars do not know if the Kwale Ware ceramics made their way into these regions due to people moving, due to the techniques for making these pots moving via knowledge transfers, or if it was a mix of both. We also don't know conclusively what language the people making/using these pots spoke, although there is a broad consensus that many spoke Bantu languages due to Kwale Ware's association with ironworking sites and its stylistic similarities with ceramics from other parts of eastern, central, and southern Africa.[13]

In the late fifth century, a different ceramic style called the Early Tana Tradition (ETT) began supplanting Kwale Ware. ETT ceramics are found at a huge range of sites, including the littoral and offshore islands between northern Kenya and southern Mozambique and in the coastal hinterlands as far as hundreds of kilometers inland. Like the Kwale Ware sites, the people living in these places produced and used iron tools. Since they emerged at a more recent time depth than EIA settlements, scholars call sites associated with ETT ceramics Middle Iron Age (MIA). Radiocarbon dates from these sites indicate that these ceramic styles thrived between 600–900 CE.[14] Moreover, because ETT ceramics are found in the earliest archaeological contexts in coastal Swahili towns, they provide one key

144   APPENDIX 1

piece of evidence for archaeologists studying the local roots of urban centers that began to form along the littoral during the late first millennium.[15] Some scholars debate whether ETT emerged from Kwale Ware, or if the former represents a different ceramic style that simply replaced the latter.[16] Regardless, it is clear that people living along huge swaths of coastal East Africa produced and used related ceramic styles over the entirety of the first millennium. Furthermore, the diversity and geographic reach of both EIA and ETT ceramics show—conclusively—that the ubiquitous material cultures from the first millennium existed beyond any single social group or linguistic community.[17]

In the past, some scholars have tried to draw direct lines between ceramics and language groups, proposing, for instance, that Kwale ceramics are representative of proto–Northeast Coast Bantu groups and that ETT's assumed "evolution" from this earlier tradition is an indication of the divergence and spread of subsequent speech communities.[18] But as I noted above, most archaeologists reject the premise that there ever existed a one-to-one correspondence between pots and language groups. Nevertheless, Northeast Coast speakers and their descendants were certainly among the people who used Kwale Ware and ETT ceramics.[19] They were likely not the exclusive producers and users of this pottery, and we cannot know whether the pottery had anything to do with their identities or sense of affinities with other groups that produced and used the same ceramics. But at least some of the EIA/ Kwale Ware sites must have included people speaking Northeast Coast languages and their descendants. Moreover, some—but certainly not all—of the diverse array of ETT sites were occupied by people speaking languages from the Sabaki family.

SETTLING THE EAST AFRICAN COAST

The principle of least moves suggests that proto–Northeast Coast Bantu was first spoken around central Tanzania. Proto-Sabaki speakers likely lived to the north of the Northeast Coast homeland after it diverged into four daughter languages. Scholars have speculated that the early Kwale Ware sites in southeastern Kenya, the earliest of which date to the third century, represent this move to the north. In this scenario, the flourishing of ETT sites on the immediate littoral and offshore islands starting around the sixth century—some of which emerged as early urban towns—are seen to represent the precursors to Swahili-speaking society. ETT ceramics also appeared in the Comoros Archipelago at sites dating to the eighth or ninth century, around the same time that genetic evidence indicates admixture between haplogroups from Africa and Southeast Asia in this region.[20]

As people moved offshore, their languages would have begun to slowly differentiate from each other. If we accept that post-Sabaki groups were among the people making ETT ceramics on East Africa's offshore islands (which is not in any dispute) then the intensive colonization of the littoral around the sixth and seventh centuries represents a point at which an early form of Swahili may have begun to emerge from Sabaki. The classification of Sabaki indicates that Comorian diverged later than Swahili, remaining in a core Sabaki group that included Mijikenda and Lower Pokomo. The archaeological and genetic evidence from the Comoros indicates that Comorian speakers had separated geographically from other Sabaki groups by the eighth century and allows us to conjecture that this late-Sabaki Comorian-Mijikenda-Pokomo group began to diverge by this point.

Over generations, the languages people spoke would have slowly changed as they engaged in new activities and discarded others, innovating or adopting new words along the way to suit their needs. Reconstructed lexical innovations in Sabaki and proto-Swahili support the scenario outlined above. As chapter 1 showed, proto-Sabaki speakers innovated many words related to cultivation, including words for clearing land, field types, and processing techniques. Based on the hypothetical movement of languages supported by the principle of least moves, proto-Sabaki was spoken in the region between northeastern Tanzania and the southern and central coast of modern Kenya. EIA sites in this region cluster along the fertile ridges a short distance inland from the littoral. With ample rainfall, rich soils, and abundant wild fauna to hunt and collect for supplementary foods, this environment would have provided a perfect laboratory for experimenting with new crops. Notably, then, a wealth of lexical innovations related to these activities is attributed to this period. In addition to innovations related to cultivation, Nurse and Hinnebusch identified proto-Sabaki innovations for small antelope species, such as *mfuno, which referred to a species of duiker (probably red duiker), as well as *ntope, or reedbuck.[21] Duiker and reedbuck both favored well-watered woodlands, such as were characteristic of many of the earliest settlements in the proposed proto-Sabaki region. After Sabaki languages began to diverge, proto-Swahili speakers innovated many new words referring to boat and sail types, as well as maritime flora and fauna like oysters, dugong, and mangrove species. These innovations suggest an intensification of maritime activities and expanding knowledge of the maritime environment during the proto-Swahili period.[22]

The archaeological evidence and linguistic innovations do not offer direct associations, but the datasets do correspond with one another in ways that invite informed speculation about past processes.[23] For instance, as I argued in chapter 1, Sabaki speakers' successful mastery of grain crops like sorghum would have allowed people to settle in new regions, including offshore islands. Compellingly, archaeological evidence from Juani Island in the Mafia Archipelago indicates that migrants living in EIA settlements—established in the fourth century—practiced a hunter-fisher-forager lifestyle. Then, in the seventh century, people living on the island shifted to the mixed farming subsistence practices found in settlements established on other offshore islands around the same time.[24] This indicates that as EIA groups began colonizing some offshore islands during the early first millennium, they did not have extensive knowledge of grain cultivation. Crops like tubers did not grow well in the island's soils, and, as a result, they pursued other forms of subsistence. When Sabaki speakers arrived a few centuries later, they introduced new subsistence technologies that allowed settlements to thrive on the island. In the process, Sabaki, or perhaps an early form of Swahili, became the language of the Mafia Archipelago. Similar processes would have no doubt unfolded in other parts of the littoral, such that Swahili became the dominant language across East Africa's immediate coast and offshore islands within a few centuries.

Ultimately, I see the available evidence supporting the following broad chronology: Northeast Coast diverged into daughter languages—including proto-Sabaki—during the early first millennium, while proto-Sabaki itself started to diverge around the middle of the millennium. After Swahili and Elwana departed, Mijikenda, Lower Pokomo, and Comorian briefly remained as a core innovating group before Comorian emerged as a distinct language by the eighth century at the latest. Shortly after this, Mijikenda and Pokomo diverged from one another. Thus, by the late first millennium, early Mijikenda had emerged as a distinct language within the Sabaki group.

APPENDIX 2

Mijikenda Dialects

The materials below offer a synchronic picture of Mijikenda dialects, showing variation in sounds and core vocabulary in different parts of the dialect chain.[1] Drawn on a map as isoglosses, this data demonstrates that Mijikenda consists of five dialects: Digo, Duruma, Rabai, Central Mijikenda, and Giryama.[2] Digo and Giryama, being the southernmost and northernmost dialects, are the most distinct from one another, with each sharing some unique lexical and phonological features with intermediary dialects.[3] Thus, we can refer to Mijikenda as a dialect chain. Tables 3 and 4 model variability from the southern to northern contours of the Mijikenda dialect chain. Table 3 shows variation in phonology, and Table 4 shows variation in core vocabulary.

PHONOLOGICAL VARIATION

TABLE 3 Phonological Variation in Mijikenda Dialects

C = Central MK dialects (i.e., Chonyi, Kambe, Kauma, Jibana, Ribe); Di = Digo; Du = Duruma; G = Giryama; R = Rabai

Proto-Sabaki	Sound changes distinguishing Mijikenda dialects
	Southern and Northern clusters
*p	> ph (Di, Du, R) > h (C, G)
*py	> ph (Di, Du, R) > sh (C, G)
*fy	> fy (Di, Du, R) > sh (C, G)
	Duruma and Duruma-Rabai
*ky	> ky (Du) > ch (Di, R, C, G)
*k_i	> kyi (Du) > chi (Di, R, C) > ki (G)
*k_e	> kye (Du) > che (Di, R, C) > che ~ ke (G)
*ns	> tsʰ (Du, R) > s (Di, C, G)

(Continued)

146

TABLE 3 (Continued)

Proto-Sabaki	Sound changes distinguishing Mijikenda dialects
	Giryama
*vy	> vy (Di, Du, R, C) > 3 (G)
*g_e	> je (Di, Du, R, C) > je ~ ge (G)
*k_i	> kyi (Du) > chi (Di, R, C) > ki (G)
*k_e	> kye (Du) > che (Di, R, C) > che ~ ke (G)

LEXICAL VARIATION

TABLE 4 Lexical Variation in Core Vocabulary for Mijikenda Dialects, South to North

(>) indicates loanwords from a non-Mijikenda language; (?) indicates the word's source is unknown. All other terms are inherited or innovations derived from inherited vocabulary.

	Dialects in which the word appears				
Word	Digo	Duruma	Rabai	CMK	Giryama
-kulu "big"	×				
-nono "good"	×				
-phia "to go"	×				
> -ng'ata "to bite"	×				
na(mutsi) "daytime"	×				
lulaka "tongue"	×				
?mnyevu "cold"	×				
-phera "ripe"	×				
> dia "dog"	×	×			
?beshe "fish"	×	×			
mwanache (~mwanakye) "child"	×	×			
-kundu "red"	×	×			
-karya "dull, blunt"	×	×			
yuphi(e) "who?"	×	×			
mwango "mountain, hill"	×	×			
mayo "mother"	×	×	×		
-phi "where"	×	×	×		
?bomu "big"		×	×	×	×
-en(enda) "to go"		×	×	×	×
ivu "ripe"		×	×	×	×
> musoza "bone"		×	×	×	×

(Continued)

148 APPENDIX 2

TABLE 4 (Continued)

Word	Dialects in which the word appears				
	Digo	Duruma	Rabai	CMK	Giryama
> *hombo* "breast"			×	×	×
> *kuro* "dog"			×	×	×
> *t'une* "red"			×	×	×
-*fufu* "narrow"			×	×	×
muhoho "child"			×	×	×
kumba "fish"			×	×	×
hiko "where"				×	×
iji "egg"				×	×
> -*nena* "to speak"					×
> -*keresi* "to sit"					×
-*rungarara* "to stand" "stand up/be straight"					×
mukole "mountain/hill"					×
> -*ṯumi(k)a* "old, worn"					×

NOTE: These wordlists are based on interviews I conducted in 2012–2013 for core vocabulary among speakers of each of the nine Mijikenda subgroups. Most of the loanwords marked here are identified in Nurse and Hinnebusch, *Swahili and Sabaki*, Appendix 4.

APPENDIX 3

Lexical Reconstructions
and Distributions

Much of the lexical data in this appendix comes from dictionaries, wordlists, and ethnographic and archival materials cited in the bibliography while some attestations are from interviews conducted in Kenya between 2012 and 2014.[1]

1. -cum- v. "gather, trade, profit"

Sabaki semantic innovation, expanding inherited meaning "collect" with commercial connotations. From Bantu *-cùm- "buy food."[2]

COMORIAN: -shuma [-tsuma] gather, make profit (Ngazija)

MIJIKENDA: -tsuma trade, buy or sell, earn (Giryama)

POKOMO: -tsuma keep money (LP)

SWAHILI: -chuma gather, profit, trade, gain or prosper (Unguja); -tuma make profit (Mvita); -shuma conduct business, prosper (Mtang'ata); -ṯuma make money (Mwiini)

OTHER: -suma make profit (Bondei); -shuma reap, nizashuma mali reap wealth (Shambaa); -suma profit, accumulate wealth (Nyamwezi); *-suma buy, sell (Greater Yao)

SOURCES: Sacleux, Dictionnaire; Deed, Giriama; Bible Translation and Literacy, "Lower Pokomo"; Johnson, Standard English-Swahili Dictionary; Krapf, Suahili; Kisseberth and Abasheikh, Chimwiini; Whiteley, Ki-Mtangat'a; Kiango, Kibondei; Langheinrich, Schambala; Maganga and Schadeberg, Kinyamwezi; Seligman, "Encircling Value."

2. *-cang(il)- v. "collect, contribute"

Derived from *-cang- "collect," which has a secondary meaning of "contribute" in NEC and some other Eastern Bantu languages. In proto-Sabaki, the suffix *-il- gave verb the sense of "collecting for or on behalf of," hence making contributions. From Bantu *-càng- "meet, find, mix, assemble."[3]

149

150 APPENDIX 3

COMORIAN: -*tsanga* contribute, give money (for community effort), -*tsangia* contribute to, pool together (money) (Nzuani)

MIJIKENDA: -*tsanga tsandzi* collect (offering), -*tsangira* welcome, greet a stranger (Giryama); -*tsanga* ~ -*tsangirana* donate (Duruma); (*mu*)*tsango* contribution, donation; *tsango* 5 contribution (Digo)

POKOMO: -*changila* collect, contribute, assist (UP)

SWAHILI: -*ṭangia* contribute to another, *ṭ'ango* collection, contribution, donation (Mvita); -*changa* collect, -*changia* make contributions, *cango* 5 contribution (Unguja); -*ṭaanga* ~ -*ṭaangiile* contribute a share for collective use (money or things); *shṭaango* 7 collection, cooperative effort to raise funds (Mwiini)

OTHER NEC: -*sanga* collect taxes, *sango* tax (Zigua); -*thanga* collect or make contributions (Pare); -*hanga* gather, collect, cooperate, join, *hanzo* contribution (Gogo); -*hanga* ~ -*hangila* share (Kagulu); *shango* levy (Shambaa)

OTHER: -*canga* contribute, *ncango* contribution (Makonde); -*sangila* share resources, *msaango* debt (Nyamwezi); -*thanga* collect, contribute (Gweno); -*sangirya* collect, make contributions, save (Mashami); -*sanga* collect, make contributions, *mcango* contribution (Kahe)

SOURCES: Ahmed-Chamanga, *Lexique Comorien*; Ottenheimer, *Comorian*; Deed, *Giryama*; Hamamoto, "Duruma"; Mwalonya et al., *Mgombato*; Ndurya et al., *Musemat'o*; Author's fieldnotes; Krapf, *Suahili*; Madan, *Swahili*; Sacleux, *Dictionnaire*; Kisseberth and Abasheikh, *Chimwiini*; Kisbey, *Zigula*; Mreta, *Chasu*; Rugemalira, *Cigogo*; Petzell, *Kagulu*; Langheinrich, *Schambala*; Rugemalira, *Cimakonde*; Maganga and Schadeberg, *Kinyamwezi*; Sewangi, *Kigweno*; Rugemalira, *Kimashami*; Kahigi, *Kikahe*.

3. *kikola n., cl. 7/8 "sharing arrangement (for sharing foods, resources, or labor)"

Sabaki innovation. Derivation unclear, possibly from verb *-kód- "choke."[4]

COMORIAN: *shikoa* community savings arrangement, people pooling money together with each making a contribution (Nzuani)

MIJIKENDA: *chikola* work party, work share of men (Rabai)

POKOMO: *kikola* cooperation, partnership (LP)

SWAHILI: *kikoa* group meal, food share (Unguja)

SOURCES: Ottenheimer, *Comorian*; Ahmed-Chamanga, *Lexique-Comorien*; Krapf, *Nika*; Author's fieldnotes; Johnson, *Standard English-Swahili Dictionary*.

4. *mukiWa n., cl. 1/2 "poor person, abandoned person" (proto-Sabaki form)

Inland areal term in Northeast Coast, Chaga-Taita, and Thagicu. Derived from proto-Bantu verb -*kíd*- "pass over, surpass" with passive extension, giving sense of one who is "passed over" or "surpassed."[5]

CHAGA-TAITA: *nkivya* poor person, orphan (Meru); *nkibha* poor person (Mashami); *mkiva* poor person (Kahe); *mkibha* poor person (Gweno); *mkiwa* orphan (Taita-Saghala); *mchiwa* poor person (Kami)

LEXICAL RECONSTRUCTIONS AND DISTRIBUTIONS   151

THAGICU: *ngia* poor person, pauper (Gikuyu); *ngya* poor person (Kamba)

SABAKI: *mukiya ~ mchiya* abject person, poor person (Mijikenda); *mukepha* (Elwana); *mukipha* (UP); *mkiwa* poor person, person who is helpless or abandoned (Swahili)

OTHER NEC: *muciwa* bereaved person, poor person, orphan (Gogo); *mukiwa* poor person (Kaguru); *mkiwa* poor person, beggar (Shambaa); *mkiwa* poor person (Zigua); *mkiwa* beggar, orphan (Bondei); *mntu mkiva* poor person (Pare).

OTHER: *mokeva* pauper (Mbugwe)

SOURCES: Rubanza, *Kimeru*; Rugemalira, *Kimashami*; Kahigi, *Kikahe*; Sewangi, *Kigweno*; Wray, *Taita*; Velten, *Kikami*; Benson, *Kikuyu*; African Inland Mission Language Committee, *Kikamba*; Taylor, *Giryama*; Mwalonya et al., *Mgombato*; Author's fieldnotes; Nurse and Hinnebusch, *Swahili and Sabaki*; Sacleux, *Dictionnaire*; Rugemalira, *Cigogo*; Petzell, *Kagulu*; Langheinrich, *Schambala*; Steere, *Shambala*; Kisbey, *Zigula*; Woodward, *Boondei*; Kagaya, *Pare*; Mous, "Mbugwe."

5. *muzuka* n., cl. 3/4 "nature spirit, shrine"

New gloss in Southern Mijikenda (Digo, Duruma) likely related to innovation in practice. In proto-Sabaki, *muzyuka n., cl. 3/4 "apparition."[6]

MIJIKENDA: *mzuka* nature spirit, shrine (Digo); *muzuka* spirit type, place of spirits (located in trees or caves) (Duruma); *muzuka* shrine in Digo (CMK); *muzuka* devil (Giryama)

OTHER SABAKI AND NEC: *mzuka* apparition, spirit (appear suddenly) (Unguja); *muzuka* evil person (LP); *muzuka* evil or possessed person, evil spirit (UP); *mzuka* ghost, apparition (Bondei); *mzuka* apparition (Zigua); *mizuka* malevolent spirits (Zaramo); *muzukule* apparition, zombie (Gogo)

SOURCES: Mwalonya et al., *Mgombato*; Ndurya et al., *Musemat'o*; Author's fieldnotes; Deed, *Giryama*; Johnson, *Standard English-Swahili Dictionary*; Bible Translation and Literacy, "Lower Pokomo"; Kiango, *Kibondei*; Mochiwa, *Kizigula*; Beidelman, *Matrilineal Peoples*; Rugemalira, *Cigogo*.

6. *nkoma n., cl. 9/10 "spirit (of deceased)"

Areal spread between Kenya Coast, Central Highlands, and northern parts of Easter Arc Mountains. Possibly derived from Bantu verb *-kóm- "hit with hammer, beat, kill," meaning "cease, come to an end" in proto-Sabaki.[7]

SABAKI: *k'oma* "spirt of the dead" (Mrima, Pemba, Mvita); *nkoma* spirits (ancestral spirits and nature spirits) (UP); *nkoma* "agrarian celebration" (Nzuani); *koma* ancestral spirit (Digo); *k'oma* shade, spirit of dead (Giryama)

OTHER: *nkoma* skull (which is worshipped) (Shambaa); *nkoma* skull of ancestor, spirit of dead person (Pare); *mukoma mvula* rain catcher (Gogo); *ngoma* shrine (Taita); *ngoma* spirit of dead person (Gweno); *ngoma* evil spirit, spirit of departed (Gikuyu); *nkoma* spirit (Chuku); *ndere na nkoma* "spirit of dead person" (Tharaka).

SOURCES: Krapf, *Suahili*; Sacleux, *Dictionnaire*; Bunger, "Islamization"; Ahmed-Chamanga, *Lexique Comorien*; Mwalonya et al., *Mgombato*; Deed, *Giryama*; Cory, "Tambiko"; Kimambo, *Political History*; Rugemalira, *Cigogo*; Harris, *Casting Out Anger*; Nurse and Philippson, "Tanzania Language Survey"; Benson, *Kikuyu*.

152 APPENDIX 3

7. *-tac- v. "make offering, sacrifice"

Proto-Chaga-Taita term that spread into neighboring inland languages. Loanword in Mijikenda, borrowed from interactions in Taita Hills/interior.[8]

MIJIKENDA: -hatsa ~ -hats'a name, bless (blowing water); -hatsira koma call for the blessings of the ancestors (Duruma); -hadza [-hatsa] name (Rabai); -hasa bless, invoke spirits (Giryama); -hasa make offering for ancestors (Digo); muhaso "medicine" (all dialects)

CHAGA-TAITA: -rasa provide offering to spirit, protect against evil; mrasa spirit rapper (Meru); -dasa sacrifice, make offering; mdasa spirit rapper (Kahe); -tatha sacrifice, make offering; (Gweno); -idasa make offering (Bosho); -ir*asaa make offering (Machame, Siha); kir*aso sacrifice (Machame, Vunjo); -tasa performance to call for blessings or supplicate spirit by spraying mouthfuls of water and ritual utterances (Taita-Dawida)

OTHER: -tasa pray, ask for help (Kagulu); -tatha worship, make offerings for the dead or spirits; mtatho sacrifice; mtatho wa mvua offerings for rain (Pare); -taza worship (Shambaa); -taza serve, provide, help (Gogo)

SOURCES: Hamamoto, "Duruma"; Krapf, Nika; Taylor, Giryama; Author's fieldnotes; Rubanza, Kimeru; Kahigi, Kikahe; Sewangi, Kigweno; Nurse and Philippson, "Tanzania Language Survey"; Harris, Casting Out Anger; Petzell, Kagulu; Mreta, Chasu; Cory, "Tambiko"; Rugemalira, Cigogo.

8. *-palo ~ *-pala n., cl. 7, 5 "meeting area"

Relic areal or Kaskazi? Derived from proto-Bantu v. *-pád- "scrape, scratch." Potential relationship to proto-Mashariki *-ipala "furnace, smithy"—i.e., specialized activity areas, often in the bush?[9]

MIJIKENDA: chiphalo place to meet and perform dances (Digo, Duruma); pala ~ p'ala cleared space in forest (for feasts, healing ceremonies) (Giryama)

OTHER SABAKI: kivaa palisade (Swahili: Tikuu); para 5 field, area for gardens (Lower Pokomo)

OTHER: kivaro/ivaro meeting place (for warriors, hearing disputes) (Embu); kihaaro/ ihaaro land used as meeting place (for tribunal, dances) (Gikuyu) kipalo plot of ground (Daiso); kivalo "district" (Kamba); cibalu circumcision camp (Gogo); hala 5 protective wall (Shambaa); yapala open space (Ndengeleko); kiwalàkate arid place (Luganda).

SOURCES: Mwalonya et al., Mgombato; Hamamoto, "Duruma"; Ndurya et al., Musemat'o; Deed, Giryama; Wolfe, Vigango; Sacleux, Dictionnaire; Bible Translation and Literacy, "Lower Pokomo"; Saberwal, Traditional Political System; Benson, Kikuyu; Nurse, Inheritance, Contact; African Inland Mission Language Committee, Kikamba; Rigby, Cattle and Kinship; Langheinrich, Schambala; Nurse and Philippson, "Tanzania Language Survey"; Snoxall, Luganda.

9. rungu n., cl. 5 "shrine in bush (for storing sacred objects)"

Mijikenda specific gloss possibly derived from *-dùngù n., cl. 5 "plain; open space; desert; loneliness." In proto-Great Lakes Bantu *-rungu n., cl. 5/6 "wilderness." In different noun class, proto-Ruvu attested a related noun, *-lungu n., cl. 3 "'potentially malevolent spirit' that moved within unsettled, neglected wilderness areas," which itself was derived from a Kaskazi term.[10]

MIJIKENDA: *rungu* ancestral shrine; small hut in the bush for healing pots (Digo); *rungu* meeting place or shrine in bush for secret societies (Duruma); *rungu* ~ *kurungu* clearing in bush for keeping sacred drum (Giyama); *rungu* place in *kaya* for storing charms and initiation objects (Rabai)

SWAHILI: *ungu* clear area, field or *uwanda* (Pemba)

OTHER: *ungu* plot of land with burnt grass surrounding it (Zigua); *irungu* hole, ditch, channel (Kahe)

SOURCES: Gerlach, "Social Organisation"; Bergman, "Willingness to Remember"; Hamamoto, "Duruma"; Brantley, box 16, int. 55; Udvardy, "Kifudu"; Krapf, *Nika*; Krapf, *Suahili*; Kisbey, *Zigula*; Kahigi, *Kikahe*.

10. *ndala* n., cl. 9/10 "healer's workplace, place for healing"

Areal in Mijikenda dialects (except northernmost Giryama) and Bondei. Derived from proto-Bantu *-dáad- "lie down, sleep; spend night; be fallow (field)," healing grounds = place for rest and recovery.[11]

MIJIKENDA: *ndala* place of seclusion for healing, healer's workplace, treatment ground (CMK, Digo, Duruma, Rabai); also place where elders sit during funeral (Duruma); *ndala* ~ *kidala* place where members of the *bahasi* healing group are honored (Rabai)

OTHER: *ndala* forested area where healers treat patients (Bondei)

SOURCES: Author's fieldnotes; Hamamoto, "Duruma"; Ndurya et al., *Musemat'o*; Krapf, *Nika*; Dale, "Account."

11. *kinyaka* ~ *chinyaka* n., cl. 7/8 "place for meetings, performing dances"

Loanword in more northern Mijikenda dialects from Kamba.

MIJIKENDA: *chinyaka* meeting place, place for performing dances (CMK, Rabai) *kinyaka* "open space for meetings or dances (Giryama)

OTHER: *kinyaka* field, dance, clearing for dances or gatherings, located between neighboring villages (Kamba)

SOURCES: Deed, *Giryama*; Taylor, *Giryama*; Krapf, *Nika*; Author's fieldnotes; Mbiti, *English-Kamba*; African Inland Mission Language Committee, *Kikamba*; Mutuku et al., "Social."

12. *chete* n., cl. 7/8 "market"

Areal spread in geographic block of languages between Mombasa and the Mrima coast, associated with interior markets. /t/ indicates it is a loanword in Mijikenda dialects. Nurse and Hinnebusch propose it originates from proto-Southern Cushitic k^w'atara^{y}a, meaning "cattle transaction" with links to markets.[12]

154   APPENDIX 3

MIJIKENDA: *chete* market, meeting place for barter (Digo, Duruma, Giryama)

SWAHILI: *chete* market, place of market—associated with Digo (Mvita, Mrima); market, market day, place of market—associated with areas to north like Mombasa and Tanga (Unguja); *kete* market (Vumba)

OTHER: *chete* market (Taita-Dawida/Saghala); *kyeete* market (Kamba); *kiete* market (Pare); *chete* market (Daiso)

SOURCES: Mwalonya et al., *Mgombato*; Ndurya et al., *Musemat'o*; Deed, *Giryama*; Krapf, *Suahili*; Johnson, *Standard English-Swahili Dictionary*; Sacleux, *Dictionnaire*; Lambert, *Ki-Vumba*; Nurse, *Chaga*; African Inland Mission Language Committee, *Kikamba*; Kagaya, *Pare*; Nurse, *Inheritance, Contact.*

13. **kicambi* n., cl. 7/8 "cloth textile"

Areal innovation between Mijikenda, Lower Pokomo, and Mombasa Swahili dialects. Derived from the verb *-camb- "wash, wash self after evacuating," which also yields a related (proto-Northeast Coast?) term, *-cambo (n., cl. 7/8), meaning "loincloth." Attestations in other Swahili dialects plus Upper Pokomo, Taita, and Kwere are loans based on their form.[13]

MIJIKENDA: *chitsambi* cloth type frequently worn by women, used for possession rituals, protection from evil spirits, and burials (Duruma); *kitsambi* colored cloth (Giryama); *lutsambo* cloth waistband, worn by women (Duruma, Giryama, Rabai)

POKOMO: *kitsambi* a special cloth put around the waist for readiness of a journey (LP); *kitambi* cloth type (UP)

SWAHILI: *kitambi* piece of cloth (five- to six-arm lengths) (Mvita); *kitambi* length of cloth used as headwear or as loincloth (Unguja)

OTHER: *kisambo* dress made of feathers or grass (Zigua); *kisambo* loincloth, grass skirt (worn during initiations) (Shambaa); *kisambo* bark dress (worn by *wafefelezi*) (Bondei); *sambo/zisambo* cloth for carrying baby (Gogo); *ithambo* cloth (worn out) (Pare); *kitambi* white cotton cloth (initiation dress) (Kwere); *kitambi* blue and red calico (Taita-Saghala)

SOURCES: Hamamoto, "Duruma"; Ndurya et al., *Musemat'o*; Deed, *Giryama*; Taylor, *Giryama*; Krapf, *Nika*; Author's fieldnotes; Krapf, *Suahili*; Johnson, *Standard English-Swahili Dictionary*; Kisbey, *Zigula*; Langheinrich, *Schambala*; Woodward, *Boondei*; Mreta, *Chasu*; Wembah-Rashid, "Socioeconomic System"; Wray, *Taita.*

14. **-coga* n., cl. 9/10 "blood pact/friendship"

Areal spread in NEC languages or proto-NEC retained only in contiguous block. Derived from a Northeast Coast verb *-cog- "cut, incise, scar," which itself has wider distribution in some East African Bantu languages meaning "provoke," "spear," etc., and is possibly related to the root *-còng- "prod, incite."[14]

COMORIAN: *-tsoa* damaged, bruised (as in fruit); be wounded, bloody (Nzuani)

MIJIKENDA: *tsoga* scar, blood pact; *-kurya tsoga* "make blood brotherhood"; *-tsodza* scar, make incisions to apply medicine (all MK)

SWAHILI: *-toja* scratch, scarify, make incisions (Mvita); *-toga* pierce, poke (Tumbatu)

LEXICAL RECONSTRUCTIONS AND DISTRIBUTIONS   155

OTHER NEC: *soga* blood pact (Bondei); *soga* "blood pact," *-dya soga* make blood pact (Zigua); *soga* blood covenant (Ngulu); *shogha* blood pact; -shoghiana make alliance (between two men); *-sogeza* confess when trading (Shambaa); *shogha* incision, tattoo, *-shogha* make an incision, incise, *-shoghiana* make blood pact (Pare); blood covenant, *-soga* to apply (medicine to a cut) (Kagulu); *soga* tip, point (Kwere)

OTHER EAB: *-thoga* provoke, incite, poke, stab (Gikuyu); *-sogga* spear to death (Luganda); *-shogha* incise (Gweno); *kishogno* bloodied skin from slaughtered animal given as sign of friendship (Chaga)

SOURCES: Ahmed-Chamanga, *Lexique Comorien*; Ottenheimer, *Comorian*; Deed, *Giryama*; Hamamoto, "Duruma"; Mwalonya et al., *Mgombato*; Ndurya et al., *Musemat'o*; Krapf, *Nika*; Author's fieldnotes; Krapf, *Suahili*; Sacleux, *Dictionnaire*; Kiango, *Kibondei*; Kisbey, *Zigula*; Mochiwa, *Kizigula*; Beidelman, *Matrilineal Peoples*; Feierman, "Concepts of Sovereignty"; Langheinrich, *Schambala*; Mreta, *Chasu*; Beidelman, "Blood Covenant"; Legère, "Ng'hwele"; Benson, *Kikuyu*; Snoxall, *Luganda*; Sewangi, *Kigweno*; Krapf, *Travels*.

15. *dhora ~ rora* n., cl. 5/6, 14 "bargain, price, trade"

Loanword in Mijikenda from Segeju, only attested as a noun with many innovations/compounds. Verbal form has broader areal distribution in Pare, Taita.[15]

MIJIKENDA: *dhora* bargain, price, commerce; *-piga dhora* to bargain; *-tosa dhora* to finish making a deal; *-tana dhora* to fail making a deal; *-henda dhora* trade; *mwenye madhora* merchant; *munena dhora* go-between (Giryama); *thora ~ rora*; *uthora* bargain, commerce, trade; *-piga thora* to strike a bargain (Rabai)

THAGICU: *-doja* to bargain, buy (Daiso); *thooa* price, value; *-thooa* to buy (Kamba); *thogora* 5/6 price; *-thogora* barter, bargain, buy (Gikuyu)

OTHER: *-dhora ~ -zora*; *-zogora* to bargain; *zora* price (Pare); *-zogora* to bargain (Taita-Saghala); *-thoghora* to search for food during famine (Gweno)

SOURCES: Taylor, *Giryama*; Krapf, *Nika*; Nurse, *Inheritance, Contact*; Nurse, "Segeju and Daisū"; African Inland Mission Language Committee, *Kikamba*; Benson, *Kikuyu*; Kagaya, *Pare*; Wray, *Taita*; Sewangi, *Kigweno*.

16. *-dhyana* v. "spy, scout"; *mudhyani ~ muryani ~ ndiani* n., cl. 1/2, 9/10 "scout, spy, leader of trade or hunting party"

Verb is an areal spread in languages in Pare Mountains and Taita Hills, originating in Segeju or a pre-Segeju Thagicu offshoot.[16] Mijikenda likely borrowed derived noun referring to trade-party leaders from Kamba.

MIJIKENDA: *-dhyana* scout, spy; *mudhyani ~ ndiani* spy, scout, caravan leader (Giryama); *-thiana*; *muthiani ~ ndiani* spy (Rabai); *mryani* leader (of a hunting group, safari, war party) (Digo); *muryani* healer who leads hunts or safaris; *uryani* hunting medicine (Duruma).

THAGICU: *-thiana* spy, scout for an enemy; *mūthiani* spy, leader of trade, war, or hunting party (Kamba); *-thigana* spy out, reconnoiter for enemy or cattle; *mūthigani* scout, spy, tracker (Gikuyu)

156   APPENDIX 3

OTHER: -*zigana* spy (Pare); -*zigana* spy (Dawida); -*thighana* search, look for (Gweno)

SOURCES: Taylor, *Giryama*; Krapf, *Nika*; Author's fieldnotes; African Inland Mission Language Committee, *Kikamba*; Benson, *Kikuyu*; Nurse, "Segeju and Daisū"; Sewangi, *Kigweno*.

17. *charo* n., cl. 7/8/10 "journey, caravan"

Inland areal term (Mijikenda form). Likely derived from Sabaki verb *-Wal- "burst, split."[17] Likely internal innovation in Mijikenda based on (1) isolated distribution in Swahili dialects to those with heaviest contact with Mijikenda speakers; (2) irregular shape outside of Mijikenda, i.e., Kamba and Chaga based on proposed derivation; (3) association with Mijikenda in historical sources.

MIJIKENDA: *charo* journey, caravan (Digo, Duruma, Rabai, Giryama)

POKOMO: *charo* journey (LP)

SWAHILI: *charo* caravan (Unguja); caravan, journey, travel party, expedition. According to Krapf's dictionary, "Charo is originally a Kinika [Mijikenda] word for which the Suahili use 'safari,' but the Kinika expression 'charo' has been fully adopted by the Suahili" (Mvita).

OTHER: *charo* caravan (Taita-Saghala); *kyalo* caravan, (Kamba); *charo* journey (Daiso); *kyaaro* ~ *kyaro* journey, travel (Chaga languages)

SOURCES: Mwalonya et al., *Mgombato*; Ndurya et al., *Musemat'o*; Deed, *Giryama*; Krapf, *Nika*; Bible Translation and Literacy, "Lower Pokomo"; Johnson, *Standard English-Swahili Dictionary*; Krapf, *Suahili*; Wray, *Taita*; African Inland Mission Language Committee, *Kikamba*; Nurse, *Inheritance, Contact*; Nurse and Philippson, "Tanzania Language Survey."

18. *-kódè n., cl. 1/2, 9/10 "captive, booty"

Proto-Bantu term, retained in Northeast Coast and Sabaki. In Mijikenda dialects and some Swahili refers to a person taken as compensation for a crime.[18]

MIJIKENDA: *kore* fine for murder; usually a relative is given as compensation to family of deceased (Digo); damages or compensation given for killing a person or animal (Giryama)

SWAHILI: *kole* debt captive, relative seized as compensation for crime or a debt (Unguja); *kole* hostage (Mrima)

OTHER NEC: *kole* captive, war captive (Bondei); *nkole* captive (Zigula); *nkole* prisoner of war (Shambaa)

SOURCES: Mwalonya et al., *Mgombato*; Ndurya et al., *Musemat'o*; Deed, *Giryama*; Johnson, *Standard English-Swahili Dictionary*; Sacleux, *Dictionnaire*; Langheinrich, *Schambala*; Kisbey, *Zigula*; Woodward, *Boondei*.

NOTES

INTRODUCTION

1. Shipton et al., "78,000-Year-Old Record."

2. Freeman-Grenville, *East African Coast: Select Documents*, 20.

3. Hamdun and King, *Ibn Battuta*, 21.

4. Known as Mnara Mosque. The mosque's precise age is unknown, but according to Prita Meier it was built as early as the fourteenth century. Meier, *Swahili Port Cities*, 78.

5. The Arabic term in question is *barr*. See Hamdun and King, *Ibn Battuta*, 79–80, and Gibb, *Travels of Ibn Battuta*, 379.

6. Adding to the potential for errors, the travelogue was only written in its final form around 1354–1355 by a scholar from Fez who acted as Ibn Battuta's ghostwriter, creating an abridged version of three decades of globetrotting from the traveler's notes and memories. See Gibb, *Travels*, vol. 1, 1–7; Dunn, *Adventures of Ibn Battuta*, 253–260.

7. Shipton et al., "Intersections"; Helm, "Conflicting Histories."

8. James Emery's journal from his time in Mombasa in the 1820s provides the clearest indication of the frequency of these interactions: "A Journal of the British Establishment at Mombasa," the National Archives of the UK (henceforth TNA): ADM 52/3940. But see also the earlier records of Mijikenda-speaking "Mosungulos" in the city discussed in chapters 3 and 4.

9. Freeman-Grenville, *East African Coast: Select Documents*, 180, 185.

10. Owen, *Narrative*, vol. 1, 417–418, vol. 2, 154; Omar and Frankl, "Mombasa Chronicle," 107; Mbuia-Joao, "Revolt of Dom Jeronimo," 272.

11. See, for instance, al-Salimi and Jansen, *Portugal*, vol. 15; vol. 16, 203–208; 294–297.

12. Sheriff, *Dhow Cultures*, 239–258; Alpers, *Indian Ocean in World History*, 40–68.

13. Abu-Lughod, *Before European Hegemony*, 253.

14. Prange, *Monsoon Islam*.

15. Recent scholarship on nineteenth- and twentieth-century East Africa has successfully reframed interior regions as part of the Indian Ocean world. For example, see

158 NOTES

Gooding, *On the Frontiers*, and Julia Verne, "Ends of the Indian Ocean." For earlier periods, Chapurukha Kusimba and Jonathan Walz have emphasized that coastal Swahili towns were dependent upon interior regions—often featuring very distinctive social, ritual, and economic orientations—however, the full dynamics of these inland entanglements remain understudied relative to the histories of coastal towns. See discussion in Kusimba and Walz, "When Did the Swahili Become Maritime? A Reply," and Walz, "Inland Connectivity."

16. Although I'm speaking to the Indian Ocean context, my framing is inspired by Steven Feierman's writings on Africa and macronarratives of world history. See Feierman, "African Histories and the Dissolution of World History," and Feierman, "Colonizers, Scholars."

17. Taylor, *Giryama Vocabulary*, xv.

18. Freeman-Grenville, *East African Coast: Select Documents*, 20.

19. Gibb, *Travels*, vol. 2, 379.

20. Tibbetts, *Arab Navigation*, 208.

21. Pearson, *Port Cities*, 80–81.

22. Due to the island's modern population density, its archaeology visibility is poor compared to the best-known coastal archaeological sites, which consist of abandoned towns that have not been impacted by modern construction.

23. Kiriama, "Mombasa: Archaeology and History," 621.

24. Helm, "Conflicting Histories"; McConkey and McErlean, "Mombasa Island," 106.

25. Sassoon, "Excavations," 1–42.

26. Thorbahn, "Precolonial Ivory Trade"; Kusimba, Kusimba, and Dussubieux, "Beyond the Coastalscapes."

27. The nine Mijikenda are Chonyi, Digo, Duruma, Giryama, Jibana, Kambe, Kauma, Rabai, and Ribe.

28. Spear, *Kaya Complex*.

29. Willis, *Mombasa, the Swahili*. For additional details on the process of Mijikenda ethnicity formation, see Willis and Gona, "Tradition, Tribe, and State," 448–473.

30. Essays in Gearhart and Giles, eds., *Contesting Identities*, provide important correctives to the Swahili-centric focus of coastal scholarship, but they primarily address the modern period.

31. Mutoro, "Archaeological Study"; and Helm, "Conflicting Histories." Mutoro, along with George Abungu, was an early advocate for the importance of the interior for understanding East Africa's oceanic connections. See Abungu and Mutoro, "Coast-Interior Settlements."

32. Ray, *Ethnicity*.

33. Jeremy Prestholdt's *Domesticating the World* remains the classic study of East Africans' engagements of foreign goods. For examples from different parts of eastern and southern Africa, see Fleisher, "Rituals of Consumption"; Moffett and Chirikure, "Exotica in Context"; Wynne-Jones, *Material Culture*; Seligman, "Lip Ornaments."

34. For Mombasa's interior, see Kusimba, Kusimba, and Dussubieux, "Beyond the Coastalscapes."

35. For similar critiques in East African and South Asian historiography, see Kusimba and Walz, "When Did the Swahili Become Maritime? A Reply"; Walz and Gooding, "Reality and Representation"; Morrison, "Pepper in the Hills"; and Bauer, "Provincializing the Littoral."

NOTES   159

36. Ideas about identity and forms of "groupwork" certainly existed prior to this, but they are not a primary concern of in this book. On studying "groupwork" in precolonial Africa, see Schoenbrun, *Names of the Python*. On the dynamic history of collective identity in coastal East Africa, see Ray, *Ethnicity*.

37. I do so with full recognition that none of the actors considered in this book would have referred to themselves as "Mijikenda speakers," and, in many cases, if not most, they would not have considered their being part of the same "speech community" as an indicator of a collective identity.

38. Grollemund et al., "Bantu Expansion," 13296–13301.

39. See discussion of language change as it relates to Latin and other languages in Crowley and Bowern, *Historical Linguistics*, 3–19.

40. See Appendix 1 for further discussion of the classification and how I arrived at these dates. This narrative chronology largely follows the classification outlined in Derek Nurse and Thomas Hinnebusch's book, *Swahili and Sabaki: A Linguistic History*, which remains the most comprehensive classification of Sabaki languages.

41. For an overview of the first century of this scholarship, see Vansina, "Bantu in the Crystal Ball, I," and Vansina, "Bantu in the Crystal Ball, II."

42. For examples outside of Africa, see Anthony, *The Horse, the Wheel*, and Kirch and Green, *Hawaiki*.

43. A classification measures the genetic relationship between different languages based on their lexical, phonological, and morphological features. This provides a framework to understand the history of changes in the sounds, grammar, and lexicon of a group of languages, or a "language family," such as Sabaki.

44. For further discussion of words and things in historical linguistics, see de Luna and Fleisher, *Speaking with Substance*, 12–20.

45. Krapf, *Dictionary of the Suahili Language*, 270; Johnson, *Standard Swahili-English Dictionary*, 325.

46. Parkin, *Sacred Void*, 215.

47. Bastin et al., "Bantu Lexical Reconstructions 3," Main 1062 and DER 1050, henceforth, BLR3.

48. Guthrie, *Comparative Bantu*, vol. 3, 168; Schoenbrun, *Historical Reconstruction*, 182.

49. Contini-Morava, "Noun Class Markers," 22–23.

50. Kodesh, *Beyond the Royal Gaze*, 44; Colson, *Plateau Tonga*, 8–9.

51. Parkin, *Sacred Void*, 166, 208; Frank, *Habari na desturi*, 53–53; Ingrams, *Zanzibar*, 282; Middleton, *Land Tenure in Zanzibar*, 30; Knappert, *Swahili Islamic Poetry*, 73.

52. Gonzales, *Societies, Religion, and History*, 94–96; Swantz, *Medicine Man*, 18, 51–55; McVicar, "Wanguru Religion," 15–17; Beidelman, *Matrilineal Peoples*, 18–19, 33–34, 63, 71; Dale, "Account," 233–236.

53. See Frachetti, Smith, and Copp, "Pastoralist Participation," and Frachetti and Bullion, "Bronze Age Participation."

54. Much of this work is synthetic and broadly focused, for example, Bentley, *Old World Encounters*; Abu-Lughod, *Before European Hegemony*; Jennings, *Globalizations and the Ancient World*. Sanjay Subrahmanyam's approach to "connected histories" of social and political ideas represents another important model. See Subrahmanyam, "Connected Histories."

55. To be clear, such work represents an important scholarly turn by moving the focus beyond a nation-state framework and centering the ideas and actions of subaltern individuals

160   NOTES

within histories of the modern world. In the Indian Ocean, see, for instance, Alavi, *Muslim Cosmopolitanism*, and Simpson and Kresse, *Struggling with History*. For an enriching study of local practices as cosmopolitan, see Franklin, *Everyday Cosmopolitanisms*.

56. Jeremy Adelman's 2017 *Aeon* essay "What Is Global History Now?" represents one important origin point of debates about the limits of global connections. Subsequent essays—including some directly responding to Adelman—emphasize the interplay between connection and disconnection, arguing that disconnection itself is a form of global connection. In many ways, these insights were preceded by anthropological work on globalization by scholars like Anna Tsing and James Ferguson, who perceptively showed that frictions, disconnections, and fragmented engagements were key features of global interactions. See Tsing, *Friction*, and Ferguson, *Global Shadows*. For recent historical engagements with these questions, see Drayton and Motadel, "Futures of Global History"; Biedermann, "(Dis)connected History"; Wenzlhuemer et al., "Forum Global Dis:connections."

57. Green, "Waves of Heterotopia."

58. Cooper, "What Is the Concept of Globalization Good For?"; Ferguson, *Global Shadows*; Piot, *Remotely Global*; Prestholdt, *Domesticating the World*.

59. Wright, *The World and a Very Small Place*; Northrup, *Trade without Rulers*; McIntosh, *Ancient Middle Niger*; D'Avignon, *Ritual Geology*. In the case of Wright's classic study of Niumi, a small region in The Gambia, longer-term pressures of Atlantic slavery ultimately broke these tendencies, drawing it—unequally—into the Atlantic "world system." While a world systems approach emphasized integration, more recent scholarship, like D'Avignon's analysis of small-scale mining in the Bambuk region of West Africa, highlights how older ideas endured and even thrived across centuries of engagements with larger states and networks.

60. Feierman, "Colonizers, Scholars"; Schoenbrun, "Conjuring the Modern"; Janzen, *Lemba*; and d'Avignon, *Ritual Geology*, chap. 2.

61. Vaughn, "Africa and Global History," 200. For elaboration of how intra-African histories can constitute global histories, see Jimenez, "Southern Africa's Global Grain Basket."

62. For example, Oliver, "Bantu Expansion."

63. Vansina, *Paths*; Ehret, *African Classical Age*; Klieman, *Pygmies*; Schoenbrun, *Green Place*.

64. De Luna, *Collecting Food*; Stephens, *History of African Motherhood*; Saidi, *Women's Authority*; Stephens, *Poverty and Wealth*.

65. Fields-Black, *Deep Roots*; de Almeida, "Speaking of Slavery"; de Luna, "Sounding."

66. Gonzales, *Societies, Religion, and History*; Seligman, "Encircling Value"; Ray, *Ethnicity*.

67. De Luna, "Amassing Global History," 2.

68. For examples of studies taking the Indian Ocean as a unit of analysis: Chaudhuri, *Trade and Civilisation*; Risso, *Merchants of the Faith*; Sheriff, *Dhow Cultures*.

69. See Green, "Languages of Indian Ocean Studies."

70. Margariti, *Aden*; Prange, *Monsoon Islam*; Alpers and Goswami, eds., *Transregional Trade*; Um, *Merchant Houses*; Chaffee, *Muslim Merchants*.

71. Ho, *Graves of Tarim*; Machado, *Ocean of Trade*; Aslanian, *From the Indian Ocean*.

72. See, for instance, Bishara, *Sea of Debt*, and Elizabeth Lambourne, *Abraham's Luggage*.

73. Prange, "'Measuring by the Bushel,'" 214–219, and Morrison, "Christians and Spices."

NOTES 161

74. Riello, *Cotton*, chapters 2–3 provide a compelling glimpse of what this might have looked like. But compare this to work on later eras, like Chaudhuri, "Structure," and Subramanian, "Power and the Weave."

75. Margariti, *Aden*, 66. Margariti does an impressive job combing scattered written and archaeological sources to develop a sketch of towns in Aden's hinterland, which was "more populous and settled" than assumed, playing a key role in provisioning the city. But, as the author notes, a more systematic study is needed to understand the full scope of these relationships.

76. Verne, "Ends of the Indian Ocean"; Gooding, *On the Frontiers*.

77. As recent work in eastern and southern Africa shows, focusing on the local contexts in which people circulated and consumed trade goods is one way to address these shortfalls. See, for instance, Kusimba, Kusimba, and Dussubieux, "Beyond the Coastalscapes," and Moffett and Chirikure, "Exotica in Context."

78. Pearson, "Littoral Society."

79. Prange, "Scholars and the Sea," 1384.

80. Barnes, "Indian Cotton," and Guy, *Woven Cargoes*.

81. McDow, *Buying Time*.

82. Scott, *Art of Not Being Governed*, 216.

83. Boivin and Frachetti, "Introduction," 11.

84. Boivin and Frachetti, "Introduction," 11; Scott, *Art of Not Being Governed*.

1. UNMOORED FROM THE OCEAN

1. The monsoon was initiated by two tectonic "growth spurts" around 8–10 million years ago and 2.6–3.6 million years ago, respectively, which dramatically raised the mountain plateau on a short geological timescale. Zhiseng et al., "Evolution of Asian Monsoons."

2. Li and Yanai, "Onset and Interannual Variability."

3. Campbell, "Africa and the Early Indian Ocean."

4. Casson, *Periplus*.

5. See Spear and Nurse, *The Swahili*; Pouwels, *Horn and Crescent*; Horton and Middleton, *The Swahili*.

6. See, for instance, Fleisher and LaViolette, "Early Swahili Trade Village"; Fleisher, "Swahili Synoecism"; Pawlowicz, "Modeling the Swahili Past"; Wynne-Jones et al., "Urban Chronology."

7. Casson, *Periplus*.

8. Casson, *Periplus*, 132.

9. Casson, *Periplus*, 59. Menuthias is usually identified as Pemba, an island in the Zanzibar Archipelago.

10. Casson, *Periplus*, 61.

11. Casson, *Periplus*, 61.

12. Freeman-Grenville, *East African Coast: Select Documents*, 3–4.

13. Campbell, *Africa and the Indian Ocean World*, 61.

14. Horton and Middleton, *The Swahili*, 31–37; Casson, *Periplus*, 136–142; and Hughes and Post, "A GIS Approach," 135–156.

162 NOTES

15. Excavations from two sites on Zanzibar uncovered sherds of Mediterranean and Sassanian ceramics that date to the fifth or sixth century. Juma, "Swahili and the Mediterranean Worlds," 148–154, and Boivin et al., "East Africa," 243–244. Glassware fragments, glazed ceramics, and beads found in the Rufiji Delta, around the south-central coast of Tanzania, were once believed to offer direct archaeological evidence of early first-millennium Mediterranean–Indian Ocean trade. But upon reevaluation these finds were dated to the fifth or sixth century. See Chami, "Roman Beads"; Chami and Msemwa, "New Look"; Wood, "Eastern Africa."

16. Horton and Middleton, *The Swahili*, 37.

17. See, for instance, recent work on LSA communities at Kuumbi Cave on Zanzibar. Langley et al., "Poison Arrows"; Shipton et al., "Reinvestigation of Kuumbi Cave."

18. Ehret, *African Classical Age*, 275–76.

19. These settlements are associated with a regional ceramic variant that archaeologists refer to as "Kwale Ware." Archaeologist Felix Chami has suggested that some Early Iron Age/pre–Kwale Ware sites in central Tanzania may date as early as 200 BCE. However, most date the establishment of these sites around the start of the first millennium. See further discussion in Appendix 1.

20. Alpers, *Indian Ocean in World History*, 37.

21. Büntgen et al, "Cooling"; Newfield, "Climate Downturn."

22. Thambani et al., "Indian Summer Monsoon"; Gupta, "Abrupt Changes."

23. For discussion of the Indian Ocean context, see Campbell, *Africa and the Indian Ocean World*, 68–88, and Alpers, *Indian Ocean*, 39.

24. Freeman-Grenville, *Select Documents*, 14–17.

25. See LaViolette, "Swahili Cosmopolitanism," for a good overview.

26. Boivin et al., "East Africa"; Crowther et al., "Coastal Subsistence."

27. Vansina, "Slow Revolution."

28. East Africa's rainfall is affected by interactions between multiple climate phenomena, including El Niño Southern Oscillation Zone (ENSO), Indian Ocean Dipole (IOD), Sea Surface Temperatures (SST), and the Intertropical Convergence Zone (ITCZ). The movement of the ITCZ—referring to the point where the southwest and northwest trade winds meet—across the equator is traditionally understood as the key contributor to East Africa's bimodal rainfall. However, climate scientists' understanding of the exact ways the above dynamics interact remains incomplete. For discussion of how each individual factor impacts East Africa's climate, see Nicholson, "A Review of Climate Dynamics," and Marchant et al., "Indian Ocean Dipole." On the limits of the ITCZ paradigm, see Nicholson, "ITCZ."

29. Prins, *Swahili-Speaking Peoples*, 59–60; Prins, *Coastal Tribes of the North-Eastern Bantu*, 55; and Ingrams, *Zanzibar*, 275. Planting patterns vary more by microclimate inland from Mombasa. However, clearing generally takes place during the drier months preceding the long rains followed by planting either just before or immediately after the onset of the rains. See Waaijenberg, *Mijikenda Agriculture*, 106.

30. Ehret, *African Classical Age*, 12–14.

31. These interactions are evident in the array of loanwords that they adopted from Sudanic and Sahelian languages for crops (like sorghum and millet varieties) and different grain products. See Ehret, *African Classical Age*, 301–305.

32. Ehret, *African Classical Age*, 130.

NOTES   163

33. Ehret, *African Classical Age*, 130–131.

34. See Appendix 1 for discussion of the proposed settlement geography of Northeast Coast Bantu speakers.

35. Nurse and Hinnebusch, *Swahili and Sabaki*, 288, and Ehret, *African Classical Age*, 49.

36. Gonzales, *Societies, Religion, and History*, 59.

37. Gonzales, *Societies, Religion, and History*, 59. They retained the term *-tíkà, which referred to the long rainy season that lasted from March to May. While the long rains followed a similar seasonality to the eastern savanna grasslands occupied by their linguistic ancestors, the central and northeastern Tanzanian coast experienced an additional short rainy season from October to December.

38. Walsh, "Swahili Language," 122.

39. Konecky et al., "Impact of Monsoons," 17–25. The nearest climate data to the region occupied by Northeast Coast speakers comes from Lake Challa, a crater lake located about 250 kilometers inland from the coast and that flanks the eastern side of Mt. Kilimanjaro. Proxies from Lake Challa largely mirror the trends from other East African lakes, indicating that the region experienced a comparatively drier period during the first half of the first millennium, with "pronounced aridity" from 45 BCE to 57 CE. Buckles et al., "Interannual." For a summary of East Africa's climate history, see Lane and Breen, "Eastern African Coastal Landscape," 22–24.

40. Goldstein et al., "Hunter-Gatherer," 107390.

41. Goldstein et al., "Hunter-Gatherer," 107390; Roberts et al., "Late Pleistocene"; and Shipton et al., "78,000-Year-Old Record."

42. Helm, "Re-Evaluating Traditional Histories," 73.

43. Tuyere fragments and iron slag provide evidence of ironworking at Early Iron Age (EIA) sites in southeast Kenya's coastal hinterlands by the third or fourth century. See Soper, "Kwale," 3; Helm, "Conflicting Histories." EIA sites in central Tanzania show evidence of iron production from a few centuries earlier. See Appendix 1.

44. Fleisher and Wynne-Jones, "Finding Meaning."

45. Nurse and Hinnebusch, *Swahili and Sabaki*, 307, 585, 597, 601.

46. Nurse and Hinnebusch, *Swahili and Sabaki*, 290, 602.

47. For Swahili, see entries in Johnson, *Standard English-Swahili Dictionary*, 359–360. In Upper and Lower Pokomo, (-*phaiya*) and Elwana (-*phalila*) can describe weeding, hoeing, or clearing forest while compounds of these terms also describe different stages of weeding. Author's fieldnotes, August 21, 2014; October 20, 2014.

48. Nurse and Hinnebusch, *Swahili and Sabaki*, 292, 647; Gonzales, *Societies, Religion, and History*, 121, 135. While Nurse and Hinnebusch list the proto-Sabaki form as both *Wucelo and *Wucelu at different points in their book, the noun form with a final *-u has a wider distribution in Northeast Coast languages. In Sabaki languages, the term is attested in noun class 14 while Ruvu speakers attest the term in class 5. For a good description of the labors of creating this field type see Champion, *Agiryama*, 8.

49. Nurse and Hinnebusch, *Swahili and Sabaki*, 619; BLR3, Main 1509.

50. Nurse and Hinnebusch, 292, 642. This may be derived from the Bantu root -kónud- / -kónyud-, to "break off," which is associated with clearing trees in Great Lakes Bantu languages. See Schoenbrun, *Historical Reconstruction*, 56, 136, and BLR 3 DER 1947 and VAR 1932.

164   NOTES

51. Champion, *Agiryama*, 8–9; Waaijenberg, *Mijikenda Agriculture*, 168–170; Prins, *Swahili-Speaking Peoples*, 60–61; Middleton, *Land Tenure*, 16, 21.

52. Ethnographic records make this distinction, although it is not entirely consistent across the coastal region. See Prins, *Swahili-Speaking Peoples*, and Middleton, *Land Tenure*. It is hard to discern the precise distinction between *mugunda and *nkonde using comparative ethnographic evidence because Mijikenda and Pokomo have dropped one term or the other, respectively.

53. Nurse and Hinnebusch, *Swahili and Sabaki*, 289, 648.

54. Nurse and Hinnebusch, *Swahili and Sabaki*, 292, 634, 644. In subsequent centuries most daughter languages discarded one or the other type of grain storage with just a few Swahili dialects retaining both terms. For descriptions in Sabaki languages, see Johnson, *Standard English-Swahili Dictionary*, 486, 508; Parkin, *Sacred Void*, 100; Krapf, *Dictionary of the Suahili Language*, 413; and Charles Sacleux, *Dictionnaire*, 927–928, 976.

55. Nurse and Hinnebusch, *Swahili and Sabaki*, 559, 621, 634.

56. Nurse and Hinnebusch, *Swahili and Sabaki*, 292, 618.

57. Nurse and Hinnebusch, *Swahili and Sabaki*, 292, 639, 646–647.

58. Krapf, *Nika-English*, 216; Krapf, *Suahili*, 423; and Sacleaux, *Dictionnaire*, 1015.

59. Vansina, "Slow Revolution," and de Luna, *Collecting Food*.

60. These dates place the cultivation of these crops in the coastal region near the end of the proto-Sabaki period or shortly after. However, the "lack of systematic archaeobotany at any earlier coastal sites (particularly those dating to the EIA/Kwale period), suggest that a seventh century date for the arrival of African crops on the east coast should be considered a *terminus ante quem*." Boivin et al., "East Africa," 237. See also Crowther et al., "Subsistence Mosaics," 108–113; Walshaw, "Converting to Rice," 141–142; and Helm, et al., "Exploring Agriculture."

61. Nurse and Hinnesbusch, *Swahili and Sabaki*, 620. Archaeobotanical records similarly demonstrate that the cultivation of cowpeas was underway at coastal ironworking sites by the seventh century at the latest. See Crowther at al., "Subsistence Mosaics," 108, 112.

62. Attesting to the importance of small land mammals, Nurse and Hinnebusch proposed that the lexicon of proto-Sabaki speakers included new terms for "reedbuck" (*ntope) and a "duiker sp.," probably red duiker, (*mfuno). See Nurse and Hinnebusch, *Swahili and Sabaki*, 292, 637, 643. Both terms are also distributed in regular form in some neighboring Seuta languages and the Ruvu language, Kwere, indicating they may be Sabaki-era areal spreads or earlier Northeast Coast innovations.

63. The best faunal records come from the last few centuries of the first millennium, and they therefore provide a picture of diets in the period shortly after Sabaki began to diverge into separate languages. Records from the immediate interior, coastal belt, and offshore islands show that people in all of these regions relied heavily on locally available wild fauna. See Helm, "Conflicting Histories," 255–59; Mudida and Horton, "Subsistence at Shanga"; Crowther et al., "Coastal Subsistence"; Prendergast et.al., "Dietary Diversity."

64. De Luna, *Collecting Food*, 67, and Vansina, *Paths in the Rainforest*, 83–92.

65. Helm, "Conflicting Histories," 135–137; Wilson, "Spatial Analysis."

66. Lane and Breen, "Eastern African Coastal Landscape," 22–24. Climate proxies from Lake Challa indicate increased rainfall between 600–1000 CE, which represented the wettest period of the last 2200 years. Buckles et al., "Interannual," 1256.

NOTES   165

67. Crowther et al., "Subsistence Mosaics," 115; Boivin et al., "East Africa," 261–264.

68. Crowther et al., "Subsistence Mosaics," 115; Prendergast et al., "Dietary Diversity," 634.

69. LaViolette, "Swahili Cosmopolitanism," 30–35; Wynne-Jones, *Material Culture*, 29–34.

70. Fleisher and Wynne-Jones, "Ceramics."

71. Fleisher and Wynne-Jones, "Ceramics," 274.

72. Wynne-Jones, *Material Culture*, 39.

73. Miers and Kopytoff's articulation of "rights in persons" from their edited volume *Slavery in Africa* represents a classic modeling of the concept. See Guyer, "Wealth in People, Wealth in Things," 86, fn. 20, for examples of this broad observation in the secondary literature.

74. Guyer and Belinga, "Wealth in People."

75. Stephens, *Poverty and Wealth*, 11. As Stephens shows, concepts and wealth varied considerably across the diversity of speech communities living in a relatively compact region. Wealth could include possession of people (often wives), livestock, crops, and prestige goods. But it also encompassed abstract and emotional concepts, such as notions of wealth as possessing power or honor.

76. Ray, "Defining the Swahili," 73–74.

77. Ehret, *African Classical Age*, 150.

78. Ray, "Defining the Swahili," 74.

79. Ehret, *African Classical Age*, 149–150, and Gonzales, *Societies, Religion, and History*, 103. These two words are the Mashariki forms of *lukolo and *mulyongo, with the latter representing a merging of words meaning "lineage," "line (of objects)," and "door." See Ray, *Ethnicity*, 42–44.

80. Ehret, *African Classical Age*, 151. See also Ray, "Disentangling Ethnicity," 108–110, which builds from Ruel, "Structural Articulation." In most Northeast Coast languages, modern reflexes of *nyumba have taken the more general meaning of "house." However, the gendered connotation is retained among some. See, for instance, Beidelman, *The Kaguru*; Rigby, *Cattle and Kinship*; Prins, *Swahili-Speaking Peoples*, 78; Gerlach, "Social Organisation," 180.

81. Ruel, "Structural Articulation," 70–71.

82. Schoenbrun, *Green Place*, 98.

83. Ray, "Defining the Swahili," 73–74. While it is common to adopt an anthropological lens when studying past societies, and to view social organization as based around narrowly defined "matrilineal" or "patrilineal" descent practices, scholars of early Africa have demonstrated that ideas about descent and kinship were flexible and subject to historical change. See discussion in Stephens, *African Motherhood*, 10–11.

84. Ehret, *African Classical Age*, 146–149.

85. Ehret, *African Classical Age*, 252.

86. Specifically, the titles *-àmì and *-kúmú. In early Mashariki society, according to Ehret, these words referred to ritual leaders who were responsible for matters related to cultivation, harvests, and ancestor veneration. Kathryn de Luna posits that proto-Mashariki speakers used *-àmì to refer to an "agent of protection and prosperity" who could attract, provide nourishment for, and protect people among their web of contacts. The *-kúmú,

166   NOTES

meanwhile, was a very old position among Bantu speakers, referring to an "honored person," the reflexes of which came to mean things like "big man," "chief," and "doctor-diviner" in different Bantu languages. Based on a close reading of the term's aspect and morphology, de Luna has shown that the "honor" associated with *-kúmú was not directed at the person occupying this position. Instead, they cultivated a sense of collective honor that "dispersed across the community." See Ehret, *African Classical Age*, 146–147, and de Luna, *Collecting Food*, 47–49, 88–89. For broader discussion of these roots in other ancient Bantu social histories, see also Schoenbrun, *Green Place*, 104–105, 109–111; Klieman, *Pygmies*, 75; Vansina, *Paths in the Rainforest*, 274; and de Almeida, "Speaking of Slavery," 128–133.

87. Ehret, *African Classical Age*, 148. Ehret suggests that these associations linking "kin leaders to their dependents" may date to the proto-Bantu period or earlier.

88. Ray, "Defining the Swahili," 73. These associations endure in the ethnographic sources from many Northeast Coast daughter languages that used compound forms of *-éné to describe a lineage head or chief who also acted as the "owner" of the land or village occupied by the lineage. For example, in Sabaki: Mijikenda (Giriama), *mwenye t'si* or *mwenye mudzi* and Swahili (Amu), *mwenye mui*; in Seuta: Shambaa, *ng'wenye shi* or *ng'wenye mzi*; and in Ruvu: Sagara, *mwenyegoha* and Luguru *mwenye mulunga*. See Taylor, *Giryama Vocabulary*; El Zein, *Sacred Meadows*; Feierman, *Peasant Intellectuals*; and Beidelman, *Matrilineal Peoples*.

89. Ray, "Defining the Swahili," 73–74.

90. See Schoenbrun, *Historical Reconstruction*, 103–104; BLR3 2721; Guthrie, *Comparative Bantu*, vol. 4, 85.

91. Gonzales, *Societies, Religion, and History*, 107, 130–131.

92. Ruel, "Structural Articulation," 70.

93. Ray, "Defining the Swahili," 74.

94. For the limited Sabaki distribution of the meaning "village quarter," see Nurse and Hinnebusch, *Swahili and Sabaki*, 621. I also confirmed this distribution during language consultations in Mijikenda, Pokomo, and Elwana.

95. While Sabaki languages employ different terms to refer to these enclosures, Horton theorizes that they originated from an earlier practice in spatial organization. See Horton, "Swahili Architecture," 151–155, and Horton and Middleton, *The Swahili*, 121–123.

96. Kopytoff, *African Frontier*, 40–48.

97. Scholars of early Africa emphasize that leaders attracted a following not only through material redistribution, but also by monopolizing healing technologies, expanding their ritual networks, and by cultivating their own reputations. See, for instance, approaches in Schoenbrun, *Green Place*; de Luna, *Collecting Food*; Kodesh, *Beyond the Royal Gaze*; Vansina, *Paths in the Rainforest*.

98. Seligman, "Encircling Value," 40.

99. Appendix 3, no. 1.

100. Appendix 3, no. 2. See also Bresnahan, "Greatness," 370.

101. Nurse and Hinnebusch, *Swahili and Sabaki*, 610. Schoenbrun posits that the root *-túul- "give gift, tribute" and its nominal form date to proto-Mashariki. Schoenbrun, *Historical Reconstruction*, 170.

102. The earliest archaeological evidence of consumption rituals, such as communal feasts, dates to the early second millennium. See Fleisher, "Rituals of Consumption"; Wynne-Jones, "Remembering and Reworking."

NOTES 167

103. Appendix 3, no. 3.

104. Some Giryama homesteads included a section of land called kikola, which was worked collectively. See Parkin, *Sacred Void*, 113.

105. The mutual support offered by these common meals was especially important during the rainy season or in times of scarcity. The institution is best documented in literary sources, including proverbs and epic poetry about the Swahili/Pokomo folk hero Fumo Liongo. See Anon., *Hadithi za Kiunguja*, 53; Scheven, *Swahili Proverbs*, 244, 264–265, 268, 285–86; and Mbele, "Kikoa Incident."

106. Schoenbrun, "Violence, Marginality," 45.

107. Schoenbrun, "Violence, Marginality," 45. Although it follows regular sound correspondences, the term's distribution indicates that *muja may have spread from the Sabaki language along interior trade routes. See also Nurse and Hinnebusch, 616, and BLR3 Main 1391.

108. The antiquity of this term is uncertain. Nurse and Hinnebusch list it as a "proto-Swahili" innovation while also including the meaning in their proto-Sabaki lexis based on its regular form in a range of Swahili and Comorian dialects. See *Swahili and Sabaki*, 295, 616. The term also has a wider distribution in eastern and southern Africa, indicating its possible spread since the proto-Sabaki period. See Schoenbrun, "Violence, Marginality," 45, and BLR3 Comp 6464.

109. Appendix 3, no. 4.

110. On linguistic associations between being bereft or kinless and poverty, see Stephens, *Poverty and Wealth*.

111. Nurse and Hinnebusch, *Swahili and Sabaki*, 291, 613.

112. Bresnahan, "Greatness," 370–371.

2. LOOKING INLAND, TO THE WORLD

1. On Frank's biography, see Martin Walsh, "From Ribe Scribe to Nationalist Poet," July 10, 2010, https://notesandrecords.blogspot.com/2010/07/from-ribe-scribe-to-nationalist-poet.html.

2. Frank, *Habari na Desturi*, 8–12.

3. For discussion of the evolution of Swahili building materials, see Spear and Nurse, *The Swahili*, 16–22; Horton and Middleton, *The Swahili*, 119.

4. Meier, *Swahili Port Cities*, 37.

5. For a similar argument about Mijikenda political organization in relation to modern political categories, see Mkangi, "Democratic Roots." For other examples in Africa, see McIntosh, "Pathways to Complexity," and Fitzsimons, "Warfare, Competition."

6. Horton and Middleton, *The Swahili*, 42–46, quoting 46.

7. Many important insights have come from archaeologists writing on Pemba Island. See, for instance, LaViolette and Fleisher, "Urban History"; Fleisher, "Swahili Synoecism"; Wynne-Jones et al., "Urban Chronology." On connections with interior regions, see Pawlowicz, "Modeling the Swahili Past."

8. See Prange, *Monsoon Islam*, and Sheriff, *Dhow Cultures*.

9. This proto-Sabaki term was derived from an ancient Bantu word meaning "town" or "village." Nurse and Hinnebusch, *Swahili and Sabaki*, 619, and BLR3 Main 6466.

10. See Middleton, *World of the Swahili*, 102; Mwalonya et al., *Mgombato*, 118; Deed, *Giryama-English*, 66; Krapf, *Nika-English Dictionary*, 268–269; Munyaya, "Sense Relations,"

168 NOTES

69, 146; Ahmed-Chamanga, *Lexique Comorien*, 153–154; Bible Translation and Literacy, "Lower Pokomo Dictionary"; Krapf, *Dictionary of the Suahili Language*, 230; Johnson, *English-Swahili*, 282; Sacleux, *Dictionnaire*, 540. The exception is Elwana, where the term refers exclusively to a hamlet or family home. See Nurse, *Inheritance, Contact*.

11. Lobben, "Semantic Classification," 137.

12. Griffiths, "Glimpses," 268; Prins, *Swahili-Speaking Peoples*, 104; Walker, *Islands*, 94.

13. To borrow a phrase and argument from Fleisher and LaViolette, "Early Swahili Trade Village."

14. Wright, "Comoros and Their Early History."

15. Wynne-Jones, "Creating Urban Communities"; Chittick, *Kilwa*.

16. Horton, *Shanga*. Thus, Shanga's documented material changes and enduring spatial organization offer a model for understanding how humble villages grew over time into Islamic stone towns. See, for example, discussion of the town in Spear and Nurse, *The Swahili*, 19–21.

17. Fleisher, "Town and Village," 202.

18. Fleisher and LaViolette, "Early Swahili Trade Village." On domestic production see Flexner et al., "Bead Grinders."

19. Casson, *Periplus*, 140.

20. LaViolette and Fleisher, "Urban History."

21. LaViolette and Fleisher, "Urban History"; Fleisher, "Swahili Synoecism."

22. Wynne-Jones et al., "Urban Chronology," 33. Towns like Unguja Ukuu and Mikindani provide other good examples of varied trajectories on the Swahili coast. See Juma, *Unguja Ukuu*, and Pawlowicz, "Modeling."

23. Pawlowicz's work on Mikindani offers the clearest elaboration of this point.

24. Helm, "Conflicting Histories," 159.

25. Helm, "Conflicting Histories," 206–208.

26. Helm, "Conflicting Histories," 173.

27. Helm, "Conflicting Histories"; Shipton et al., "Intersections, Networks," 427–438.

28. These surveys were conducted by the National Museums of Kenya in the 1990s. For a visualization of the results of the surveys, see Helm, "Re-evaluating," 75–78.

29. Helm, "Conflicting Histories," 137–138, 275–294. See 301–348 for a gazetteer of these sites.

30. Helm, "Conflicting Histories," 287–290.

31. Ray, "Recycling Interdisciplinary Evidence," 121. Ray develops this idea by following the lead of coastal East African oral historians. He argues that professional historians should treat oral historians as "interpreters and theorists of the past rather than mere conveyers of evidence."

32. Spear and Nurse, *The Swahili*, 70–79. Many scholars view the Shirazi traditions as an explanation of the interplay between local and outside forces, as small coastal villages transformed into oceanic trading centers during the early second millennium, rather than representing the past as it happened. Spear and Nurse, *The Swahili*, 78–79; Pouwels, *Horn and Crescent*, 35–37. However, recent DNA analysis of skeletal remains adds support for the veracity of these traditions, showing that people in multiple Swahili towns had Asian genetic ancestry as the result of genetic mixing between Persian men and African women starting around 1000 CE. Brielle et al., "Entwined."

33. Abdulaziz, *Muyaka*, 19–21.

NOTES   169

34. Berg, "Swahili Community," 41–44.

35. Berg, 35–56. See also chap. 5 for more details on the twelve *miji*, also known as the Twelve Tribes.

36. As scholarship on oral traditions in other parts of eastern Africa has shown, generic tropes, spatial images, and chronicles of conflicts and disputes in oral traditions can yield important insights into past processes and changes. See Schoenbrun, *Names of the Python*; Kodesh, *Beyond the Royal Gaze*; and Shetler, *Imagining Serengeti*.

37. For analysis of this ritual and its role in the myth, see Dingley, "Kinship, Capital," 66–137; Walsh, "Mung'aro," 11–22.

38. For a synthesis of oral traditions following this arc, see Spear, *Kaya Complex*.

39. Spear, *Kaya Complex*, 106–128; Brantley, "Gerontocratic Government." On the *kayas* as sacred groves, see Nyamweru et al., "Kaya Forests," and Bresnahan, "Forest Imageries."

40. These phases correspond to the aspects of traditions discussed in chap. 2, 3, and 5 of Spear's *Kaya Complex*. See also, Helm, "Re-evaluating Traditional Histories," 80–81.

41. Helm analyzed oral traditions associated with over one hundred archaeological sites, including but not limited to *kayas*.

42. As Helm explains, "the 'dispersed' settlement pattern" that scholars often associated with the nineteenth century in fact "had its roots in an earlier pattern of settlement dynamics." Helm, "Re-evaluating Traditional Histories," 82.

43. Thomas Spear, *Mijikenda Historical Traditions*, no. 29 (Thomas Spear papers, 1969–2012, University of Wisconsin-Madison Archives), henceforth Spear, *MHT*.

44. See, for instance, Ray's analysis of Spear's interview with Thomas Govi in "Recycling Interdisciplinary Evidence," 116–126.

45. Brantley, box 16, folder 31, interviews 120 and 126; Spear, *MHT* 4, 58, 21; Griffiths, "Glimpses," 267; Champion, *Agiryama*, 4–5.

46. Spear, *MHT* 2, 8, 29, 43, 44, 67, 68; Helm Research Deposit, Fort Jesus Museum Library; Interview, Kambe, July 26, 2014.

47. Spear, *MHT* 8, 12, 20, 21, 23, 29, 32, 58.

48. Kodesh, "Networks of Knowledge," and *Beyond the Royal Gaze*. On clan activities in precolonial East Africa, see also Shetler, *Imagining Serengeti*, chap. 2, and Schoenbrun, *Names of the Python*.

49. This discussion of Sabaki clanship draws on Ray, "Disentangling Ethnicity," 139–217. For a discussion of medicines following clans in Mijikenda ethnography, see Udvardy, "Gender and the Culture of Fertility," 113, 119, 166.

50. See discussion of Helm's surveys and excavations in the section of this chapter titled "Port Cities and Other Possibilities."

51. See Spear, *MHT* 3, 23, 27, 67, and Brantley, box 16, folder 28, interview 11.

52. Spear, *MHT* 4, 16, 58.

53. Spear, *MHT* 4, 8, 12, 23, 31, 33, 43, 58; Brantley, box 16, folder 34.

54. To borrow from Schoenbrun, *Names of the Python*, 26. See also Walsh, "Mijikenda Origins," 10, for a similar observation on Mijikenda oral traditions.

55. Ray, "Recycling Interdisciplinary Evidence," 105.

56. Willis, *Mombasa, the Swahili*, 22.

57. My thinking here is influenced by Schoenbrun's writing on the contingent nature of groupwork in *Names of Python*.

170 NOTES

58. This description is developed from the ethnographic and oral sources cited in the following section.

59. Nurse and Hinnebusch, *Swahili and Sabaki*, 624; BLR3 Main 2545.

60. Kayamba, "Notes on the Wadigo," 91; Bergman, "Willingness to Remember," 54–58; Gerlach, "Social Organisation," 170–174. For examples in other NEC languages, see Dale, "Account," 223, 234–235; Baumann, *Usambara*, 140; Kisbey, *Zigula-English*, 9; Kimambo, *Political History*, 75, 87; Sacleux, *Dictionnaire*, 222; Horton, "Swahili Architecture," 155.

61. McIntosh, *Edge of Islam*, 178–181; Interview in Giryama, July 3, 2014. See discussion of this term in the introduction for linguistic and comparative ethnographic evidence.

62. Appendix 3, no. 5. For ethnographic accounts, see Kayamba, "Notes on the Wadigo," 85; Bergman, "Willingness to Remember," 128–136.

63. The ability to ritually occupy the space of a village through technologies like ancestral shrines was a key strategy for societies that regularly moved their settlements, as Jan Bender Shetler has shown for the western Serengeti region of Tanzania. See *Imagining Serengeti*, 103–114.

64. Parkin, *Sacred Voidi* 207–208; R. Ngala, *Nchi na Desturi*, 35; Griffiths, "Glimpses," 275; S. Ngala, "Mila za Mijikenda." Digo speakers are the exception. They appeased their *koma* at burial areas located outside of the settled area of their *midzi*. Gerlach, "Social Organisation," 142; Mwalonya et al., *Mgombato*, 74. During the mid-nineteenth century, Krapf indicated that *koma* huts were erected in *kayas*; he also noted *koma* located outside of villages, indicating that the practice of placing them inside the village may be a more recent adaptation. Krapf, *Travels, Researches*, 150, 176.

65. Brown, "Miji Kenda Grave," 37.

66. Bergmann, "Willingness to Remember," 232; Parkin, *Sacred Void*, 206–215; Champion, *Agiryama*, 28; New, *Life, Wanderings*, 106, 120–22.

67. Appendix 3, no. 6, and Nurse and Hinnebusch, *Swahili and Sabaki*, 669.

68. Bunger, *Islamization*, 93–96; Harris, *Casting Out Anger*, 32, 83–84. In the nearby Pare Mountains, people placed the skulls of exhumed ancestors in pots, referring to both the skull pots and the ancestral spirits as *nkoma*. See Kimambo, *Political History*, 191.

69. Appendix 3, no. 7. For a summary of the Chaga-Taita group (also called Kilimanjaro-Taita), see Nurse, "Towards a Historical Classification," 5.

70. Kusimba, Kusimba, and Dussubieux, "Beyond the Coastalscapes," 406–416.

71. Harris, *Casting Out Anger*, 25–26.

72. Fitzgerald, *Travels in the Coastlands*, 104–105; Brantley, box 12, folder 31; Interview in Giryama, July 10, 2014.

73. See discussion in de Luna, *Cultivating Foods*, 121–125.

74. In proto-Sabaki, their older forms referred to a "grassland" (*nyika) and "thicket, brush" (*įcaka), according to Nurse and Hinnebusch. See *Swahili and Sabaki*, 623, 644; BLR3 Main 423 and 3347. In Mijikenda dialects, Krapf, *Nika*, 54, 309; Mwalonya et al., *Mgombato*, 138, 175; Deed, *Giryama-English*, 83, 98,

75. See Appendix 3, no. 8, and descriptions in Rigby, *Cattle and Kinship*, 207; Kenyatta, *Facing Mount Kenya*, 36, 217; Saberwal, *Traditional Political System*, 76; Sacleux, *Dictionnaire*, 922–923; Kayamba, "Notes on the Wadigo"; Interview in Digo, September 4, 2014.

76. Nurse and Hinnebusch, *Swahili and Sabaki*, 646; Spear, *Kaya Complex*, 47–48. Some dialects also retained the more general meaning of an "open tract of land" for *lwanda*. Deed, *Giryama-English*, 58; Krapf, *Nika*, 217; Interview in Ribe, July 23, 2014.

77. For details on the terms appearing in the table, see Nurse and Hinnebusch, *Swahili and Sabaki*, 333 (*moro*); Walsh, "Segeju Complex," 43 (*rome/dhome*); and Appendix 3, nos. 8, 9, 10, 11.

78. Ehret posited that Mijikenda began to form into dialects by 1000 CE, while Phillip Sedlak proposed Digo and Giryama began to diverge as early as the mid-eighth century (±120) with CMK dialects and Giryama only distinguishing themselves around the start of the seventeenth century (±70). See Ehret, *African Classical Age*, 186; Sedlak, "Sociocultural Determinants," 143. These dates are derived from a method called glottochronology, which posits that languages tend to replace core vocabulary at a standard rate of approximately twenty-seven words over one thousand years. Figures derived from lexicostatistics (computing shared cognate rates in the core vocabulary of languages) can help produce a rough estimate for the date at which languages diverged from one another. In studies of Mijikenda dialects, linguists have determined that internal averages in shared cognates are 73.3 percent with a median of 73.5 (Nurse and Hinnebusch, one hundred items) and 74.7 percent with a median of 78 percent (Sedlak, two hundred items). I calculated 78.7 percent internal average with a median of 81.5 percent based on one hundred item lists that I collected in Kenya in 2012–2013 (I attribute this slightly higher cognition rate compared to previous studies to the heavy influence of Swahili on Nurse and Hinnebusch's Digo lists and Sedlak's use of a two-hundred-word list). These figures are consistent with a broad estimate that Mijikenda began to diverge into dialects by the early second millennium CE.

79. I use the name Central Mijikenda (CMK) to refer to the speech of Chonyi, Jibana, Kambe, Kauma, and Ribe. While these communities maintain distinct social identities, there are few lexical differences among them, and they are identical in terms of their sounds and grammar. As a result, I treat them as one dialect while respectfully acknowledging that speakers themselves may refer to their language differently, i.e., Chichonyi vs. Chijibana/ Chidzihana.

80. On lexical and morphological differences in Digo, see Nurse and Hinnebusch, *Swahili and Sabaki*, 537–539.

81. See Appendix 2 for outline of sound changes in the Mijikenda dialects. "Core" refers to words that are culturally neutral and therefore less resistant to change. Typical items include personal pronouns, numerals one through five, and common verbs like "to go," "to sit," and "to stand." Linguists use lists of one hundred to two hundred basic vocabulary items to establish genetic relationships between languages.

82. As a result of these frequent and enduring interactions, I am cautious about placing the words outlined in the chart precisely in time. Because words can easily be invented or borrowed at one end of the dialect chain and spread to adjacent dialects, it is often hard to determine exactly where and when a word was invented. This is especially true if the words under consideration are not affected by any sound changes. Since most of the words in the chart postdate the proto-Sabaki period, however, what they do illuminate is the substantial degree of innovation related to meeting places in Mijikenda society.

83. Appendix 3, no. 11. On the use of this space in the ethnography: Parkin, *Sacred Void*, 113; Tinga, "Spatial Organization"; Interview in Chonyi, October 14, 2014; Interview in Rabai, August 13, 2014. On the *kinyaka* in Kamba, see Mutuku et al., "Social and Cultural Antecedents," 108.

84. For descriptions of the *p'ala*: Wolfe, *Vigango*, 38–47; Parkin, *Sacred Void*, 108–09; Johnston, "Dispute Settlement," 293–94; Brantley, box 16, folder 28, int. 1, 9, 108.

172 NOTES

85. Appendix 3, no. 10. In the ethnography: Bergman, "Willingness to Remember," 222–223; Dale, "Account," 213–214, 235–236; Interview in Digo, October 18, 2013; Interview in Kambe, August 12, 2014; Interview in Rabai, August 13, 2014; Interview in Chonyi, October 14, 2014. In Giryama interviews, I was told *p'ala* is equivalent to *ndala* in other Mijikenda dialects. Interview, July 14, 2014.

86. Gerlach, "Social Organisation," 181–182; Bergman, "Willingness to Remember," 216–217. Among Duruma speakers, *rungu* was also used by members of male healing groups. Griffiths, "Glimpses," 292–293.

87. Brantley, box 16, int. 55; Dingley, "Kinship, Capital," 271; Udvardy, "*Kifudu*," 137–152.

88. Appendix 3, no. 8.

89. Appendix 3, no. 9. On agricultural terms, see discussion of *-palil- in chap. 1.

90. Schoenbrun, *Historical Reconstruction*, 60.

91. Gonzales, *Societies, Histories, Religion*, 97. This term is retained in some Mijikenda, i.e., *mulungu*: "An evil spirit supposed to cause sickness." Krapf, *Nika-English*, 285.

92. This evidence for various types of forested meeting places and ritual groves supports Willis's assertion that during the twentieth century a "diverse set of settlement sites and places of power may have been reinterpreted as *kayas*." See Willis, "Northern Kayas," 96. For a discussion of how this unfolded during the colonial period, see Bresnahan, "Forest Imageries." Beyond the ubiquitous example of the *fingo* charms in *kaya* narratives, many of the other spaces discussed in this section are incorporated into some historical representations of the *kayas*. See Tinga, "Spatial Organization," 35–41.

93. Krapf, *Nika*, 268.

94. Feierman, "Colonizers, Scholars."

95. See Feierman, "Colonizers, Scholars"; Kodesh, *Beyond the Royal Gaze*; Schoenbrun, "Conjuring the Modern."

96. Janzen, *Lemba*.

97. Nurse and Hinnebusch, *Swahili and Sabaki*, 616.

98. Ray, "Recycling Interdisciplinary Evidence," 117.

99. Ray, "Disentangling Ethnicity," 141–145.

100. Nurse and Hinnebusch, *Swahili and Sabaki*, 616; BLR3 Main 1332.

101. Nurse and Hinnebusch, *Swahili and Sabaki*, 616; BLR3 Main 861; Der 392 and 393. I follow anthropologist Diane Ciekawy in referring to *utsai* as harmful magic. See Ciekawy, "Utsai as Ethical Discourse." In other Sabaki languages, see Bunger, *Islamization*, 99–100; Middleton, *World of the Swahili*, 181–183.

102. Ciekawy, "Witchcraft Eradication," 64–65.

103. Ray, "Disentangling Ethnicity," 208–209. On the close relationship between medicines that healed and medicines that harmed in precolonial Africa, see Feierman, *Peasant Intellectuals*, chap. 2–3; Schoenbrun, *Green Place*, 110–111; Janzen, *Lemba*, 13–16.

104. Nurse and Hinnebusch, *Swahili and Sabaki*, 596; BLR3 Main 872.

105. For details in Mijikenda, Swahili, and Pokomo, see Johnston, "Dispute Settlement"; Krapf, *Nika*, 178, and *Travels*, 173–174; New, *Life, Wanderings*, 111–112; and Kayamba, "Notes on the Wadigo," 93–96; Johnson, *Swahili*, 18; Sacleux; *Dictionnaire*, 344; Bunger, *Islamization*, 99.

106. New, *Life, Wanderings*, 111–112.

107. On protective *virapho* in Mijikenda dialects, see Prins, *Coastal Tribes*, 78; Brantley, "Oaths," in box 12, folder 32 and box 16, int. 29; Griffiths, "Glimpses," 277–278; Ngala, "Mila

NOTES   173

za Mijikenda"; Krapf, *Nika*, 178. Swahili speakers used *viapo* (Standard Swahili form) to protect fields and property. See Krapf, *Dictionary of the Suahili Language*, 135; Stigand, *Land of Zinj*, 128. In Pokomo, people used *vilaфo* as "traps" to protect fields, homes, and animals from thieves. Author's email communications with Swaleh Odha, August 2022.

108. Monica Udvardy, "Gender and the Culture of Fertility," 23; Griffiths, "Glimpses," 277–278, 287–288; Spear, *MHT* 31, 45, 58, 63.

109. Ray, "Disentangling Ethnicity," 208–215.

110. Griffiths, "Glimpses," 288; Udvardy, "Culture of Fertility," 123.

111. Each of these has dialectical variations so they are also rendered and in the historical and ethnographic literature as: *kinyenze, gohu, mvaya, bahasi*, and *kifudu*. Apart from *habasi ~ bahasi*, all are cognates. In most sources *phaya* is written as *vaya*.

112. Brantley, box 16, folder 31, int. 125; Krapf, *Nika*, 178. See Parkin, *Sacred Void*, 153–154, for a description of an early twentieth-century *fisi* oath.

113. New, *Life, Wanderings*, 113.

114. Digo speakers also practiced *virapho* in the sense of administering judicial oaths and medicines. The absence of medicinal groups outside of *vifudu* may be due to Digo speakers' widespread adoption of Islam beginning in the mid-1800s or other factors, as several aspects of Digo political organization are distinct from other Mijikenda groups. See Prins, *Coastal Tribes*, 76, and Kayamba, "Notes on the Wadigo," 81–84.

115. BRL3 Main 2110; See Nurse and Hinnebusch, *Swahili and Sabaki*, 624. The original source item in Sabaki is the term * įfų̠lu ~ * įfų̠vų̠, meaning "tortoise." In Mijikenda and some Swahili, it refers to an empty shell or coconut shell with its Mijikenda form being attested with a new noun prefix giving the connotation of "small, shelled thing" hence, coconut shell/medicinal pot.

116. Udvardy, "Culture of Fertility," 143–178; Udvardy, "Gender Metaphors," 50; Bergman, "Willingness to Remember," 215–221; Gerlach, "Social Organisation," 161–170.

117. Krapf, *Nika*, 244; Parkin, *Sacred Void*, 209; Champion, *Agiryama*, 36; Ngala, "Mila za Mijikenda."

118. Udvardy, "Culture of Fertility," 93–106; Parkin, *Sacred Void*, 137–150; Mwalonya, et al., *Mgombato*, 191; Hamamoto, "Order of the Homestead."

119. Dingley, "Kinship, Capital," 249.

120. See Spear, *MHT* 8, 12, 16, 23, 58. Some traditions claim that the Laa—the hunter-foragers said to have guided people to their *kayas* and who ultimately joined their clans—introduced medicines that cured this affliction.

121. Parkin, *Sacred Void*, 209–210. On the *vifudu*'s role in reproduction, see Udvardy, "Gender, Power," 146–147, and "Kifudu." My framing of the complementary relationship between these two male and female groups draws from Udvardy's discussion of the *vifudu* and *vigango* in "Gender Metaphors," 47–48.

122. The initiation feast is called *nyambura*, where *gophu* initiates received their carved armlet, the ritual adornments that marked their status. The verb *kurura* or *kudhura* referred to the act of receiving these initiation honors. On the loanwords, see Walsh, "Segeju Complex," 42. On the initiations, see George Gona, "AGiryama the Rise of Tribe and Its Traditions," n.p., 98–100, in Brantley, box 16, folder 32; Orchardson-Mazrui, "Socio-Historical Perspective," 173–177; Dingley, "Kinship, Capital," 244–251.

123. Wolfe, *Vigango*, 56–75.

124. Wolfe, *Vigango*; Orchardson-Mazrui, "Socio-Historical Perspective," 179–185.

174   NOTES

125. Champion, *Agiryama*, 23.

126. Spear, *Kaya Complex*, 106.

127. As Rhiannon Stephens observed for proto-Gwe-Saamia speakers, the "small-scale nature of political authority" along with a long settlement history in the Lake Victoria Nyanza region "created space for wealthier people to assert themselves in the community." Similar social/spatial dynamics may have contributed to the tight relationship between wealth and power in Mombasa's interior. See Stephens, *Poverty and Wealth*, 92–93.

128. Spear, *MHT* 32, 33, 38, 43, 44, 63, 66. See also Champion, *Agiryama*, 23.

129. Champion, *Agiryama*, 35.

130. McIntosh, "Pathways to Complexity," 11. McIntosh's argument builds on Northrup, *Trade without Rulers*, 107–113.

131. Champion, "Report by ADC-Giriama, October 28, 1913," KNA 72/6/11/12; Brantley, "Notes on Giryama Government," box 12, folder 28. Notably, Champion and Brantley both emphasize in their fieldnotes and informal commentaries the centrality of healing groups in the absence of a formal government. However, these observations stand in contrast to their later published accounts that tried to fit these practices into a story of formal government institutions.

3. THE INLAND UNDERPINNINGS OF INDIAN OCEAN COMMERCE

1. On gateway communities, see Hirth, "Interregional Trade." While this traditionally refers to market towns and urban entrepôt, I believe the gateway concept is also useful for understanding decentralized rural communities like Mijikenda because it draws attention to their role controlling the entry and exit of trade goods within a specific region: Mombasa and its adjacent inland ridges. Thus, Mijikenda commercial advantages rested on their geography as well as the commercial, ritual, military, and political strategies they mobilized to manage control of this metaphorical "gate."

2. See, for instance, Kusimba, Kusimba, and Dussubieux, "Beyond the Coastalscapes"; Walz, "Routes to a Regional Past"; Denbow, Klehm, and Dussubieux, "Glass Beads of Kaitshaa"; Wilmsen, "Tsodilo Hills"; Chirikure, "Land and Sea"; Moffett, Hall, and Chirikure, "Crafting Power"; Moffett and Chirikure, "Exotica in Context."

3. Seligman, "Encircling Value," and de Luna, *Collecting Food*, chap. 5.

4. For discussion of reframing "hinterland" regions in eastern and southern Africa, see Gonzales, *Societies, Religion, and History*, chap. 2, and de Luna, *Collecting Food*, chap. 5.

5. Shipton et al., "Intersections, Networks," 434.

6. Shipton et al., "Intersections, Networks," 438.

7. Helm et al., "Exploring Agriculture," 54–59. Excavations have also yielded lithic artifacts at late first-millennium sites associated with Middle Iron Working settlements, indicating that the occupants of these sites held trading relationships with the communities that produced stone technologies. See, also, Helm, "Conflicting Histories," 146–153, 159–172.

8. Especially since many sites established during the late first millennium were strategically placed to give their occupants access to a range of wild and domestic resources. See Mutoro, "Archaeological Study," 44–102; Abungu and Mutoro, "Coast-Interior Settlements," 694–704.

9. Helm et al., "Exploring Agriculture," 46–47; Shipton et al., "Intersections, Networks" 442–443; Helm, "Conflicting Histories," 145–181.

NOTES   175

10. McConkey and McErlean, "Mombasa Island," 106; Sassoon, "Excavations," 1–42.

11. Krapf, *Dictionary of the Suahili Language*, 282. See also Willis, *Mombasa, the Swahili*, 27–28.

12. "This area is broadly differentiated into the eastern-facing foot plateau (comprising the Pingilikani, Lutsangani and Dzitsoni uplands) and the western coastal range (comprising the Kaloleni, Kwale, Rabai and Kinango uplands, the Shimba Plateau in the south and Mwangea Hill in the north)." Shipton et al., "Intersections, Networks," 429–30.

13. This paragraph draws from Moomaw, *Plant Ecology*; Helm, "Conflicting Histories," 72–100; and Shipton et al., "Intersections, Networks," 428–430.

14. Thorbahn, "Precolonial Ivory Trade."

15. See Kusimba, Kusimba, and Wright, "Development and Collapse"; Kusimba, Kusimba, and Dussubieux, "Beyond the Coastalscapes"; and Wright, "New Perspectives."

16. Thorbahn developed a chronology for ivory procurement in Tsavo by studying historical records for tusk weights for ivory exported from East Africa. He determined that the average tusk weight declined steadily between the sixteenth and nineteenth centuries and suggested that by the 1700s elephant herds in East Africa were being overexploited.

17. Kusimba, Kusimba, and Wright, "Development and Collapse," 244.

18. My framing of this later point is influenced by Stahl, "Political Economic Mosaics." For a critique of the use of mosaics in African history and archaeology, see de Luna, *Collecting Food*, 14.

19. Bravman, *Making Ethnic Ways*, 23.

20. Kusimba, Kusimba, and Wright, "Development and Collapse," 247. See also Wakefield and Johnston, "Routes," 314, and Hobley, *Kenya*, 63–64.

21. Kusimba, Kusimba, and Dussubieux, "Beyond the Coastalscapes," 409.

22. Kusimba and Kusimba, "Preindustrial Water Management," 34–36.

23. Kusimba, Kusimba, and Dussubieux, "Beyond the Coastalscapes," 416.

24. On marine glass beads at different inland sites, see Kusimba, Kusimba, and Dussubieux, "Beyond the Coastalscapes," 418; Kusimba and Walz, "Maritime Myopia," 436; Helm, "Conflicting Histories," 194; Shipton et al., "Intersections, Networks," 445; Dussubieux et al., "Trading of Ancient Glass."

25. Kusimba, Kusimba, and Dussubieux, "Beyond the Coastalscapes," 417–418. See also Wynne-Jones, *Material Culture*, chap. 5.

26. Walz, "Routes to a Regional Past," 272–274. On Mtsengo, see Helm, "Conflicting Histories," 181–196, and Shipton et al., "Intersections, Networks," 445.

27. Walz, "Routes to a Regional Past," 245, 272–273.

28. Walz, 274.

29. Freeman-Grenville, *East African Coast: Select Documents*, 20, 23.

30. Kusimba and Killick, "Ironworking," 114–115.

31. Kusimba and Killick, "Ironworking," 106; Kusimba and Walz, "Maritime Myopia," 436.

32. Kusimba, Kusimba, and Wright, "Development and Collapse," 251.

33. In oral traditions, see Spear, *MHT* 1, 2, 16, 23, 29, 45, 68. For additional discussion of Mijikenda arrow poison, see Parker, *Ivory Crisis*, 33–40; Steinhart, *Black Poachers*, 26–29; Walker, "Giriama Arrow Poison," 226–28; and Walsh, "Elephant Shrews."

34. Freeman-Grenville, *East African Coast: Select Documents*, 179; Theal, *Records*, vol. 6, 249–250.

176   NOTES

35. Kusimba, Kusimba, and Dussubieux, "Beyond the Coastalscapes," 408.

36. Wood and Ehret, "Origins and Diffusion," 14.

37. Wood and Ehret, "Origins and Diffusion," 9–10.

38. Wood and Ehret, "Origins and Diffusion," 13–14.

39. Appendix 3, no. 12.

40. Nurse and Hinnebusch, *Swahili and Sabaki*, 304. See Ehret, *Historical Reconstruction*, 269 for details on the proto–Southern Cushitic item.

41. Ehret, *History and Testimony*, 174–213, and Ehret and Nurse, "Taita Cushites." It is unclear precisely when Mijikenda speakers adopted the term other than sometime after the proto-Sabaki period (based on the word's phonetic shape in Mijikenda languages). Based on archaeological evidence from Tsavo and the established chronology for Southern Cushitic languages in the region, sometime during the first half of the second millennium is a safe estimate.

42. For a broader discussion of how global trade relied on translocal circulations in goods and decentralized and often mobile trading agents, see essays in Boivin and Frachetti, eds., *Globalization in Prehistory*.

43. Theal, *Records*, vol. 3, 80–82; Freeman-Grenville, *East African Coast: Select Documents*, 51–53.

44. Dua, *Captured at Sea*, 163–164.

45. Hamdun and King, *Ibn Battuta*, 16–17.

46. Freeman-Grenville, *East African Coast: Select Documents*, 51.

47. Theal, *Records*, vol. 3, 80–81.

48. Casson, *Periplus*, 61.

49. Horton, "Swahili Corridor," 86–93; Alpers, "Ivory Trade," 353.

50. Freeman-Grenville, *East African Coast: Select Documents*, 14–15.

51. Zhao also wrote that Asian elephants tusks weighed only "ten to twenty or thirty catties" in contrast to "large specimens" from African elephants weighing "from fifty to a hundred catties." A catty is a Chinese measurement equaling about six hundred grams, meaning the largest tusks from African elephants weighed over one hundred pounds (an accurate estimate based on modern figures). Hirth and Rockhill, *Chau Ju-kua*, 232.

52. Machado, *Ocean of Trade*, 169–170.

53. The reason ivory exports from southeast Africa are better documented is because Portuguese influence there was more enduring and because Portuguese traders also had better access to interior regions. See Pearson, *Port Cities*, 81–87.

54. Dames, *Book of Duarte Barbosa*, 21.

55. Foster, *English Factories*, 57.

56. Freeman-Grenville, *East African Coast: Select Documents*, 156. See also Jenson, *Journal*, 45.

57. Astley and Green, *New General Collection*, vol. 3, 389.

58. Al-Salimi and Jansen, *Portugal*, vol. 16, 208.

59. Al-Salimi and Jansen, *Portugal*, vol. 16, 237, 348; Astley and Green, *New General Collection*, 389.

60. On the inner workings of maritime trade superintendencies, see Chaffee, *Muslim Merchants*, 86–89.

61. The entry on ivory in book 2 notes that it originated in Arabia, specifically Mirbat. However, entries on Zanzibar and the Berber Coast in book 1 note that both places produced elephant tusks. See Hirth and Rockhill, *Chau Ju-kua*, 116, 126, 128, 232.

NOTES   177

62. For a discussion of Waata hunting techniques, see Steinhart, *Black Poacher*, 24–29; Parker, *Ivory Crisis*, 34–40. Steinhart suggests that these hunting techniques date back to the first millennium.

63. Hirth and Rockhill, *Chau Ju-kua*, 232.

64. On bow hunting with poisoned arrows, see Marks, "Hunting Behavior," 25. Regarding other techniques, see de Luna, "Collecting Food," 210; Forssman et al., "How Important Was the Presence of Elephants," 81–83.

65. Kusimba, Kusimba, and Dussubieux, "Beyond the Coastalscapes," 409.

66. Spear, *MHT* 1, 2, 16, 23, 29, 45, 68.

67. Kirkman, "Muzungulos of Mombasa," 78–79.

68. According to Resende's early seventeenth-century account, ivory procured from inland merchants was also shipped from Mtwapa, a smaller Swahili town fifteen kilometers north of Mombasa that similarly sat at the end of an estuarian creek that connected the town to Mijikenda-speaking settlements along the coastal ridge. Freeman-Grenville, *East African Coast: Select Documents*, 186.

69. Emery, "Short Account," 283.

70. Gray, *British in Mombasa*, 61–62.

71. Krapf, "Journal Descriptive of a Journey Made to Ukambani, 1849," CMS/B/OMS/C A5 O16/174.

72. Prestholdt, *Domesticating the World*, 74–74.

73. Burton, *Lakes Region*, 536–538. See also Sunseri, "Political Ecology," 206–207.

74. More precisely, these coastal forests were "dry lowland or hill-land forests sandwiched between the Indian Ocean littoral and the Eastern Arc montane rainforests." See Sunseri, "Political Ecology," 202–204.

75. Crowther et al., "Use of Zanzibar Copal."

76. The best evidence of its use in southern Arabia comes from extensive finds at Sharma, a tenth- to twelfth-century settlement on the southern coast of Yemen. Copal is also mentioned among the merchandise imported to the port city of Aden during the late thirteenth century. See Regert et al., "Reconstructing."

77. Theal, *Records*, vol. 3, 213, 83; al-Salimi and Jansen, *Portugal*, vol. 1, 194, and vol. 2, 179.

78. Brady, *Commerce and Conquest*, 75.

79. Jenson, *Journal*, 73. According to French traders at Kilwa, Mombasa remained a main port of call for English ships to obtain ivory, ambergris, and copal throughout the eighteenth century. See Freeman-Grenville, *French at Kilwa*, 221.

80. Burton, *Lakes Region*, 537. On Mijikenda copal procurement during the mid-nineteenth century, see New, *Life, Wanderings*, 84; Sperling, "Growth of Islam," 44, fn. 5; and Spear, *MHT* 10.

81. The word copal is itself a loan in European languages from Meso-America, originally deriving from a Nahuatl word meaning "incense."

82. Sunseri, "Political Ecology," 204.

83. Taylor, *Giryama*, 28, 46; Krapf, *Nika*, 259. This term is also attested in an areal form in neighboring languages like Taita and Kamba. See Shaw, *Pocket Vocabulary*, 35, and Wray, *Elementary Introduction*, 98. Elwana also attests a cognate form, *moogolo*, which refers to a "certain shrub and its resin (used as resin)," possibly indicating that the Mijikenda term dates to proto-Sabaki. See Nurse, *Inheritance, Contact*.

178   NOTES

84. Mijikenda and Zaramo (a Ruvu language) share a linguistic heritage, both being part of the Northeast Coast group of languages.

85. On the importance of inland material interests, see Prestholdt, *Domesticating the World*; Seligman, "Lip Ornaments."

86. Shipton et al., "Intersections, Networks," 441–445.

87. The main evidence of textile production industries comes from spindle whorls recovered from Swahili towns. In some towns, artisans continued to produce cotton, weaving together locally produced cotton with imported threads to produce new color patterns and styles. Horton, "Artisans," 73–75.

88. Hirth and Rockhill, *Chau Ju-kua*, 126.

89. Theal, *Records*, vol. 3, 83, and vol. 6, 250. On Cambay, see Machado, *Ocean of Trade*, 122–125.

90. Machado, *Ocean of Trade*, 120.

91. Horton and Middleton, *The Swahili*, 111–112.

92. Freeman-Grenville, *East African Coast: Select Documents*, 37.

93. Theal, *Records*, vol. 1, 66–67.

94. Dames, *Book of Duarte Barbosa*, 27–28. See also Freeman-Grenville, *East African Coast: Select Documents*, 110; Pearson, *Port Cities*, 48, and Horton, "Artisans," 74.

95. Freeman-Grenville, *East African Coast: Select Documents*, 185.

96. Freeman-Grenville, *East African Coast: Select Documents*, 180.

97. Barnes, "Indian Cotton," 15–30.

98. Horton, "Artisans," 74.

99. Quoted in Pearson, *Port Cities*, 48.

100. Parthasarathi, *Why Europe Grew Rich*, 21–50; Riello, *Cotton*, 110–134.

101. The remainder of this section expands on a short essay I wrote for *World History Commons*. See Bresnahan, "Short Teaching Module."

102. For a similar discussion of globally circulating commodities more generally, see Um, *Shipped*, 2–3.

103. See Prestholdt, *Domesticating the World*; Seligman, "Wealth"; Wynne-Jones, *Material Culture*, especially chap. 5; and Biginagwa, "Historical Archaeology."

104. For a good discussion of textiles' names during the nineteenth century, see Fee, "'Cloths with Names.'"

105. Nurse and Hinnebusch, *Swahili and Sabaki*, 640.

106. Appendix 3, no. 13. In Northeast Coast languages, reflexes of *-cambo are articulated in noun classes 5, 7, 11.

107. Al-Salimi and Jansen, *Portugal*, vol. 16, 266.

108. Krapf, *Nika*, 158; Orchardson-Mazrui, "Socio-Historical Perspective," 114–115; Adamson, *Peoples of Kenya*, 298, 312. *Visambo* (grass skirts) were also worn for initiations among Shambaa speakers in the Usambara Mountains. Hans Cory, "Samba Initiation Schools. Songs in the Vernacular," EAF.Cory.177A, University of Dar es Salaam East Africana Collection.

109. Champion, *Agiryama*, 22–23; Orchardson-Mazrui, "Socio-Historical Perspective," 89.

110. Orchardson-Mazrui, "Expressing Power and Status," 93; New, *Life, Wanderings*, 121.

111. On *mizimu*: Ngala, "Mila za Mijikenda." On *koma*: Adamson, *Peoples of Kenya*, 285, 292, 322; Fitzgerald, *Travels in the Coastlands*, 104; Champion, *Agiryama*, 24–25; and Wolfe, *Vigango*, 51–52.

NOTES   179

112. To borrow from Prestholdt's work on consumption in East Africa. See *Domesticating the World*.

113. For good examples of scholarship attentive to the ritual contexts that supported oceanic imports and exports, see Kohl, "Seven Tusks"; Wilmsen, "Hills"; Fleisher, "Rituals of Consumption"; Andaya, "Flights of Fancy."

114. For a discussion of how material culture enabled this sort of transoceanic imagining in a Swahili context, see Meier, "Unmoored."

115. Emery, "Short Account," 282–283.

116. Nurse and Hinnebusch, *Swahili and Sabaki*, 580, 588.

117. See chap. 1 and Appendix 3, no. 1.

118. Spear, *MHT* 29, 33; Beidelman, "Blood Covenant," 325; Meyer, *Across East African Glaciers*, 206; Barret, "Notes," 34–35; Griffiths, "Glimpses," 287; Herlehy, "Ties That Bind."

119. Spear, *Kenya's Past*, 115.

120. Appendix 3, no. 14.

121. Alternatively, the word could have originated in proto-Northeast Coast Banu but was only preserved by speakers of adjacent daughter languages. However, its irregular form in Pare/Chasu -*shogha* (reg. would be -*thogha*) suggests the former scenario.

122. This hypothesis is based on three factors: (1) The term is attested in all four languages of the Seuta subgroup, (2) Seuta languages border all the other NEC daughter languages where reflexes of *-coga are attested, and (3) Seuta is believed to have diverged into separate languages after Mijikenda, Pare, and Kagulu were established as distinct languages within their respective subgroups. For a map of proto-Seuta and adjacent languages, see Gonzales, *Societies, Religion, and History*, map 6.

123. On post-NEC interactions between Sabaki and Seuta speakers, see Nurse and Hinnebusch, *Swahili and Sabaki*, 308.

124. Herlehy, "Ties That Bind," 299–30, and Spear, *MHT* 65, 46, 38.

125. Spear, *MHT* 29, 33, 35.

126. Cummings, "Aspects of Human Porterage," 103–104; Krapf, "Excursion to Dshembo, Dshogni, Likoni, Rabbay Empia and the Vicinity of the Latter," March 1845, CMS/B/OMS/C A5 O16/167., and Krapf, Journal, May 22, 1847, CMS/B/OMS/C A5 O16/171-172. On blood pacts and these settlement patterns: Herlehy, "Ties That Bind," 303; Spear, *MHT* 35.

127. White, "Blood Brotherhood Revisited."

128. Spear, *MHT* 29, 33, 35, 65.

129. Herlehy, "Ties That Bind," 298–305.

130. Curtin, *Cross-Cultural Trade*, is the classic study. See also Aslanian, *From the Indian Ocean*, and Trivellato, *Familiarity of Strangers*.

131. Lambourn, *Abraham's Luggage*, 89–92, and Prange, *Monsoon Islam*, 66–67.

132. See Wynne-Jones, *Material Culture*, 119–120, for discussion of the limits of this framing.

133. Kusimba, Kusimba, and Wright, "Development and Collapse," 243–265. For discussion of similar developments in the Pare Mountains, see Walz, "Routes to a Regional Past," 263, 269–70.

134. Appendix 3, no. 15.

135. Taylor, *Giryama*, 11, 47, 62, 90, 106. See also Walsh, "Loanwords," 22–23, which first drew my attention to these innovations.

180 NOTES

136. Walsh, "Segeju Complex," 36. See also, Krapf, *Nika*, 335. Krapf also recorded a seemingly related verb -*rumiria* glossed as "to return with goods from a journey."

137. Appendix 3, no. 16; Nurse, "Segeju and Daisū," 186, 206–7; Walsh, "Segeju Complex," 29.

138. Cummings, "Aspects of Human Porterage"; Osborne, *Ethnicity and Empire*, 28–33; and Steinhart, *Black Poachers*, 47.

139. Spear, *Kaya Complex*, 89–90. As in Kamba, the title could also refer to leaders of hunting parties.

140. Krapf, *Nika*, 180, *Suahili*, 155, *Travels*, 222–223; Ndurya, *Jadi ya Muduruma*, 21. On other uses, see Griffiths, "Glimpses," 295; Hamamoto, "Duruma Dictionary"; and Walsh, "Mung'aro," 7. Trade party leader themselves were considered powerful healers. Brantley, box 16, folder 28, int. 2; Interview in Digo, September 3, 2013; Interview in Duruma, September 3, 2014.

141. Bosha, *Taathira za Kiarabu*, 180–181.

142. Appendix 3, no. 17.

143. Contini-Morava, "Noun Class Markers," 27.

144. Schadeberg and Bostoen, "Word Formation," 189.

145. I thank an anonymous peer reviewer for pointing out this alternative interpretation. On traders splitting up: Spear, *MHT* 29, 33.

146. Rebmann, "Journey to Jagga," CMS/B/OMS/C A5 O24/52B. See also, Krapf, "Journey to Usambara," July to December 1848, CMS/B/OMS/C A5 O16/173; Emery, "Short Account," 282–283; and discussion in Spear, *Kaya Complex*, 65–75.

147. Walz, "Routes to History," 72.

148. Rebmann, "Journey to Jagga." See also Walz, "Routes to History," 72.

149. Rebmann, "Rebmann's Second Journey to Jagga," in Krapf, *Travels*, 255.

4. INLAND VILLAGES AND OCEANIC EMPIRES

1. Al-Salimi and Jansen, *Portugal*, vol. 16, 203–208.

2. Scott, *Art of Not Being Governed*.

3. On maroon communities in the Americas, see Thompson, *Flight to Freedom*; Price, *Maroon Societies*; Diouf, *Slavery's Exiles*. For maroon economies see Sweeney, "Market Marronage." On the memory of warfare within maroon-colonial alliances, see McKee, "From Violence to Alliance."

4. On smaller-scale political organization as an advantageous strategy in warfare in precolonial Africa, see Fitzsimons, "Warfare, Competition." This chapter's arguments build on ideas developed in Bresnahan, "In Mombasa."

5. We can positively associate "Musungulos" with Mijikenda speakers since descriptions of them sometimes refer to specific communities like the Chonyi and Rabai.

6. Freeman-Grenville, *East African Coast: Select Documents*, 177–180.

7. Freeman-Grenville, *East African Coast: Select Documents*, 73–75.

8. Pearson, *Port Cities*; Sheriff, *Dhow Cultures*, 310–314; Kusimba, *Rise and Fall*, 155–177.

9. Strandes, *Portuguese Period*, 21–23.

10. Freeman-Grenville, *East African Coast: Select Documents*, 108–111.

11. Pearson, *Port Cities*, 141; Mbuia-Joao, "Revolt of Dom Jeronimo," 175–179.

NOTES 181

12. Strandes, *Portuguese Period*, 111; Casale, "Global Politics," 292.

13. Casale, *Ottoman Age*, 163–179.

14. Prange, *Monsoon Islam*, 187.

15. Mbuia-Joao, "Revolt of Dom Jeronimo," 241–284 and Strandes, *Portuguese Period*, 165–170.

16. Mbuia-Joao, "Revolt of Dom Jeronimo," 272.

17. Mbuia-Joao, 281–283 and Strandes, *Portuguese Period*, 170.

18. Freeman-Grenville, *East African Coast: Select Documents*, 178.

19. Mbuia-Joao, "Revolt of Dom Jeronimo," 305–309; 314–317.

20. Mbuia-Joao, 332.

21. Freeman-Grenville, *Mombasa Rising*.

22. Strandes, *Portuguese Period*, 179–180.

23. Strandes, *Portuguese Period*, 182.

24. Strandes, *Portuguese Period*, 183–192, and Mbuia-Joao, "Revolt of Dom Jeronimo," 439–462.

25. Freeman-Grenville, *East African Coast: Select Documents*, 141.

26. Freeman-Grenville, *East African Coast: Select Documents*, 182.

27. Freeman-Grenville, *East African Coast: Select Documents*, 149. For more details on the Zimba, see discussion and analysis of these events in Casale, *Ottoman Age*, 174–179, and Casale, "Global Politics."

28. Casale, "Global Politics," 296, n. 78.

29. The exception is António Boccaro's secondhand account of Chingulia's revolt, published in Goa in 1635, which described the band of inland warriors who attacked Fort Jesus as a combination of Zimbas and Musungulos. See Mbuia-Joao, "Revolt of Dom Jeronimo," 362.

30. Casale, "Global Politics," 295.

31. Quoted in Mbuia-Joao, "Revolt of Dom Jeronimo," 282.

32. Al-Salimi and Jansen, *Portugal*, vol. 16, 294–296.

33. Freeman-Grenville, *East African Coast: Select Documents*, 142.

34. Dames, *Book of Duarte Barbosa*, 21.

35. Seligman, "Wealth"; Machado; *Ocean of Trade*; Prestholdt, "As Artistry Permits."

36. Kusimba, Kusimba, and Wright, "Development and Collapse," 243–265. For discussion of similar developments in the Pare Mountains, see Walz, "Routes to a Regional Past," 269–70.

37. Kusimba, "Archaeology of Slavery."

38. Nearly all of these loanwords were adopted during interactions with speakers of Southern Cushitic languages between 1000 BCE and the start of the current era. See Ehret, *History and the Testimony*, 58–67.

39. Helm, "Conflicting Histories," 261–274. This evidence is replicated at first-millennium coastal sites as well. See Mudida and Horton, "Subsistence at Shanga"; and Prendergast et al., "Dietary Diversity."

40. Helm, "Conflicting Histories," 261–274, for discussion of Mtsengo and trends at contemporaneous sites. See also Mutoro, "Archaeological Study," 242–250.

41. Theal, *Records*, vol. 3, 214.

42. Spear, *MHT* 16, 21, 27, 31, 65. See also Walsh, "Segeju Complex," 32.

182   NOTES

43. All the loanwords listed in Table 2 are also attested in Pare. The phonetic shape of the loans in Mijikenda and other languages indicates that they date to a similar period of contact. For details on their status in Mijikenda and Pare, see Walsh, "Segeju Complex," 33, and Nurse, "Segeju and Daisū," 186, 202, 206–208. See also Nurse, *Classification of the Chaga Dialects*, 514, 534, for wider distributions for "dog" and "bull."

44. Beyond the loanwords attested in Mijikenda and Pare, there is another set of loans specific to Mijikenda dialects that include meanings such as "tend livestock" (-*dhorima/-roroma*) and "rumen, tripe" (*kitaphira/chitamvira*). The shape of these items indicates that Mijikenda speakers borrowed them directly from Segeju/Daiso speakers. In addition, there is a larger inventory of Thagicu loanwords in Mijikenda that cannot conclusively be attributed to Segeju/Daiso. Based on their phonetic shape they may be recent loans from Kamba. This loan set includes terms that refer to actions such as "marking" and "branding" livestock and "copulate (animals)." See Walsh, "Segeju Complex," 33–34.

45. On Segeju history, see Baker, "Notes"; Nurse, "Segeju and Daisū," 175–208; and Ridhiwani, "Habari za kale." Daiso is a daughter language of the Thagicu group of Mashariki Bantu languages (also called Central Kenyan Bantu). The Thagicu group includes some of the most widely spoken Bantu languages in Kenya, such as Gikuyu and Kamba. The name Daiso is cognate with Thagicu while Segeju is a variant of both (although noncognate, being the Mijikenda form). Today, Daiso is spoken by a community around Bwiti, in northeastern Tanzania. Groups in far-southern Kenya and northern Tanzania also have a separate sense of identity as "Segeju," although they now speak a variant of Digo. Evidence from lexicostatistics suggests that proto-Thagicu began to diverge around the eleventh and twelfth centuries CE. Thagicu first diverged into Northern and Southern branches before the Southern group further divided into Western and Eastern branches. Among Thagicu daughter languages, Segeju/Daiso is most closely related to Kamba, forming the Eastern subbranch of Thagicu, or proto-Kamba-Daiso. The available linguistic data does not allow us to determine precisely when proto-Kamba-Daiso diverged into two separate languages. However, pairing linguistic evidence with historical records suggests that this began sometime after the twelfth century but prior to the sixteenth-century arrival of a distinctive "Segeju" group on the Kenya coast. For an outline of the subclassification, see Walsh, "Segeju Complex," 31. For shared retention of core vocabulary of some Thagicu languages, see Bastin, Coupez, and Mann, *Continuity and Divergence*, 211.

46. Håkansson, "Socio-ecological Consequences," and Håkansson, "Politics, Cattle, and Ivory."

47. Lobo, Le Grand, and Johnson, *Voyage to Abyssinia*, 10. On Oromo trade, see Spear, *Kaya Complex*, 67–68, and Marshall, "Spatiality," 363–366.

48. Buckles et al., "Interannual," 1243–1263, and Buckles et al., "Short-term Variability," 1177–1218. Coral records from Malindi similarly indicate strong rainfall on the coast from 1680 to 1775. Pluvial conditions are recorded elsewhere in Kenya around this same time. See Lane and Breen, "Eastern African Coastal Landscape," 24; Konecky et al., "Impact of Monsoons," 20–22.

49. Wynne-Jones, *Material Culture*, 124. On the nature of these circulations in oral traditions, see Spear, *MHT* 1, 2, 4, 29, 44, 45, 59, 71.

50. Freeman-Grenville, *East African Coast: Select Documents*, 178.

51. Kirkman, "Muzungulos of Mombasa," 79; al-Salimi and Jansen, *Portugal*, vol. 16, 294, 263–266. See also Harries, "Founding of Rabai," 142–143.

NOTES   183

52. Freeman-Grenville, *East African Coast: Select Documents*, 184.

53. Sperling, "Growth of Islam," 40–41, 49.

54. Emery's journal, quoted in Gray, *British in Mombasa*, 120.

55. On Portuguese civilization discourses on the East African coast, see Prestholdt, "Portuguese Conceptual Categories."

56. Spear, *Kaya Complex*, 58–65; Brantley, "Gerontocratic Government," 250–254. For discussion of *rika* as a tool of military organization, see Ray, "Disentangling Ethnicity," 259–261.

57. Spear, *Kaya Complex*, 60. See also, Griffiths, "Glimpses," 293–294; Champion, *Agiryama*, 16–17; Gerlach, "Social Organisation," 247–250.

58. Walsh, "Mung'aro," 7.

59. Ibn Ruzaiq, *History of the Imâms*, 209.

60. See discussion in chap. 2 and Helm, "Conflicting Histories."

61. Much in the manner described by Scott for southeast Asia's uplands in *Art of Not Being Governed*.

62. Adding to this synergy, Spear dated Mijikenda adoption of age sets to the sixteenth or seventeenth century, and Martin Walsh has argued that they may have adopted aspects of the *mung'aro* ritual from Segeju speakers who also offered access to valued animal husbandry knowledge. See Walsh, "Mung'aro," 8–9, and Spear, *Kaya Complex*, 65. For a discussion of the interpretation of *mung'aro* ritual at different historical moments from the sixteenth century to the present, see Dingley, "Kinship," 66–137.

63. Pearson, *Port Cities*, 159; Wilkinson, *Arabs and the Scramble*, 24.

64. Al-Salimi and Jansen, *Portugal*, vol. 10, 289; Strandes, *Portuguese Period*, 200–201.

65. On the text's authorship, see Kirkman, "Muzungulos of Mombasa," 77; Strandes, *Portuguese Period*, 237, fn. 2.

66. According to Strandes, the Junta was formally set in March of 1697, but it "had been operating for a year previous to this on the basis of temporary arrangements made in Goa." See *Portuguese Period*, 211. Another account, *Planta da Ilha da Mombaça*, written by a Portuguese officer who spent three months in Fort Jesus as part of the first relief after the start of the siege, indicates that the Junta was imposed in February 1695. See Kirkman, "Muzungulos of Mombasa," 79.

67. Strandes, *Portuguese Period*, 211–212. See also Alpers, *Ivory and Slaves*, 77–79.

68. Al-Salimi and Jansen, *Portugal*, vol. 15, 105; Kirkman, "Muzungulos of Mombasa," 78–79.

69. Al-Salimi and Jansen, *Portugal*, vol. 15, 101–102.

70. On their many thwarted attempts to reach Fort Jesus with provisions, see al-Salimi and Jansen, *Portugal*, vol. 15, 103–104; 109; 120–121; 132; 170–176.

71. Al-Salimi and Jansen, *Portugal*, vol. 15, 105. This is also discussed by the author of *Planta da Ilha da Mombaça*. See excerpt in Kirkman, "Muzungulos of Mombasa," 78–79.

72. In the document, he's referred to as "Rey do Chone"—probably referring to the senior elder of the main *kaya*, or settlement, of Chonyi, a Mijikenda-speaking group located northwest of Mombasa.

73. Kirkman, "Muzungulos of Mombasa," 79–80.

74. Al-Salimi and Jansen, *Portugal*, vol. 15, 106.

75. In the document this appears as "Muinhe Chambe," or, more correctly, *Mwinyi*, an honorific title that captures meanings such as "owner," "chief," or "town trustee" in Swahili.

184   NOTES

This title indicates that Chambe was a representative of one of Mombasa's Twelve Tribes, local confederations that provided a check on foreign power in Mombasa by managing relationships with Mijikenda-speaking communities. See Berg, "Swahili Community," 40–41; Pouwels, *Horn and Crescent*, 91; Ray, "Disentangling Ethnicity," 114.

76. Al-Salimi and Jansen, *Portugal*, vol. 15, 106.

77. Al-Salimi and Jansen, *Portugal*, vol. 15, 106. Oral traditions from Chonyi and neighboring settlements also describe defending their forested hilltop settlements from an Arab invasion, indicating historical memories of these events. See Spear, *MHT* 12, 27, 32.

78. This quote appears in al-Salimi and Jansen, *Portugal*, vol. 15, 163. See also 107 in the same volume.

79. Al-Salimi and Jansen, *Portugal*, vol. 15, 168.

80. Al-Salimi and Jansen, *Portugal*, vol. 15, 133, 180, 183.

81. Al-Salimi and Jansen, *Portugal*, vol. 15, 186–187.

82. While it is not clear exactly how or even when Oman finally took full control of the town, by December 1698 Portuguese ships approaching the harbor saw Oman's red flag flying at Fort Jesus. Different rumors of the fort's fall circulated to the Portuguese fleet: some claimed that the Omanis overpowered those remaining at Fort Jesus in a swift attack, while others suggested that the remaining holdouts simply surrendered. See al-Salimi and Jansen, *Portugal*, vol. 15, 203–205, and Strandes, *Portuguese Period*, 233.

83. For a discussion of rivalries in the Indian Ocean, see McPherson, "Anglo-Portuguese."

84. Strandes, *Portuguese Period*, 239–240; Wilkinson, *Arabs and the Scramble*, 24–25. See also al-Salimi and Jansen, *Portugal*, vol. 16, 207–208.

85. Al-Salimi and Jansen, *Portugal*, vol. 16, 59.

86. Al-Salimi and Jansen, *Portugal*, vol. 16, 54–55; 236.

87. Al-Salimi and Jansen, *Portugal*, vol. 16, 258–264; 299–304; Strandes, *Portuguese Period*, 246–248.

88. Al-Salimi and Jansen, *Portugal*, vol. 16, 265–266.

89. Al-Salimi and Jansen, *Portugal*, vol. 16, 94.

90. Strandes, *Portuguese Period*, 253.

91. Sources give a variety of dates for this trip between 1729 and 1731. But Portuguese records clearly document that Mombasa locals and Mijikenda allies began attacking Portuguese forts in April 1729. They gained control of Fort Jesus by November and ships from Oman arrived a month later. Based on monsoon travel patterns, the trip most likely took place around May or June of 1729.

92. Owen, *Narrative*, vol. 1, 418.

93. In the order they appear in the document: Ribe, Chonyi, Kambe, Kauma, Jibana, Rabai, Jibana, Duruma, Shimba, Lunga, and Digo. Shimba and Lunga are both locations within Digo-speaking areas.

94. This split was formalized in 1732–1733, when Bal'arab bin Himyar was elected the imam at Nizwa. See John Wilkinson, *Imamate Tradition*, 223–224.

95. According to chronicles, Saif bin Sultan II's fourth election as imam took place on April 2, 1728. See Miles, *Countries and Tribes*, 250–52; Ibn Ruzaiq, *History of the Imâms*, 130–132.

96. Owen, *Narrative*, vol. 1, 418.

97. Al-Salimi and Jansen, *Portugal*, vol. 16, 318.

98. Owen, *Narrative*, vol. 1, 417–418.

NOTES 185

99. During the latter part of the siege some were reportedly kicked out of the fort to conserve the remaining provisions. al-Salimi and Jansen, *Portugal*, vol. 16, 107, 314.

5. FROM MIJIKENDA CITY TO BUSAIDI BACKWATER

1. The document uses the Arabic form of this word rather than the common Swahili form *hati*, which is a loanword from Arabic. The chair is of particular interest, being an object associated with political power and status in Swahili society. See Allen, "Kiti Cha Enzi."

2. Omar and Frankl, "Mombasa Chronicle," 107; MS 373394 SOAS Special Collections.

3. This paragraph builds from the extensive literature on East Africa's coast and interior during the nineteenth century. See Sheriff, *Slaves, Spices, and Ivory*; Prestholdt, *Domesticating the World*; McDow, *Buying Time*; Rockel, *Carriers of Culture*; Gooding, *On the Frontiers*.

4. Al-Salimi and Jansen, *Portugal*, vol. 16, 265–266.

5. Mbuia-Joao, "Revolt of Dom Jeronimo," 272.

6. Hollis, "Notes on the History of Vumba," 279–280.

7. Owen, *Narrative*, vol. 2, 154; Gray, *British in Mombasa*, 138.

8. The title is also rendered as *mwana ngira* or *mwana ndia* in different sources, representing the Giryama and Mvita forms. See Spear, *Kaya Complex*, 72, 106; "Safari by A.D.C., Giriama among WaNyika," July 9, 1913, KNA: MP/296; Dundas, "Native Laws," 221.

9. Al-Mazrui, *History of the Mazru'i*, 34–42. See also, Berg, "Swahili Community," 49–51.

10. Wilkinson, *Imamate Tradition*, 225.

11. Ray, "Disentangling Ethnicity," 243–244.

12. The migrants from Malindi themselves became part of the Mvita group of the Nine Tribes. Berg, "Mombasa under the Busaidi," 42–48, and Berg, "Swahili Community," 35–56.

13. *Thelatha Taifa* allied with Digo and Duruma Mijikenda groups, while members of *Tisa Taifa* formed similar coalitions with more central and northern Mijikenda groups. See Guillain, *Documents*, vol. 3, 244–245; Prins, *Swahili-Speaking Peoples*, 98–99; and portrayals in al-Mazrui, *History of the Mazru'i*.

14. Strandes, *Portuguese Period*, 183; Martin, *History of Malindi*, 35–36.

15. Historical chronicles on Mombasa have many references to people—including deposed Mazrui leaders—fleeing Mombasa for the "Nyika" to seek refuge and assistance. See bin Stamboul, "Early History of Mombasa," 32–36; "Mombasa Chronicle" in Owen, *Narrative*, vol. 1, 414–422; and Guillain, *Documents*, vol. 1, 614–622.

16. Krapf, Journal, September 25, 1844, "Mission Books 1842–1846." CMS/B/OMS/C A5 M1. The following analysis of *heshima* builds on Ray, "Disentangling Ethnicity," 229–230. This section expands on Bresnahan "In Mombasa."

17. Krapf, Journal, September 25, 1844.

18. Krapf, Journal, March 25, 1845, "Excursion to Dshembo, Dshogni, Likoni, Rabbay Empia and the Vicinity of the Latter Place," March 1845, CMS/B/OMS/C A5 O16/167.

19. Krapf, Journal, September 25, 1844.

20. Krapf, Journal, March 25, 1845.

21. Bosha, *Taathira za Kiarabu*, 51. The Swahili word comes from the Arabic root *ḥašm*, which means "to shame, put to shame; to be ashamed to face; to be reticent, modest, shy, bashful, diffident." Cowan, *Hans Wehr Dictionary*, 210.

22. Krapf, *Suahili*, 100.

186 NOTES

23. Iliffe, *Honour in African History*, 32–33.

24. McMahon, *Slavery and Emancipation*, 8.

25. El Zein, *Sacred Meadows*; Middleton, *World of the Swahili*, 194.

26. Ray, "Disentangling Ethnicity," 229.

27. On Arabic loaning in Swahili, see Nurse and Hinnebusch, *Swahili and Sabaki*, 321–331.

28. In Mijikenda dialects, /h/ comes from one of two sources: *t and, in northern dialects, *p (which becomes /β/in southern dialects). Nurse and Hinnebusch suggest that in proto-Mijikenda the proto-Sabaki phonemes *t > *ɽ and *p > *ɸ. It is unclear, however, precisely when these sound changes occurred.

29. Similar practices of collecting "taxes"—called *hongo*—on trade goods developed in the nineteenth century along caravan routes in central Tanzania. Chiefs collected *hongo* from passing caravans in exchange for "safe transit and access to local resources." Like *heshima, hongo* often consisted of cloth. See Rockel, *Carriers of Culture*, 53, 67.

30. Krapf, Journal, March 25, 1845.

31. Berg, "Mombasa under the Busaidi," 42; Willis, *Mombasa, the Swahili*, 36–37.

32. Krapf, Journal, March 25, 1845.

33. Burton and Speke, "Coasting Voyage," 195; Krapf, "Journal Descriptive of a Journey Made to Ukambani, 1849," CMS/B/OMS/C A5 O16/74.

34. Emery's journal, quoted in Gray, *British in Mombasa*, 122.

35. Ray, "Muyaka's Lament," 12.

36. Bishara, *Sea of Debt*, 30–31; Wilkinson, *Imamate Tradition*, 50–53.

37. Ibn Ruzaiq, *Imâms and Seyyids*, 209.

38. On Mombasa's larger sphere of influence during the eighteenth and nineteenth centuries, see al-Mazrui, *History of the Mazru'i*, 22–23, 48; al-Salimi and Jansen, *Portugal*, vol. 16, 79–80; Owen, *Narrative*, vol. 2, 143; Guillain, *Documents*, vol. 1, 546–549.

39. Pouwels, "Battle of Shela"; Sheriff and Biersteker, *Mashairi Ya Vita*.

40. Al-Mazrui, *History of the Mazru'i*, 80–83; Owen, *Narrative*, vol. 2, 141–142.

41. For an overview, see Sheriff, *Slaves, Spices, and Ivory*, 24–30. For different accounts in historical chronicles, see Ibn Ruzaiq, *Imâms and Seyyids*, 348–349; al-Mazrui, *History of the Mazru'i*, 97–122; Harries, "Swahili Traditions of Mombasa." See also Gray, *British in Mombasa*, 173–192, and Guillain, *Documents*, vol. 1, 602–605.

42. Bishara, *Sea of Debt*, 6.

43. Bishara; McDow, *Buying Time*, especially chap. 2.

44. Sheriff, *Slaves, Spices, and Ivory*; Glassman, *Feasts and Riot*, 38–54.

45. Spear, *Kaya Complex*, 112–113.

46. Spear, 98–101, and Willis, *Mombasa, the Swahili*, 22–23.

47. Krapf, "A Memoir on the East African Slave Trade," CMS/B/OMS/C A5 O16/179; Ibn Ruzaiq, *Imâms and Seyyids*, 349.

48. Spear, *MHT* 2, 23, 29, 31. For a discussion of enslaved Africans in Arabia, see Hopper, *Slaves of One Master*.

49. See Emery, "A Journal of the British Establishment at Mombasa," TNA: ADM 52/3940; Willis, *Mombasa, the Swahili*, 49–50.

50. Krapf, Journal, March 24 and 25.. See also, Spear, *Kaya Complex*, 136–138.

51. Willis, *Mombasa, the Swahili*, 52–59, and Champion, *Agiryama*, 18–20.

52. De Almeida, "Speaking of Slavery," 154. While de Almeida proposes that this innovation took place in Narrow West Bantu, the word's distribution and associated practices in NEC languages indicate deeper antiquity.

NOTES 187

53. Appendix 3, no. 18.

54. Kayamba, "Notes on the Wadigo," 94–96; Griffiths, "Glimpses," 286; Champion, *Agiryama*, 19–20.

55. Depending on the context, the debt could be quite large. Around 1814, for instance, the Kubo, or leader of the Digo, reportedly killed the *liwali* of Mtangata while he was traveling from Mombasa. The "blood price" in this case was set at twelve elephant tusks and twenty-five slaves. Al-Mazrui, *History of the Mazru'i*, 74–77.

56. These are very clearly loanwords from Swahili since "t" is not an inherited sound in Mijikenda languages. If they were inherited meanings, they would be pronounced *muhoro*, *heka*, and *muhumwa*. Notably, they did retain *muhumwa*, which is an inherited term, but they used this word to refer to a messenger, servant, or person exchanged for a fine, making this distinct from the Swahili form and meaning. See Krapf, *Nika*, 277; Deed, *Giryama*, 68. In proto-Sabaki, see Nurse and Hinnebusch, *Swahili and Sabaki*, 616.

57. Johnson, *English-Swahili Dictionary*, 263; Krapf, *Suahili*, 365; Mwalonya et al., *Mgombato*, 96; Ndurya et al., *Musemat'o*, 73. For its source, the Sabaki verb, *-tek-, see Nurse and Hinnebusch, *Swahili and Sabaki*, 608.

58. Johnston, "Dispute Settlement"; Champion, *Agiryama*, 18–20; Bergman, "Willingness to Remember," 154–157.

59. Vernet, "Slave Trade and slavery."

60. Al-Salimi and Jansen, *Portugal*, vol. 16, 77–78; 261; 294; Gray, *British in Mombasa*, 80–81.

61. Freeman-Grenville, *French at Kilwa Island*, 221.

62. Morton, *Children of Ham*, 2.

63. Cooper, *Plantation Slavery*, 70–82.

64. Hopper, *Slaves of One Master*, 42–46, and Glassman, *Feasts and Riot*, 55–78.

65. Willis, *Mombasa, the Swahili*, 57–59; Cooper, *Plantation Slavery*, 128–129.

66. Krapf, *Suahili*, 167.

67. Krapf, Journal, January 30, 1845, "Excursion to the Country of the Wanika Tribe at Rabbay, and Visit of the Wakamba People at Endila," CMS/B/OMS/C A5 O16/166.

68. New, *Life, Wanderings*, 128.

69. Krapf, Journal, January 30, 1845.

70. For comparable transformations in a West-Central African context, see Ferreira, *Cross Cultural Exchange*, 52–87.

71. Willis, *Mombasa, the Swahili*, 53–54.

72. See Willis, 55–62, 70–71, for greater details on the strategies described in this paragraph.

73. For the latter, see al-Mazrui, *History of the Mazru'i*, 77–78.

74. Wilkinson, *Arabs and the Scramble*, 72.

75. Krapf to Venn, March 14, 1853, "Mission Books, 1846–1856," CMS/B/OMS/C A5 M2.

76. Krapf to Venn, March 14, 1853.

77. Krapf to Venn, March 14, 1853.

78. Rebmann to Venn, April 4, 1853, "Mission Books, 1846–1856," CMS/B/OMS/C A5 M2.

79. See, for instance, Cooper, *Plantation Slavery*; Morton, *Children of Ham*; Sheriff, *Slaves, Spices, and Ivory*.

80. Alpers, *Ivory and Slaves*, 264. On Nyamwezi caravans, see Rockel, *Carriers of Culture*.

81. Prestholdt, *Domesticating the World*, chap. 3; Seligman, "Lip Ornaments."

82. Glassman, *Feasts and Riot*, and Fabian, *Making Identity*.

83. See Spear, *Kaya Complex*, 106–145.

188 NOTES

84. Willis, *Mombasa, the Swahili*, 10. During the late nineteenth century, Pangani's agriculture focused on large plantation crops like sugarcane. Mombasa, by contrast, focused more on grain crops, which gave small-scale producers greater control over agricultural production.

85. Krapf, Journal, September 25, 1844.

86. Ray, "Disentangling Ethnicity," 294.

87. Guillan, *Documents*, vol. 1, 244–245.

88. Glassman, *Feasts and Riot*.

89. Willis, *Mombasa, the Swahili*; Sperling, "Growth of Islam," 42–43; 66.

90. For a discussion of Islam in Mijikenda communities, see Sperling, "Growth of Islam."

91. Sperling, "Growth of Islam," 90–92; Spear, *Kaya Complex*, 115–122; Berg, "Mombasa under the Busaidi," 88; 107–108; Willis and Miers, "Becoming."

CONCLUSION

1. Different versions of the story of Mijikenda settlement on Mombasa are documented in oral traditions from nearly every Mijikenda community. In the early 1970s, Spear recorded versions of the elephant hunter story in Chonyi, Digo, Duruma, Jibana, and Ribe. Two decades later, Mohamed Karisa Gohu and Richard Helm recorded stories of different Mijikenda groups passing through Ngomeni on Mombasa Island before reaching their *kayas* in Digo, Duruma, Kambe, and Ribe. Rabai elders also have stories about elephant hunters at Ngomeni. Spear, *MHT* 13, 16, 20, 27, 31, 38, 65, 67; Helm, transcripts on "Origin and Migration Pattern of the Mijikenda," Research Deposit, Fort Jesus Museum Library; Author's interview, September 29, 2014.

2. Knappert, "Chronicle of Mombasa."

3. This observation, of course, builds on the work of many scholars, as I hope is clear from secondary literature cited throughout this book. For some recent exemplary scholarship, see essays in Boivin and Frachetti, *Globalization in Prehistory*, and Franklin, *Everyday Cosmopolitanisms*.

4. Riello, *Cotton*, 61–65, 80–82, and Sinopoli, *Political Economy*, 173–190.

5. Chaudhuri, "Structure," 138; Machado, *Ocean of Trade*, 141–149.

6. Riello, *Cotton*, 64.

7. Sinopoli, *Political Economy*, 177.

8. Riello, *Cotton*, 30–33; Ray, "Far-Flung Fabrics," 30–31.

9. Quote from Riello, *Cotton*, 29; see also Barnes, ed., *Textiles*, for discussion of other contexts.

10. Prange, *Monsoon Islam*.

11. Morrison, "Pepper in the Hills," 121–122; Prange, "Measuring by the Bushel," 215–216.

12. Prange, "Measuring by the Bushel," 214–219. For a discussion of western India's hinterland networks and the distinctive cultural production resulting from the region's engagements with maritime trade, see Malekandathil, "Dynamics of Trade."

13. Morrison and Lycett, "Forest Products," 134.

14. Morrison and Lycett, "Forest Products," 131; Morrison, "Pepper in the Hills," 109–111.

15. Morrison, "Christians and Spices," 283–397.

NOTES 189

16. See Villiers, "Great Plenty of Almug."

17. On centering the agency of small-scale societies to understand Southeast Asia's global trading connections, see Hoogervorst and Boivin, "Invisible Agents."

18. This paragraph draws from Andaya, "Flights of Fancy."

19. On the global circulation of kingfisher feathers and other avian products, see Reyes, "Glimpsing," and Ptak, "Chinese Bird Imports."

20. Hirth and Rockhill, *Chau Ju-Kua*, 222–223, 193, 235.

21. Chaffee, *Muslim Merchants*, 140–144.

22. See discussion in Green, "Languages of Indian Ocean."

23. In an Indian Ocean context, see Green, "Waves of Heterotopia," and Becker and Cabrita, "Performing Citizenship." For larger debates on this topic among global historians, see Adelman, "What Is Global History Now?"; Drayton and Montadel, "Futures of Global History."

APPENDIX 1: PLACING EAST AFRICAN LANGUAGES IN TIME AND SPACE

1. For discussion of NEC languages, see Nurse and Hinnebusch, *Swahili and Sabaki*, 19–23; 214–22; 463–473.

2. Sabaki may have also included a sixth member, called Mwani, spoken in modern Mozambique, which was heavily influenced by surrounding non-NEC Bantu languages. It is unclear whether Mwani was an independent member of Sabaki or part of the Southern Swahili dialect cluster. According to Nurse and Hinnebusch, the latter scenario makes the most sense diachronically, and thus I do not treat it as a sixth Sabaki language in this book. See Nurse and Hinnebusch, *Swahili and Sabaki*, 527.

3. For shared Mijikenda-Comorian-Lower Pokomo innovations, see Nurse and Hinnebusch, 374, 427, 476–480. For discussion of Mijikenda and Lower Pokomo as a Sabaki subgroup, see 436–438; 533–544. On the convergence of Upper and Lower Pokomo, see 544–549.

4. On the application of these principles, see Dimmendaal, *Historical Linguistics*, 336–345; Ehret, *History and the Testimony*, 46–47.

5. In applying the theory, scholars must also account for geographic factors—such as mobility along sea lanes in the Swahili case—as well as phenomena like historical climate change or warfare in prompting human migrations and language movements. See Dimmendaal, *Historical Linguistics*, 339–345; Crowley and Bowern, *Historical Linguistics*, 313–316.

6. For a discussion of the movement of languages through such varied processes, see Vansina, "New Linguistic Evidence"; Klieman, *Pygmies*, 35–65; Schoenbrun, *Green Place*, 43–45; 65–90.

7. Ehret, *History and the Testimony*, 123–125.

8. De Luna and Fleisher, *Speaking with Substance*, 95–97. For a broader discussion of criticisms and approaches to linguistic dating techniques among linguists, see Crowley and Bowern, *Historical Linguistics*, 149–151, and Dimmendaal, *Historical Linguistics*, 71–74.

9. Ehret, *History and the Testimony*, 112–115.

10. See, for instance, Ashley, "Socialised Archaeology"; Croucher and Wynne-Jones, "People, Not Pots"; Lane, "Ethnicity,"; and Dores Cruz, "Pots Are Pots."

190 NOTES

11. A published dialogue between historian Kathryn de Luna and archaeologist Jeffrey Fleisher offers an important critique of the problems of past interdisciplinary approaches to the histories of coastal East African groups. In this dialogue, de Luna outlines how scholars have often relied on inconsistent and, in some cases, incommensurable data when making arguments about the chronology of proto–Northeast Coast, proto-Sabaki, and proto-Swahili. As a result, de Luna questioned the commonly accepted chronology of theses protolanguages' divergences. I agree with de Luna's critique of past correlations approaches as well as her suggestion that an approach based on multiple direct associations between archaeological records and linguistic evidence will provide the most accurate chronology. That said, I think the chronology described below—which largely mirrors that of Nurse and Hinnebusch—remains the most plausible estimate based on the evidence available at present. For their dialogue, see de Luna and Fleisher, *Speaking with Substance*, 107–113.

12. Chami, "Review," and Spear, "Early Swahili History," 266–268.

13. See Phillipson, *African Archaeology*, 49–69, for a summary of this archaeological evidence. Among historical linguists, see Gonzales, *Societies, Religion, and History*, 56–57; Schoenbrun, *Green Place*, 33–36; 46–47; Ehret, *African Classical Age*.

14. For a thorough overview of ETT ceramics, see Fleisher and Wynne-Jones, "Ceramics," 245–278.

15. Fleisher and Wynne-Jones, "Ceramics," 247; Chami, "Review"; Spear, "Early Swahili."

16. See M'Mbogori, *Population*; Chami, "Review of Swahili Archaeology"; Helm, "Conflicting Histories," 279–283.

17. Fleisher and Wynne-Jones, "Ceramics."

18. See Spear, "Early Swahili History," 265–275, for a summary of this approach. Ehret and Gonzales have attributed Kwale to an entirely different language group that they call, respectively, "Uplands" and "Azanian" Bantu. They propose that ETT ceramics marked the beginning of the divergence of Northeast Coast. However, this argument does not hold up based on the geographic distribution of both Kwale and ETT ceramics, which indicate that these were regional styles, as described above.

19. See also Nurse and Hinnebusch, *Swahili and Sabaki*, 490. For a critical assessment, see de Luna and Fleisher, *Speaking with Substance*, 108–112.

20. This genetic evidence is seen to represent intermarriage between Sabaki Bantu speakers and Austronesians by the eighth century. Brucato et al., "Comoros," 64–65. On ceramic assemblages in the Comoros, see Wright et al., "Early Seafarers." For discussion of Comoros within the ETT, see Wright, "Trade and Politics," and Fleisher and Wynne-Jones, "Ceramics."

21. Nurse and Hinnebusch, *Swahili and Sabaki*, 292, 637, 643. Both terms are also distributed in regular form in neighboring Seuta languages, indicating they are early Sabaki-Seuta areal spreads. See Kisbey, *Zigula*, 10, 89; Kiango, *Kibondei*, 15, 59; Langheinrich, *Schambala*, 62, 378.

22. See proto-Swahili innovations in Nurse and Hinnebusch, *Swahili and Sabaki*, 295–297.

23. On dating through direction associations between linguistic and archaeological records, see de Luna, "Surveying the Boundaries."

24. Crowther et al., "Subsistence Mosaics," 101–120; Crowther et al., "Coastal Subsistence," 211–237.

NOTES 191

APPENDIX 2: MIJIKENDA DIALECTS

1. This table draws from Nurse and Hinnebusch's analysis of Sabaki phonology in *Swahili and Sabaki*, chap. 2. I expand on their analysis by adding data from all "Central Mijikenda" dialects and by parsing distinguishing phonological features of different areas in the Mijikenda speech community beyond the "Northern" and "Southern" division. This better establishes that (1) Mijikenda is a dialect chain and (2) it features greater phonological variability than a Northern and Southern Mijikenda allows (which is something Nurse and Hinnebusch acknowledge but did not fully explore as their primary focus was the not the history of Mijikenda dialects). See Bresnahan, "Contours of Community," 37–52, 310–320, for further discussion.

2. An isogloss refers to a line drawn on a map that marks the limits of a particular word or linguistic feature. Isoglosses tend to bunch closely together, forming isogloss bundles that allow us to identify variations in regional speech patterns or dialects.

3. Several additional morphological and phonological innovations distinguish Digo from other Mijikenda dialects. See Nurse and Hinnebusch, *Swahili and Sabaki*, 537–539, for a summary.

APPENDIX 3: LEXICAL RECONSTRUCTIONS AND DISTRIBUTIONS

1. Among Sabaki languages, Comorian, Mijikenda, Pokomo, and Swahili all have distinct dialects. I have only included attestations from multiple dialects of a given language when it is relevant to my analysis of the word, for example, to show differences in a word's form within dialects of a language or variations in a word's meaning.

2. BLR3 Main 717; Nurse and Hinnebusch, *Swahili and Sabaki*, 290, 538; Seligman, "Encircling Value," 367–369. Extension of meaning of older root in Seuta languages, Yao, and Nyamwezi through commercial contacts with Swahili.

3. BLR3 Main 462; Nurse and Hinnebusch, *Swahili and Sabaki*, 581.

4. BLR3 Main 1876; Nurse and Hinnebusch, *Swahili and Sabaki*, 592.

5. BLR3 Main 717; Nurse and Hinnebusch, *Swahili and Sabaki*, 291, 616.

6. Nurse and Hinnebusch, *Swahili and Sabaki*, 615.

7. BLR3 Main 1914; Nurse and Hinnebusch, *Swahili and Sabaki*, 593, 669.

8. The regular form in Duruma and Rabai seems to be related to a separate, unrelated sound shift where the inherited nasal cluster *ns becomes /ts/ but becomes /s/ in other dialects.

9. BLR3 Main 2353; Nurse and Hinnebusch, *Swahili and Sabaki*, 602. For *ipala see Seligman, "Encircling Value," 305. While Mijikenda and Thagicu forms are clearly cognates, the relationship with other attestations is less clear. Not a loan in Mijikenda from Thagicu based on its form in Digo and Duruma.

10. BLR3 4491; Schoenbrun, *Historical Reconstruction*, 60–61; Gonzales, *Societies, Religion, and History*, 97–98; 128–129.

11. BLR3 Main 795.

12. Nurse and Hinnebusch list this as Southern Dialect "innovation" via loaning from interior, *Swahili and Sabaki*, 304. See Ehret, *Southern Cushitic*, 269, for possible proto item.

13. BLR3 Main 434; Nurse and Hinnesbusch, *Swahili and Sabaki*, 581.

192 NOTES

14. BLR3 DER 667. The loss of the nasal may explain verb's form in Mijikenda and some Swahili: PSA *g > j / dz, which is not anomalous in Sabaki. See Nurse and Hinnebusch, *Swahili and Sabaki*, 108.

15. Thagicu *c > /dh/ ~ /r/ in Mijikenda dialects, as is evidenced in many loanwords. Mijikenda form would be -*tsogora* if inherited. See Walsh, "Segeju Complex," 37; Nurse, "Segeju and Daisū," 206.

16. Mijikenda would be -*tsigana* if inherited. See also Walsh, "Segeju Complex," 37; Nurse, "Segeju and Daisū," 207.

17. Nurse and Hinnebusch, *Swahili and Sabaki*, 613.

18. BLR3 DER 1881, derived from Main 6999; Vansina, *Paths*, 279; Almeida, "Speaking of Slavery," 150–156; 366–367.

BIBLIOGRAPHY

ARCHIVAL AND LIBRARY COLLECTIONS

Bible Translation and Literacy East Africa, Library Collection, Nairobi
Church Missionary Society Archives, University of Birmingham, Cadbury Research Library
Cynthia Brantley Papers, University of California, Davis Library
Derek Nurse Papers, USIU Africa Library, Nairobi
East Africana Collection, University of Dar es Salaam Library
Fort Jesus Museum Library, Mombasa
Kenya National Archives, Nairobi
National Archives of Britain, Public Records Office, Kew
Special Collections, School of Oriental and African Studies, London
Thomas Spear Papers, 1969–2012, University of Wisconsin-Madison Archives

DICTIONARIES AND LANGUAGE MATERIALS

African Inland Mission Language Committee. *A Kikamba-English Dictionary.* Nairobi: Literacy Centre of Kenya for Afrolit Association, 1970.

Ahmed-Chamanga, Mohamed. *Lexique Comorien (Shinzuani) Français.* Paris: L'Harmattan, 1992.

Baraza la Kiswahili la Zanzibar. *Kamusi la Lahaja ya Kipemba.* Oxford: Oxford University Press, 2012.

Baraza la Kiswahili la Zanzibar. *Kamusi la Lahaja ya Kitumbatu.* Oxford: Oxford University Press, 2012.

Bastin, Yvonne, André Coupez, and Michael Mann. *Continuity and Divergence in the Bantu Languages: Perspectives from a Lexicostatistic Study.* Tervuren: Musee Royal de l'Afrique Centrale, 1999.

194   BIBLIOGRAPHY

Bastin, Yvonne, André Coupez, Evariste Mumba, and Thilo C. Schadeberg. "Bantu Lexical Reconstructions 3." Tervuren: Royal Museum for Central Africa, 2002.

Benson, T. G. *Kikuyu-English Dictionary*. Oxford: Clarendon Press, 1964.

Besha, Ruth M. *A Classified Vocabulary of the Shambala Language with Outline Grammar*. Tokyo: Institute for the Study of Languages and Cultures of Asia and Africa, 1993.

Bible Translation and Literacy. "Lower Pokomo Dictionary." Nairobi, n.d.

Bosha, Ibrahim. *Taathira za Kiarabu Katika Kiswahili Pamoja na Kamusi Thulathiya*. Dar es Salaam: University of Dar es Salaam Press, 1993.

Cowan, J. M., ed. *The Hans Wehr Dictionary of Modern Written Arabic*. Urbana: Spoken Languages Series, 1994.

Deed, Florence. *Giryama-English Dictionary*. Kampala: East African Literature Bureau, 1964.

Ehret, Christopher. *The Historical Reconstruction of Southern Cushitic Phonology and Vocabulary*. Berlin: Reimer, 1980.

Fischer, François. *Grammaire-Dictionnaire Comorien*. Strasbourg: Société d'édition de la Basse Alsace, 1949.

Fourshey, Catherine Cymone, Christine Saidi, and Rhonda Gonzales. "Bantu Historical Linguistic Database." African Matrilineal Histories website. Last modified 2018. https:// africanmatrilinealhistories.bucknell.edu/database.php.

Guthrie, Malcolm. *Comparative Bantu: An Introduction to the Comparative Linguistics and Prehistory of the Bantu Languages*. Vols. 1–4. Farnborough: Gregg Press, 1967–1971.

Hamamoto, Mitsuru. "Duruma Dictionary." n.p.

Johnson, Frederick. *A Standard Swahili-English Dictionary*. London: Oxford University Press, 1939.

Kagaya, Ryohei. *A Classified Vocabulary of the Pare Language*. Tokyo: Institute for the Study of Languages and Cultures of Asia and Africa, 1989.

Kahigi, Kulikoyela. *Kikahe: Msamiati wa Kikahe-Kiswahili-Kiingereza na Kiingereza-Kikahe-Kiswahili*. Dar es Salaam: Languages of Tanzania Project, 2008.

Kiango, John. *Kibondei: Msamiati Wa Kibondei-Kiswahili-Kiingereza*. Dar es Salaam: Languages of Tanzania Project, 2008.

Kisbey, Walter Henry. *Zigula-English Dictionary*. London: Society for Promoting Christian Knowledge, 1906.

Kisseberth, Charles. "Chimiini-English Dictionary and Chrestomathy." n.p.

Kisseberth, Charles, and Mohammad Imam Abasheikh. *The Chimwiini Lexicon Exemplified*. Tokyo: Research Institute for Languages and Cultures of Asia and Africa, Tokyo University of Foreign Studies, 2004.

Krapf, J. L. *A Dictionary of the Suahili Language*. Farnborough: Gregg Press, 1964.

Krapf, J. L. *A Nika-English Dictionary*. London: Society for Promoting Christian Knowledge, 1887.

Krapf, J. L. *Vocabulary of Six East African Languages: Kiswahili, Kinika, Kikamba, Kipokomo, Kihiau, Kigalla*. Farnborough: Gregg Press, 1967.

Lafon, Michel. *Lexique Français-Comorien (Shingazidja)*. Paris: L'Harmattan, 1991.

Lambert, H. E. *Chi-Chifundi, a Dialect of the Southern Kenya Coast*. Kampala: East African Swahili Committee, 1957.

BIBLIOGRAPHY 195

Lambert, H. E. *Chi-Jomvu and Ki-Ngare, Subdialects of the Mombasa Area*. Kampala: East African Swahili Committee, 1958.

Lambert, H. E. *Ki-Vumba, A Dialect of the Southern Kenya Coast*. Kampala: East African Swahili Committee, 1957.

Langheinrich, F. *Schambala-Wörterbuch*. Hamburg: L. Friederichsen and Co., 1921.

Legère, Karsten. "Trilingual Ng'hwele-Swahili-English and Swahili-Ng'hwele-English Wordlist." n.p., 2021.

Madan, A. C. *Swahili-English Dictionary*. Oxford: Clarendon Press, 1903.

Maganga, Clement, and Thilo Schadeberg. *Kinyamwezi: Grammar, Texts, Vocabulary*. Köln: R. Köppe, 1992.

Mbiti, John S. *English-Kamba Vocabulary*. Nairobi: Kenya Literature Bureau, 1981.

Meeussen, A. E. *Bantu Lexical Reconstructions*. Tervuren: Koninklijk Museum voor Midden-Afrika, 1980.

Mochiwa, Zacharia. *Kizigula: Msamiati Wa Kizigula-Kiswahili-Kiingereza*. Dar es Salaam: Languages of Tanzania Project, 2008.

Mous, Maarten. "A Sketch of Mbugwe (Bantu F34, Tanzania)." n.p., n.d.

Mreta, Abel Y. *Chasu: Kamusi Ya Chasu-Kiingereza-Kiswahili*. Dar es Salaam: Languages of Tanzania Project, 2008.

Muntuggagga, Jobs. *Dala Ufi: Kamusi Ya Kipokomo*. Mombasa, 2014.

Mwalonya, Joseph, et al. *Mgombato: Digo-English-Swahili Dictionary*. Nairobi: Digo Language and Literacy Project, 2004.

Ndurya, Raphael Mkala, et al. *Musemat'o Wa Chiduruma, Chidzomba Na Chizungu*. Nairobi: Bible Translation and Literacy, 1989.

Nurse, Derek. *Inheritance, Contact, and Change in Two East African Languages*. Köln: Köppe, 2000.

Nurse, Derek. "Lexicon for Ki-Bajuni." n.p., 2010.

Nurse, Derek, and Thomas Hinnebusch. *Swahili and Sabaki: A Linguistic History*. Berkeley: University of California Press, 1993.

Nurse, Derek, and G. Philippson. "Tanzania Language Survey." n.p., 1975.

Octávio Gonçalves, Nelly. *Vocabulário de Kimwani*. Nampula: SIL Moçambique, 2010.

Ottenheimer, Harriet Joseph. *Comorian-English/English-Comorian (Shinzwani) Dictionary*. Manhattan, KS, 2011.

Petzell, Malin. *The Kagulu Language of Tanzania: Grammar, Texts and Vocabulary*. Köln: Köppe, 2008

Rubanza, Yunis I. *Kimeru: Msamiati wa Kimeru-Kiswahili-Kingereza Na Kiingereza-Kimeru-Kiswahili*. Dar es Salaam: Languages of Tanzania Project, 2008.

Rugemalira, Josephat M. *Cigogo: Kamusi Ya Kigogo-Kiswahili-Kiingereza*. Dar es Salaam: Languages of Tanzania Project, 2009.

Rugemalira, Josephat M. *Cimakonde: Kamusi Ya Kimakonde-Kiingereza-Kiswahili*. Dar es Salaam: Languages of Tanzania Project, 2013.

Rugemalira, Josephat M. *Kimashami: Kamusi ya Kimashami-Kiingereza-Kiswahili*. Dar es Salaam: Languages of Tanzania Project, 2009.

Sacleux, Charles. *Dictionnaire Swahili-Français*. Vols. 1–2. Paris: Institut d'ethnologie, 1939.

Sanderson, George Meredith. *A Yao Grammar*. London: MacMillan, 1922.

196 BIBLIOGRAPHY

Schoenbrun, David. *The Historical Reconstruction of Great Lakes Bantu Cultural Vocabulary: Etymologies and Distributions*. Köln: Rüdiger Köppe Press, 1997.

Sewangi, Seleman S. *Kigweno: Msamiati Wa Kigweno-Kiswahili-Kiingereza*. Dar es Salaam: Languages of Tanzania Project, 2008.

Shaw, Archibald. *A Pocket Vocabulary of the ki-Swahili, ki-Nyika, ki-Taita, and ki-Kamba Languages*. London: Society for Promoting Christian Knowledge, 1885.

Snoxall, R. A. *Luganda-English Dictionary*. Oxford: Clarendon Press, 1967.

Steere, Edward. *Collections for a Handbook of the Shambala Language*. Zanzibar, 1867.

Taylor, M. E. *Giryama Vocabulary and Collections*. London: Society for Promoting Christian Knowledge, 1891.

Velten, Carl. *Kikami, die Sprache der Wakami in Deutsch-Ostafrika*. Reichsdruckerei, 1899.

Walsh, Martin. "Duruma Wordlist." n.p., 1987.

Walsh, Martin. "Loanwords of Central Kenya Bantu Origin in Mijikenda." n.p., 2007.

Whiteley, W. E. *Ki-Mtang'ata: A Dialect of the Mrima Coast, Tanganyika*. Kampala: East African Swahili Committee, Makerere College, 1956.

Woodward, H. W. *Collections for a Handbook of the Boondei Language*. London: Society for Promoting Christian Knowledge, 1882.

Wray, Joseph. *An Elementary Introduction to the Taita Language, Eastern Equatorial Africa*. London: Society for Promoting Christian Knowledge, 1894.

OTHER PRIMARY AND SECONDARY SOURCES

Abdulaziz, Mohamed H. *Muyaka: 19th Century Swahili Popular Poetry*. Nairobi: East African Literature Bureau, 1979.

Abu-Lughod, Janet. *Before European Hegemony: The World-System AD 1250–1350*. New York: Oxford University Press, 1991.

Abungu, George, and Henry Mutoro. "Coast-Interior Settlements and Social Relations in the Kenya Hinterland." In *The Archaeology of Africa: Food, Metals, and Towns*, edited by Shaw et al., 694–704. London: Routledge, 1993.

Adamson, Joy. *The Peoples of Kenya: Epilogue*. London: Collins and Harvill P, 1967.

Adelman, Jeremy. "What Is Global History Now?" *Aeon*, March 2017. https://aeon.co/essays/is-global-history-still-possible-or-has-it-had-its-momentdelman.

Al-Mazrui, Al-Amin bin. *The History of the Mazru'i Dynasty of Mombasa*. Translated by J. McL. Ritchie. New York: Oxford University Press, 1995.

Al-Salimi, Abdulrahman, and Michael Jansen, eds. *Portugal in the Sea of Oman: Religion and Politics: Research on Documents*. 17 vols. Hildesheim: Georg Olms Verlag, 2015–2018.

Alavi, Seema. *Muslim Cosmopolitanism in the Age of Empire*. Cambridge: Harvard University Press, 2015.

Allen, James de Vere. "The Kiti Cha Enzi and Other Swahili Chairs." *African Arts* 22, no. 3 (1989): 53–63.

Alpers, Edward. "Indian Ocean Studies: How Did We Get Here and Where Are We Going? A Historian's Perspective." *Journal of Indian Ocean World Studies* 5, no. 2 (2021): 314–336.

Alpers, Edward. *The Indian Ocean in World History*. Oxford: Oxford University Press, 2013.

Alpers, Edward. *Ivory and Slaves in East Central Africa: Changing Patterns of Internal Trade to the Late Nineteenth Century*. London: Heinemann, 1975.

Alpers, Edward. "The Ivory Trade in Africa: An Historical Overview." In *Elephant: The Animal and Its Ivory in African Culture*, edited by Doran Ross, 349–386. Los Angeles: Fowler Museum of Cultural History, 1992.

Alpers, Edward, and Chhaya Goswami, eds. *Transregional Trade and Traders: Situating Gujarat in the Indian Ocean from Early Times to 1900*. Oxford University Press, 2019.

Andaya, Leonard. "Flights of Fancy: The Bird of Paradise and Its Cultural Impact." *Journal of Southeast Asian Studies* 48, no. 3 (2017): 372–389.

Anon. *Hadithi za Kiunguja: Short Stories Related by Natives of Zanzibar*. Zanzibar: Central African Mission Press, 1867.

Anthony, David. *The Horse, the Wheel, and Language: How Bronze-Age Riders from the Eurasian Steppes Shaped the Modern World*. Princeton: Princeton University Press, 2007.

Ashley, Ceri Z. "Towards a Socialised Archaeology of Ceramics in Great Lakes Africa." *African Archaeological Review* 27 (2010): 135–163.

Aslanian, Sebouh David. *From the Indian Ocean to the Mediterranean: The Global Trade Networks of Armenian Merchants from New Julfa*. Berkeley: University of California Press, 2014.

Astley, Thomas, and John Green, *A New General Collection of Voyages and Travels*. Vol. 3. London, 1745.

Baker, E. C. "Notes on the History of the Wasegeju." *Tanganyika Notes and Records* 27 (1949): 16–41.

Barnes, Ruth. "Indian Cotton for Cairo: The Royal Ontario Museum's Gujarati Textiles and the Early Western Indian Ocean Trade." *Textile History* 48, no. 1 (2017): 15–30.

Barret, W. E. "Notes on the Customs and Beliefs of the Wa-Giriama, etc. British East Africa." *Journal of the Royal Anthropological Institute of Great Britain and Ireland* 41 (1911): 20–39.

Bauer, Andrew. "Provincializing the Littoral in Indian Ocean Heritage: Coastal Connections and Interior Contexts of the Southern Deccan." In *Bridging the Gulf: Maritime Cultural Heritage of the Western Indian Ocean*, edited by Himanshu Prabha Ray, 101–119. Manohar: India International Center, 2016.

Baumann, Oskar. *Usambara und seine nachbargebiete: allgemeine darstellung des nordöstlichen Deutsch-Ostafrika und seiner bewohner auf grund einer im auftrage der Deutsch-Ostafrikanischen gesellschaft in jahre 1890 ausgeführten reise*. Dietrich Reimer, 1891.

Becker, Felicitas, and Joel Cabrita. "Introduction: Performing Citizenship and Enacting Exclusion on Africa's Indian Ocean Littoral." *Journal of African History* 55, no. 2 (2014): 161–171.

Beidelman, T. O. "The Blood Covenant and the Concept of Blood in Ukaguru." *Africa: Journal of the International Africa Institute* 33, no. 4 (1963): 321–342.

Beidelman, T. O. *The Kaguru: A Matrilineal People of East Africa*. New York: Holt, Rinehart, and Winston, 1971.

Beidelman, T. O. *The Matrilineal Peoples of Eastern Tanzania (Zaramo, Luguru, Kaguru, Ngulu, etc.)*. London: International African Institute, 1967.

Bentley, Jerry H. *Old World Encounters: Cross-Cultural Contacts and Exchanges in Pre-Modern Times*. Oxford: Oxford University Press, 1993.

Berg, F. J. "Mombasa under the Busaidi Sultanate: The City and Its Hinterlands in the Nineteenth Century." PhD diss., University of Wisconsin-Madison, 1971.

198   BIBLIOGRAPHY

Berg, F. J. "The Swahili Community of Mombasa, 1500–1900." *Journal of African History* 9, no. 1 (1968): 35–56.

Bergman, Jeanne Louise. "A Willingness to Remember: The Persistence of Duruma Culture and Collective Memory." PhD diss., University of California, Berkeley, 1997.

Biedermann, Zoltán. "(Dis)connected History and the Multiple Narratives of Global Early Modernity." *Modern Philology* 119, no. 1 (2021): 13–32.

Biginagwa, Thomas. "Historical Archaeology of the 19th Century Caravan Trade in Northeastern Tanzania: A Zooarchaeological Perspective." PhD diss., University of York, 2012.

Bin Stamboul, Sheikh Omari. "An Early History of Mombasa and Tanga, Translated by EC Baker." *Tanganyika Notes and Records* 31 (1951): 32–36.

Bishara, Fahad. *A Sea of Debt: Law and Economic Life in the Western Indian Ocean, 1780–1950.* Cambridge: Cambridge University Press, 2017.

Boivin, Nicole, et al. "East Africa and Madagascar in the Indian Ocean World." *Journal of World Prehistory* 26, no. 3 (2013): 213–281.

Boivin, Nicole, and Michael D. Frachetti, "Introduction: Archaeology and the 'People without History.'" In *Globalization in Prehistory: Contact, Exchange, and the 'People Without History,'* edited by Nicole Boivin and Michael D. Frachetti, 1–14. Cambridge: Cambridge University Press, 2018.

Brady, Cyrus Townsend. *Commerce and Conquest in East Africa.* Salem: Essex Institute, 1950.

Brantley, Cynthia. "Gerontocratic Government: Age-Sets in Pre-Colonial Giriama." *Africa: Journal of the International African Institute* 48, no. 3 (1978): 248–264.

Bravman, Bill. *Making Ethnic Ways: Communities and Their Transformations in Taita, Kenya, 1800–1950.* Portsmouth: Heineman, 1998.

Bresnahan, David. "The Contours of Community on the East African Coast: A View from the Hinterlands." PhD diss., University of Wisconsin-Madison, 2018.

Bresnahan, David. "Forest Imageries and Political Practice in Colonial Coastal Kenya." *Journal of Eastern African Studies* 12, no. 4 (2018): 655–673.

Bresnahan, David. "Greatness Is Like a Rubbish Hole: Social Frictions and Global Connections in the Early-Swahili World." *Journal of World History* 31, no. 2 (2020): 361–390.

Bresnahan, David. "In Mombasa They Are 'Like Prisoners' to the Mijikenda: Martiality, Trade, and Inland Influences on a Swahili Port City." In *Making Martial Races: Gender, Society, and Warfare in Africa,* edited by Myles Osborne, 25–49. Athens: Ohio University Press, 2024.

Bresnahan, David. "Short Teaching Module: Precolonial Kenya, A Small-Scale History." *World History Commons,* 2022. https://worldhistorycommons.org/short-teaching-module -precolonial-kenya-small-scale-history.

Brielle, Esther S., et al. "Entwined African and Asian Genetic Roots of Medieval Peoples of the Swahili Coast." *Nature* 615, no. 7954 (2023): 866–873.

Brown, Jean Lucas. "Miji Kenda Grave and Memorial Sculptures." *African Arts* 13, no. 4 (1980): 36–39.

Brucato, Nicolas, et al. "The Comoros Show the Earliest Austronesian Gene Flow into the Swahili Corridor." *American Journal of Human Genetics* 102, no. 1 (2018): 58–68.

Buckles, Laura K., et al. "Short-term Variability in the Sedimentary BIT Index of Lake Challa, East Africa over the Past 2200 Years: Validating the Precipitation Proxy." *Climate of the Past* 11, no. 2 (2015): 1177–1218.

BIBLIOGRAPHY 199

Buckles, Laura K., et al. "Interannual and (Multi-)Decadal Variability in the Sedimentary BIT Index of Lake Challa, East Africa, over the Past 2200 Years: Assessment of the Precipitation Proxy." *Climate of the Past* 12, no. 5 (2016): 1243–1262.

Bunger, Robert. *Islamization among the Upper Pokomo.* Syracuse: Maxwell School of Citizenship and Public Affairs, 1979.

Büntgen, Ulf, et al. "Cooling and Societal Change during the Late Antique Little Ice Age from 536 to around 660 AD." *Nature Geoscience* 9, no. 3 (2016): 231–236.

Burton, Richard Francis. *The Lakes Region of Central Africa.* New York: Dover Publishers, 1995.

Burton, Richard Francis, and J. H. Speke. "A Coasting Voyage from Mombasa to the Pangani River: Visit to Sultan Kimwere: And Progress of the Expedition into the Interior, Visit to Sultan Kimwere; and Progress of the Expedition into the Interior." *Journal of the Royal Geographic Society of London* 28 (1858): 188–226.

Campbell, Gwyn. "Africa and the Early Indian Ocean World Exchange System in the Context of Human-Environmental Interaction." In *Early Exchange between Africa and the Wider Indian Ocean World*, edited by Gwyn Campbell, 1–24. London: Palgrave Macmillan, 2016.

Campbell, Gwyn. *Africa and the Indian Ocean World from Early Times to circa 1900.* New York: Cambridge University Press, 2019.

Casale, Giancarlo. "Global Politics in the 1580s: One Canal, Twenty Thousand Cannibals, and an Ottoman Plot to Rule the World." *Journal of World History* 18, no. 3 (2007): 267–296.

Casale, Giancarlo. *The Ottoman Age of Exploration.* Oxford: Oxford University Press, 2010.

Casson, Lionel. *The Periplus Maris Erythraei: Text with Introduction, Translation, and Commentary.* Princeton: Princeton University Press, 1989.

Chaffee, John. *The Muslim Merchants of Premodern China: The History of a Maritime Asian Trade Diaspora, 750–1400.* Cambridge University Press, 2017.

Chami, Felix. "A Review of Swahili archaeology." *African Archaeological Review* 15, no. 3 (1998): 199–218.

Chami, Felix. "Roman Beads from the Rufiji Delta, Tanzania: First Incontrovertible Archaeological Link with the *Periplus.*" *Current Anthropology* 40, no. 2 (1999): 237–242.

Chami, Felix, and Paul Msemwa. "A New Look at Culture and Trade on the Azanian Coast." *Current Anthropology* 38, no. 4 (1997): 673–677.

Champion, Arthur. *The Agiryama of Kenya*, edited by John Middleton. London: Royal Anthropological Institute of Great Britain and Ireland, 1967.

Chaudhuri, Kirti N. "The Structure of Indian Textile Industry in the Seventeenth and Eighteenth Centuries." *Indian Economic and Social History Review* 11, no. 2–3 (1974): 127–182.

Chaudhuri, Kirti N. *Trade and Civilisation in the Indian Ocean: An Economic History from the Rise of Islam to 1750.* New York: Cambridge University Press, 1985.

Chirikure, Shadreck. "Land and Sea Links: 1500 Years of Connectivity between Southern Africa and the Indian Ocean Rim Regions, AD 700 to 1700." *African Archaeological Review* 31 (2014): 705–724.

Chittick, Neville. *Kilwa: An Islamic Trading City on the East African Coast.* 2 vols. Nairobi: British Institute in Eastern Africa, 1974.

Ciekawy, Diane. "Utsai as Ethical Discourse: A Critique of Power from Mijikenda in Coastal Kenya." In *Dialogues of "Witchcraft": Anthropological and Philosophical Exchanges,* edited by George Clement Bond and Diane Ciekawy, 158–189. Athens: Ohio University Press, 2001.

Ciekawy, Diane. "Witchcraft Eradication as a Political Process in Kilifi District, Kenya, 1955–1988." PhD diss., Columbia University, 1992.

Colson, Elizabeth. *The Plateau Tonga of Northern Rhodesia: Social and Religious Studies.* Manchester: Manchester University Press, 1962.

Contini-Morava, Ellen. "(What) Do Noun Class Markers Mean?" In *Signal, Meaning, and Message: Perspectives on Sign-Based Linguistics*, edited by Wallis Reid, Ricardo Otheguy, and Nancy Stern, 3–64. Amsterdam: John Benjamins, 2002.

Cooper, Frederick. *Plantation Slavery on the East Coast of Africa.* New Haven: Yale University Press, 1977.

Cooper, Frederick. "What Is the Concept of Globalization Good For? An African Historian's Perspective." *African Affairs* 100, no. 399 (2001): 189–213.

Cory, Hans. "Tambiko (fika)." *Tangnyika Notes and Records*, nos. 58–59 (1962): 274–282.

Croucher, Sarah, and Stephanie Wynne-Jones. "People, Not Pots: Locally Produced Ceramics and Identity on the Nineteenth-Century East African Coast." *International Journal of African Historical Studies* 39, no. 1 (2006): 107–124.

Crowley, Terry, and Claire Bowern. *An Introduction to Historical Linguistics.* 4th ed. Oxford: Oxford University Press, 2010.

Crowther, Alison, et al. "Coastal Subsistence, Maritime Trade, and the Colonization of Small Offshore Islands in Eastern African Prehistory." *Journal of Island and Coastal Archaeology* 11, no. 2 (2016): 211–237.

Crowther, Alison, et al. "Subsistence Mosaics, Forager-Farmer Interactions, and the Transition to Food Production in Eastern Africa." *Quaternary International* 489 (2018): 101–120.

Crowther, Alison, et al. "Use of Zanzibar Copal (Hymenaea Verrucosa Gaertn.) as Incense at Unguja Ukuu, Tanzania in the 7–8th Century CE: Chemical Insights into Trade and Indian Ocean Interactions." *Journal of Archaeological Science* 53 (2014): 374–390.

Cummings, Robert. "Aspects of Human Porterage with Special Reference to the AKamba of Kenya; Towards an Economic History, 1820–1920." PhD diss., UCLA, 1975.

Curtin, Phillip. *Cross-Cultural Trade in World History.* Cambridge: Cambridge University Press, 1985.

D'Avignon, Robyn. *A Ritual Geology: Gold and Subterranean Knowledge in Savanna West Africa.* Durham: Duke University Press, 2022.

Dale, Godfrey. "An Account of the Principle Customs and Habits of the Natives Inhabiting the Bondei Country, Compiled Mainly for the Use of European Missionaries in the Country." *Journal of the Anthropological Institute of Great Britain and Ireland* 25 (1896): 181–239.

Dames, M. L. *The Book of Duarte Barbosa: An Account of the Countries Bordering on the Indian Ocean and Their Inhabitants: Written by Duarte Barbosa, and Completed about the Year 1518 AD.* London: Hakluyt Society, 1918.

De Almeida, Marcos Abreu Lelitão. "Speaking of Slavery: Slaving Strategies and Moral Imaginations in the Lower Congo (Early Times to the Late 19th Century)." PhD diss., Northwestern University, 2020.

De Luna, Kathryn M. "Amassing Global History." *Cyber Review of Modern Historiography* (2021).

De Luna, Kathryn M. *Collecting Food, Cultivating People: Subsistence and Society in Central Africa*. New Haven: Yale University Press, 2016.

De Luna, Kathryn M. "Collecting Food, Cultivating Persons: Wild Resource Use in Central African Political Culture, c. 1000 BCE to c. 1900." PhD diss., Northwestern University, 2008.

De Luna, Kathryn M. "Sounding the African Atlantic." *William and Mary Quarterly* 78, no. 4 (2021): 581–616.

De Luna, Kathryn M. "Surveying the Boundaries of Historical Linguistics and Archaeology: Early Settlement in South Central Africa." *African Archaeological Review* 29 (2012): 209–251.

De Luna, Kathryn M., and Jeffrey Fleisher. *Speaking with Substance: Methods of Language and Materials in African History*. New York: Springer, 2019.

Denbow, James, Carla Klehm, and Laure Dussubieux. "The Glass Beads of Kaitshàa and Early Indian Ocean Trade into the Far Interior of Southern Africa." *Antiquity* 89, no. 344 (2015): 361–377.

Dimmendaal, Gerrit J. *Historical Linguistics and the Comparative Study of African Languages*. Amsterdam: John Benjamins Publishing Company, 2011.

Dingley, Zebulon. "Kinship, Capital, and the Occult on the South Coast of Kenya." PhD diss., University of Chicago, 2018.

Diouf, Sylviane A. *Slavery's Exiles: The Story of the American Maroons*. New York: New York University Press, 2014.

Dores Cruz, Maria. "'Pots Are Pots, Not People:' Material Culture and Ethnic Identity in the Banda Area (Ghana), Nineteenth and Twentieth Centuries." *Azania: Archaeological Research in Africa* 46, no. 3 (2011): 336–357.

Drayton, Richard, and David Motadel. "Discussion: The Futures of Global History." *Journal of Global History* 13, no. 1 (2018): 1–21.

Dua, Jatin. *Captured at Sea: Piracy and Protection in the Indian Ocean*. Berkeley: University of California Press, 2019.

Dundas, Charles. "Native Laws of Some Bantu Tribes of East Africa." *Journal of the Royal Anthropological Institute of Great Britain and Ireland* 51 (1921): 217–278.

Dunn, Ross. *The Adventures of Ibn Battuta: A Muslim Traveler of the Fourteenth Century, with a New Preface*. Berkeley: University of California Press: 2012.

Dussubieux, L., et al. "The Trading of Ancient Glass Beads: New Analytical Data from South Asian and East African Soda-Alumina Glass Beads." *Archaeometry* 50, no. 5 (2008): 797–821.

Ehret, Christopher. *An African Classical Age: Eastern and Southern Africa in World History 1000 BC to AD 400*. Charlottesville: University of Virginia Press, 1998.

Ehret, Christopher. *History and the Testimony of Language*. Berkeley: University of California Press, 2011.

Ehret, Christopher, and Derek Nurse. "The Taita Cushites." *Sprache und Gesschichte in Afrika* 3 (1981): 125–168.

El Zein, Abdul Hamid. *The Sacred Meadows: A Structural Analysis of Religious Symbolism in an East African Town*. Evanston: Northwestern University Press, 1974.

Emery, James. "Short Account of Mombas and the Neighboring Coast of Africa." *Journal of the Royal Geographic Society of London* 3 (1833): 280–283.

BIBLIOGRAPHY

Fabian, Steven. *Making Identity on the Swahili Coast: Urban Life, Community, and Belonging in Bagamoyo.* Cambridge: Cambridge University Press, 2019.

Fee, Sarah. "'Cloths with Names': Luxury Textile Imports to Eastern Africa, c. 1800–1885." *Textile History* 48, no. 1 (2017): 49–84.

Feierman, Steven. "African Histories and the Dissolution of World History." In *Africa and the Disciplines: The Contributions of Research in Africa to the Social Sciences and Humanities,* edited by Robert Bates, V. Y. Mudimbe, and Jean O'Barr, 167–212. Chicago: University of Chicago Press, 1993.

Feierman, Steven. "Colonizers, Scholars, and the Creation of Invisible Histories." In *Beyond the Cultural Turn: New Directions in the Study of Society and Culture,* edited by Victoria E. Bonnell and Lynn Hunt, 182–216. Berkeley: University of California Press, 1999.

Feierman, Steven. "Concepts of Sovereignty among the Shambaa and their Relation to Political Action." PhD diss., Oxford University, 1972.

Feierman, Steven. *Peasant Intellectuals: Anthropology and History in Tanzania.* Madison: University of Wisconsin Press, 1990.

Ferguson, James. *Global Shadows: Africa in the Neoliberal World Order.* Durham: Duke University Press, 2006.

Ferreira, Roquinaldo. *Cross-Cultural Exchange in the Atlantic World: Angola and Brazil during the Era of the Slave Trade.* Cambridge University Press, 2012.

Fields-Black, Edda. *Deep Roots: Rice Farmers in West Africa and the African Diaspora.* Bloomington: Indiana University Press, 2008.

Fitzgerald, William. *Travels in the Coastlands of British East Africa and the Islands of Zanzibar and Pemba; Their Agricultural Resources and General Characteristics.* London: Chapman and Hall, 1898.

Fitzsimons, William. "Warfare, Competition, and the Durability of 'Political Smallness' in Nineteenth-Century Busoga." *Journal of African History* 59, no. 1 (2018): 45–67.

Fleisher, Jeffrey. "Rituals of Consumption and the Politics of Feasting on the Eastern African Coast, AD 700–1500." *Journal of World Prehistory* 23, no. 4 (2010): 195–217.

Fleisher, Jeffrey. "Swahili Synoecism: Rural Settlements and Town Formation on the Central East African Coast, A.D. 750–1050." *Journal of Field Archaeology* 35, no. 3 (2010): 265–282.

Fleisher, Jeffrey. "Town and Village." In *The Swahili World,* edited by Stephanie Wynne-Jones and Adria LaViolette, 194–204. New York: Routledge, 2018.

Fleisher, Jeffrey, and Adria LaViolette. "The Early Swahili Trade Village of Tumbe, Pemba Island, Tanzania, AD 600–950." *Antiquity* 87, no. 388 (2013): 1151–1168.

Fleisher, Jeffrey, and Stephanie Wynne-Jones. "Ceramics and the Early Swahili: Deconstructing the Early Tana Tradition." *African Archaeological Review* 28, no. 4 (2011): 245–278.

Fleisher, Jeffrey, and Stephanie Wynne-Jones. "Finding Meaning in Ancient Swahili Spatial Practices." *African Archaeological Review* 29, nos. 2–3 (2012): 171–207.

Flexner, J. L., et al. "Bead Grinders and Early Swahili Household Economy: Analysis of an Assemblage from Tumbe, Pemba Island, Tanzania, 7th–10th Centuries AD." *Journal of African Archaeology* 6, no. 2 (2008): 161–181.

Forssman, Tim, et al. "How Important Was the Presence of Elephants as a Determinant of the Zhinzo Settlement of the Greater Mapungubwe Landscape?" *Journal of African Archaeology* 12, no. 1 (2014): 75–87.

BIBLIOGRAPHY   203

Foster, William. *The English Factories in India, 1618–1621; A Calendar of Documents in the India Office, British Museum and Public Record Office.* Oxford: Clarendon Press, 1906.

Frachetti, Michael D., and Elissa Bullion. "Bronze Age Participation in a 'Global' Ecumene: Mortuary Practice and Ideology across Inner Asia." In *Globalization in Prehistory: Contact, Exchange, and the 'People Without History,'* edited by Nicole Boivin and Michael D. Frachetti, 102–130. Cambridge: Cambridge University Press, 2018.

Frachetti, Michael D., C. Evan Smith, and Cody Copp. "Pastoralist Participation (PastPart): A Model of Mobility and Connectivity across the Inner Asian Mountain Corridor." In *New Geospatial Approaches to the Anthropological Sciences*, edited by Glenn C. Conroy and Robert L. Anemone, 171–188. Albuquerque: University of New Mexico Press, 2018.

Frank, William. *Habari na desturi za Waribe.* Sheldon Press, 1953.

Franklin, Kate. *Everyday Cosmopolitanisms: Living the Silk Road in Medieval Armenia.* Berkeley: University of California Press, 2021.

Freeman-Grenville, G.S.P. *The East African Coast: Select Documents from the First to the Earlier Nineteenth Century.* Oxford: Clarendon Press, 1962.

Freeman-Grenville, G.S.P. *The French at Kilwa Island: An Episode in Eighteenth-Century East African History.* Oxford: Clarendon Press, 1965.

Freeman-Grenville, G.S.P., ed. and trans. *The Mombasa Rising against the Portuguese, 1631: From Sworn Evidence.* London: Oxford University Press, 1980.

Gearhart, Rebecca, and Linda Giles, eds. *Contesting Identities: The Mijikenda and Their Neighbors in Kenyan Coastal Society.* Trenton: Africa World Press, 2014.

Gerlach, Luther P. "The Social Organisation of the Digo of Kenya." PhD diss., School of Oriental and African Studies, 1960.

Gibb, H.A.R. *The Travels of Ibn Battuta, Translated with Notes.* Vol 2. Cambridge: Hakluyt Society, 1963.

Glassman, Jonathon. *Feasts and Riot: Revelry, Rebellion, and Popular Consciousness on the Swahili Coast, 1856–1888.* Portsmouth: Heinemann, 1995.

Goldstein, Steven T., et al. "Hunter-Gatherer Technological Organization and Responses to Holocene Climate Change in Coastal, Lakeshore, and Grassland Ecologies of Eastern Africa." *Quaternary Science Reviews* 280 (2022): 107390.

Gonzales, Rhonda. *Societies, Religion, and History: Central-East Tanzanians and the World They Created, c. 200 BCE to 1800 CE.* New York: Columbia University Press, 2009.

Gooding, Phillip. *On the Frontiers of the Indian Ocean World: A History of Lake Tanganyika, c.1830–1890.* Cambridge: Cambridge University Press, 2022.

Gray, John. *The British in Mombasa: 1824–1826, Being the History of Captain Owen's Protectorate.* London: MacMillan, 1957.

Green, Nile. "The Languages of Indian Ocean Studies: Models, Methods and Sources." *World History Compass*, special issue (2021): 1–15.

Green, Nile. "The Waves of Heterotopia: Toward a Vernacular Intellectual History of the Indian Ocean." *The American Historical Review* 132, no. 3 (2018): 846–887.

Griffiths, J. B. "Glimpses of a Nyika Tribe (Waduruma)." *Journal of the Royal Anthropological Institute of Great Britain and Ireland* 65 (1935): 267–296.

Grollemund, Rebecca, et al. "Bantu Expansion Shows That Habitat Alters the Route and Pace of Human Dispersals." *Proceedings of the National Academy of Science of the United States of America* 112, no. 43 (2015): 13296–13301.

204 BIBLIOGRAPHY

Guillain, Charles. *Documents sur l'histoire, le géographie et le commerce de l'Afrique Orientale*. 3 vols. Paris: Bertrand, 1856.

Gupta, Anil. "Abrupt Changes in the Asian Southwest Monsoon during the Holocene and Their Links to the North Atlantic Ocean." *Nature* 421 (2003): 354–357.

Guy, John. *Woven Cargoes: Indian Textiles in the East*. London: Thames and Hudson, 1998.

Guyer, Jane. "Wealth in People, Wealth in Things—Introduction." *Journal of African History* 36, no. 1 (1995): 83–90.

Guyer, Jane, and Samuel M. Eno Belinga. "Wealth in People as Wealth in Knowledge: Accumulation and Composition in Equatorial Africa." *Journal of African History* 36, no. 1 (1995): 99–120.

Håkansson, Thomas. "Politics, Cattle, and Ivory: Regional Interaction and Changing Land-Use Prior to Colonialism." In *Culture, History and Identity: Landscapes of Inhabitation in the Mount Kilimanjaro Area, Tanzania*, edited by Timothy Clark, 141–154. Oxford: Archaeopress, 2009.

Håkansson, Thomas. "Socio-ecological Consequences of the East African Ivory Trade." In *Ecology and Power: Struggles over Land and Material Resources in the Past, Present, and Future*, edited by Alf Hornborg, Brett Clark, and Kenneth Hermele, 124–142. London and New York: Routledge, 2012.

Hamamoto, Mitsuru. "Order of the Homestead and Its Boundaries: The Duruma Concept of Homestead (mudzi) and Sexuality." n.p.

Hamdun, Said, and Noel King. *Ibn Battuta in Black Africa*. Princeton: Marcus Weiner Publishers, 1995.

Harries, Lyndon. "The Founding of Rabai: A Swahili Chronicle by Midani bin Mwidad." *Swahili, Journal of the East African Swahili Committee* 31, no. 1–2 (1960): 140–149.

Harries, Lyndon. "Swahili Traditions of Mombasa." *Afrika und Übersee: Sprachen, Kulturen* 43, no. 2 (1959): 81–105.

Harris, Grace Gredys. *Casting Out Anger: Religion among the Taita of Kenya*. Cambridge: Cambridge University Press, 1978.

Helm, Richard. "Conflicting Histories: The Archaeology of the Iron-Working, Farming Communities in the Central and Southern Coast Region of Kenya." PhD diss., University of Bristol, 2000.

Helm, Richard. "Re-evaluating Traditional Histories on the Coast of Kenya: An Archaeological Perspective." In *African Historical Archaeologies*, edited by Andrew Reid and Paul Lane, 59–89. New York: Kluwer Academic/Plenum Publishers, 2004.

Helm, Richard, et al. "Exploring Agriculture, Interaction, and Trade on the Eastern African Littoral: Preliminary Results from Kenya." *Azania: Archaeological Research in Africa* 47, no. 1 (2012): 39–63.

Herlehy, Thomas. "Ties That Bind: Palm Wine and Blood-Brotherhood at the Kenya Coast during the 19th Century." *International Journal of African Historical Studies* 17, no. 2 (1984): 285–308.

Hirth, Friedrich, and W. W. Rockhill, *Chau Ju-kua: His Work on the Chinese and Arab Trade in the Twelfth and Thirteenth Centuries, entitled Chu Fan Chï*. St. Petersburg: Imperial Academy of Sciences, 1912.

Hirth, Kenneth G. "Interregional Trade and the Formation of Prehistoric Gateway Communities." *American Antiquity* 43, no. 1 (1978): 35–45.

Ho, Engseng. *The Graves of Tarim: Genealogy and Mobility across the Indian Ocean.* Berkeley: University of California Press, 2006.

Hobley, Charles. *Kenya, from Chartered Company to Crown Colony: Thirty Years of Exploration and Administration in British East Africa.* London: H. F. and G. Witherby, 1929.

Hollis, A. C. "Notes on the History of Vumba, East Africa." *Journal of the Royal Anthropological Institute* 30 (1900): 275–300.

Hoogervorst, Tom, and Nicole Boivin. "Invisible Agents of Eastern Trade: Foregrounding Island Southeast Asian Agency in Pre-Modern Globalisation." In *Globalization in Prehistory: Contact, Exchange, and the 'People Without History,'* edited by Nicole Boivin and Michael D. Frachetti, 205–231. Cambridge: Cambridge University Press, 2018.

Hopper, Matthew. *Slaves of One Master: Globalization and Slavery in Arabia in the Age of Empire.* New Haven: Yale University Press, 2015.

Horton, Mark. "Artisans, Communities, and Commodities: Medieval Exchanges between Northwestern India and East Africa." *Ars orientalis* 34 (2006): 62–80.

Horton, Mark. *Shanga: An Early Muslim Trading Community on the Coast of Eastern Africa.* London: British Institute in Eastern Africa, 1996.

Horton, Mark. "Swahili Architecture, Space and Social Structure." In *Architecture and Order: Approaches to Social Space,* edited by Michael Parker Pearson and Colin Richards, 145–165. London: Routledge, 1997.

Horton, Mark. "The Swahili Corridor." *Scientific American* 257, no. 3 (1987): 86–93.

Horton, Mark, and John Middleton. *The Swahili: The Social Landscape of a Mercantile Society.* Oxford: Blackwell Publishers, 2000.

Hughes, Carl, and Ruben Post. "A GIS Approach to Finding the Metropolis of Rhapta." In *Early Exchange between Africa and the Wider Indian Ocean World,* edited by Gwyn Campbell, 135–156. London: Palgrave Macmillan, 2016.

Ibn Ruzaiq, Ḥumaid Ibn-Muḥammad. *History of the Imâms and Seyyids of 'Omân: From AD 661–1856.* London: Hakluyt Society, 1871.

Iliffe, John. *Honour in African History.* Cambridge: Cambridge University Press, 2005.

Ingrams, W. H. *Zanzibar: Its History and Its People.* London: Witherby, 1924.

Janzen, John M. *Lemba 1650–1930: A Drum of Affliction in Africa and the New World.* New York and London: Garland Publishing, 1982.

Jennings, Justin. *Globalizations and the Ancient World.* Cambridge: Cambridge University Press, 2010.

Jenson, John, ed. *Journal and Letter Book of Nicholas Buckeridge, 1651–1654.* Minneapolis: University of Minnesota Press, 1973.

Jimenez, Raevin. "Southern Africa's Global Grain Basket." In AHR History Lab "On Transnational and International History." *American Historical Review* 128, no. 1 (2023): 291–296.

Johnston, Marguerite. "Dispute Settlement among the Giriama of Kenya." PhD diss., University of Pennsylvania, 1976.

Juma, Abdulrahman M. "The Swahili and the Mediterranean Worlds: Pottery of the Late Roman Period from Zanzibar." *Antiquity* 70 (1996): 148–154.

Juma, Abdulrahman M. "Unguja Ukuu on Zanzibar: An Archaeological Study of Early Urbanism." PhD diss., Uppsala University, 2004.

Kayamba, H. Martin T. "Notes on the Wadigo." *Tanganyika Notes and Records* 23 (1947): 80–96.

Kenyatta, Jomo. *Facing Mount Kenya: The Tribal Life of the Gikuyu*. London: Secker and Warburg, 1938.

Kimambo, Isaria. *A Political History of the Pare of Tanzania, 1500–1900*. Nairobi: East African Publishing House, 1969.

Kirch, Patrick Vinton, and Roger C. Green. *Hawaiki, Ancestral Polynesia: An Essay in Historical Anthropology*. Cambridge: Cambridge University Press, 2001.

Kiriama, Herman. "Mombasa: Archaeology and History." In *The Swahili World*, edited by Stephanie Wynne-Jones and Adria LaViolette, 620–628. New York: Routledge, 2018.

Kirkman, James. "The Muzungulos of Mombasa." *International Journal of African Historical Studies* 16, no. 1 (1983): 73–82.

Klieman, Kairn. *The Pygmies Were Our Compass: Bantu and Batwa in the History of West Central Africa, Early Times to c. 1900 C.E.* Portsmouth: Heinemann 2003.

Knappert, Jan. "The Chronicle of Mombasa." *Swahili: Journal of the East African Swahili Committee* 34 (1964): 21–27.

Knappert, Jan. *Swahili Islamic Poetry*. Leiden: Brill, 1971.

Kodesh, Neil. *Beyond the Royal Gaze: Clanship and Public Healing in Buganda*. Charlottesville: University of Virginia Press, 2010.

Kodesh, Neil. "Networks of Knowledge: Clanship and Collective Well-being in Buganda." *Journal of African History* 49, no. 2 (2008): 197–216.

Kohl, Karl-Heinz. "The Elephant with the Seven Tusks: Maritime Commodities in the East Indonesian Clan Houses and Marriage Cycles." In *Cargoes in Motion Materiality and Connectivity across the Indian Ocean*, edited by Burkhard Schnepel and Julia Verne, 269–286. Athens: Ohio University Press, 2022.

Konecky, Bronwen, et al. "Impact of Monsoons, Temperature, and CO_2 on the Rainfall and Ecosystems of Mt. Kenya during the Common Era." *Palaeogeography, Palaeoclimatology, Palaeoecology* 396 (2014): 17–25.

Kopytoff, Igor. *The African Frontier: The Reproduction of Traditional African Societies*. Bloomington: Indiana University Press, 1987.

Krapf, J. L. *Travels, Researches, and Missionary Labours, during an Eighteen Years' Residence in Eastern Africa*. 2nd ed. London: Frank Cass, 1968.

Kusimba, Chapurukha M. "Archaeology of Slavery in East Africa." *African Archaeological Review* 21, no. 2 (2004): 59–88.

Kusimba, Chapurukha M. *The Rise and Fall of Swahili States*. Walnut Creek: AltaMira Press, 1999.

Kusimba, Chapurukha M., and David Killick. "Ironworking on the Swahili Coast of Kenya." In *East African Archaeology: Foragers, Potters, Smiths, and Traders*, edited by Chapurukha Kusimba and Sibel Kusimba, 99–115. Philadelphia: University of Pennsylvania Press, 2003.

Kusimba, Chapurukha M., and Sibel Kusimba. "Preindustrial Water Management in Eastern Africa." *Global Journal of Archaeology and Anthropology* 1, no. 2 (2017): 29–41.

Kusimba, Chapurukha M., and Jonathan Walz. "When Did the Swahili Become Maritime?: A Reply to Fleisher et al. (2015), and to the Resurgence of Maritime Myopia in the Archaeology of the East African Coast." *American Anthropologist* 120, no. 3 (2018):

429–443. Kusimba, Chapurukha M., Sibel Kusimba, and Laure Dussubieux. "Beyond the Coastalscapes: Preindustrial Social and Political Networks in East Africa." *African Archaeological Review* 30, no. 4 (2013): 399–426.

Kusimba, Chapurukha M., Sibel Kusimba, and David Wright. "The Development and Collapse of Precolonial Ethnic Mosaics in Tsavo, Kenya." *Journal of African Archaeology* 3, no. 2 (2005): 243–265.

Lambourn, Elizabeth. *Abraham's Luggage: A Social Life of Things in the Medieval Indian Ocean World*. Cambridge: Cambridge University Press, 2018.

Lane, Paul J. "Ethnicity, Archaeological Ceramics, and Changing Paradigms in East African Archaeology." In *Ethnic Ambiguity and the African Past Materiality, History, and the Shaping of Cultural Identities*, edited by Francois G. Richard and Kevin C. MacDonald, 245–271. New York: Routledge, 2015.

Lane, Paul, and Colin Breen. "The Eastern African Coastal Landscape." In *The Swahili World*, edited by Stephanie Wynne-Jones and Adria LaViolette, 19–35. New York: Routledge, 2018.

Langley, Michelle, et al. "Poison Arrows and Bone Utensils in Late Pleistocene Eastern Africa: Evidence from Kuumbi Cave, Zanzibar." *Azania: Archaeological Research in Africa* 52, no 2 (2016): 155–177.

LaViolette, Adria. "Swahili Cosmopolitanism in Africa and the Indian Ocean World, A.D. 600–1500." *Archaeologies: Journal of the World Archaeological Congress* 4, no. 1 (2008): 24–49.

LaViolette, Adria, and Jeffrey Fleisher. "The Urban History of a Rural Place: Archaeology and Pemba Island, Tanzania, AD 700–1500." *International Journal of African Historical Studies* 42, no. 3 (2009): 433–455.

Li, Chengfeng, and Michio Yanai. "The Onset and Interannual Variability of the Asian Summer Monsoon in Relation to Land-Sea Thermal Contrast." *Journal of Climate* 9, no. 2 (1996): 358–375.

Lobben, Marit. "Semantic Classification in Category-Specific Semantic Impairments Reflected in the Typology of Bantu Noun Class Systems." In *Selected Proceedings of the 41st Annual Conference on African Linguistics: African Languages in Contact*, edited by Bruce Connell and Nicholas Rolle, 361–404. Somerville: Cascadilla Proceedings Project, 2012.

Lobo, Jerónimo, Joachim Le Grand, and Samuel Johnson. *A Voyage to Abyssinia*. A. Bettesworth, and C. Hitch, 1735.

Machado, Pedro. *Ocean of Trade: South Asian Merchants, Africa, and the Indian Ocean, c. 1750–1850*. Cambridge: Cambridge University Press, 2014.

Malekandathil, Pius. "Dynamics of Trade, Faith and the Politics of Cultural Enterprise in Early Modern Kerala." In *Clio and Her Descendants: Essays in Honour of Kesavan Veluthat*, edited by Manu V. Devadevan, 157–198. Primus Books, 2018.

Marchant, Rob, et al., "The Indian Ocean Dipole–The Unsung Driver of Climatic Variability in East Africa." *African Journal of Ecology* 45, no. 1 (2007): 4–16.

Margariti, Roxani Eleni. *Aden and the Indian Ocean Trade: 150 Years in the Life of a Medieval Arabian Port*. Chapel Hill: University of North Carolina Press, 2007.

Marks, Stuart. "Hunting Behavior and Strategies of the Valley Bisa in Zambia." *Human Ecology* 5, no. 1 (1977): 1–36.

BIBLIOGRAPHY

Marshall, Lydia. "Spatiality and the Interpretation of Identity Formation: Fugitive Slave Community Creation in Nineteenth-Century Kenya." *African Archaeological Review* 29, no. 4 (2012): 355–381.

Martin, Esmond Bradley. *The History of Malindi: A Geographical Analysis of an East African Coastal Town from the Portuguese Period to the Present*. Nairobi: East African Literature Bureau, 1973.

Mbele, Joseph. "The Kikoa Incident in the Liongo Epic." *Kiswahili* 66 (2003): 39–48.

Mbuia-Joao, Tome Nhamitambo. "The Revolt of Dom Jeronimo Chingulia of Mombasa, 1590–1637 (An African Episode in the Portuguese Century of Decline)." PhD diss., Catholic University of America, 1990.

McConkey, Rosemary, and Thomas McErlean. "Mombasa Island: A Maritime Perspective." *International Journal of Historical Archaeology* 11, no. 2 (2007): 99–121.

McDow, Thomas. *Buying Time: Debt and Mobility in the Western Indian Ocean*. Athens: Ohio University Press, 2018.

McIntosh, Janet. *The Edge of Islam: Power, Personhood, and Ethnoreligious Boundaries on the Kenya Coast*. Durham: Duke University Press, 2009.

McIntosh, Roderick J. *Ancient Middle Niger: Urbanism and the Self-Organizing Landscape*. Cambridge: Cambridge University Press, 2005.

McIntosh, Susan Keech. "Pathways to Complexity: An African Perspective." In *Beyond Chiefdoms: Pathways to Complexity in Africa*, edited by Susan Keech McIntosh, 1–30. Cambridge: Cambridge University Press, 1999.

McKee, Helen. "From Violence to Alliance: Maroons and White Settlers in Jamaica, 1739–1795." *Slavery and Abolition* 39, no. 1 (2018): 27–52.

McMahon, Elisabeth. *Slavery and Emancipation in Islamic East Africa: From Honor to Respectability*. Cambridge: Cambridge University Press, 2013.

McPherson, Kenneth. "Anglo-Portuguese Commercial Relations in the Eastern Indian Ocean from the Seventeenth to the Eighteenth Centuries." *South Asia: Journal of South Asian Studies* 19 (1996): 41–57.

McVicar, Thomas. "Wanguru Religion." *Primitive Man* 14, no. 1/2 (1941): 13–30.

Meier, Prita. *Swahili Port Cities: The Architecture of Elsewhere*. Bloomington: Indiana University Press, 2016.

Meier, Prita. "Unmoored: On Oceanic Objects in Coastal Eastern Africa, circa 1700–1900." *Comparative Studies of South Asia, Africa, and the Middle East* 37, no. 2 (2017): 355–367.

Meyer, Hans. *Across East African Glaciers: An Accunt of the First Ascent of Kilimanjaro*. London: G. Philips and Son, 1891.

Middleton, John. *Land Tenure in Zanzibar*. London: H. M. Stationery Office, 1961.

Middleton, John. *The World of the Swahili: An African Mercantile Civilization*. New Haven: Yale, 1992.

Miers, Suzanne, and Igor Kopytoff, eds. *Slavery in Africa: Historical and Anthropological Perspectives*. Madison: University of Wisconsin Press, 1977.

Miles, Samuel Barret. *The Countries and Tribes of the Persian Gulf*. England: Harrison and Sons, 1919.

Mkangi, Katama. "The Democratic Roots in Mijikenda Polity." In *Contesting Identities: The Mijikenda and Their Neighbors in Kenya*, edited by Rebecca Gearhard and Linda Giles, 189–197. Trenton: Africa World Press, 2014.

M'Mbogori, Freda Nkirote. *Population and Ceramic Traditions: Revisiting the Tana Ware of Coastal Kenya (7th–14th Century AD)*. Oxford: Archaeopress, 2015.

Moffett, Abigail J., and Shadreck Chirikure. "Exotica in Context: Reconfiguring Prestige, Power and Wealth in the Southern African Iron Age." *Journal of World Prehistory* 29 (2016): 337–382.

Moffett, Abigail J., Simon Hall, and Shadreck Chirikure. "Crafting Power: New Perspectives on the Political Economy of Southern Africa, AD 900–1300." *Journal of Anthropological Archaeology* 59 (2020): 101180.

Moomaw, James. *Plant Ecology of the Coast Region of the Kenya Colony, British East Africa*. Nairobi: Kenya Department of Agriculture, 1960.

Morrison, Kathleen D. "Christians and Spices: Hidden Foundations and Misrecognitions in European Colonial Expansions to South Asia." In *Globalization in Prehistory: Contact, Exchange, and the 'People Without History,'* edited by Nicole Boivin and Michael D. Frachetti, 283–297. Cambridge: Cambridge University Press, 2018.

Morrison, Kathleen D. "Pepper in the Hills." In *Forager-Traders in South and Southeast Asia: Long-Term Historiesi* edited by Kathleen Morrison and Laura Junker, 105–130. Cambridge: Cambridge University Press, 2002.

Morrison, Kathleen D., and Mark Lycett. "Forest Products in a Wider World: Early Historic Connections across Southern India." In *Connections and Complexity: New Approaches to the Archaeology of South Asia*, edited by Shinu Anna Abraham et al., 127–142. London: Routledge, 2013.

Morton, Fred. *Children of Ham: Freed Slaves and Fugitive Slaves on the Kenya Coast, 1873–1907*. Boulder: Westview Press, 1990.

Mudida, Nina, and Mark Horton. "Subsistence at Shanga: The Faunal Record." In *Shanga: The Archaeology of a Muslim Trading Community on the Coast of East Africa*, 378–393. London: British Institute in Eastern Africa, 1996.

Munyaya, Elizabeth Jumwa. "Sense Relations and Lexical Pragmatic Processes in Linguistic Semantics: A Description of the Kigiryama System of Meaning." PhD diss., Pwani University, 2016.

Mutono, Diana, et al. "Social and Cultural Antecedents of Kalambya Boys and Sisters Kamba Popular Band." *Journal of African Research and Development* 2, no. 3 (2018): 102–123.

Mutoro, Henry. "An Archaeological Study of the Mijikenda Kaya Settlements on Hinterland Kenya Coast." PhD diss., UCLA, 1987.

Ndurya, Raphael Mkala. *Jadi ya Muduruma chitabu cha Phiri*. Duruma Language and Literacy Project, 2001.

Ngala, Ronald. *Nchi na Desturi za Wagiriama*. Nairobi: Eagle Press, 1949.

Ngala, Samuel. "Mila za Mijikenda." n.p.

New, Charles. *Life, Wanderings, and Labours in Eastern Africa*. London: Frank Cass and Co. LTD., 1971.

Newfield, Timothy P. "The Climate Downturn of 536–50." In *The Palgrave Handbook of Climate History*, edited by Sam White, Christian Pfister, and Franz Mauelshagen, 447–493. London: Palgrave Macmillan, 2018.

Nicholson, Sharon E. "A Review of Climate Dynamics and Climate Variability in Eastern Africa." In *Limnology, Climatology and Paleoclimatology of the East African Lakes*, edited by Thomas C. Johnson and Eric O. Odada, 25–56. New York: Routledge, 1996.

Nicholson, Sharon E. "The ITCZ and the Seasonal Cycle over Equatorial Africa." *Bulletin of the American Meteorological Society* 99, no. 2 (2018): 337–348.

Northrup, David. *Trade without Rulers: Pre-colonial Economic Development in South-Eastern Nigeria*. Oxford: Oxford University Press, 1978.

Nurse, Derek. *Classification of the Chaga Dialects: Language and History on Kilimanjaro, the Taita Hills, and the Pare Mountains*. Hamburg: Buske, 1979.

Nurse, Derek. "Segeju and Daisū: A Case Study of Evidence from Oral Tradition and Comparative Linguistics." *History in Africa* 9 (1982): 175–208.

Nurse, Derek. "Towards a Historical Classification of East African Bantu Languages." In *Bantu Historical Linguistics: Theoretical and Empirical Perspectives*, edited by Jean-Marie Hombert and Larry M. Hyman, 1–41. Stanford: CSLI Publications, 1999.

Nyamweru, Celia, et al. "The Kaya Forests of Coastal Kenya: 'Remnant Patches' or Dynamic Entities." In *African Sacred Groves: Ecological Dynamics and Social Change*, edited by Michael Sheridan and Celia Nyamweru, 62–86. Athens: Ohio University Press, 2007.

Omar, Yahya Ali, and Peter J. L. Frankl. "The Mombasa Chronicle." *Afrika und Übersee* 73, no. 1 (1990): 101–128.

Oliver, Roland. "The Problem of the Bantu Expansion." *Journal of African History* 7, no. 3 (1966): 361–376.

Orchardson-Mazrui, Elizabeth. "Expressing Power and Status through Aesthetics in Mijikenda Society." *Journal of African Cultural Studies* 11, no. 1 (1998): 85–102.

Orchardson-Mazrui, Elizabeth. "A Socio-Historical Perspective of the Art and Material Culture of the Mijikenda of Kenya." PhD diss., School of African and Oriental Studies, 1986.

Osborne, Myles. *Ethnicity and Empire in Kenya: Loyalty and Martial Race among the Kamba c. 1800 to the Present*. Cambridge: Cambridge University Press, 2014.

Owen, W.F.W. *Narrative of Voyages to Explore the Shores of Africa, Arabia, and Madagascar*. 2 vols. London: Bentley, 1833.

Parker, Ian. *Ivory Crisis*. London: Hogarth Press, 1983.

Parkin, David. *Sacred Void, Spatial Images of Ritual and Work among the Giriama of Kenya*. Cambridge: Cambridge University Press, 1991.

Parthasarathi, Prassannan. *Why Europe Grew Rich and Asia Did Not: Global Economic Divergence, 1600–1850*. Cambridge: Cambridge University Press, 2011.

Pawlowicz, Matthew. "Modeling the Swahili Past: The Archaeology of Mikindani in Southern Coastal Tanzania." *Azania: Archaeological Research in Africa* 47, no. 4 (2012): 488–508.

Pearson, Michael. "Littoral Society: The Concept and the Problems." *Journal of World History* 17, no. 4 (2006): 353–373.

Pearson, Michael. *Port Cities and Intruders: The Swahili Coast, India, and Portugal in the Early Modern Era*. Baltimore: Johns Hopkins University Press, 2002.

Phillipson, David W. *African Archaeology*. Cambridge: Cambridge University Press, 2005.

Piot, Charles. *Remotely Global: Village Modernity in West Africa*. Chicago: University of Chicago Press, 1999.

Pouwels, Randall. "The Battle of Shela: The Climax of an Era and a Point of Departure in the Modern History of the Kenya Coast." *Cahiers d'Études Africaines* 123 (1991): 362–389.

Pouwels, Randall. *Horn and Crescent: Cultural Change and Traditional Islam on the East African Coast, 800–1900*. Cambridge: Cambridge University Press, 1987.

Prange, Sebastian. "'Measuring by the Bushel': Reweighing the Indian Ocean Pepper Trade." *Historical Research* 84, no. 224 (2011): 212–235.

Prange, Sebastian. *Monsoon Islam: Trade and Faith on the Medieval Malabar Coast.* Cambridge University Press, 2018.

Prange, Sebastian. "Scholars and the Sea: A Historiography of the Indian Ocean." *History Compass* 6, no. 5 (2008): 1382–1393.

Prendergast, Mary E., et al. "Dietary Diversity on the Swahili Coast: The Fauna from Two Zanzibar Trading Locales." *International Journal of Osteoarcheology* 27 (2017): 621–637.

Prestholdt, Jeremy. "As Artistry Permits and Custom May Ordain: The Social Fabric of Material Consumption in the Swahili World, circa 1450–1600." Program in African Studies, Northwestern University, working paper, no. 3 (1998): 1–49.

Prestholdt, Jeremy. *Domesticating the World: African Consumerism and the Genealogies of Globalization.* Berkeley: University of California Press, 2008.

Prestholdt, Jeremy. "Portuguese Conceptual Categories and the 'Other' Encounter on the Swahili Coast." *Journal of Asian and African Studies* 36, no. 4 (2001): 383–406.

Price, Richard, ed. *Maroon Societies: Rebel Slave Communities in the Americas.* 3rd ed. Baltimore: Johns Hopkins University Press, 1996.

Prins, A.J.H. *The Coastal Tribes of the North-Eastern Bantu (Pokomo, Nyika, Teita).* London: International African Institute, 1952.

Prins, A.J.H. *The Swahili-Speaking Peoples of Zanzibar and the East African Coast: Arabs, Shirazi, and Swahili.* London: International African Institute, 1967.

Ptak, Roderich. "Chinese Bird Imports from Maritime Southeast Asia, c. 1000–1500." *Archipel* 84 (2012): 197–245.

Ray, Daren E. "Defining the Swahili." In *The Swahili World*, edited by Stephanie Wynne-Jones and Adria LaViolette, 67–80. New York: Routledge, 2018.

Ray, Daren E. "Disentangling Ethnicity in East Africa, ca. 1–2010 CE: Past Communities in Present Practices." PhD diss., University of Virginia, 2014.

Ray, Daren E. *Ethnicity, Identity, and Conceptualizing Community in Indian Ocean East Africa.* Athens: Ohio University Press, 2023.

Ray, Daren E. "Muyaka's Lament: The Surrender of Mombasa, 1815–1840." Paper at the Rocky Mountain Workshop on African History, virtual, August 21, 2021.

Ray, Daren E. "Recycling Interdisciplinary Evidence: Abandoned Hypotheses and African Historiologies in the Settlement History of Littoral East Africa." *History in Africa* 49 (2022): 97–130.

Ray, Himanshu Prabha. "Far-flung Fabrics—Indian Textiles in Ancient Maritime Trade." In *Textiles in Indian Ocean Society*, edited by Ruth Barnes, 16–34. New York: Routledge, 2005.

Regert, M., et al. "Reconstructing Ancient Yemeni Commercial Routes during the Middle Ages Using Structural Characterization of Terpenoid Resins." *Archaeometry* 50, no. 4 (2008): 668–695.

Reyes, Raquel. "Glimpsing Southeast Asian Naturalia in Global Trade, c. 300 BCE–1600 CE." In *Environment, Trade and Society in Southeast Asia*, edited by David Henley and H.G.C. Schulte Nordholt, 96–119. Leiden: Brill, 2015.

Ridhiwani, Pera. "Habari za kale za kabila la Wasegeju." n.p.

Riello, Giorgio. *Cotton: The Fabric That Made the Modern World.* Cambridge: Cambridge University Press, 2013.

Rigby, Peter. *Cattle and Kinship among the Gogo: A Semi-pastoral Society of Central Tanzania*. Ithaca: Cornell University Press, 1969.

Risso, Patricia. *Merchants of the Faith: Muslim Commerce and Culture in the Indian Ocean*. Boulder: Westview Press, 1995.

Roberts, Patrick, et al. "Late Pleistocene to Holocene Human Palaecology in the Tropical Environments of Coastal Eastern Africa." *Palaeogeography, Palaeoclimatology, Palaeoecology* 537 (2020): 1–18.

Rockel, Stephen. *Carriers of Culture: Labor on the Road in Nineteenth Century East Africa*. Portsmouth: Heinemann, 2006.

Ruel, Malcolm. "The Structural Articulation of Generations in Africa." *Cahiers d'Études Africaines* 42 (2002): 51–81.

Saberwal, Satish. *The Traditional Political System of the Embu of Central Kenya*. Kampala: Makerere Institute of Social Research, 1970.

Saidi, Christine. *Women's Authority and Society in Early East-Central Africa*. Rochester: University of Rochester Press, 2010.

Sassoon, Homo. "Excavations at the Site of Early Mombasa." *Azania: Journal of the British Institute in Eastern Africa* 15, no. 1 (1980): 1–42.

Schadeberg, Thilo, and Koen Bostoen. "Word Formation." In *The Bantu Languages*, edited by Mark Van de Velde, Koen Bostoen, Derek Nurse, and Gérard Philippson, 172–203. New York: Routledge, 2019.

Scheven, Albert. *Swahili Proverbs: Nia zikiwa moja, Kilicho mbali huja*. Washington: University Press of America, 1981.

Schoenbrun, David L. "Conjuring the Modern in Africa: Durability and Rupture in Histories of Public Healing Between the Great Lakes of East Africa." *American Historical Review* 111, no. 5 (2006): 1403–1439.

Schoenbrun, David L. *A Green Place, A Good Place: Agrarian Change, Gender, and Social Identity in the Great Lakes Region to the 15th Century*. Portsmouth: Heinemann, 1998.

Schoenbrun, David L. *The Names of the Python: Belonging in East Africa, 900–1930*. Madison: University of Wisconsin Press, 2021.

Schoenbrun, David L. "Violence, Marginality, Scorn, and Honour: Language Evidence of Slavery to the 18th Century." In *Slavery in the Great Lakes Region of Africa*, edited by Henri Médard and Shane Doyle, 38–75. Oxford: James Curry, 2007.

Scott, James. *The Art of Not Being Governed: An Anarchist History of Upland Southeast Asia*. New Haven: Yale University Press, 2009.

Sedlak, Phillip. "Sociocultural Determinants of Language Maintenance and Language Shift in a Rural Coastal Kenyan Community." PhD diss., Stanford University, 1974.

Seligman, Yaari F. [published under the author's former legal name] "Encircling Value: Inland Trade in the Precolonial East African-Indian Ocean World, ca. 1st–17th Centuries." PhD diss., Northwestern University, 2014.

Seligman, Yaari F. [published under the author's former legal name] "Lip Ornaments and the Domestication of Trade Goods: Fashion in Sixteenth and Seventeenth Century Central East Africa." *History in Africa* 42, no. 1 (2015): 357–373.

Seligman, Yaari F. [published under the author's former legal name] "Wealth Not by Any Other Name: Inland African Material Aesthetics in Expanding Commercial Times, c. 16th–20th Centuries." *International Journal of African Historical Studies* 48, no. 3 (2015): 449–469.

Sheriff, Abdul. *Dhow Cultures of the Indian Ocean: Cosmopolitanism, Commerce, and Islam.* London: Hurst, 2010.

Sheriff, Abdul. *Slaves, Spices, and Ivory in Zanzibar: Integration of an East African Commercial Empire into the World Economy, 1770–1873.* Athens: Ohio University Press, 1987.

Sheriff, Ibrahim Noor, and Ann Biersteker. *Mashairi Ya Vita Vya Kuduhu: War Poetry in Kiswahili Exchanged at the Time of the Battle of Kuduhu.* Lansing: Michigan State University Press, 1995.

Shetler, Jan Bender. *Imagining Serengeti: A History of Landscape Memory in Tanzania from Earliest Times to the Present.* Athens: Ohio University Press, 2007.

Shipton, Ceri, et al. "78,000-Year-Old Record of Middle and Later Stone Age Innovation in an East African Tropical Forest." *Nature Communications* 9, 1832 (2018): 1–8.

Shipton, Ceri, et al. "Intersections, Networks, and the Genesis of Social Complexity on the Nyali Coast of East Africa." *African Archaeological Review* 30, no. 4 (2013): 427–453.

Shipton, Ceri, et al. "Reinvestigation of Kuumbi Cave, Zanzibar Reveals Later Stone Age Coastal Habitation, Early Holocene Abandonment and Iron Age Reoccupation." *Azania: Archaeological Research in Africa* 52, no. 2(2016): 197–233.

Simpson, Edward, and Kai Kresse, eds. *Struggling with History: Islam and Cosmopolitanism in the Western Indian Ocean.* New York: Columbia University Press, 2008.

Sinopoli, Carla. *The Political Economy of Craft Production: Crafting Empire in South India, c. 1350–1650.* Cambridge: Cambridge University Press, 2003.

Soper, Robert. "Kwale: An Early Iron Age Site in Southeastern Kenya." *Azania: Journal of the British Institute in Eastern Africa* 2, no. 1 (1967): 1–17.

Spear, Thomas. "Early Swahili History Reconsidered." *International Journal of African Historical Studies* 33, no. 2 (2000): 257–290.

Spear, Thomas. *The Kaya Complex: A History of the Mijikenda Peoples of the Kenya Coast to 1900.* Nairobi: Kenya Literature Bureau, 1978.

Spear, Thomas. *Kenya's Past: An Introduction to the Historical Methods in Africa.* Essex: Longman, 1981.

Spear, Thomas, and Derek Nurse. *The Swahili: Reconstructing the History and Language of an African Society.* Philadelphia: University of Pennsylvania Press, 1985.

Sperling, David. "The Growth of Islam among the Mijikenda of the Kenya Coast, 1826–1933." PhD diss., School of Oriental and African Studies, 1988.

Stahl, Ann Brower. "Political Economic Mosaics: Archaeology of the Last Two Millennia in Tropical Sub-Saharan Africa." *Annual Review of Anthropology* 33 (2004): 145–172.

Steinhart, Edward. *Black Poachers, White Hunters: A Social History of Hunting in Colonial Kenya.* Athens: Ohio University Press, 2006.

Stephens, Rhiannon. *A History of African Motherhood: The Case of Uganda, 700–1900.* Cambridge: Cambridge University Press, 2013.

Stephens, Rhiannon. *Poverty and Wealth in East Africa: A Conceptual History.* Durham: Duke University Press, 2022.

Stigand, C. H. *The Land of Zinj.* London: Constable and Co. LTD., 1913.

Strandes, Justus. *The Portuguese Period in East Africa.* 4th ed. Nairobi: Kenya Literature Bureau, 1989.

Subrahmanyam, Sanjay. "Connected Histories: Notes towards a Reconfiguration of Early Modern Eurasia." *Modern Asian Studies* 31, no. 3 (1997): 735–762.

214   BIBLIOGRAPHY

Subramanian, Lakshmi. "Power and the Weave: Weavers, Merchants and Rulers in Eighteenth-Century Surat." In *Politics and Trade in the Indian Ocean World: Essays in Honor of Flashin Das Gupta*, edited by Rudrangshu Mukherjee and Lakshmi Subramanian, 52–82. Delhi: Oxford University Press, 1998.

Sunseri, Thaddeus. "The Political Ecology of the Copal Trade in the Tanzanian Coastal Hinterlands, 1820–1905." *Journal of African History* 48, no. 2 (2007): 201–220.

Swantz, Lloyd. *The Medicine Man among the Zaramo of Dar es Salaam*. Uddevalla: Nordic Africa Institute, 1990.

Sweeney, Shauna J. "Market Marronage: Fugitive Women and the Internal Marketing System in Jamaica, 1781–1834." *William and Mary Quarterly* 76, no. 2 (2019): 197–222.

Thambani, Meloth, et al. "Indian Summer Monsoon Variability during the Holocene as Recorded in Sediments of the Arabian Sea: Timing and Implications." *Journal of Oceanography* 63, no. 6 (2007): 1009–1020.

Theal, George McCall, ed. *Records of South-Eastern Africa Collected in Various Libraries and Archive Departments in Europe Records*. 9 vols. Cape Town, 1898–1903.

Thompson, Alvin O. *Flight to Freedom: African Runaways and Maroons in the Americas*. Mona: University Press of the West Indies, 2006.

Thorbahn, P. F. "The Precolonial Ivory Trade of East Africa: Reconstruction of a Human-Elephant Ecosystem." PhD diss., University of Massachusetts, 1979.

Tibbetts, Gerald R. *Arab Navigation in the Indian Ocean before the Coming of the Portuguese: Being a Translation of Kitāb al-Fawā 'id fī uṣūl al-baḥr wa 'l-qawā 'id of Aḥmad b. Mājid al-Najdī*. Royal Asiatic Society of Great Britain and Ireland, 1971.

Tinga, Kaingu. "Spatial Organization of a Kaya." *Kenya Past and Present* 29 (1997): 35–41.

Trivellato, Francesca. *The Familiarity of Strangers: The Sephardic Diaspora, Livorno, and Cross-Cultural Trade in the Early Modern Period*. New Haven: Yale University Press, 2012.

Tsing, Anna Lowenhaupt. *Friction: An Ethnography of Global Connection*. Princeton: Princeton University Press, 2005.

Udvardy, Monica. "Gender and the Culture of Fertility among the Giriama of Kenya." PhD diss., University of Uppsala, 1990.

Udvardy, Monica. "Gender Metaphors in Maladies and Medicines: The Symbolism of Protective Charms among the Giriama of Kenya." In *Culture, Experience and Pluralism: Essays on African Ideas of Illness and Healing*, edited by Anita Jacobson-Widding and David Westerlund, 45–57. Stockholm: Almquist and Wiksell International, 1989.

Udvardy, Monica. "Gender, Power and the Fragmentation of Fertility among the Giriama of Kenya." In *Body and Space: Symbolic Models of Unity and Division in African Cosmology and Experience*, edited by Anita Jacobson-Widding. 143–154. Stockholm: Almquist and Wiksell International, 1991.

Udvardy, Monica. "*Kifudu*: A Female Fertility Cult among the Giriama." In *The Creativity Communion: African Folk Models of Fertility and the Regeneration of Life*, edited by Anita Jacobson-Widding and Walter van Bleek, 137–152. Stockholm: Almquist and Wiksell International, 1990.

Um, Nancy. *The Merchant Houses of Mocha: Trade and Architecture in an Indian Ocean Port*. Seattle: University of Washington Press, 2009.

Um, Nancy. *Shipped But Not Sold: Material Culture and the Social Protocols of Trade during Yemen's Age of Coffee*. Honolulu: University of Hawaii Press, 2017.

Vansina, Jan. "Bantu in the Crystal Ball, I." *History in Africa* 6 (1979): 287–333.

Vansina, Jan. "Bantu in the Crystal Ball, II." *History in Africa* 7 (1980): 293–325.

Vansina, Jan. "New Linguistic Evidence and 'the Bantu Expansion.'" *Journal of African History* 36, no. 2 (1995): 173–195.

Vansina, Jan. *Paths in the Rainforest: Toward a History of Political Tradition in Equatorial Africa*. Madison: University of Wisconsin Press, 1990.

Vansina, Jan. "A Slow Revolution: Farming in Subequatorial Africa." *Azania: Archaeological Research in Africa* 29–30, no. 1 (1994): 15–26.

Vaughan, Megan. "Africa and Global History." In *Writing the History of the Global: Challenges for the 21st Century*, edited by Maxine Berg, 200–201. Oxford: Oxford University Press, 2013.

Verne, Julia. "The Ends of the Indian Ocean: Tracing Coastlines in the Tanzanian 'Hinterland.'" *History in Africa* 46 (2019): 359–383.

Vernet, Thomas. "Slave Trade and Slavery on the Swahili Coast (1500–1750)." In *Slavery, Islam, and Diaspora*, edited by B. A. Mirzai, I. M. Montana, and P. Lovejoy, 37–76. Trenton: Africa World Press, 2009.

Villiers, John. "Great Plenty of Almug Trees: The Trade in Southeast Asian Aromatic Woods in the Indian Ocean and China, 500 CE-AD 1500." *The Great Circle* 23, no. 2 (2001): 24–43.

Waaijenberg, Henk. *Mijikenda Agriculture in Coast Province of Kenya*. Amsterdam, KIT Publishers, 1994.

Wakefield, Thomas, and Keith Johnston. "Routes of Native Caravans from the Coast to the Interior of Eastern Africa, Chiefly from Information Given by Sádi bin Ahédi, a Native of a District Near Gazi, in Udigo, a Little North of Zanzibar." *Journal of the Royal Geographic Society of London* 40 (1870): 303–339.

Walker, D. A. "Giriama Arrow Poison: A Study in African Pharmacology and Ingenuity." *Central African Journal of Medicine* 3, no. 6 (1957): 226–28.

Walker, Iain. *Islands in a Cosmopolitan Sea: A History of the Comoros*. New York: Oxford University Press, 2019.

Walsh, Martin. "Elephant Shrews and Arrow Poison." *EANHS Bulletin* 22, no. 2 (1992): 18–21.

Walsh, Martin. "Mijikenda Origins: A Review of the Evidence." *Transafrican Journal of History* 21 (1992): 1–18.

Walsh, Martin. "Mung'aro, the Shining: Ritual and Human Sacrifice on the Kenya Coast." *Kenya Past and Present* 40 (2013): 11–22.

Walsh, Martin. "The Segeju Complex? Linguistic Evidence for the Precolonial Making of the Mijikenda." In *Contesting Identities: The Mijikenda and Their Neighbors in Kenyan Coastal Society*, edited by Rebecca Gerhart and Linda Giles, 25–51. Trenton: Africa World Press, 2013.

Walsh, Martin. "The Swahili Language and Its Early History." In *The Swahili World*, edited by Stephanie Wynne-Jones and Adria LaViolette, 121–131. New York: Routledge, 2018.

Walshaw, Sarah. "Converting to Rice: Urbanization, Islamization and Crops on Pemba Island, Tanzania, AD 700–1500." *World Archaeology* 42, no. 1 (2010): 137–154.

Walz, Jonathan. "Inland Connectivity in Ancient Tanzania." *Islamic Africa* 8 (2017): 217–227.

Walz, Jonathan. "Routes to History: Archaeology and Being Articulate in Eastern Africa." In *The Death of Prehistory*, edited by Peter Schmidt and Stephen Mrozowski, 69–91. Oxford: Oxford University Press, 2014.

BIBLIOGRAPHY

Walz, Jonathan. "Routes to a Regional Past: An Archaeology of the Lower Pangani (Ruvu) Basin, Tanzania, 500–1900 C.E." PhD diss., University of Florida, 2010.

Walz, Jonathan, and Philip Gooding. "Reality and Representation of Eastern Africa's Past: Archaeology and History Redress the 'Coast-Inland Dichotomy.'" *African Studies Quarterly* 20, no. 4 (2021): 56–85.

Wembah-Rashid, J.A.R. "The Socio-economic System of Wakwere: An Ethnographic Study of a Matrilineal People of Central Eastern Tanzania." PhD diss., University of Dar es Salaam, 1978.

Wenzlhuemer, Roland, et al. "Forum Global Dis:connections." *Journal of Modern European History* 21, no. 1 (2023): 2–33.

White, Luise. "Blood Brotherhood Revisited: Kinship, Relationship, and the Body in East and Central Africa." *Africa* 64, no. 3 (1994): 359–372.

Wilkinson, John C. *The Arabs and the Scramble for Africa.* Sheffield: Equinox Publishers, 2015.

Wilkinson, John C. *The Imamate Tradition of Oman.* Cambridge: Cambridge University Press, 1987.

Willis, Justin. *Mombasa, the Swahili,. and the Making of the Mijikenda.* Oxford: Claredon Press, 1993.

Willis, Justin. "The Northern Kayas of the Mijikenda: A Gazetteer, and an Historical Reassessment." *Azania: Archaeological Research in Africa* 31 (1996): 75–98.

Willis, Justin, and George Gona. "Tradition, Tribe, and State in Kenya: The Mijikenda Union, 1945–1980." *Comparative Studies in Society and History* 55, no. 2 (2013): 448–473.

Willis, Justin, and Suzanne Miers. "Becoming a Child of the House: Incorporation, Authority and Resistance in Giryama Society." *Journal of African History* 38, no. 3 (1997): 479–495.

Wilmsen, Edwin N. "Hills and the Brilliance of Beads: Myths and the Interpretation of Iron Age Sites in Southern Africa." *Southern African Humanities* 21, no. 1 (2009): 263–274.

Wilmsen, Edwin N. "The Tsodilo Hills and the Indian Ocean: Small-Scale Wealth and Emergent Power in Eighth to Eleventh-Century Central-Southern Africa." In *Globalization in Prehistory: Contact, Exchange, and the 'People Without History,'* edited by Nicole Boivin and Michael D. Frachetti, 263–282. Cambridge: Cambridge University Press, 2018.

Wilson, Thomas. "Spatial Analysis and Settlement Patterns on the Coast of East Africa." *Paideuma* 28 (1982): 201–219.

Wolfe III, Ernie. *Vigango: Commemorative Sculpture of the Mijikenda of Kenya.* Williamstown: Williams College Museum of Art, 1986.

Wood, L. J., and Christopher Ehret. "The Origins and Diffusion of the Market Institution in East Africa." *Journal of African Studies* 5, no. 1 (1978): 1–17.

Wood, Marilee. "Eastern Africa and the Indian Ocean World in the First Millennium CE: The Glass Bead Evidence." In *Early Exchange between Africa and the Wider Indian Ocean World,* edited by Gwyn Campbell, 173–193. London: Palgrave Macmillan, 2016.

Wright, David. "New Perspectives on Early Regional Interaction Networks of East African Trade: A View from Tsavo National Park, Kenya." *African Archaeological Review* 22, no. 3 (2005): 111–140.

Wright, Donald R. *The World and a Very Small Place in Africa: A History of Globalization in Niumi, the Gambia.* 3rd ed. New York: Routledge, 2010.

Wright, Henry. "The Comoros and Their Early History." In *The Swahili World*, edited by Stephanie Wynne-Jones and Adria LaViolette, 66–76. New York: Routledge, 2018.

Wright, Henry T. "Trade and Politics on the Eastern Littoral of Africa, AD 800–1300." In *The Archaeology of Africa: Food, Metals and Towns*, edited by Bassey Andah, Alex Okpoko, and Thurson Shaw, 658–672. London: Routledge, 1993.

Wright, Henry T., et al. "Early Seafarers of the Comoro Islands: The Dembeni Phase of the IXth–Xth centuries AD." *Azania: Journal of the British Institute in Eastern Africa* 19, no. 1 (1984): 13–59.

Wynne-Jones, Stephanie. "Creating Urban Communities at Kilwa Kisiwani, Tanzania, A.D. 800–1300." *Antiquity* 81, no. 312 (2007): 368–380.

Wynne-Jones, Stephanie. "Lines of Desire: Power and Materiality along a Tanzanian Caravan Route." *Journal of World Prehistory* 23, no. 4 (2010): 219–237.

Wynne-Jones, Stephanie. *A Material Culture: Consumption and Materiality on the Coast of Precolonial Africa*. Oxford: Oxford University Press, 2016.

Wynne-Jones, Stephanie. "Remembering and Reworking the Swahili Diwanate: The Role of Objects and Places at Vumba Kuu." *International Journal of African Historical Studies* 43, no. 3 (2010): 407–427.

Wynne-Jones, Stephanie, et al. "Urban Chronology at a Human Scale on the Coast of East Africa in the 1st Millennium A.D." *Journal of Field Archaeology* 46, no. 1 (2021): 21–35.

Zhiseng, A., et al., "Evolution of Asian Monsoons and Phased Uplift of the Himalaya-Tibetan Plateau since Late Miocene Times." *Nature* 411, no. 6833 (2001): 62–66.

INDEX

Abu al-Fida, 74
Abu-Lughod, Janet, 2
Acokanthera schimperi tree, 79
Adelman, Jeremy, 160n56
Aden, port city of, 83, 161n75, 177n76
Africa, 30, 32, 51, 165n83; ancient languages of,
9; central, 129; early, 51, 165n83, 166n97;
equatorial, 38, 54, 124; haplogroup admixture
with Southeast Asia, 144; narratives of
the global and, 13; precolonial, 32, 60, 139;
southern, 34, 68, 69, 79, 100, 126, 143, 161n77,
167n108; West Africa, 13. *See also* East Africa
aganga [Mijikenda] (swearing of oath
by accused), 62
agriculture, 38, 59, 73, 188n84; irrigation, 73;
knowledge of soils and rainfall patterns,
30; large farm plots, 42; microclimate and,
162n29; root crops, 25, 26, 31, 34; "slow
revolution" in, 24, 32; swidden clearings, 30,
52, 95, 136, 140; words for clearing land, 26,
28, 29. *See also* farming communities;
specific crops
Ahmad ibn Majid, 6
Aksum, 23
Almeida, Marcos de, 124, 186n52
Alpers, Edward, 2
ambergris, 77, 94, 108, 126, 177n79
*-àmi [Mashariki] ("agent of protection and
prosperity"), 165n86
ancestors, 66, 165n86; ancestral shrines, 56,
170n63; ancestral spirits, 53, 61; matrilineal, 59;

memorial posts for, 55; textiles in rituals
associated with, 85
Andaya, Leonard, 137–38
animal husbandry, 64, 102, 133.
See also cattle keeping
animals, wild: danger of, 93; small land
mammals, 30
Arabia, 5, 6, 20, 22, 23, 93; East Africa's political
links with, 22; ivory trade and, 79; merchants
from, 1; Mijikenda speakers' trip to, 114;
Portuguese invasion of southern coast, 107;
trade winds and, 25
Arabic language and speakers, 5, 6, 81, 119, 120,
133, 185n21
archaeology, 4, 6, 8, 12, 14, 158n22;
archaeobotanical records, 30, 164n61;
ceramics and language groups, 143–44; of
earliest farming communities, 26; evidence
of production and exchange in Mombasa's
interior, 73–76; evidence of smaller
settlement patterns, 106; historical linguistics
and, 68–69; imported trade goods and,
47; at Shanga, 45–46, 168n16; on splitting
and settlement diffusion, 64; tracking of
material changes and, 31; zooarchaeological
records, 30
architecture, coral stone, 6, 45, 46, 70
arrowheads, iron, 74–75, 80
arrow poison, 75–76, 79–80, 99, 105
Atlantic "world system" economy, 13, 160n59
Azanian languages, 22

219

Bal'arab bin Himyar, 184n94
banditry, 95
"Bantu expansions," 14
Bantu languages, 4, 9, 25, 55, 189n2; Great Lakes, 59; Narrow West Bantu, 186n52; proto-Bantu, 9, 11, 156; "Uplands" or "Azanian," 190n18
Bantu speakers, 21, 24, 25; in coastal forests, 81; food procurement practices, 25; newcomers adopted into settlements, 51
Barbosa, Duarte, 78, 101–2
beeswax, 6, 70, 77, 80, 85, 106; Mijikenda access to, 101; Southeast Asian connections to global exchange networks and, 137; traded by "King of Chonyi," 108
Berg, F. J., 117
bird of paradise feathers, 134, 137–38
Bishara, Fahad, 122–23
blood pacts, cross-cultural commerce and, 86–89, 93
Boccaro, António, 181n29
Bondei language, 151, 153, 155, 156
Brantley, Cynthia, 174n131
Braudel, Ferdinand, 14
bubonic plague, 24
Buganda Kingdom, 42
al-Busaidi, Said bin Sultan. See Said, Seyyid
Busaidi Sultanate, 19, 115, 117; oceanic empire of, 131; shifts in western Indian Ocean politics and, 121–23; slavery and, 123–28, 130
bushcraft, 14
Bwana Dau bin Bwana Shaka, 109

Cairo, 15, 84
Cambay (Gujarat, India), port city of, 82, 94
*-cambo [NEC Bantu] ("loincloth"), 84
camphor, 137, 138
*-cang(il)- [NEC Bantu] ("collect, contribute"), 36, 37, 39, 149–50
caravans, 104, 129, 130; Arab-Swahili, 86, 91; knowledge of long-distance trade and, 89–93; provisioning of, 131
Casale, Giancarlo, 100–101
cattle keeping, 42, 80, 87, 90; cattle rustling, 89; economic vocabulary and, 75, 113; healing/magic practices and, 61; herds as markers of political status, 104; Mombasa trade with interior and, 80; Segeju influence on Mijikenda speakers, 102–4; trade parties and, 87, 91
Central Asia, 138
Central Mijikenda (Mijikenda dialects), 59, 146, 151, 191n1 (App 2); areas of, 58map;

communities of, 171n79; emergence of, 171n78; lexical variation of, 147–48table; phonological variation of, 146–47table
ceramics, 6, 23, 32; Early Tana Tradition (ETT), 31, 143–44, 190n18; ethnolinguistic identities and, 143; foreign, 31, 43, 46; glazed, 82, 162n15; Kwale Ware, 143, 144, 162n19; Sassanian and Chinese, 70, 162n15
cereal cultivation, 17, 21, 25–26, 29, 32, 34. See also millet; sorghum
Chaga languages, 75, 92, 155, 156
Chaga-Taita languages, 38, 56, 150, 152
Challa, Lake, 163n39, 164n66
Chambe, Mwinyi, 108, 109, 118, 183–84n75
Chami, Felix, 162n19
Champion, Arthur, 66, 174n131
charo [Mijikenda] ("journey, caravan"), 91–93, 123, 156
chete [Mijikenda] ("market"), 75–76, 153–54, 176n41
"chiefship," 34, 166nn86,87,88
chifudu (virapho specialist group), 60, 63–64, 173n115
China, 6, 15, 77, 82
Chingulia, Dom Jeronimo, 96, 98–99, 101, 181n29
chinyenze (virapho specialist group), 63
chiphalo [Digo and Duruma] (place for medicine and dance), 56–57, 57table, 59
chirapho (oathing practice), 62, 63, 66
chitsambi or kitsambi [Mijikenda] (dyed cotton textiles), 84
Chombo, settlement of, 47–48
Chonyi (Mijikenda dialect and speakers), 107–9, 114, 171n79, 183n72; delegation to Muscat and, 111, 184n93; phonological variation of, 146table; provisions supplied to Fort Jesus, 118. See also Central Mijikenda
Chonyi, King of (Rey do Chone), 108, 183n72
Christianity, 99
Christian Topography (Cosmas Indicopleustes), 23
Church Missionary Society of England, 118, 128
Chwaka, urban center of, 46
climate changes, 23–24, 162n28, 189n5; drier periods, 26, 31, 163n39; wet periods, 31, 164n66
cloves, 115, 126, 130
coconuts, 126, 136
*-coga [NEC languages] ("blood pact/friendship"), 87, 88, 154–55, 179nn121,122
*-cogora [Thagicu] ("to buy, bargain"), 90

Comorian language, 9, 10*fig.*, 36, 144; dialects of, 191n1 (App 3); dispersal to offshore islands, 142; divergence from Sabaki, 141; emergence of, 145; lexical reconstructions and, 149, 150, 154; redistribution terms, 37–38

Comoros Islands, 31, 37, 40, 45, 125

Congo Basin, 115

copal. *See* gum copal

Cosmas Indicopleustes, 23, 24

cosmopolitanism, 13, 23

cow pea (*lukunde), 30, 164n61

cowries, 47, 70

*-cum- [Sabaki] ("to buy food, collect"), 36, 86, 149

Cushitic speakers, 23, 26

da Gama, Vasco, 76–77, 96, 101

Daiso language, 64, 152, 154, 155, 184n45. *See also* Segeju language and speakers

Dawida language and speakers, 55–56, 87, 90, 103, 156

debts, social, 39–40, 124

de Luna, Kathryn, 69, 165n86, 190n11

dhora ~ rora [Segeju] ("bargain, price, trade"), 90, 155

-dhyana/-ryana [Mijikenda] ("to spy" or "to scout"), 89, 155–56

diasporic communities, 14, 133, 135, 138, 139

Digo (Mijikenda dialect and speakers), 55, 146, 151; areas of, 58*map*; conversion to Islam, 131; delegation to Muscat and, 111, 184n93; distinctiveness of, 59; emergence of, 171n78; lexical reconstructions and, 153; lexical variation of, 147–48*table*; phonological variation of, 146–47*table*; settlement history of Digo speakers, 47; *Thelatha Taifa* and, 185n13

disconnections, global interactions and, 13, 160n56

disease, 51, 52, 60, 61, 64, 94

dispersed settlement, 65, 169n42

documentary records, scarcity of, 9

Domesticating the World (Prestholdt), 158n33

droughts, 16, 52, 61; climate changes and, 26; crops resistant to, 30, 34; rainmaking during, 52

Duruma (Mijikenda dialect and speakers), 55, 59, 146, 151, 152; areas of, 58*map*; delegation to Muscat and, 111, 184n93; lexical reconstructions and, 153, 154; lexical variation of, 147–48*table*; phonological variation of, 146–47*table*; sound shift in, 191n8; *Thelatha Taifa* and, 185n13

Early Iron Age (EIA), 30, 143–45

Early Tana Tradition (ETT) ceramics, 31, 143–44, 190n18

East Africa, 5, 6, 8, 20, 43, 94; connections with other world regions, 4, 13; "copal belt" of, 81; early interactions with trading networks, 22; French interest in, 128; Great Lakes region, 15; plantation economy in, 129; settlement of East African coast, 44, 144–45; "slow revolution" in first millennium, 24–26, 28–30; "wealth in people" in first millennium, 32–36. *See also* Mombasa inland region

Eastern Arc Mountains, 38

Edward Bonaventure (English ship), 81

Egypt, 83

Ehret, Christopher, 34, 142–43, 190n18

elephant hunters, 15, 74; poison-tipped arrows used by, 75, 79–80; as settlers of Mombasa, 132, 188n1. *See also* ivory

Elwana language and speakers, 9, 10*fig.*, 35, 163n47, 177n83; areas of, 142; divergence from proto-Sabaki, 141; lexical reconstructions and, 151

Emery, James, 121, 157n8

*-éné [NEC Bantu] ("lineage head"), 34, 36–38, 166n88. *See also* lineage heads

environmental conditions, 23–24

Estado da Índia (Portuguese India), 98, 99, 101, 109, 110, 117. *See also* Portuguese empire

ethnography, 4, 8

exchange networks, 7, 23, 24, 75, 137; global, 24; inland/interior, 68, 70

famine, 42, 123–24, 127; harmful magic and, 61; splitting of clans following, 52

farming communities, 26, 31, 40, 70, 104. *See also* agriculture

faunal records, 30, 103, 164n63

Feierman, Steven, 158n16

Felber-Seligman, Yaari, 69, 102

Ferguson, James, 160n56

fingo ("fetish, charm"), 54, 172n92

fisi ("hyena oath"), 63

Fleisher, Jeffrey, 31, 46, 190n11

forests, 26, 29, 67, 143; coastal, 79, 177n74; emergence of agriculture and, 30; forest shrines, 53; on Kasigau massif, 73; on upland ridges, 1, 95; of Western Ghats (India), 136

Fort Jesus, 5, 83, 96, 97, 98, 118; Mijikenda militias' capture of (1729), 112, 185n29; Omani capture of, 107–10, 184n82; Portuguese traders at, 132; retaken by Portuguese forces, 99, 116

222   INDEX

Frank, William, 42, 43
Funan polity, 23

Gambia, The, 160n59
Ganda speakers, 11
Geography (Ptolemy), 22–23
Gikuyu language, 151, 155, 184n45
Giryama (Mijikenda dialect), 4, 5, 59, 146; areas
of, 58*map*; blood pacts and, 87; emergence
of, 171n78; lexical reconstructions and, 151,
152, 153, 156; lexical variation of, 147–48*table*;
oathing practices and, 85; phonological
variation of, 147*table*
Giryama Vocabulary and Collections
(Taylor), 90
glass, imported, 70
glass beads, 74, 82, 84, 105
Glassman, Jonathon, 130
globalization, 13, 160n56
glottochronology, 142, 171n78
Goa (Portuguese India), 2, 95, 98, 99, 107
Gogo language, 150, 151, 152, 154
gold trade, trans-Saharan, 13
Gonja, settlement of, 72*map*, 74
Gonzales, Rhonda, 14, 59, 190n18
gophu/gohu (*virapho* healing specialist group),
63, 64–65, 90, 173n122
Green, Nile, 13
"groupwork," 159n36, 169n57
Gujarat (India), 15
gum copal, 2, 18, 69, 177n76; archaeological
records of, 81; consumer demand in
industrializing countries and, 115; Mijikenda
access to, 101; as second-most important
export, 80; uses of, 80
Gupta polity (India), 23
Gweno language, 150, 151, 152; lexical
reconstructions and, 155, 156; loanwords
from Segeju, 103

Habari na desturi za WaRibe ["History and
Customs of the Ribe"] (Frank), 42
habasi (*virapho* specialist group), 62, 63, 85
Hamad bin Said, 121–22
Hamilton, Capt. Alexander, 78
al-Hasan ibn Ahmed, Sultan, 98, 101
healing ideas/rituals, 7, 51; access to medicines,
52; bush associations with, 56; governance
and, 61; healing associations, 13; innovating
medicines, 60–67; leaders' monopoly on
healing technologies, 166n97; *muzimu* spirits
and, 12; "oaths" and, 62–67; specialized
medicines/medicinal groups, 18, 42; trade

party leaders as healers, 91, 93; wealth and
gendered forms of healing, 65
Helm, Richard, 7, 50, 169n42
Herlehy, Thomas, 88
heshima (honor) tributes, 115, 122, 123, 130, 131,
185n21; *kore* (debt) and, 19, 124–28; Seyyid
Said's relation to Mijikenda and, 128; tributes
as autonomy, 118–21
-heshimu [Swahili] ("to honor"), 114, 119
Hinnebusch, Thomas, 141, 145, 153, 171n78,
190n11
História de Mombaça, 107, 108, 109–10
honey, wild, 70, 73, 78
hongo (taxes on trade goods), 186n29
Hormuz, port city of, 78
Horton, Mark, 35, 45, 166n95
hunter-forager/gatherer groups, 26, 50, 51, 70
hunting. *See* elephant hunters
Hymenaea verrucosa tree, 80, 81

Ibn Battuta, 1–2, 5–6, 77, 157n6
*icaka [Sabaki] ("thicket, brush"), 170n74
identity, 8, 87, 159nn36–37; ethnic, 7, 8; gender,
55; religious, 15, 131
al-Idrisi, Muhammad, 5, 74
*ifulu ~ *ifuvu [Sabaki] ("tortoise"), 173n115
imperialism, oceanic, 17, 102, 113
incorporative practices, 49
India, 5, 23, 25, 77; British governors of, 122;
hinterland networks, 136; Malabar coast, 2,
15, 135–37; port cities of western India, 93;
Portuguese, 19, 112; textile industry in, 84, 135
Indian Ocean world, 1, 7, 8, 139; disaggregated
histories of port cities, 14–17; early African
history and, 12–14; Indian Ocean as "Muslim
Lake," 2, 4; interior regions as part of, 4,
157n15; monsoon trade winds, 20–21, 24,
40, 85, 161n1; multidirectional trading
networks in, 68; port cities of, 6; resurgence
of commercial networks in, 40; as space of
"heterotopia," 13; trade networks and, 21
Indonesia, 137
iron mines, 74
ironworking, 26, 31, 163n43; archaeological
evidence of ironworking centers, 73; bush
associations with, 56; Late Stone Age
(LSA) communities and, 70; small-scale
communities and, 40; *uganga* medicine
and, 61; as village resource brought by
newcomers, 38
Islam, 2, 24, 49; adopted by coastal towns, 42;
coastal commerce and urban Islamic society,
130; Digo speakers' adoption of, 173n114;

Mazrui dynasty and, 117; Mijikenda-speaking groups and, 4; port cities and, 133; reciprocal trading arrangements and, 88; Swahili speakers converted to, 47. *See also* Muslims

isoglosses, 146, 191n2 (App 2)

ivory, 2, 18, 22, 69, 77, 85, 133; circulation of, 94; consumer demand in industrializing countries and, 115; Junta do Comércio and, 108; Mijikenda speakers and, 79–80, 101, 102, 177n68; Mombasa as a center of ivory trade, 78, 81, 94, 105, 177n79; quality of African ivory, 77–78, 176n51; supplied to Indian Ocean markets, 77, 129; traded to China, 79, 138; trade party leaders and, 91; traders' obtaining of, 89; in Tsavo region, 71, 175n16. *See also* elephant hunters

Janzen, John, 61

Jibana (Mijikenda dialect and speakers), 111, 114, 146*table*, 171n79, 184n93. *See also* Central Mijikenda

Kabaka (Buganda king), 42

Kagulu language, 150, 152, 155

Kaguru language, 151

Kahe language, 150, 152

Kamba language, 90, 177n83, 184n45; blood pacts and, 87, 88; lexical reconstructions and, 151, 152, 153, 154, 155, 156

Kambe (Mijikenda dialect and speakers), 111, 146*table*, 171n79, 184n93. *See also* Central Mijikenda

Kami language, 150

Kasigau, Mount, 72–73, 72*map*, 73, 74

Kauma (Mijikenda dialect and speakers), 111, 146*table*, 171n79, 184n93. *See also* Central Mijikenda

Kaya Complex, The (Spear, 1978), 6

Kaya Kwale, settlement of, 47

kayas (fortified settlements), 50–51, 52, 53; diverse places reinterpreted as, 172n92; founding narratives for, 54; meeting house for clans of, 57; *vitio* outbreaks and splitting of, 64

*-kazi [Sabaki] ("wife"), 38

Kenya, 40, 50, 81, 145; Central Kenya, 38; southeast interior, 48, 61, 89; Tsavo National Park, 71

Kenya-Uganda Railway, 5

khatti (contract agreement), 114

*kicambi ("cloth textile"), 154

*kikola [Sabaki] ("sharing arrangement"), 37–38, 39, 150

*kilapo [Sabaki] (oathing practices), 62

Kilifi, port city of, 3*map*, 58*map*, 71, 72*map*

Kilimanjaro, Mount, 51, 72*map*, 91, 92–93, 163n39

Kilindini Harbor, 5, 131

Kilwa, port city of, 1, 3*map*, 6, 25, 45, 143; Busaidi Sultanate and, 121; Portuguese empire and, 97; textile industry in, 82

kinship, 11, 15, 36, 166n87; imagined, 88; multiple strategies for reckoning descent, 33, 165n83

kinyaka ~ chinyaka [Northern Mijikenda and Kamba] ("place for meetings, performing dances"), 57*table*, 59, 85, 153

kiraho cha tsoka [Central Mijikenda] ("ordeal of the axe"), 62

Kirongwe (ironworking center), 73

kitambi [Swahili] (cloth as unit of measure), 84

knowledge networks, 51, 53–54

*-kódè [Bantu] ("captive, booty"), 124, 156

koma [Mijikenda] (memorial posts for ancestors), 55, 56, 65, 85, 170n64

Kongowea, settlement of, 49

Kopytoff, Igor, 165n73

kore (person exchanged to settle a debt), 19, 115; balance with *heshima* (honor), 124–27; as permanent "debt imprisonment," 126

Krapf, Johann Ludwig, 118–20, 124, 127, 156; on *koma* huts, 170n64; on *kore* debt, 126; on Mijikenda and Seyyid Said, 128, 129

*-kųmų [Bantu] ("honored person"), 165–66n86

kurya tsoga [Mijikenda] ("to eat the scar"), 87–89, 92

Kusimba, Chapurukha, 71, 102, 158n15

Kusimba, Sibel, 71

kutasa ancestral rituals, 56

Kwa Jomvu, town of, 80

Kwale Ware ceramics, 143, 144, 162n19

Kwere language, 154, 155

Laa or Langulo (hunter-forager group), 51, 132, 173n120

Lamu Archipelago, 45, 122, 125

Late Antique Little Ice Age, 23

Late Stone Age (LSA) communities, 70

Lemba (healing cult), 61

lineage heads, 34, 40, 44; efforts to expand influence, 36; female newcomers married to, 38; "mother-derived grouping" and, 35; rivalries among, 39. *See also* *-éné

linguistics, historical, 4, 7, 8, 54; absence of documentary records and, 14; archaeology and, 68–69; "principle of least moves" theory, 141–42, 189n5; social incorporation practices and, 12

224 INDEX

"Little Ice Age," 105
littoral societies, 15, 94, 139
Lower Congo, 61
Lower Pokomo language, 9, 84, 144, 152, 163n47.
 See also Pokomo languages
Luganda language, 152, 155
lukolo*lukolo [NEC Bantu] ("clan"), 33, 165n79
Lunga, settlement of, 111, 184n93
*luWambe [Sabaki] ("chaff"), 29
*luWanda [Sabaki] ("open area"), 57
lwanda [Mijikenda] (clearing, open land), 50,
 57, 170n76

Machado, Pedro, 82, 102
Madagascar, 79, 125
Mafia Archipelago, 143, 145
Mafia Island, 3map
magic, harmful. See utsai [Mijikenda]
Makonde language, 150
Makupa Creek, Portuguese-built forts at, 96, 98,
 110, 111
male bonding, cross-societal, 88
Malindi, port city of, 3map, 5, 58map, 72map,
 104; inland communities' influence on, 106;
 iron exported from, 74; ivory trade and, 78;
 Portuguese empire and, 77, 96, 97, 100
Margariti, Roxani Eleni, 161n75
marginality, terms for, 39, 41
marine resources, 30, 145
Mashami language, 150
Mashariki Bantu languages, 25, 26, 35, 165n79,
 184n45; Kaskazi branch, 33, 57, 153;
 proto-Mashariki, 165n86, 166n101
al-Masudi, 24, 77
mateka [Swahili] ("captives"), 125, 187n56
material changes, tracking of, 30–32
matrilineal descent, 33, 59, 165n83
Mazrui, Mbaruk, 122
al-Mazrui, Muhammad bin Uthman, 117
Mazrui family (Omani dynasty), 5, 117, 118, 121,
 123, 127
Mbugwe language, 151
McIntosh, Susan Keech, 66
Mediterranean region, 15, 17, 21, 24
meeting grounds, 54; healing practices and,
 60–67; in Mijikenda dialects, 57table;
 rock outcroppings as, 75
Meier, Prita, 157n4
Menuthias (fishing settlement), 22
merchants, 5, 21, 126, 133; Chinese, 78–79;
 coastal, 7; diasporic, 135, 138; European,
 130; Gujarati, 82, 83; Hadhrami, 125; healing

practices and, 61; heshima (honor) tributes
 and, 119, 120; houses of, 43; Muslim, 138
Meroe, 23
Meru language, 150
*mfuno ("duiker"), 145, 164n62
microclimates, 40, 52, 162n29; of coastal uplands,
 73; rainfall fluctuations and, 71
Middle Iron Age (MIA), 143
Miers, Suzanne, 165n73
miji ("towns"), 49
Mijikenda languages, 4, 36, 54, 178n84; Arabic
 loanwords in, 120; areas of, 142; core
 vocabulary, 59, 171n81; dialectal terms for
 meeting places, 57table; dialects of, 58map,
 59, 146–48, 171n78; divergence from Sabaki,
 141; divergence from Swahili, 5; economic
 vocabulary, 86, 89, 90; emergence of, 145;
 history of, 8–9; lexical reconstructions
 and, 149, 150, 152–56; proto-Mijikenda, 120,
 186n28; proto-Sabaki as ancestor of, 9, 10fig.;
 redistribution terms, 37; Segeju loanwords in,
 90, 103, 104table, 182n44; Swahili loanwords
 denoting slavery, 125, 187n56
Mijikenda speakers, 1, 9, 21, 35, 67, 83, 159n37;
 arrival in Mombasa inland region, 6;
 changing relationship with coastal society,
 130–31; choice to engage with maritime
 trading networks, 69; commercial influence
 in Mombasa, 19; East Africa's global
 connections and, 13; ethnic identity of,
 7, 8; as gateway society, 68, 115–16, 174n1;
 heshima (honor) tributes and, 118–20; Indian
 Ocean networks and, 41; interactions with
 Indian Ocean world, 43; ivory trade and,
 80; Mombasa delegation to Muscat, 110–12,
 114, 184n91; Muslims, 131; oceanic trade and,
 2; oral traditions of, 6, 49–53; participation
 in Indian Ocean commercial/political
 dynamics, 12; political capital from trade, 8;
 political influence on Mombasa and imperial
 powers, 95; in Portuguese accounts, 13, 97;
 "rights of retaliation" wielded by, 129–30;
 rika age-set system, 106, 183n62; role as
 trade brokers between Mombasa and
 interior, 80; settlement areas of, 3map;
 slavery and, 124–25; ties with neighboring
 inland groups, 18; trading strategies of, 7.
 See also "Musungulos"
Mijikenda speakers, textile tributes paid to, 2,
 100, 104, 110, 112, 116; betrayal of Hasan and,
 98; British protectorate at Mombasa and, 121;
 heshima practice and, 115; sultan of Vumba

INDEX 225

Kuu and, 116–17; threat of raids and, 95; viewed by Portuguese as extortion, 101, 105
Mikindani, town of, 168n22
millet, 25, 162n31; as drought-resistant crop, 34; finger millet, 30, 70; increasing cultivation of, 28; pearl millet, 30, 70; processing techniques for, 29. *See also* cereal cultivation
Minnagar, 23
Mir Ali Beg, 97, 100
Mirbat (Oman), town of, 79, 176n61
missionaries, European, 63, 126, 127, 128
*mizịmu [Bantu] ("offerings to spirits"), 54
Mkisi, Mwana (queen mother), 49
Mogadishu, port city of, 3*map*, 6, 25; Ibn Battuta in, 77; textile industry in, 82
Mombasa, port city of, 1, 3*map*, 20, 45, 58*map*, 72*map*; British protectorate at (1824), 121–22; built landscape of, 43; under Busaidi Sultanate, 19, 115, 117, 132; defense of, 75; as distribution center for trade goods, 69; as East Africa's most important port, 18; emergence as major port, 67, 68, 93; English ships at, 177n79; *heshima* rituals and, 120; imperial shifts and influence of inland communities, 97–101; ivory trade and, 78, 81, 105, 177n79; livestock supplied by mainland, 105; merchants of, 2; Mijikenda-speaking groups and, 4–8; as node of interconnected Indian Ocean world, 134; Old Town, 5; under Omani control, 94, 110, 184n82; Omani siege of, 107–10, 118; oral traditions about origins of, 49–50; under Portuguese control, 76–77, 84, 89, 96–97; prosperity of, 6; recaptured by Portuguese (1728), 110; slave trade and, 125–26; textile tribute payments to interior communities, 114
Mombasa Chronicle, 111, 112
Mombasa inland region, 43, 55, 71, 72*map*, 97; ecological diversity of, 69–70; fertile ridges, 47, 49, 57, 145; geography of, 1, 2, 20; global trade provisioned by, 104–7; as "great wilderness," 92; healing and ritual knowledge in, 60; history, 1; homestead-based settlements, 66; limits of Omani authority in, 128–30; slave raiding in, 125; smaller settlements in, 52; splitting and expansion of settlements, 48–49; trade and conflicts prior to Portuguese era, 101–2; upland regions, 71, 175n12; wealth and power in, 174n127
Mombasa Island, 6, 47, 76, 132
Monsoon Islam (Prange), 136
moro [Mijikenda] (assembly of elders), 57*table*

Morrison, Kathleen, 136
mosaics, trading, 71, 74
mosques, 1, 2, 5, 93; in coral stone architecture, 46, 70; Mnara Mosque, 157n4; in Shanga, 45
Mozambique, 31, 40, 105, 143, 189n2
Mteza, settlement of, 47–48
Mtongwe, settlement of, 131
mtoro [Swahili] ("runaway slave"), 125, 187n56
Mtsangnyiko, trading center of, 131
Mtsengo, settlement of, 48, 72*map*, 74
mtumwa [Swahili] ("slave"), 125, 187n56
Mtwapa, port city of, 3*map*, 71, 72*map*, 177n68
*mucele [Sabaki] ("cleaned grain"), 29
mudhyani ~ muryani ~ ndiani [Mijikenda] ("scout, spy, leader of trade or hunting party"), 91, 93, 155–56
mudzi [Mijikenda] (village), 60
*mugunda [Sabaki] ("garden plots"), 28, 164n52
*muja [Sabaki] ("newcomer"), 38
*mujakazị [Sabaki] ("newcomer wife"), 38
*muji [Sabaki] ("settlements" or "placenta"), 44–45, 167n9
*mukiWa [Sabaki] ("poor person, abandoned person"), 38, 39, 150–51
*mulungu [Kaskazi] (spirit of unsettled areas), 59
*mulyongo [NEC Bantu] ("lineage"), 33, 165n79
mung'aro initiation ritual, 106, 183n62
Muscat, 19, 95, 107, 112; Mijikenda delegation to, 110–12, 114, 184n91; Omani siege of Mombasa and, 108
Muslims, 13, 111, 131. *See also* Islam
"Musungulos" (Portuguese term for Mijikenda speakers), 94, 96, 98, 114, 180n5; attack on Fort Jesus and, 181n29; Omani siege of Mombasa and, 109; Portuguese attacked by, 111; raids on Mombasa, 106; textile tributes paid to, 101; visits to Mombasa, 116. *See also* Mijikenda speakers
*mutala [Sabaki] ("quarter of a village"), 35, 36
mūthiani [Kamba] (trade party leaders, war leaders, expert hunters), 91
Mutoro, Henry, 7
muzimu (Swahili: place of sacrifice or worship; Mijikenda: nature spirits), 10–12
muzuka [Southern Mijikenda] ("nature spirit, shrine"), 55, 151
*muzyuka [Sabaki] ("apparition"), 55
Mvita, Shehe (Sheikh), 49
mwana njira ("child of the path"), 117, 185n8
Mwani language, 189n2
mwanza (drum associated with *virapho*), 63
*mwavị [Sabaki] (oathing practices), 62

226 INDEX

Names of the Python, The (Schoenbrun), 169n57
*ncungu [Sabaki] ("waste heaps"), 29
ndala [Mijikenda] ("healer's workplace, place for healing"), 57*table*, 59, 153
Ndenge, Kathungi, 51
New, Charles, 62, 63, 126
ngoma [Dawida] (ancestral shrine), 56
Ngulu language, 155
*nguWo [Sabaki] ("clothing"), 84
Nilotic languages, 75
Nine Tribes (Swahili: *Tisa Taifa*), 117, 185n13
*nkoma ("spirit of deceased"), 55, 151
*nkonde [Sabaki] ("cultivated field"), 28, 164n52
Northeast Coast (NEC) Bantu languages and speakers, 9, 11, 33, 34, 54, 75, 178n84; divergence of, 26, 141, 143, 190n18; lexical reconstructions and, 150, 155, 156; proto-NEC Bantu, 141–42; "slow revolution" in agriculture and, 30; terms for social reciprocity, 36, 37. *See also* Ruvu languages; Seuta languages
*ntope (reedbuck), 145, 164n62
*ntuuzo [Sabaki] ("gift"), 37
Nurse, Derek, 141, 145, 153, 171n78, 190n11
nyambura (*gophu* initiation feast), 173n122
Nyamwezi language and speakers, 129, 150
*nyika [Sabaki] ("grassland"), 170n74
nyika [Bantu] ("wilderness"), 56, 70–71
*nyumba [NEC Bantu] ("house"), 33, 35, 165n80

oathing practices, 62–63
Omani empire, 19, 78, 133; civil war in, 110, 111; limits of authority in Mombasa interior, 128–30; Mijikenda speakers described by, 106; Mombasa under control of, 110; rivalry with Portuguese empire, 84, 94, 95; siege of Mombasa, 107–10, 118; textile tributes paid to Mijikenda speakers, 110. *See also* Busaidi Sultanate; Mazrui family
Opônê, port city of, 22
oral traditions, 4, 6, 8, 12, 14, 184n77; about children kidnapped during famines, 124; about Chombo and Mteza, 47; on blood pacts, 87; conflicts and disputes chronicled in, 50, 169n36; elephant hunters as settlers of Mombasa, 132, 188n1; founding narratives for *kayas*, 54; healing practices and, 61; on ivory trade and elephant hunting, 80; knowledge of long-distance trade and, 86; meeting places and, 57; Mijikenda, 49–53; poisons used by hunters, 75; splitting and settlement diffusion, 64; on splitting of trade parties, 92

Oromo speakers, 50, 87, 104–5
Ottoman empire, 97, 100–101, 112

*-pád- [Sabaki] ("scrape, scratch"), 59
p'ala [Mijikenda] (healer's workplace), 57*table*, 59, 60, 172n85
palm wine, 42, 55, 56, 65
*-palo ~ *-pala ("meeting area"), 152
Pangani, town of, 3*map*, 122, 129, 188n84
Pangani River, 72*map*, 142
Papua New Guinea, 137
Pare language, 26, 90, 141; areas of, 27*map*; lexical reconstructions and, 150, 152, 154, 156; loanwords from Segeju, 103, 104*table*
Pare Mountains, 72*map*, 74, 75, 90, 170n68
patrilineal descent, 33, 165n83
Pearson, Michael, 15
Pemba Island, 3*map*, 46, 58*map*, 72*map*, 105; Mazrui dynasty and, 122; plantation economy on, 129; Portuguese empire and, 98; textile trade and, 83
pepper, from Malabar hinterland, 15, 134, 135–37, 140
Periplus Maris Erythraei (Greco-Roman merchant's guide), 22–24, 46, 77
Persia, 5, 6, 93, 121, 133, 138; merchants from, 1; "Shirazi tradition" of Swahili origins, 49, 168n32
Persian Gulf, 22, 31, 78, 125
phaya (*virapho* specialist group), 63, 65, 85
Planta da Ilha de Mombaça, 183n66
Pokomo languages and speakers, 35, 55, 141; areas of, 142; divergence from Sabaki, 141; lexical reconstructions and, 149, 150, 154. *See also* Lower Pokomo language; Upper Pokomo language
port cities, 43, 93, 133; emergence of, 32; fees imposed on visiting merchants, 82–83; smaller settlements and, 44–49
Port Reitz, 47
Portuguese empire, 2, 6, 19, 83, 133; Junta do Comércio, 107, 183n66; Mombasa under partial control of, 84, 89, 96–97, 98; rivalry with Omani empire, 84, 94, 95. *See also* Estado da Índia
Prange, Sebastian, 2, 136
Prestholdt, Jeremy, 102, 158n33
Ptolemy, 22–23

Quanzhou (China), port city of, 78, 79, 138

Rabai (Mijikenda dialect and speakers), 59, 98, 111, 146, 150, 152, 184n93; areas of, 58*map*;

Krapf and, 118; lexical reconstructions and, 154, 155; lexical variation of, 147–48; phonological variation of, 146–47*table*; sound shift in, 191n8

rainfall fluctuations, 24, 25, 39, 162nn28–29; knowledge of soils and weather patterns, 53; microclimates and, 71; rainy season on Tanzania coast, 26, 163n37

rainmaking, 52, 61

Ray, Daren, 7, 14, 34; on "cosmopolitan ethic," 49; on Mijikenda oral historians, 52, 168n31; on social and ecological issues facing clans, 52

Rebmann, Johannes, 92, 128

redistribution practices, 33, 36, 39–40, 166n97

Red Sea, 22, 99, 121

Resende, Pedro Barreto de, 96, 105, 112, 177n68

Rhapta, ancient town of, 22–23

rhinoceros horn, 6

Ribe (Mijikenda dialect and speakers), 111, 114, 118–19, 146*table*, 171n79, 184n93. *See also* Central Mijikenda

"rights in persons," 32, 124, 165n73

rock crystal, 47, 71, 73

rock outcroppings, 54, 73, 75, 76

rome, dhome [Mijikenda] (place for storytelling by elders), 57*table*

Rukanga (ironworking center), 73

rungu [Mijikenda] ("shrine in bush"), 57*table*, 59, 60, 63, 152–53

Ruvu languages, 12, 26, 141; areas of, 27*map*; blood pacts and, 87; proto-Ruvu, 59; terms for markets, 75

Sabaki (proto-Sabaki) language, 26, 151, 164n63; areas of, 27*map*, 141–42; divergence of, 9, 10*fig.*, 141, 143, 159n43; economic vocabulary, 86; phonemes transformed in proto-Mijikenda, 120, 186n28; reconstructed lexical innovations, 145, 149–51; "slow revolution" in agriculture and, 30

Sabaki speakers, 21, 28, 40, 71; lexical innovations of, 29; settlements categorized in expansive terms, 44, 45; Swahili urbanism and, 46; villages in range of microclimates, 40

safari [Arabic] (caravans), 91

Sahelian languages, 25, 162n31

Said, Seyyid, 122, 128, 129, 130

Saif bin Sultan II, 111, 117

Saphar, 23

Sassanian polity, 23

Saubatha, 23

Schoenbrun, David L., 38, 166n101

Scott, James, 95

secret societies, 57*table*, 66, 153

Sedlak, Phillip, 171n78

Segeju language and speakers, 64, 155; migrants from Central Kenya, 102; in Portuguese accounts, 100; Segeju identity in Kenya and Tanzania, 184n45. *See also* Daiso language

Seligman, Yaari, 14

settlement design, 35–36

Seuta languages, 12, 26, 141; areas of, 27*map*; blood pacts and, 87, 179n22; terms for markets, 75

Shambaa language and speakers, 150–56, 178n108

Shanga, settlement of, 45–46, 82, 168n16

Sharma (Yemen) settlement of, 177n76

shell beads, 46, 70

shellfish, 23, 30

Sheriff, Abdul, 2

Shimba, settlement of, 111, 184n93

"Shirazi tradition," 49, 168n32

Shungwaya (mythical homeland), 6, 50, 51, 103, 132

Silk Road, 138

slavery, Atlantic, 14, 160n59

slavery, in East Africa, 115–16, 119; in context of shifting balance honor and debt, 123–28; slave raiding in Mombasa inland region, 125

Slavery in Africa (Miers and Kopytoff, eds.), 165n73

social reciprocity, terms associated with, 36–39, 41

Somalia, 22, 31, 79

sorghum, 25, 26, 162n31; as drought-resistant crop, 34; in Early Iron Age sites, 30; increasing cultivation of, 28; Late Stone Age (LSA) communities and, 70; processing techniques for, 29. *See also* cereal cultivation

South Asia, 20, 22, 94

Southeast Asia, 15, 135, 137–38

Southern Cushitic language, 75, 76, 176n41, 181n38

Spear, Thomas, 6, 7, 51, 88, 183n62

spices, 76, 77, 136, 137, 138

spirit mediums, 13

Srivijaya empire, 137

Stephens, Rhiannon, 32, 165n75, 174n127

Stone Age, 6, 23

Subrahmanyam, Sanjay, 159n54

subsistence innovations and strategies, 21, 33, 35

Sudanic languages, 25, 162n31

suhba (Islamic trading arrangement), 88

Sultan bin Saif, 107

Sultan bin Saif II, 111

Swahili and Sabaki (Nurse and Hinnebusch, 1993), 141

228   INDEX

Swahili coast, 8, 15, 41; emergence of port cities, 24; as most important ivory-exporting region, 78; Ottoman empire and, 100–101; "pre-Swahili" coast, 22–24; Swahili culture seen as Middle Eastern import, 21; urbanism on, 45, 46

Swahili language, 1, 5, 36, 55; Arabic loanwords, 91; dictionaries of, 10; dispersal to offshore islands, 142; divergence from proto-Sabaki, 141; as dominant language on East African coast, 145; Giryama and, 4; lexical reconstructions and, 149, 153, 154, 156; Modern Standard Swahili, 35; proto-Sabaki as ancestor of, 9, 10*fig.*; proto-Swahili, 190n11

Swahili speakers, 21, 41, 46, 48; Mijikenda speakers and, 4–5, 7, 71; on Mombasa Island, 70

Tabula RogerianaI (al-Idrisi), 5

-tac- [Chaga-Taita] ("make offering, sacrifice"), 56, 152

Taita Hills, 56, 72, 72*map*, 73, 87; farmers' abandonment of lower slopes, 102; trading vocabulary in, 90

Taita language, 177n83

Taita-Saghala language, 150, 151, 154, 156

Takaungu, trading center of, 131

-tambik- [Sabaki] ("to make a sacrifice"), 56

Tanga, port city of, 58*map*, 142, 154

Tanzania, 9, 12, 23, 26; Kwale Ware ceramics in, 143; Northeast Coast Bantu languages in, 144; Northeast Coast languages in, 142; Pemba Island and, 46; South Pare Mountains, 74

Taylor, W. E., 90

textiles, 42, 69, 105, 154; ancestor rituals and, 85; circulation of, 94; from Gujarat, 15; as most important inland trade of Mombasa, 82; ritual and protective uses of, 84–85, 178n108; South Asian, 82; village economies and cotton textiles, 134–35. *See also* Mijikenda speakers, textile tributes paid to

textual records, inland connections in, 76–82

Thagicu languages, 38, 150, 151, 155, 191n9; divergence of, 184n45; economic vocabulary, 89; loanwords in Mijikenda from, 182n44; terms for markets, 75. *See also* Daiso language; Segeju language

Tharaka language, 151

Thorbahn, P. F., 71

Three Tribes (Swahili: *Thelatha Taifa*), 117, 118, 185n13

Tonga speakers, 11

tortoise shell, 22, 94, 108

trade, long-distance, 18, 69, 85–86, 89; blood pacts and cros-cultural commerce, 86–89; proto-caravans and knowledge of, 89–93

trade goods, 22, 76, 98; control over access to, 19; "domestication" of, 7; long-distance, 46; maritime, 70; moved through "down the line" exchanges, 89; in Portuguese documentation, 77

tsaka [Bantu] ("forest"), 56

Tsavo region, 71, 72, 105, 175n16; archaeological sites in, 73–74; elephant-hunting specialists of, 75; pastoralists of, 102; proto-caravans in, 89, 91, 92

Tsing, Anna, 160n56

Tumbe, settlement of, 46, 47

-tuuzy- [Sabaki] ("to give as a gift"), 37

Twelve Tribes (Swahili: *Thenashara Taifa*), 111, 184n75; *heshima* (honor) tributes and, 120; rival political factions within, 117

Uganda, 11, 32

uganga [Mijikenda] (medicine, specialized knowledge), 61, 65, 66, 67, 91

Ukambani region, 72*map*, 87, 92

Umba River, 72*map*

Unguja Ukuu, town of, 5, 168n22

Upper Pokomo language, 9, 10*fig.*, 154, 163n47. *See also* Pokomo languages

Usambara Mountains, 72*map*

utsai [Mijikenda] (harmful magic), 52, 56, 61–62, 66, 172n101

Vansina, Jan, 24

Venn, Henry, 128

vifudu ("tortoise") containers, 63, 64, 173n121

vigango (memorial posts for *gophu*), 65, 85, 173n121

village/bush dichotomy, 56, 60

virapho oathing practices, 62–63, 65–66, 67, 85, 173n114

virumbi (staffs with protective charms), 91

vitio (disease from sexual transgressions), 64

vitsambi [Mijikenda] (cloth), 84, 85

Vumba Kuu, town of, 72*map*, 116, 154

Waata hunters/communities, 87, 105

*Waganga [Sabaki] (healers), 61

Walz, Jonathan, 158n15

Wanyika or Nyika [Swahili] ("wilderness dwellers"), 71, 111, 112, 122, 185n15

warfare, 83, 95, 96

"wealth in people," 32–36, 165n73, 165n75
"What Is Global History Now?"
    (Adelman, 2017), 160n56
White, Louise, 88
*-Wil- [Sabaki] ("to owe"), 39
Willis, Justin, 6–7, 127, 172n92
wire, 80, 86, 87, 89, 91, 115
Wright, David, 71
Wright, Donald R., 160n59
*WucaWi [Sabaki] (harmful magic), 61
*Wucelu [Sabaki] ("cleared fields"), 28, 29, 163n48
*Wuishwa [Sabaki] ("chaff"), 29
Wynne-Jones, Stephanie, 31

Yao people, 129
Yemen, 22

Yusuf bin Hasan Chingulia. *See* Chingulia,
    Dom Jeronimo

Zambia, 11
Zanzibar, 19, 79; Busaidi Sultanate and, 121;
    copal trade and, 81; French designs on, 128;
    plantation economy on, 129; rise of, 130;
    textile trade and, 83
Zanzibar Archipelago, 31, 98, 105, 115
Zaramo language, 151, 178n84
Zaramo speakers, 12, 81
Zhao Rukua, 78–79, 138, 176n51
Zhu Fan Zhi [*Records of Various Foreign Peoples*]
    (Zhao Rukua), 78–79, 138, 176n61
Zigua language, 150, 151, 153, 154, 155, 156
"Zimba" warriors, 100, 181n29

Founded in 1893,
UNIVERSITY OF CALIFORNIA PRESS
publishes bold, progressive books and journals
on topics in the arts, humanities, social sciences,
and natural sciences—with a focus on social
justice issues—that inspire thought and action
among readers worldwide.

The UC PRESS FOUNDATION
raises funds to uphold the press's vital role
as an independent, nonprofit publisher, and
receives philanthropic support from a wide
range of individuals and institutions—and from
committed readers like you. To learn more, visit
ucpress.edu/supportus.